FRENCH.

Æsop. Fables in French. With a Dictionary. 18mo. $0 65

Bibliothèque d'Instruction et de Recréation.

Achard—Clos-Pommier, et les Prisonniers, par Xavier de Maistre, 85 cents. *Bédolliere*—Mère Michel. New Vocabulary, by Pylodet, 75 cents. *Biographies* des Musiciens Célèbres, $1.25. *Erckman-Chatrian* Conscrit de 1813. With Notes, $1.10. *Fallet*—Princes de l'Art, $1.50. *Feuillet*—Roman d'un Jeune Homme Pauvre, $1.10 *Foa*—Contes Biographiques. With Vocab., $1.00. ——Petit Robinson de Paris. With Vocab., 85 cents. *Macé*—Bouchée de Pain. With Vocab., $1.25. *Porchat*—Trois Mois sous la Neige, 85 cents. *Pressensé*—Rosa. With Vocab., $1.25. *Saint Germain*—Pour une Epingle. With Vocab., $1.00. *Sand*—Petite Fadette, $1.25. *Segur*—Contes (Petites Filles Modèles: Les Gouters de la Grand'-Mère), $1.00. *Souvestre*—Philosophe sous les Toits, 75 cents.

Borel. Cours de Thèmes. 12mo.............. 75

——— Grammaire Française. 12mo.............. 1 60

Buckingham's-Eugène. French Grammar and Exercises. 12mo...... 1 60

——— Elementary French Lessons. 12mo.............. 75

Delille. Condensed French Instruction. 18mo.............. 50

Fisher. Easy French Reading. With Vocabulary. 16mo.............. 59

Fleury. Histoire de France. 12mo.............. 1 40

——— Ancient History. Translated, with Notes. 12mo.............. 85

Gasc. French-English Dictionary. 8vo.............. 3 75

——— Do do 18mo. Pocket Edition, $1.40; 2 vols. 1 60

———Translator. (English into French).............. 1 25

Gibert. Introductory French Manual. 12mo.............. 85

Janon, De. Recueil de Poésies. 16mo.............. 1 00

Lacombe. Histoire du Peuple Française. 16mo.............. 75

Maistre (X de). Œuvres Complètes. 12mo.............. 1 40

——— Voyage autour de ma Chambre. 12mo. Paper.............. 40

Moutonnier. Les Premiers pas dans L'Étude du Français. 12mo...... 1 25

Musset. Un Caprice (Comédie). 12mo. Paper.............. 30

Otto. French Conversation Grammar. 12mo. Roan, $1.60; Key...... 75

———Bôcher's French Reader. 12mo. Roan.............. 1 40

———First Book in French. 16mo. Boards.............. 40

———Introductory French Lessons.............. 1 25

———Introductory French Reader. 12mo. Boards.............. 1 00

Parlez-vous Français? or, Do you Speak French? 18mo. Boards...... 50

Plays. *College Series of Modern French Plays.* With English Notes by Prof. Bôcher. 12mo. Paper. La joie Fait Peur, 30 cents; La Bataille des Dames, 35 cents; La Maison de Penarvan, 35 cents; La Poudre aux Yeux, 35 cents; Les Petits Oiseaux, 35 cents; Mademoiselle de la Seiglière, 35 cents; Le Roman d'un Jeune Homme Pauvre, 35 cents; Les Dogits de Fée, 35 cents; Jean Baudry, 35 cents. The foregoing in two volumes. 12mo. Cloth. Each vol.............. 1 60

Modern French Comedies. Le Village, 25 cents: La Cagnotte, 35 cents; Les Femmes qui Pleurent, 25 cents; Les Petites Misères de la Vie Humaine, 25 cents; La Niaise de St. Flour, 25 cents; Trois Proverbes, 30 cents; Valerie, 30 cents: Le Collier de Perles, 30 cents. The three last named have vocabularies.

French Plays for Children. With Vocabularies. 12mo. Paper. La Vieille Cousine: Les Ricochets, 25 cents; Le Testament de Madame Patural; La Mademoiselle de St. Cyr, 25 cents; La Petite Maman; Le Bracelet, 25 cents; La Lotterie de Francfort; Jeune Savante, 25 cents.

Students' Collection of Classic French Plays. 12mo. Paper. With full notes by Prof. E. S. Joynes. **Corneille.** Le Cid, 50 cents. **Racine.**

Athalie. 50 cents. **Molière.** Le Misanthrope, 50 cents. The foregoing in 1 vol. 12mo. Cloth, $1.50. **Molière.** L'Avare, 50 cents. **Racine.** Esther, 40 cents. **Corneille.** Cinna........................

Pylodet's Beginning French. 16mo. Boards........................ 55
——— Beginner's French Reader. With illustrations. 16mo. Boards.... 55
——— Second French Reader. With illustrations........................ 1 10
——— La Litérature Française Classique. 12mo........................ 1 60
——— La Litérature Française Contemporaine. 12mo........................ 1 40
——— Gouttes de Rosée. French Lyric Poetry. 18mo........................ 65
——— Mère L'Oie. Illustrated. 8vo. Boards........................ 50
Riodu. Lucie. French and English Conversations. 12mo........................ 75
Sadler. Translating English into French. 12mo........................ 1 25
Sauveur. Introduction to Teaching. 12mo. Paper........................ 25
——— De L'Enseignement des Langues Vivantes. Paper........................ 25
——— Entretiens sur la Grammaire. 12mo........................ 1 75
——— Causeries avec mes Élèves. 12mo. Illustrated........................ 1 50
——— Petites Causeries. 12mo........................ 1 25
——— Causeries avec les Enfants. 12mo........................ 1 25
——— Fables de la Fontaine. 12mo........................ 1 50
Stern and Méras. Étude Progressive de La Langue Française. 12mo. 1 50
Witcomb and Bellenger. French Conversation. 18mo........................ 65
Zender. Abécédaire, French and English Primer. 12mo. Boards...... 50

GERMAN.

☞ *The prices are for paper covers, unless otherwise expressed.*

Andersen. Bilderbuch ohne Bilder. With Notes. 12mo........................ $0 30
——— Die Eisjungfrau, etc. With Notes. 12mo........................ 50
Carove. Das Märchen ohne Ende........................ 25
Evans. Otto's German Reader. Half Roan........................ 1 35
Eichendorf. Aus dem Leben eines Taugenichts. 12mo........................ 50
Elz. Three German Comedies. 12mo........................ 35
Fouqué. Undine. With Vocabulary. 12mo........................ 40
Goethe. Egmont. With Notes........................ 50
——— Herrman und Dorothea. With Notes. 12mo........................ 35
Grimm. Venus von Milo; Rafael und Michel-Angelo. 12mo........................ 50
Heine. Harzreise und Das Buch Le Grand. 12mo. Cloth........................
Heness. Der Leitfaden. 12mo. Cloth........................ 1 50
——— Der Sprechlehrer unter seinen Schülern........................ 1 35
Heyse. Anfang und Ende. 12mo........................ 30
——— Die Einsamen. 12mo........................ 25
Keetels. Oral Method with German. 12mo. Half roan........................ 1 60
Koerner. Zriny. With Notes........................ 60
Klemm. Lese und Sprachbuecher. In 8 concentrischen Kreisen. 12mo
———Geschichte der Deutschen Literatur........................ 1 50
Lessing. Minna von Barnhelm. In English with German Notes, 12mo.. 50
——— Emilia Galotti. 12mo........................ 40
Lodeman. German Conversation Tables. 12mo. Boards........................ 35
Mügge. Riukan Voss. 12mo........................ 30
———Signa die Seterin. 12mo........................ 30
Nathusius. Tagebuch eines armen Fräuleins. 12mo........................ 60
Otto. German Grammar. 12mo. Roan, $1.60; Key........................ 75
——— Evans' German Reader. With Notes and Vocab. 12mo. Roan.. 1 35
——— First Book in German. 12mo. Boards........................ 35
——— Introductory Lessons; or, Beginning German. 12mo. Cloth...... 95
——— Introductory Reader. With Notes and Vocabulary. 12mo. Cloth 1 20
———Translating English into German, $1.00. Key........................ 1 00
Prinzessin Ilse. With Notes. 12mo........................ 25

COMPENDIOUS

GERMAN GRAMMAR

BY

WILLIAM D. WHITNEY

PROFESSOR OF SANSKRIT AND INSTRUCTOR
IN MODERN LANGUAGES IN
YALE COLLEGE.

FIFTH EDITION, REVISED.

NEW YORK
HENRY HOLT AND COMPANY
F. W. CHRISTERN
BOSTON: CARL SCHŒNHOF

TROW'S
PRINTING AND BOOKBINDING CO.,
201-213 *East 12th St.*,
NEW YORK.

PREFACE.

The author of a new German grammar, in a community where so many are already in use, and with so much approval, may well feel called upon to explain and defend his undertaking —especially, when his work is almost entirely wanting in those practical exercises, for writing and speaking, which make the principal part of the other grammars now most in use.

That system of instruction in modern languages of which the Ollendorff grammars are popularly regarded as the type, has its unquestionable advantages where learning to speak is the main object directly aimed at, and where the smallness of the classes, and the time spent with the instructor, render it possible for the latter to give each pupil that amount of personal attention and drilling which is needed in order to make the system yield its best results.

But in our schools and colleges this is for the most part impracticable. Their circumstances and methods of instruction render translation and construction the means by which the most useful knowledge and the best discipline can be gained. To the very great majority of those who learn German, ability to speak is an object inferior in importance to ability to understand accurately and readily the language as written or printed and the attainment of the former is properly to be made posterior to that of the latter. One who has mastered the principles of grammar, and acquired by reading a fair vocabulary and a feeling for the right use of it, will learn to speak and to write rapidly and well when circumstances require of him that ability.

Moreover, there is a large and increasing class of students, whose philological training has to be won chiefly or altogether in the study of the modern languages, instead of the classical—and who must win it by methods somewhat akin with those so long and so successfully followed in classical study. For the class referred to, German offers peculiar advantages, quite superior to those presented by any other modern language. In words, forms, and constructions, it is enough unlike English to call forth and exercise all the pupil's powers of discrimination, to sharpen his attention to the niceties of word and phrase, and train his philological insight: while, at the same time, the fundamental relation of German to the most central and intimate part of English makes the study instinct with practical bearings on our own tongue, and equivalent to a historical and comparative study of English itself: and, both on the esthetic and the practical side, there is no other modern literature so rich in attraction and so liberal of reward to us as the German.

It has appeared to me that, in these aspects of the study, hardly sufficient assistance was furnished the teacher and learner by the grammars hitherto accessible. Three subjects especially have called for more careful exposition: the derivation of German words from one another; the construction of sentences; and the correspondences between German and English. I have also desired to see in some respects a more acceptable arrangement of the ordinary subject-matter of a grammar—one having in view the history of words and forms, although not obtruding the details of that history unnecessarily upon pupils unprepared for their study.

At the same time, I have endeavored to make a really compendious and simple grammar, according to the promise of the title-page, a grammar which might answer the needs even of young scholars, although containing some things which they would not fairly understand and appreciate until later. That I shall have satisfied others' ideal of a compendious grammar, by including all they may deem essential and omitting the unessen tial, I do not venture to hope: but only trust that I may have come pretty near to meeting the wants of many.

A careful distinction of the contents of the book by variety of type, according to their degree of immediate importance, has been attempted throughout. Especially, I have meant to put into the largest type (sm. pica) just about so much as the scholar ought to learn carefully and thoroughly in his first course of grammar-lessons, preparatory to reading. This a class should acquire, according to the age and capacity and previous training of its members, in from twelve to twenty-five lessons; and should then at once be put into reading, while the grammar is taken up again, and such part of what was before omitted is learned as the judgment of the intelligent teacher shall direct. It is solely as auxiliary to the first course of lessons that the Exercises are intended—to furnish, namely, to the teacher the opportunity of drilling his pupils in the practical application of the more important rules and principles while they are learning them, or gaining practice in parsing, subject by subject, instead of leaving the whole work to be taken up at once when reading is begun. While believing that they will be found valuable in this way, I would not press their use, but would leave it to each one's decision whether to employ or neglect them.

Nothing has been put in the largest type after the subject of conjugation is finished, nor anything anywhere in syntax: the main principles of construction, and the use of particles, are sufficiently alike in English and German to allow the pupil to begin reading without having studied them especially in German.

After enough reading to have given some familiarity with forms and constructions, I would have the writing of exercises begun; and I feel confident that a better result in reading and writing together will be won thus, in a given time, than by any other method. I have myself been accustomed to prepare exercises for my classes, for turning into German, from whatever text the class were reading; taking a sentence or paragraph, and putting its phrases into a different shape from that presented in the text, so that the student shall have his main vocabulary before him on the page, instead of having to hunt for proper expressions in the dictionary, with knowledge insufficient for the task. This method I would recommend to others; but, for the aid of those who may desire such aid, I purpose to prepare a series of practical and progressive exercises as a supplement to this grammar, and to have it ready by the time that those who begin their study of German with the grammar shall be ready for its use.

Some of the subjects treated in the grammar (especially word-derivation, and the relation of English and German), need support from the lexicon. Considering the general deficiency of information on these subjects in the accessible dictionaries, I am endeavoring to give the beginner help till he can make his analyses and comparisons for himself, in the Vocabulary to a German Reader, which is published as a companion-book to the present one.* From its pages have been drawn a large part of the examples given in the Grammar, and I have now and then taken the liberty to refer to it (by page and line), in illustration of some exceptional or anomalous point which was under treatment.

Of course, I have consulted, and more or less used, a good many grammars while engaged in the preparation of this one, deriving more or less of valuable information or suggestion from each and all of them. But I do not feel that I need to make special acknowledgments save to one—the work of Heyse (in its two editions, the *Schul-Grammatik* and the *Ausführliches Lehrbuch*). To it my obligations have been more constant and various than I can well point out in detail: hence this general confession of indebtedness. Those familiar with Heyse will have no difficulty in tracing its influence in many parts (for

* The text of the Reader is already published, and it is expected that the Notes and Vocabulary will be ready by the end of 1869.

example, in the classification of verbs of the Old conjugation, which I have taken almost without modification from that authority); while they will also find that I have nowhere followed it slavishly.

It has everywhere been my intention so to set forth the facts of the language as to favor the recognition of language as a growth, as something which has been gradually converted into what it is, from a very different condition, by those who have used it—a recognition which is the first need, if one would really understand language, and which must lead the way to those deeper studies into the history of languages and of language, constituting so important a branch of modern science.

The study of German is so rapidly increasing in prevalence that there is pressing need of raising it to a somewhat higher plane. I trust it will be found that this volume contributes its part, though a small one, to so desirable an end.

W. D. W.

YALE COLLEGE, New Haven, Aug. 1869.

PREFACE TO THE FOURTH EDITION.

SINCE the first publication of this work, the series of which it forms a part has been extended, as promised, by adding to the Reader a Vocabulary and Notes, and to the Grammar a set of Exercises for translating from English into German (both in September, 1870). The Grammar is now completed by a detailed Index, which, but for untoward circumstances, would have formed a part of it when originally issued. I have also made such slight alterations in the work itself, here and there, as seemed most called for, having been either found desirable by myself or suggested by others. And I have only further to direct attention here to one or two features in the plan of the work, which, although pointed out above, have been by some overlooked or misunderstood.

In the first place, the Exercises scattered through the Grammar are simply and solely parsing exercises, helps along the way through a course that is meant to lead at the earliest possible moment to the reading of German authors. If they had been anything else, I should have expended much more labor upon them, and submitted them to thorough revision by a native German. For their intended purpose, they were as good as if every sentence had been an extract from Goethe or Schiller.

In the second place, the Grammar was never meant to be learned in bulk, or studied through in the order in which it is written—unless perhaps by advanced scholars, who desire to systematize knowledge previously gained. With beginners, especially, it should be gone over briefly, in the manner indicated above (p. v.), with inclusion only of the parts in largest type, and of the paradigms; and the author's design was to produce a work which, being so used, would carry a pupil prepared for it (such as compose the classes in our high schools and collegiate institutions of various kinds) through the essentials of German grammar, and enable him to begin to read easy German intelligently, *in a shorter time than was possible by any other text-book in use*, putting distinctly before him what he ought first and most to know, and, at the same time, in such form as would fit well, without alteration, into the more complete knowledge which he should acquire later. As a fuller explanation of this design, I add below a sketch of a course of twenty lessons, preparing for reading:—

1. lesson in pronunciation; no recitation.
2. chief rules of pron. (6, 7, 55); parts of speech (56); declension (57–60); articles (63).
3. declension of nouns (68–71); first decl., first class (75–9).
4. Ex. I.; second class (81–5).
5. Ex. II.; third class (87–90), and Ex. III.
6. second declension (91–4); Ex. V.
7. adjective declension (114–22); Ex. VI., VII. (a sentence or two of each).
8. Ex. VIII.; adj. as noun and as adverb (129–30); Ex. IX. (part).
9. comparison of adj. (134–6, 140); Ex. X. (part); pronouns, personal pron. (150–1).
10. pronouns (153–5, 157, 159, 163–5, 172–4, 177); Ex. XI., XII. (parts of each).
11. numerals (197, 203); Ex. XIII.
12. conjugation (231); simple forms of verb (235); lieben, geben (236).
13. auxiliaries (238–9); haben, sein, werden (239).
14. Ex. XIV. (part); complete conj. of haben and sein (244); Ex. XV.
15. conjugations (245–6); New conjugation (247–8); Ex. XVI.
16. Old conjugation (261–2, 268–71, 273).
17. Ex. XVIII.; passive voice (274–7).
18. reflexive and impersonal verbs (283–5, 291–2); Ex. XIX.
19. compound verbs, separable (297–300).
20. compound verbs, inseparable, etc. (302–4, 308–11); Ex. XX.

This scheme is, of course, intended only as a suggestion, for each teacher to modify in accordance with his own judgment and the needs and capacities of his class. Some may prefer to go more slowly over the ground, including the more important items of the second size of print; and, on the other hand, there are classes (as I have myself made experience) who can do the whole task well in from twelve to fifteen lessons.

W. D. W.

July, 1871.

TABLE OF CONTENTS.

The references are to paragraphs and pages.

LIST OF EXERCISES.

GERMAN GRAMMAR

ALPHABET.

1. The German language is usually printed in an alphabet having the same origin as our own, and the same extent; but in the form of its characters nearly resembling what we call "Old English," or "Black-letter."

This is one of the derivative forms of the old Latin alphabet, a product of the perverse ingenuity of monkish scribes in the Middle Ages. It was in general use throughout Europe at the time of the invention of printing, but was abandoned by one nation after another for the simpler, neater, and more legible character which we call "Roman," and which the Germans know as "Latin" (lateinisch). For scientific literature, the latter is in more common use among the Germans themselves, and many of the best German scholars are in favor of the entire relinquishment of the other.

2. The letters of the ordinary German alphabet, with their "Roman" equivalents, and the names by which the Germans call them, are as follows:

German letters.	Roman equiv'ts.	German name.	German letters.	Roman equiv'ts.	German name.
𝔄, 𝔞	a	â (*ah*)	𝔑, 𝔫	n	ĕn
𝔅, 𝔟	b	bā (*bay*)	𝔒, 𝔬	o	o
ℭ, 𝔠	c	tsā	𝔓, 𝔭	p	pā
𝔇, 𝔡	d	dā	𝔔, 𝔮	q	kū (*koo*)
𝔈, 𝔢	e	ā	ℜ, 𝔯	r	ĕr
𝔉, 𝔣	f	ĕf	𝔖, ſ, 𝔰	s	ĕs
𝔊, 𝔤	g	gā	𝔗, 𝔱	t	tā
ℌ, 𝔥	h	hâ	𝔘, 𝔲	u	ū (*oo*)
ℑ, 𝔦	i	ē (*ee*)	𝔙, 𝔳	v	fou (*found*)
ℑ, 𝔧	j	yōt	𝔚, 𝔴	w	vā
𝔎, 𝔨	k	kâ	𝔛, 𝔵	x	ĭx
𝔏, 𝔩	l	ĕl	𝔜, 𝔶	y	ipsilon
𝔐, 𝔪	m	ĕm	ℨ, 𝔷	z	tsĕt

3. Certain points concerning this alphabet require special notice on the part of the learner:

1. Of the two forms of small *s*, the second, or short ꞩ, is used only at the end of a word; the other, or long ſ, in other situations: thus, las; but leſen, ſo.

If a word ending in s is followed by another in composition, it is still written with short s: thus, losgehen (los and gehen), deshalb (des and halb).

2. Some of the letters are modified in form by combination with one another: thus, ch, *ch*; ck, *ck*; ß, *sz*; tz, *tz*.

3. Some letters resemble one another so much as to be easily confounded by the beginner:

Thus, B, *b*, and V, *v*; C, *c*, and E, *e*; G, *g*, and S, *s*; K, *k*, N, *n*, and R, *r*; D, *d*, O, *o*, and Q, *q*; also, b, *b*, d, *d*, and h, *h*; f, *f*, and ſ, *s*; k, *k*, and t, *t*; r, *r*, and x, *x*.

4. There is a special written alphabet, as well as a printed, for the German. The forms of its letters, and specimens of written texts, will be given at the end of this work. The beginner had better not concern himself with it, as he can make practical use of it to advantage only when he has already gained considerable familiarity with the language.

When German is written or printed in the "Latin" character, each German letter is represented by its Latin equivalent, with the single exception that for the compound ß, *sz*, is usually and preferably substituted *ss*.

5. The German uses capital initial letters

1. As the English, at the beginning of sentences, of lines in poetry, and of direct quotations.

2. For all nouns, common as well as proper, and for words used as nouns.

Words used as nouns are especially adjectives (**129**) and infinitives (**340**). As no fixed line divides their ordinary from their substantive use, there are doubtful cases in each class, with regard to which usage is conflicting.

3. For pronouns of the third person, when used in address, with the value of those of the second person (**153**).

That is, especially, Sie, with its oblique cases, and its corresponding possessive Ihr; but not its reflexive, ſich.

Pronouns of the second person properly take capitals only when intended to come under the eye of the person addressed (as in letters, etc.); in such a case, ſich also is written Sich.

Respecting the indefinite pronouns Jedermann, 'every one,' Jemand, 'any one,' Niemand, 'no one,' etc., and the pronominal adjectives used substantively, such as alles, 'everything,' mancher, 'many a one,' einige, 'some,' usage is very various. Some write ein with a capital when it is emphatic, or means 'one.'

4. For adjectives derived from names of persons or places, usually; but not for adjectives of nationality, as englisch, 'English, französisch, 'French.'

Adjectives of title, or those used in respectful and complimentary address, also usually take capital initials: thus, Eure Königliche Hoheit, 'your royal highness,' Sie, Wohlgeborener Herr, 'you, excellent sir.'

PRONUNCIATION.

6. The precise mode of production of German articulated sounds, taken singly or in combination, as well as the general tone and style of utterance, can only be acquired through means of oral instruction, and by long practice. The following rules, however, will help the learner, with or without a teacher, to approximate to the true pronunciation of German words.

The subject is a comparatively easy one to deal with, because

1. There are no silent letters, either vowels or consonants.

Excepting sometimes h (28).

2. As a rule, the same letter receives the same sound under all circumstances.

Exceptions, b, c, d, g, s, v—see those letters, below.

3. The German, however, like many other languages, writes certain simple sounds, vowel or consonant, with digraphs and even trigraphs—i.e., with combinations of two and of three letters.

VOWELS.

7. Each simple vowel sound is either long or short, varying in quantity, or time of utterance, without at the same time varying, like our English vowels, to any notable extent in quality, or nature of sound.

The distinction of long and short vowels must to a great extent be learned by practice; but the following rules will be found of service:

1. A vowel doubled, or followed by h, is long.

2. A vowel is short before a double consonant, and

more usually before a group of two consonants—unless the latter of the pair or group belongs to an appended ending or suffix.

8. **A, a.**—A has always the sound of our open or Italian *a*, in *far*, *father*.

It is long in Aal, Haar, Bahn, nah, Namen.

It is short in Ball, Mann, hatte, Hand, scharf, hat, bald.

Particularly avoid the flattening of this vowel, or its reduction to a sound at all resembling that of our "short *a*" in *hat*, *can*.

9. **E, e.**—E is pronounced nearly as our *e* in *they*, or our "long *a*" in *fate*, only without the distinct vanishing-sound of *ee* into which our *ā* passes at its close. Short e is nearly our "short *e*" in *met*, *men*.

It is long in Heer, mehr, Reh.

It is short in denn, schnell, nett, Herr, Welt.

In long syllables—and by some authorities also in short ones—is distinguished a closer and an opener utterance of the e, the latter inclining very slightly toward our "short *a*" (in *hat*, *can*). The difference is analogous with that between the French *é* and *è*. Thus, e is said to be close in mehr, Reh, jeder (first syllable), and open in (the first syllables of) Leben, geben, beten. No rules are to be given respecting the occurrence of this distinction; nor is it much to be insisted on.

Unlike the other vowels, e is notably slighted and obscured in sound when unaccented. Especially before a consonant, in a syllable following the accent, it acquires nearly the tone of our "short *u*" (in *but*), and becomes very inconspicuous.

Guard against giving to final e the sound of English *e*; it should have a very open utterance, and in parts of Germany even becomes like our "short *u*" (in *but*, *puff*).

10. **I, i.**—I has the sound of our *i* in *pique*, *machine*, or of our "long *e*," or double *ee*. When short, it is more like our "short *i*" (in *pin*), yet somewhat less removed than that is from our "long *e*."

It is long in ihn, ihr, Igel, dir, Mine.

It is short in billig, bitten, hinter, ist, Trift.

I is never written double, and it is followed by h only in the personal pronouns ihn, ihm, ihr, ihrer, ihnen, and the possessives ihr and ihrig. To indicate its long sound, an e is generally added, making the digraph, or compound vowel, ie (**18**).

11. O, o.—O has always the tone of our "long *o*," except the distinct vanishing-sound of *u* (*oo*) with which the latter ends.

It is long in Moor, Bohne, Ton, Gebot, Moder.

It is short in soll, Gott, offen, Molke, Topf.

Never give to o the quality of our "short *o*" in *hot*, *on*, etc.; this is no proper *o*-sound, but pretty nearly the German short a.

12. U, u.—U long is our *u* in *rule*, or *oo* in *boot*; u short is nearly our *u* in *pull*, or *oo* in *book*, but less removed from long u.

It is long in Uhr, nun, gut, ruhen.

It is short in Brust, Stunde, Null.

U is never doubled.

Be especially careful not to give to u, under any circumstances, the pronunciation of English *u* in *union*, *mute*, *cure*; to do so is to put a *y* before it.

13. Y, y.—Y is found only in foreign words (except, according to the usage of some, in the digraphs ay, ey: see below, **19.**3), and is ordinarily pronounced as an i would be in the same situation.

Examples: Syrup, Asyl, lyrisch, Myrte.

Some require that in words from the Greek, of more learned and less popular use, it should have the sound of ü (**17**).

Modified Vowels.

14. 1. The modified vowels are, historically, products of the mixture with a, o, u, of an e or i-sound, or of the phonetic assimilation of the former to the latter in a succeeding syllable. They were written Ae, Oe, Ue, ae, oe, ue, and are still usually so written when the vowel modified is a capital; but when small letters were used, the e came to be first written above the other vowel—thus, aͤ, oͤ, uͤ—and then, for convenience, was reduced in common use to a couple of dots—as, ä, ö, ü.

2. They are never doubled; and hence, a noun containing in the singular a double vowel, if requiring modification in the plural, loses one vowel: thus, Saal forms Säle, Aas forms Aeser.

15. Ae, ä.—Ae has the sound of an open e—that is to say, of an e very slightly approaching our "short *a*;" it is every where hardly distinguishable from an e in the same situation.

It is long in Kläger, prägen, Aeser, Späher, Mähre.

It is short in Hände, Aepfel, hätte, Bäcker, fällen.

16. Oe, ö.—Oe is really produced by a combination of that position of the tongue in which e (*e* in *they*) is uttered, and of that position of the lips in which o is uttered; but it is not easily given by a conscious effort so to dispose the organs. It is nearest in tone to our *u* in *hurt*, but is notably different from this, verging considerably toward the *e* of *they*. It is closely akin with the French *eu*-sounds.

It is long in Oefen, mögen, schön, hören, Oel.

It is short in könnte, öffnen, Hölle, Spötter, Oerter.

To form ö, therefore, endeavor to hit an intermediate sound between the vowels of *hurt* and *hate*.

The German poets frequently make ö rhyme with the simple e, and in parts of Germany the two are hardly distinguished. But their real difference, as properly pronounced, is quite marked, and should never be neglected.

17. Ue, ü.—Ue is produced by a combination of that position of the tongue in which i (*i* in *pique*, *pin*) is uttered, and of that position of the lips in which u (*u* in *rule*, *pull*) is uttered. It is the same sound with the French *u*. To utter it, first round the lips to the u-position, and then, without moving them, fix the tongue to say i (*ee*)—or *vice versâ*.

It is long in Uebel, Schüler, müde, kühn, kühl, über.

It is short in Glück, Mütter, Ueppigkeit, füllen, Hütte, dünn.

The sounds of ö and ü are, among the German vowels, much the hardest to acquire, and cannot be mastered without assiduous practice under a teacher.

Diphthongs and Vowel Digraphs.

18. For Ae, Oe, Ue, see Modified Vowels, above (**14–17**).

Ie, as already noticed (**10**), is an i made long by the addition of an e, instead of by doubling, or the addition of h.

Historically, ie often represents an original combination of separate vowels.

Examples: die, tief, liegen, Frieden, Riemen.

At the end of a few words (mostly coming from the Latin, and accented on the preceding syllable), the e of ie has its own proper sound, and the i is pronounced like *y* before it, or else forms an independent syllable: thus, Linien, Glorie, Familie, Tragödie; also Knie (plural of Knie, and sometimes spelt Kniee).

19. 1. **Ai.**—Ai is a combination of letters representing a true diphthongal sound, which is composed of the two elements a (*a* in *far*) and i (*i* in *pique*). It is pronounced nearly as the English *aye* (meaning 'yes'); or like the "long *i*" of *aisle*, *isle*, but with the first constituent of that sound made very slightly opener and more conspicuous, a little dwelt on. It occurs in very few words.

Examples: Hain, Waise, Mai.

2. **Ei.**—Ei represents the same sound, and is of very much more frequent occurrence, being the ordinary German equivalent of our "long *i*."

Examples: Bein, Beil, Eimer, sei, Ei, Eitelkeit.

3. Ay and ey were formerly written in certain words instead of ai and ei: they are now gone nearly out of use, only a few authors retaining them. Examples: May, seyn, sey, Polizey.

20. **Au.**—Au combines the two sounds a (in *far*) and u (in *rule*), and is pronounced almost precisely like the English *ou*, *ow*, in *house*, *down*, but with the first element, the *a*-sound, a shade more distinct.

Examples: Haus, kaufen, Auge, Sau, braun, Maul.

21. 1. **Eu.**—Eu is most nearly like the English *oi*, *oy*, in *boil*, *boy*, differing chiefly in having the first element briefer and less conspicuous. Theoretically, its final element is the ü-sound.

Examples: heute, neu, Euter, Freunde, euer.

2. **Aeu, äu.**—Aeu is the modified diphthong corresponding to au, as ä to a. It is pronounced in the same manner as eu.

Examples: Aeugler, Häute, bräunen, Träume.

22. **Ui.**—Ui is found only in hui, pfui, and is pronounced like *we*.

CONSONANTS.

23. **B, b.**—B has the same sound as in English, when followed in the same syllable by a vowel or semivowel (r, l), or when doubled.

Examples: Biber, Bube, haben, ober, Blei, brechen, Ebbe.

In other situations—i.e., when final, or followed by a consonant in general—it loses its sonant character, and is converted into the corresponding surd, p.

Examples: Stab, gehabt, ob, schub, Habsburg.

24. C, c.—C, in words properly German, is found only in the combinations ch, ck, sch, for which see below, **43, 44, 48.**

In words borrowed from other languages and not Germanized in spelling, it is, as in English, hard before a, o, u, l, n, r, but soft before e, i, y: in the former case, it is pronounced as k, in the latter, as *ts* (German z: **42**).

Examples: Cato, Carcer, Concert, Cicero, Claudius, Ocean.

25. D, d.—D, like b, has its own proper sonant sound, that of English *d*, before a vowel, or any consonant that may intervene between it and a vowel, in the same syllable; also when doubled.

Examples: Damm, dick, Dorf, du, adel, drei, Dwall, Trobbel.

At the end of a word, or of a syllable before another consonant, it is changed to the corresponding surd, t.

Examples: Brod, Stadt, mild, Abend, tödten.

26. F, f.—F has always the same sound as in English.

27. G, g.—G, like the other sonant mutes, b and d, has its proper hard sound (as English *g* in *go*, *give*, *get*) when doubled, or when followed in the same syllable by a vowel or liquid (l, n, r). It is never softened before e or i—as it also is not in any English word of Germanic origin.

Examples: Gans, gegen, Gier, gut, groß, Glas, Gnade, Dogge.

In the same situations in which b and d become p and t, g is also changed to a surd; it does not, however, assume the value of k, but rather that of ch (43).

Examples: Tag, zog, Zug, Vogt, Magd, ruhig, täglich.

There is much difference of usage among Germans, and of opinion among German orthoepists, as to the pronunciation of g. All, indeed, agree to give it the hard sound when initial. But in other situations, some always soften it to ch—e. g., in Degen, Ziege. Others do not allow it anywhere the precise ch-sound, especially not after the hard vowels (a, o, u), but pronounce it nearly as k, or as something between a g and k, or between a k and ch—and so on.

28. H, h.—H has the sound of English *h* when it begins a word (or either of the suffixes heit, haft). Elsewhere it is silent, serving either to lengthen the preceding vowel, or to make a hiatus between two vowels

Th (37) is pronounced as simple t. For ch and sch, see below (43, 48).

Examples: hin, her, ha, Hof, Hut, höher, ruhen, Kindheit, hafthaft, Ahn, Ehre, eher, ihm, Ohr, thun, rathen, roth.

29. **J, j.**—J is always pronounced like our *y* consonant.

Examples: Jahr, jung, jeder, Johann, bejahen.

30. **K, k.**—K has always the sound of English *k*. Instead of double k is written ck (which, however, if separated in syllabication, becomes k-k).

Examples: kann, kennen, Kleid, Kreide, Knie, Knabe, Glocke, drukken (but drucken).

31. **L, l; M, m.**—These letters have the same sounds as their English correspondents.

32. **N, n.**—N has usually the same sound as English *n*. Like the latter, it has before k the value of *ng:* thus, sinken, Dank.

For the digraph ng, see below (45).

33. **P, p.**—P is pronounced as in English. For the digraph ph, see below (46.2).

34. **Q, q.**—Q, as in English, is always followed by u, and qu is pronounced as *kv*, but with the pure labial utterance of the *v*-sound, as explained below (under w, 39).

Examples: Qual, quer, Quirl, quoll.

35. **R, r.**—R has a decidedly more distinct and forcible utterance than in English, being more or less rolled or trilled, and so, of course, formed a little further forward in the mouth than our *r*. In every situation, it must be clearly heard.

Examples: Rand, reden, Ritter, roth, rund, her, Herr, Arbeiter, Führer, vermerken, marmorner, erlernbarer.

36. **S, ſ, s.**—S, after a manner analogous with b, d, and g, has its proper surd or hissing sound only when doubled, final, or standing before a consonant; before a vowel (not before a semivowel; nor when preceded by a surd consonant, as t, ch, or a liquid, l, m, n, r) it approaches a sonant or buzzing sound, that of our *z*, and in the usage of some localities, or of some classes, it is a full *z*; according, however, to the better supported pronunciation, it

is a compromise between *s* and *z*, a kind of *sz*. Before t and p at the beginning of a word, the weight of authority is in favor of its utterance as *sh* (but less broadly and conspicuously than our common *sh*); but the pronunciation as written has also good usage (especially in Northern Germany) in its favor.

Double s (ss, ss) is always surd or hissing; for ß, see **49**.

Examples: Glas, Hast, Bosheit, wissen, Lootse, emsig, also, Sohn, Seele, Besen, Gesang, steif, Strang, Spur, springen.

37. T, t.—T, in words properly German, has always the ordinary sound of English *t*. In certain terminations (especially tion) of words from the Latin or French, it is pronounced like *ts* (German z).

Th is pronounced like simple t; its h has usually no historical, but only a phonetic ground, as sign of the long quantity of the neighboring vowel. For tz, see **51**.

Examples: hat, hast, Tafel, tragen, thut, Muth, Thräne, Station.

38. V, v.—V is rarely found except at the beginning of a word, and there has the sound of English *f*. In the few cases where it occurs in the interior of words, before a vowel, it is pronounced as our *v*; as also, in words taken from foreign languages which give it the latter sound.

Examples: Vater, viel, Verfall, freveln, Sklave, Vacanz, Venedig.

39. W, w.—W, when not preceded by a consonant in the same syllable, is commonly and correctly pronounced precisely as the English *v*, or between the edges of the upper teeth and lower lip. Another mode of its utterance, which is also supported by good authority, excludes the action of the teeth, and produces the sound between the edges of the lips alone. As thus made, it is still distinctly a *v* (not a *w*), though one of a different quality from our *v*: the difference, however, is not conspicuous to an unpractised ear. All authorities agree in requiring this purely labial pronunciation after a consonant (which consonant is nearly always a sibilant, sch or z): and the same belongs, as above noticed (**34**), to the u of the combination qu.

Examples: Welle, Wahn, Wuth, wollen, schwer, zwei, Twiel, Dwall.

40. X, x.—X is found in only an exceedingly small number of words originally German. It has the sound of English *x* (*ks*), whether as initial or elsewhere.

Examples: Axt, Hexe, Text, Xenophon, Xenien, Xylographie.

41. Y, y.—Y in German is a vowel only (13).

42. Z, z.—Z is always pronounced as *ts*, except in the combination ß (see below, 49): its two constituents should be sharply and distinctly uttered. Instead of double z, is written tz (51).

Examples: Zinn, Zoll, zu, zerziehen, zagen, heizen, Prinz, Holz, Herz, Platz, zwei.

Consonantal Digraphs and Trigraphs.

43. 1. Ch, ch.—Ch, in all situations, is a rough breathing, an *h*, rasped out with conspicuous force through as nearly as possible the same position of the organs in which the preceding vowel was uttered. According, then, as the vowel is one produced in the throat—namely, a, o, u—or one which comes forth between the flat of the tongue and the palate—namely, e, i, y, ä, ö, ü—or as it is a diphthong whose final constituent is of each class respectively—namely, au on the one hand; ai, ei, äu, eu on the other—it has a different pronunciation, guttural or palatal. The guttural ch (after a, o, u, au) is the throat-clearing or hawking sound; the palatal approaches our *sh*, but is notably different from it, being formed further back upon the roof of the mouth, and lacking the full sibilant quality (before a vowel, nearly as English *hy*). Ch after a consonant has the softer or palatal sound.

As above noticed (27), g not followed by a vowel etc. has the sound which ch would have in the same situation.

Examples—guttural ch: Bach, doch, Buch, auch, Macher, Achtung, Tochter, Tag, zog, Zug;

palatal ch: Pech, recht, ich, nichts, sicher, Bücher, füchten, Fächer, Löcher, reich, euch, feucht, däuchte, durch, Dolch, mancher, Weg, richtig, Mägde, beugte, Aeuglein, Zwerg.

The fault particularly to be avoided in practising the ch-sound is the closure of the organs, forming a mute consonant, a kind of *k* or *g*. If such a mispronunciation is once acquired, it cannot be unlearned without great trouble. Much better utter a mere breathing, an *h*, at first, depending upon further practice to enable one by degrees to roughen it to the desired point of distinctness.

2. Ch before s, when the s belongs to the theme of the word, and not to an added suffix or inflectional ending, loses its peculiar sound, and is uttered as k (i.e., chs as x).

Examples: Wachs, Ochse, Fuchs, Büchse.

3. Ch in foreign words is usually pronounced as in the languages from which the words are taken—in Greek words, as *k*, in French, as *sh*. As initial, before i or e, it is palatal.

44. Ck, ck.—Ck, as already explained (**30**), is the written equivalent of a double k.

45. Ng, ng.—Ng is the guttural nasal, the equivalent of English *ng*, standing related to k and g as n to t and d, and m to p and b. Its g is not separately uttered, as g, before either a vowel or a consonant: thus, Finger like *singer*, not like *finger*; hungrig like *hangrope*, not like *hungry*.

Examples: jung, singen, Gang, Gänge, länger, dringlich.

46. 1. **Pf, pf.**—Pf is often etymologically the equivalent of our *p* (Pfund, *pound*, Pfahl, *pale*), but is uttered as a combination of p and f.

2. **Ph, ph.**—Ph is found only in words of foreign origin, and has the sound of f, as in English.

Examples: Pfeffer, Pferd, topf, rupfen, Phase, Phosphor, Graphit.

47. Qu, qu.—This combination has been already explained (**34, 39**).

48. Sch, sch.—Sch is the equivalent of our *sh*.

Examples: Schiff, schön, scheu, Asche, Fisch, Schnur, Schwan, Schloß, Schmerz, schreiben, kindisch.

49. Sz, ß.—Sz is pronounced as a double s (ss, **36**), the z losing its distinctive character in the combination. Double ss is not written at the end of a word, nor before a consonant (t), nor after a long vowel or diphthong, ß being in such situations substituted for it.

Examples: laß, laßt (from lassen), Schoß (but Schösse), genießen, Strauß and Sträuße, Haß, häßlich, haßte (but hassen).

As was remarked above (4), when German is written or printed in the Roman character, ß should be represented by *ss*.

50. **Th, th.**—Th, as noticed above (37), is equivalent to t simply.

51. **Tz, tz.**—Tz is the written equivalent of a double z, and is pronounced in the same manner as a single z.

Examples: Platz, Plätze, ſitzen, Mütze, jetzt, plötzlich.

General Supplementary Rules.

52. 1. Other combinations of letters than those treated of above, whether of vowels or of consonants, are pronounced as the single letters of which they are made up.

2. Doubled consonants, however, are not pronounced double, but in the same manner as single ones.

Double consonants, in general, have no etymological ground, but are an orthographical device for indicating the short quantity of the preceding vowel.

53. But doubled consonants, or double vowels, or any of the foregoing combinations of vowels or consonants, if produced by the coming together of the final and initial letters of the parts making up a word—either by composition or by the addition of prefixes or of suffixes of derivation beginning with a consonant—are pronounced as in those parts taken separately. Thus,

beerdet (be=erdet)	not as	Beere ;	geirrt (ge=irrt)	not as	Geier ;
beurtheilt (be=urtheilt)	"	Beute ;	Handdruck (Hand=druck)	"	Edda ;
Mittag (Mit=tag)	"	Mitte ;	wegging (weg=ging)	"	Egge ;
Abbild (Ab=bild)	"	Ebbe ;	auffallt (auf=fallt)	"	Affe ;
vielleicht (viel=leicht)	"	Welle ;	dennoch (den=noch)	"	Henne ;
verreiſt (ver=reiſt)	"	ſperren ;	dasſelbe (das=ſelbe)	"	deſſen ;
wachſam (wach=ſam)	"	wachſen ;	ungar (un=gar)	"	Ungar ;
Häuschen (Häus=chen)	"	haſchen ;	Hauszins (Haus=zins)	"	außer ;
Hutzucker (Hut=zucker)	"	Hitze ;	wegeſſen (weg=eſſen)	"	gegeſſen ;
Abart (Ab=art)	"	Abend ;	Handeiſen (Hand=eiſen)	"	handeln.

54. 1. Respecting the pronunciation of foreign words occurring in German texts, no special rules can or need be given. The degree of their conformity with the rules of utterance of the language to which they properly belong on the one hand, or of the German on the other, depends upon the less or greater completeness of their adoption into German.

2. In pronouncing the classical languages, Latin and Greek, the Germans follow, in general, the rules of utterance of their own letters, both vowels and consonants. But, in reading Latin, *g* is always hard, and *v* has the sound of English *v* (German w), not of German v (English *f*).

ACCENT.

55. The accentuation of German words is so generally accordant in its principles with that of English words, that it occasions little difficulty, even to the beginner, and can be left to be learned by practice, without detailed exposition and illustration. The following are its leading rules:

1. The accent ordinarily rests, in words uncompounded, on the radical or chiefly significant syllable—never on terminations of declension or conjugation, almost never on suffixes of derivation, and never on the inseparable prefixes of verbs (**302**), either in the forms of conjugation or in derivative words.

Exceptions are: the suffix ei (**408**); the i or ie of verbs ending in the infinitive in iren or ieren (**404**); and a few wholly anomalous words, as leben'dig (from le'ben, le'bend).

2. In compound words, except compound particles, the accent rests, as in English, upon the first member. The separable prefixes of verbs are treated as forming compounds, and receive the accent, in the verbal forms and in most verbal derivatives.

Exceptions are: many compounds with all, as allmäch'tig, 'almighty,' allein', 'alone,' allererst', 'first of all;' compound words of direction, like Südost', 'south-east;' and a number of others, as Jahrhun'dert, 'century, leibei'gen, 'vassal,' willkom'men, 'welcome.'

3. Compound particles usually accent the final member: thus, dahin', 'thither,' obgleich', 'although,' zufol'ge, 'according to,' zuvor', 'previously.'

Exceptions are: many adverbs which are properly cases of compound nouns or adjectives; and some others: compare **425**.

4. The negative prefix un has the accent commonly, but not always (compare **416**.*4b*).

5. Words from foreign languages regularly retain the accent belonging to them in those languages—yet with not a few, and irregular, exceptions. As the greater part of them are French, or Latin with the unaccented syllables at the end dropped off, they more usually accent the final syllable.

PARTS OF SPEECH.

56. The parts of speech are the same in German as in English.

They are classified according to the fact and the mode of their grammatical variation, or inflection.

1. NOUNS, ADJECTIVES, and PRONOUNS are declined.

Among these are here included ARTICLES, NUMERALS, and PARTICIPLES, which are sometimes reckoned as separate parts of speech.

2. VERBS are conjugated.

3. ADVERBS, PREPOSITIONS, and CONJUNCTIONS are uninflected.

4. INTERJECTIONS are a class by themselves, not entering as members into the construction of the sentence.

DECLENSION.

57. Declension is the variation of nouns, adjectives, and pronouns for number, case, and gender.

58. There are two NUMBERS, *singular* and *plural*, of which the value and use are in general the same as in English.

For special rules concerning the use of the numbers in German, see **211.**

59. There are four CASES in German, as in the oldest known form of English (Anglo-Saxon).

1. The *nominative*, answering to the English nominative.

The nominative case belongs to the subject of a sentence, to a word in apposition with it, or a predicate noun qualifying it; it is also used in address (as the Latin vocative). See **212–14.**

2. The *genitive*, answering nearly to the English possessive, or objective with *of*.

It is therefore most often dependent upon a noun, but is also used as the object of certain adjectives, verbs, and prepositions; and it stands not infrequently without a governing word, in an adverbial sense. See **215–20.**

3. The *dative*, corresponding to the Latin and Greek dative, or to the English objective with *to* or *for*.

The dative stands as indirect object of many verbs, transitive or intransitive, and also follows certain adjectives, and prepositions. Sometimes it sustains an "ablative" relation, such as we express by *from*. See **221–5.**

4. The *accusative*, nearly the same with our objective

This is especially the case of the direct object of a transitive verb; certain prepositions are followed by it; it is used to express measure (including duration of time and extent of space), also the time when anything is or is done; and it occasionally stands absolutely, as if governed by *having* understood. See **226-30**.

A noun in apposition with a noun standing in any of these relations is put in the same case with it.

60. There are three GENDERS, masculine, feminine, and neuter.

Each noun is of one or the other of these genders, yet not wholly according to the natural sex of the object indicated by it. The names of most objects having conspicuous sex are, indeed, masculine or feminine, according as those objects are male or female; but there are not infrequent exceptions; and the names of objects destitute of sex have a grammatical gender, as masculine, feminine, or neuter, according to rules of which the original ground is in great part impossible to discover, and which do not admit of succinct statement.

This system of artificial or grammatical gender was an original characteristic of all the languages with which the German is related; it belonged equally to the English in the Anglo-Saxon period, and was only lost in connection with the simplification of English grammar by the loss of the distinctive endings of words. See the author's "Language and the Study of Language," p. 77.

61. In the main, therefore, the gender of German words must be learned outright, by experience; but the following practical rules will be found of value:

1. *Exceptions to the natural gender of creatures having sex.*

a. All diminutives formed by the suffixes chen and lein (**410**) are neuter: thus, das Mädchen, 'the girl,' das Fräulein, 'the young lady.'

b. Besides the special names which designate the male and female of certain species, there is a neuter name for the young, or for the species, or for both: thus, der Eber, 'the boar,' die Sau, 'the sow,' das Ferkel, 'the pig,' das Schwein, 'the hog.' Other species are called by the masculine or feminine name properly belonging to one sex only: thus, der Hase, 'the hare,' die Nachtigall, 'the nightingale.'

c. Of anomalous exceptions, only das Weib, 'woman,' requires special notice.

2. *Attribution of gender to classes of inanimate objects.*

a. Names of the seasons, months, and days of the week, of the points of compass, and of stones, are masculine: thus, der Winter,

'winter,' der Mai, 'May,' der Montag, 'Monday,' der Nord, 'north, der Kiesel, 'flint.'

b. Most names of rivers, and of plants, fruits, and flowers (usually ending in e), are feminine: thus, die Donau, 'the Danube,' die Fichte, 'the pine,' die Pflaume, 'the plum,' die Nelke, 'the pink.

c. Most names of countries and places, of metals, the names of the letters, and other parts of speech used as nouns, are neuter: thus: das Italien, 'Italy,' das Berlin, 'Berlin,' das Eisen, 'iron,' das X, 'the letter *x*,' das Ja und Nein, 'the *yes* and *no*.'

3. *Gender as determined by derivation or termination* (for further details, see **408–11**).

a. Masculine are the greater number of derivatives formed from roots without suffix, by change of vowel; also (though with numerous exceptions) of words in el, en, and er; and all derivatives formed by ing and ling.

Thus, der Spruch, 'the speech,' der Nagel, 'the nail,' der Regen, 'the rain,' der Finger, 'the finger,' der Deckel, 'the cover,' der Bohrer, 'the gimlet,' der Findling, 'the foundling.'

b. Feminine are most derivatives in e and t, and all those formed by the secondary suffixes ei, heit, keit, schaft, ung, and in (or inn).

Thus, die Sprache, 'speech,' die Macht, 'might,' die Schmeichelei, 'flattery,' die Weisheit, 'wisdom,' die Eitelkeit, 'vanity,' die Freundschaft, 'friendship,' die Ordnung, 'order,' die Freundin, 'the female friend.'

c. Neuter are all diminutives formed with chen and lein (as already noticed), most nouns formed by the suffixes sel, sal, niß, and thum, most collectives and abstracts formed by the prefix ge, and all infinitives used as nouns.

Thus, das Männchen, 'the mannikin,' das Knäblein, 'the little boy,' das Räthsel, 'the riddle,' das Schicksal, 'fate,' das Gleichniß, 'the likeness,' das Königthum, 'the kingdom,' das Gefieder, 'plumage,' das Gespräch, 'talk,' das Stehen, 'the act of standing.'

4. *Gender of compound nouns.*

Compound nouns regularly and usually take the gender of their final member.

Exceptions are die Antwort, 'answer' (das Wort, 'word'), der Abscheu, abhorrence' (die Scheu, 'fear'), several compounds of der Muth, 'spirit,' as, die Großmuth, 'magnanimity,' Sanftmuth, 'gentleness,' and Demuth, 'humility,' etc., some names of places, and a few others (**421**).

5. *Gender of nouns of foreign origin.*

Excepting a few words—which, having become thoroughly

Germanized, nave had their original gender altered by assimilation to analogous German words, or otherwise anomalously—nouns from other languages are masculine, feminine, or neuter, as in the tongues whence they come: thus, der Titel, 'the title' (Lat. *titulus*, m.), die Krone, 'the crown' (Lat. *corona*, f.), das Phänomen, 'the phenomenon' (Gr. *phainomenon*, n.): but der Körper, 'the body' (Lat. *corpus*, n.), das Fenster, 'the window' (Lat. *fenestra*, f.), die Nummer, 'the number' (Lat. *numerus*, m.).

6. Some nouns are used, commonly or occasionally, as of more than one gender: thus, der or das Theil, 'the part;' das or der Chor, 'the chorus.'

A considerable number of nouns are of more than one gender, dependent on differences of meaning—either nouns of identical derivation, as der Bund, 'the covenant,' and das Bund, 'the bundle,' der See, 'the lake,' and die See, 'the sea;' or nouns of diverse origin, whose identity of form is accidental only, as der Thor, 'the fool,' and das Thor, 'the gate.'

For the details of this variation, as well as of the cases and exceptions under the foregoing rules, the pupil may be referred to his dictionary.

62. Adjectives and most pronouns are inflected in the singular in all the three genders, in order to agree in gender with the nouns which they qualify or to which they relate. No such word makes a distinction of gender in the plural.

ARTICLES.

63. For the sake of convenience, the declension of the definite and indefinite articles is first given.

The definite article is the same with the demonstrative pronoun, in its adjective use (**164**); the indefinite is the same with the numeral ein, 'one' (**198**). Our own articles are of like origin.

Definite Article.

	Singular.			*Plural*	
	masc.	fem.	neut.	m. f. n.	
Nom.	der	die	das	die	the'
Gen.	des	der	des	der	'of the'
Dat.	dem	der	dem	den	'to the'
Acc.	den	die	das	die	'the'

Indefinite Article.

	Singular.			
N.	ein	eine	ein	'a'
G.	eines	einer	eines	'of a
D.	einem	einer	einem	'to a'
A.	einen	eine	ein	'a'

64. 1. The theme (base, stem) of the definite article is d only; of the indefinite, ein: the rest is declensional ending.

2. Notice that the declension of ein differs from that of der in that the former has no ending in the nom. masculine and the nom. and acc. neuter.

65. The acc. neuter das, and the dat. masc. and neuter dem are very frequently appended to prepositions in the form of simple s and m, being written as one word with the preposition; and, in such contracted forms, a preposition ending in n (an, in, von) loses its n before m. The dat. feminine der is in like manner cut down to r, but only after zu, forming zur.

The commonest cases of this contraction and combination are am, im, vom, zum, beim (for an dem, in dem, von dem, zu dem, bei dem), and ans, aufs, ins, fürs, vors (for an das, etc.). Much less frequent are aufm, vorm, durchs, and, with dissyllabic prepositions, übers, überm, and the like.

Rarely, the acc. masculine den is similarly treated, forming übern, hintern, and so on.

Some writers mark the omission of part of the article in these contracted forms by an apostrophe: thus, auf's, über'm, hinter'n, etc.

Very rarely, the same contraction is made after other words than prepositions (e. g., R. 73.30; 149.24).

Use of the Articles.

66. In general, the articles are used in German nearly as in English. But there are also not a few differences, the more important of which are stated below.

1. The definite article regularly stands in German before a noun used in its most comprehensive or universal sense, as indicating the whole substance, class, or kind of which it is the appellation as, das Gold ist gelb, 'gold is yellow;' die Blätter der Pflanzen sind grün, 'leaves of plants are green.'

2. By a like usage, it stands before abstract nouns, when taken without limitation: as, das Leben ist kurz, die Kunst ist lang, 'life is

short, art is long;' der Glaube macht selig, 'faith makes happy; ins Verderben locken, 'to entice to destruction.'

3. It is often used where we use a possessive pronominal adjective (161), when the connection sufficiently points out the possessor, or when the latter is indicated by a noun or pronoun in the dative, dependent on the verb of the sentence: as, der Vater schüttelte den Kopf, 'the father shook *his* head;' da ergreift's ihm die Seele, 'then it takes hold upon *his* soul.'

4. It is prefixed to words of certain classes which in English are used without it; as,

a. To the names of seasons, months, and days of the week: as, im Winter, 'in winter;' in dem (or im) Mai, 'in May,' am Freitag, 'on Friday.'

b. To names of streets and mountains, and to feminine names of countries: as, auf der Friedrichsstraße, 'in Frederick Street;' der Vesuv, 'Vesuvius;' in der Schweiz, 'in Switzerland.'

c. Often to proper names, especially when preceded by adjectives or titles: as, dem kranken Georg, 'to sick George;' das schöne Berlin, 'beautiful Berlin;'—or, when the name of an author is used for his works: as, ich lese den Schiller, 'I am reading Schiller;'—or, in a familiar or contemptuous way; as, rufe den Johann, 'call John;'—or, to indicate more plainly the case of the noun: as, der Schatten der Maria, 'Maria's shadow;' den Argwohn des Andronikus, 'the jealousy of Andronicus' (compare 104).

5. There are numerous phrases, in German as in English, in which the article is omitted, although called for by general analogies. These often correspond in the two languages: as, zu Bette, 'to bed,' bei Tisch, 'at table,' Anker werfen, 'to cast anchor;'—in other cases, the German retains the article which is omitted in English: as, in die Schule, 'to school,' im Himmel und auf der Erde, 'in heaven and on earth,' am Abend, 'at evening;'—or, less often, the article, retained in English, is omitted in the German: as, vor Augen, 'before *the* eyes,' gen Osten, 'toward *the* East.'

6. The article is usually omitted in technical phraseology before words referring to persons or things as already mentioned or to be mentioned, as besagt, gedacht, genannt, 'the aforesaid,' folgend, 'the following,' erster and letzter, 'former' and 'latter,' etc.; also before certain nouns, as Inhaber, 'holder,' Ueberbringer, 'bearer, etc.

7. In place of our indefinite article with a distributive sense, the German employs the definite article: as, so viel das Pfund, so much *a* pound;' des Abends, 'of *an* evening;' dreimal die

Woche, 'three times *a* week.' Also, in certain cases, the definite article in combination with a preposition stands where the indefinite would be expected: as, Staat um Staat sollte zur Provinz werden, 'state after state was to be turned into *a* province.'

8. The indefinite article is omitted before a predicate noun with sein and werden, and before a noun in apposition after als, 'as:' thus, er war Kaufmann, will aber jetzt Soldat werden, 'he was *a* merchant, but now wants to become *a* soldier;' ich kann es als Mann nicht dulden, 'I cannot, as *a* man, endure it.'

The above are only the leading points that require notice in comparing the German and English use of the articles. The German allows, especially in poetry, considerable irregularity and freedom in their employment, and they are not rarely found introduced—and, much more often, omitted—where general analogies would favor a contrary treatment.

67. In regard to their position—the definite article precedes all other qualifying words (except all, 'all'); and the indefinite suffers only so or solch, 'such,' welch, 'what,' and was für, 'what sort of,' before it: thus, die beiden Knaben, 'both the boys;' der doppelte Preis, 'double the price;' solch ein Mann (or ein solcher Mann), 'such a man;' welch ein Held! 'what a hero': but eine halbe Stunde, 'half an hour,' ein so armer Mann, 'so poor a man, eine ganz schöne Aussicht, 'quite a fine view.'

NOUNS.

68. In order to decline a German noun, we need to know how it forms its genitive singular and its nominative plural; and upon these two cases depends the classification of German declensions.

69. 1. The great majority of masculine nouns, and all neuters, form their genitive singular by adding s or es to the nominative. These constitute the FIRST DECLENSION; which is then divided into classes according to the mode of formation of the nominative plural.

a. The *first class* takes no additional ending for the plural, but sometimes modifies the vowel of the theme thus, Spaten, 'spade,' Spaten, 'spades;' but Vater, 'father,' Väter, 'fathers.'

b. The *second class* adds the ending e, sometimes also modifying the vowel: thus, Jahr, 'year,' Jahre, 'years;' Fuß, 'foot,' Füße, 'feet.'

c. The *third class* adds the ending er, and always modifies the vowel: thus, Mann, 'man,' Männer, 'men;' Grab, 'grave,' Gräber, 'graves.'

By modification of the vowel is meant the substitution of the modified vowels ä, ö, ü (**14**), and äu (**21**.2), for the simpler a, o, u, and au, in themes containing the latter. The change of vowel in English *man* and *men*, *foot* and *feet*, *mouse* and *mice*, and their like, is originally the same process. See the author's "Language and the Study of Language," p. 78.

2. Some feminines form their plural after the first and second of these methods, and are therefore reckoned as belonging to the first and second classes of the first declension, although they do not now take s in the genitive singular.

The German genitive ending of the first declension is historically identical with the *s* which forms our English possessives.

70. The rest of the masculine nouns add n or en to the theme to form the genitive singular, and take the same ending also in the nominative plural. Most feminines form their plural in the same way, and are therefore classified with them, making up the SECOND DECLENSION.

The feminines are classified by the form of their plurals only, because as is pointed out below, all feminine nouns are now invariable in the singular.

71. The two cases above mentioned being known, the rest of the declension is found by the following general rules:

1. *Singular. a.* Feminines are invariable in the singular.

For exceptions, see below, **95**.

b. In the masculines and neuters of the first declension, the accusative singular is like the nominative. Nouns which add only s in the genitive have the dative also like the nominative; those which add es in the genitive regularly take e in the dative, but may also omit it—it being proper to form the dative of any noun of the first declension like the nominative.

c. Masculines of the second declension have all their oblique cases like the genitive.

2. *Plural. a.* The nominative, genitive, and accusative are always alike in the plural.

b. The dative plural ends invariably in n: it is formed by adding n to the nominative plural, provided that case end in any other letter than n (namely, in e, l, or r, the only other finals that occur there); if it end in n, all the cases of the plural are alike.

72. The following general rules, applying to all declension—that of nouns, adjectives, and pronouns—are worthy of notice:

1. The acc. singular of the fem. and neuter is like the nominative.
2. The dat. plural (except of personal pronouns) ends in n.

73. It will be seen, on comparing the declension of nouns with that of the definite article (**63**), that the former is less full, distinguishing fewer cases by appropriate terminations. Besides their plural ending—which, moreover, is wanting in a considerable class of words—nouns have distinct forms only for the genitive singular and the dative plural, with traces of a dative singular—and even these in by no means all words.

What are here called the FIRST and SECOND declensions are often styled (after Grimm's example) the *strong* and *weak* declensions. A historically suitable designation would be "vowel-declension" and "*n*-declension," since the first mode of declension properly belongs to themes originally ending in a vowel (though the plural-ending er comes from themes in s); the second, to those ending in n: other consonant-endings with their peculiarities of declension have disappeared. The whole German declensional system has undergone such extensive corruption, mutilation, and transfer, that the old historical classifications are pretty thoroughly effaced, and to attempt to restore them, or make any account of them, would only confuse the learner.

First Declension of Nouns.

74. As already explained, the first declension contains all the neuter nouns in the language, all masculines which form their genitive singular by adding s or es to the nominative, and such feminines as form their nominative plural either without an added ending, or else by appending e to the theme.

FIRST CLASS.

75. The characteristic of the FIRST CLASS is that it adds no ending to form the plural: its nominatives are alike in both numbers—except that in a few words the vowel of the singular is modified for the plural.

76. To this class belong

1. Masculine and neuter nouns having the endings el, er, en (including infinitives used as nouns, 340), and one or two in em;

2. A few neuter nouns having the prefix ge and ending in e; also one masculine in e (Käse, 'cheese');

3. All neuter diminutives formed with the suffixes chen and lein;

4. Two feminines ending in er (Mutter, 'mother,' and Tochter, 'daughter').

No nouns of this class are monosyllabic (except the infinitives thun and sein). The endings el, er do not include iel, eel, ier, eer, but imply the simple vowel e as that of the termination.

77. Nouns of the first class add only s (not es) to form the genitive singular, and never take e in the dative.

Their only variation for case, therefore, is by the assumption of s in the gen. sing. (of masc. and neut. nouns), and of n in the dat. plural.

78. About twenty masculines (Apfel, 'apple,' Bruder, 'brother,' Garten, 'garden,' Vater, 'father,' Vogel, 'bird, etc.), one neuter (Kloster, 'convent'), and both feminines, modify in the plural the vowel of the principal syllable.

79. Examples:—

I. With vowel unchanged in the plural:

	Spaten, 'spade,' m.	Gebirge, 'mountain range,' n.	Käse, 'cheese,' m.
		Singular.	
N.	der Spaten	das Gebirge	der Käse
G.	des Spatens	des Gebirges	des Käses
D.	dem Spaten	dem Gebirge	dem Käse
A.	den Spaten	das Gebirge	den Käse

Plural.

N.	die Spaten	die Gebirge	die Käse
G.	der Spaten	der Gebirge	der Käse
D.	den Spaten	den Gebirgen	den Käsen
A.	die Spaten	die Gebirge	die Käse

II. With vowel modified in the plural:

	Bruder, 'brother,' m.	Kloster, 'convent,' n.	Mutter, 'mother,' f.
		Singular.	
N.	der Bruder	das Kloster	die Mutter
G.	des Bruders	des Klosters	der Mutter
D.	dem Bruder	dem Kloster	der Mutter
A.	den Bruder	das Kloster	die Mutter
		Plural.	
N.	die Brüder	die Klöster	die Mütter
G.	der Brüder	der Klöster	der Mütter
D.	den Brüdern	den Klöstern	den Müttern
A.	die Brüder	die Klöster	die Mütter

80. 1. A few nouns are of this class in the singular and of the second declension in the plural; a few others have lost an original ending n or en in the nom. (or nom. and acc.) singular, being otherwise regular. For all these, see Irregular Declension (**97**).

2. Among the infinitives used as nouns, and belonging to this class, are a few of irregular ending: namely, thun, 'to do,' and sein, 'to be,' with their compounds, some of which are in common use as nouns—e. g., Dasein, 'existence,' Wohlsein, 'welfare'—; and others which end in eln and ern; thus, Wandeln, 'walking,' Wandern, 'wandering.'

Exercise I.

Nouns of the first declension, first class.

For the words and forms in this and the following exercises, see the Glossary to the Exercises, at the end of the Grammar.

1. Der Bruder meines Vaters ist mein Onkel. 2. Er hat Gärten auf dem Gebirge. 3. In den Gärten sind Aepfel auf den Bäumchen. 4. Ich gebe dem Schüler das Messer und dem Lehrer den Hammer. 5. Des Müllers Käse sind auf den Tellern in meinem Zimmer. 6

Wo sind die Fräulein, die Töchter meiner Mutter? 7. Sie stehen vor den Spiegeln, oder schauen aus den Fenstern. 8. Die Adler sind Vögel, und haben zwei Flügel und einen Schnabel.

SECOND CLASS.

81. The characteristic of the SECOND CLASS is that it forms the plural by adding e to the singular; at the same time, the vowel of the principal syllable is usually modified in the plural: but to this there are many exceptions.

82. To this class belong

1. The greater number of masculine nouns;
2. Many neuters;
3. About thirty-five monosyllabic feminines (with their compounds, and including the compounds of kunft, not in use as an independent word), with the feminines formed by the suffixes niß (about a dozen in number) and sal (two or three).

83. Masculines and neuters form their genitive singular by adding either s or es; the dative is like the nominative, or adds e.

The ending es is more usually taken by monosyllables, s by polysyllables; but most words may assume either, according to the choice of the writer or speaker, depending partly on euphony, and partly on the style he is employing—es belonging to a more serious or elaborate style, and s being more colloquial. Excepted are words which end in a sibilant, and which therefore require an interposed e to make the genitive ending perceptible to the ear. Thus, Tages is more usual than Tags, Königs than Königes, while Schmetterlinges would hardly be tolerated; but always Floßes, Fuchses, Satzes.

The use or omission of e in the dative is nearly parallel with the use of es or s in the genitive; but it may be left off from every noun without exception.

84. Of the masculines, the great majority take the modified vowel in the plural, there being only about fifty exceptions (including some very common words, as Tag, 'day,' Arm, 'arm,' Hund, 'dog,' Schuh, 'shoe,' Zoll, 'inch'); of the neuters, only two, Floß, 'raft,' and Chor, 'choir,' require the modification, and two others, Boot, 'boat,' and Rohr, 'reed,' may take it or not; of the feminines, all except those ending in niß and sal modify the vowel.

85. Examples:—

I. With vowel modified in the plural:

	Sohn, 'son,' m.	Floß, 'raft,' n.	Hand, 'hand,' f.
		Singular.	
N.	der Sohn	das Floß	die Hand
G.	des Sohnes	des Floßes	der Hand
D.	dem Sohne	dem Floße	der Hand
A.	den Sohn	das Floß	die Hand
		Plural.	
N.	die Söhne	die Flöße	die Hände
G.	der Söhne	der Flöße	der Hände
D.	den Söhnen	den Flößen	den Händen
A.	die Söhne	die Flöße	die Hände

II. With vowel unchanged in the plural:

	Monat, 'month,' m.	Jahr, 'year,' n.	Ersparniß, 'saving,' f.
		Singular.	
N.	der Monat	das Jahr	die Ersparniß
G.	des Monats	des Jahres	der Ersparniß
D.	dem Monat	dem Jahre	der Ersparniß
A.	den Monat	das Jahr	die Ersparniß
		Plural.	
N.	die Monate	die Jahre	die Ersparnisse
G.	der Monate	der Jahre	der Ersparnisse
D.	den Monaten	den Jahren	den Ersparnissen
A.	die Monate	die Jahre	die Ersparnisse

86. Most nouns of foreign origin belong to this class. For some irregularities in their declension, as well as in that of other members of the class, see below, 97 etc.

Exercise II.

Nouns of the first declension, second class.

1. In einem Jahre sind zwölf Monate, und in einem Monate sind dreißig Tage. 2. Mein Sohn hat zwei Arme, und an jedem Arme

eine Hand. 3. Er hat Schuhe an den Füßen, und auf dem Kopfe einen Hut. 4. Die Stühle und Bänke stehen um die Tische. 5. Meine Freunde machen Flöße von Bäumen, und schicken sie mir auf dem Flusse. 6. Die Störche finden Frösche in den Bächen vor den Thoren der Stadt.

Third Class.

87. The characteristic of this class is the assumption of the ending er to form the nominative plural, along with modification of the vowel of the theme.

88. The class is composed chiefly of neuter nouns with a few masculines, but no feminines.

Besides the nouns formed by the suffix thum (which are, with two or three exceptions, neuter, and which modify the vowel of the suffix, not that of the radical syllable), there are not far from fifty neuters, and about a dozen masculines, belonging to the class; also, three or four words of foreign origin.

Among the neuters of most frequent occurrence are Bild, Blatt, Buch, Feld, Grab, Haus, Kind, Kleid, Licht, Lied, Thal, Volk, Weib, Wort, Gesicht. The masculines are Geist, Gott, Leib, Mann, Ort, Rand, Wald, Wurm, Vormund, Bösewicht, and sometimes Dorn.

89. Respecting the form of the genitive singular ending, whether s or es, and respecting the dative, whether like the nominative or adding e, the same rules apply as in the second class (83).

90. Examples:—

	Haus, 'house,' n.	Weib, 'woman,' n.	Irrthum, 'error,' m.	Mann, 'man,' m.
		Singular.		
N.	das Haus	Weib	der Irrthum	Mann
G.	des Hauses	Weibes	des Irrthums	Mannes
D.	dem Hause	Weibe	dem Irrthum	Manne
A.	das Haus	Weib	den Irrthum	Mann
		Plural.		
N.	die Häuser	Weiber	die Irrthümer	Männer
G.	der Häuser	Weiber	der Irrthümer	Männer
D.	den Häusern	Weibern	den Irrthümern	Männern
A.	die Häuser	Weiber	die Irrthümer	Männer

Exercise III.

Nouns of the first declension, third class.

1. Das erste Weib machte ein Kleid aus Blättern. 2. Bringe mir ein Buch und ein Licht aus dem Hause. 3. In den Büchern der Kinder sind viele Bilder und viele Wörter. 4. Der Leib des Mannes geht in das Grab, sein Geist geht zu Gott. 5. Das Volk singt Lieder im Hause, im Feld, im Wald, und in den Thälern.

Second Declension of Nouns.

91. To the second declension belong only masculine and feminine nouns. They form all the cases of the plural by adding n or en to the theme, and masculines take the same ending in the oblique cases of the singular.

92. 1. Nearly all the feminine nouns in the language are of this declension: namely

a. All feminines of more than one syllable, whether primitive words, as Seite, 'side,' Kugel, 'ball,' Feder, 'feather;' or primary derivatives, as Gabe, 'gift,' Sprache, 'speech;' words formed with prefixes, as Gefahr, 'danger,' or with suffixes, as Tugend, 'virtue,' Wahrheit, 'truth,' Fürstin, 'princess,' Ladung, 'loading.'

Exceptions: those having the suffixes niß or sal (see **82**.3).

b. About thirty monosyllables, as Art, 'manner,' Frau, 'woman,' Pflicht, 'duty,' That, 'deed,' Welt, 'world,' Zeit, 'time.'

c. All feminines derived from other languages, as Minute, 'minute,' Melodie, 'melody,' Nation, 'nation,' Universität, 'university.'

2. Masculines of the second declension are

a. Words of more than one syllable in e, as Bote, 'messenger,' Gatte, 'spouse,' Knabe, 'boy'—including those that have the prefix ge, as Gefährte, 'companion,' Geselle, 'fellow,' and some nouns of nationality, as Preuße, 'Prussian,' Franzose, 'Frenchman;' also a few in er and ar, as Baier, 'Bavarian,' Ungar, 'Hungarian.'

b. About twenty monosyllabic root-words, as Bär, 'bear,' Graf, 'count,' Held, 'hero,' Herr, 'master,' Mensch, 'man (human being),' Ochs, 'ox,' Thor, 'fool.'

c. Many foreign words, as Student, 'student,' Monarch, 'monarch,' Barbar, 'barbarian.'

93. Nouns ending in e, el, er, and ar unaccented, add n only to the theme; others add en.

Before this ending, the n of the suffix in is doubled: thus, Fürstin, Fürstinnen.

Herr, in modern usage, ordinarily adds n in the singular, and en in the plural, being the only masculine whose forms differ in the two numbers.

No noun of this declension modifies its vowel in the plural.

94. Examples:—

I. Feminines:

	Seite, 'side.'	That, 'deed.'	Wahrheit, 'truth.'	Nation, 'nation.'
		Singular.		
N.	die Seite	That	Wahrheit	Nation
G.	der Seite	That	Wahrheit	Nation
D.	der Seite	That	Wahrheit	Nation
A.	die Seite	That	Wahrheit	Nation
		Plural.		
N.	die Seiten	Thaten	Wahrheiten	Nationen
G.	der Seiten	Thaten	Wahrheiten	Nationen
D	den Seiten	Thaten	Wahrheiten	Nationen
A.	die Seiten	Thaten	Wahrheiten	Nationen

II. Masculines:

	Knabe, 'boy.'	Baier, 'Bavarian.'	Mensch, 'man.'	Student, 'student.'
		Singular.		
N.	der Knabe	Baier	Mensch	Student
G. D. A.	Knaben	Baiern	Menschen	Studenten
		Plural.		
N. G. D. A.	Knaben	Baiern	Menschen	Studenten

95. Formerly, many feminine nouns of this declension, like the masculines, took the declensional ending in the genitive and dative singular; and this ending is still commonly retained in certain phrases: e. g., auf Erden, 'on earth;' zu Ehren, 'in honor [of];' mit Freuden, 'with pleasure;' von Seiten, 'on the part [of].' Occasionally, also, it appears in a gen. feminine preceding the governing noun, as um seiner Seelen Heil, 'for the welfare of his soul;' and yet more rarely, by poetic license, in other situations (e. g., R. 100.23).

Exercise IV.

Nouns of the second declension.

1. Der Herr dieses Knaben ist ein Preuße, oder ein Ungar. 2. Grafen sind nur Menschen, und nicht immer Helden. 3. Die Studenten der Chemie waren meine Gefährten auf der Universität. 4. Die Frau sah den Ochsen und die Ziege ihres Gatten in Gefahr. 5. Die Erde ist eine Kugel, und auf ihrer Fläche leben die Nationen der Menschen mit ihren Monarchen. 6. Wahrheit ist die Tugend eines Boten. 7. Dieser Pole ist Advokat; sein Neffe ist Soldat.

Exercise V.

Nouns of all declensions.

1. Diese Familie besteht aus sechs Personen: die Frau ist die Mutter; der Mann ist ihr Gatte, und Vater der vier Kinder; die zwei Knaben sind ihre Söhne; die zwei Mädchen sind ihre Töchter. 2. Der Student steht an dem Pulte in seinem Zimmer; er stützt den Kopf auf seinen Arm; er hat eine Feder in der anderen Hand, und schreibt in einem Buche. 3. Mein Freund gab mir einen Apfel, den er fand unter einem Baume in seinem Garten. 4. Des Müllers Bruder hat das Messer meines Neffen. 5. Ich sehe Lichter in den Fenstern aller Häuser der Stadt.

Irregular Declension of Nouns.

96. Irregularities in the declension of nouns of foreign origin, and of proper names, will be considered below, under those titles respectively (see **101–8**).

97. *Mixed Declension.*

1. A very small number (six or eight) of masculine and neuter nouns are declined in the singular according to the first declension, and in the plural according to the second: as, Staat, 'state,' gen. sing. Staates, pl. Staaten.

2. A somewhat larger number (about twenty), form their plural according either to the first or the second declension: as, Vetter, 'cousin,' pl. Vetter or Vettern; Bett, 'bed,' pl. Bette or Betten.

Authorities are considerably at variance respecting the limits of these two classes, some rejecting as incorrect the one or the other of the two plurals.

3. Certain nouns of foreign origin are of the first declension in the singular, and the second in the plural, as Insect, 'insect,' gen sing. Insectes; pl. Insecten:—especially those ending in unaccented or (which, however, throw the accent forward, upon the or, in the plural), as Doc'tor, gen. sing. Doc'tors, pl. Docto'ren.

4. Examples:—

	Staat, 'state,' m.	Vetter, 'cousin,' m.	Doctor, 'doctor,' m.	Auge, 'eye,' n.
		Singular.		
N.	der Staat	Vetter	Doctor	das Auge
G.	des Staates	Vetters	Doctors	des Auges
D.	dem Staate	Vetter	Doctor	dem Auge
A.	den Staat	Vetter	Doctor	das Auge
		Plural.		
N., etc.	Staaten	Vettern or Vetter, etc.	Doctoren	Augen

98. *Declension with defective theme.*

1. A few masculines (six or eight), properly belonging to the first declension, first class, and having themes ending in en, more usually drop the n in the nom. sing., being otherwise regular.

2. One masculine, Schmerz, 'pain,' and one neuter, Herz, 'heart, have lost the en of their original themes in the nom. and acc sing. (Schmerz follows also the mixed declension).

3. Examples:—

	Namen, 'name,' m.	Frieden, 'peace,' m.	Herz, 'heart,' n.
		Singular.	
N.	der Name (or -men)	Friede (or -den)	das Herz
G.	des Namens	Friedens	des Herzens
D.	dem Namen	Frieden	dem Herzen
A.	den Namen	Frieden	das Herz
		Plural.	
N., etc.	Namen	Frieden	Herzen

99. *Redundant Declension.*

1. A considerable number of nouns of infrequent occurrence,

with some even that are in familiar use, are declined after more than one model, especially in the plural, less often in the singular also.

2. A less number (twenty to twenty-five) have two well-established forms of the plural, belonging to two different significations of their theme: thus, Band, n., 'bond' and 'ribbon;' Bande, 'bonds,' but Bänder, 'ribbons:' Wort, 'word;' Worte, 'words' (implying their significance), but Wörter, enumerated vocables.

See also **97.2.**

3. Sporn, 'spur,' besides its regular plurals Spornen and Sporne, has the wholly irregular Sporen.

100. *Defective Declension.*

1. In German, as in English, there are classes of nouns—especially abstracts, as Demuth, 'humility,' and names of substances, as Gold, 'gold' (unless, as is sometimes the case, they have taken on also a concrete or individualized sense, as Thorheiten, 'follies,' Papiere, 'papers')—which, in virtue of their signification, have no plural.

Some abstract nouns, when they take such a modified sense as to admit of plural use, substitute other, derivative or compound, forms: as, Tod, 'death,' Todesfälle, 'deaths' (literally, 'cases of death'); Bestreben, 'exertion,' Bestrebungen, 'exertions, efforts.'

2. A much smaller number have no singular: as, Eltern, 'parents,' Masern, 'measles,' Trümmer, 'ruins,' Leute, 'people.'

Compounds of Mann, 'man,' substitute leute for mann in the plural, when taken collectively: thus, Kaufmann, 'merchant,' Kaufleute, 'merchants;' but zwei Kaufmänner, 'two (individual) merchants.'

Nouns of Foreign Origin.

101. 1. Nouns derived from foreign languages are variously treated, according to the completeness of their naturalization.

2. The great mass of them are assimilated in inflection to German models, and belong to the regular declensions and classes, as already stated.

3. A class of nouns in um from the Latin form a plural in en; thus, Individuum, Individuen; Studium, Studien; and a few in al and il add ien: thus, Kapital, Kapitalien, Fossil, Fossilien.

4. A few, as in English, form their plurals after the manner of the languages from which they come; but are hardly capable of any other variation, except an s as sign of the genitive singular: thus, Musicus, Musici; Tempus, Tempora; Factum, Facta.

5. Some from the French and English, or other modern languages, form

the plural, as well as the genitive singular, in s: thus, seidene Sophas 'silken sofas;' die Lords, 'the lords;' die Lamas, 'the lamas.'

Sometimes, rather than add a genitive sign s to a word which in the original took none such, an author prefers to leave it, like a proper name, uninflected: thus, des Jaguar, 'of the jaguar' (R. 218.5); des Klima, 'of the climate' (R. 222.30).

Before this foreign and irregular s, some authorities set an apostrophe, both in the genitive and the plural, especially after a vowel. The same is true in proper names.

Proper Names.

102. Proper names are inflected like common nouns, unless they are names of persons, of places (towns and the like), or neuter names of countries.

103. Names of countries and places admit only the genitive ending s (not es); if, as terminating in a sibilant, they cannot take that ending, they are not declined at all: thus, die Wüsten Afrika's, 'the deserts of Africa;' die Einwohner Berlins, 'the inhabitants of Berlin;' but die Einwohner von Paris, 'the inhabitants of Paris.'

104. Names of persons were formerly more generally and more fully declined than at present; now, the article is customarily used to indicate the case, and the name itself remains unvaried after it in the singular.

But the genitive takes an ending if followed by the governing word: as des großen Friedrichs Thaten, 'Frederick the Great's deeds.'

105. When used without the article, such nouns add s in the genitive: thus, Schillers, Friedrichs. But masculine names ending in a sibilant, and feminines in e, have ens in the genitive: thus, Maxens, Sophiens.

The dative and accusative, of both genders, were formerly made to end in n or en, which ending is now more often, and preferably, omitted, and the name left unvaried in those cases.

106. The plurals of masculine names, with or without the article, have e (rarely en), with n added in the dative; of feminines, n or en. Those in o (from Latin themes in on) add ne: thus, Cato, Catone.

107. Jesus and Christus are still usually declined as Latin nouns: gen. Jesu, Christi (R. 189.23); dat. Jesu, Christo (R. 183.24); acc. Jesum, Christum. Other classical names were formerly treated in the same manner, and cases thus formed are occasionally met with, even in recent works

108. 1. A proper name following a title that has the article before it is left unvaried; if without the article, it takes the genitive sign, and the title (except Herr) is unvaried: thus; der Sohn Kaiser Friedrichs, 'the son of Emperor Frederick,' Herrn Schmidts Haus, 'Mr. Smith's house;' but Kreuzzug des Kaisers Friedrich, 'the crusade of Emperor Frederick.'

2. An appended title is declined, whether the preceding name be declined or not; thus, Alexanders des Großen Geschichte, 'Alexander the Great's history;' die Thaten des Königs Friedrich des Zweiten, 'the deeds of King Frederick the Second.'

3. Of two or more proper names belonging to the same person, only the last is liable to variation under the preceding rules: thus, Herrn Johann Schmidts Haus, 'Mr. John Smith's house;' but, if the last be a family name preceded by von, it takes the genitive ending only before the governing noun: thus, Friedrich von Schillers Werke, but die Werke Friedrichs von Schiller, 'the works of Frederick von Schiller.'

MODIFYING ADJUNCTS OF THE NOUN.

109. A noun may enter as an element into the structure of the sentence not only by itself, but as modified and limited by adjuncts of various kinds.

110. 1. The most usual adjunct of a noun is an adjective (including under this term the pronominal and numeral adjectives and the articles); namely

a. An attributive adjective, preceding the noun, and agreeing with it in gender, number, and case: as, ein guter Mann, 'a good man;' der schönen Frau, 'of the beautiful woman;' diesen artigen Kindern, 'to these well-behaved children' (see **115**).

b. An appositive adjective, following the noun, and in German not varied to agree with it (treated, rather, as if the predicate of an adjective clause): thus, ein Lehnstuhl reich geschnitzt und wunderlich, 'an arm-chair richly carved and quaint' (see **116**.2).

But an adjective may follow a noun, as if appositive, and yet be declined, being treated as if having a noun understood after it: thus, die Feinde, die mächtigen, siegen, 'the enemies, the mighty, prevail;' wenn ich vergang'ner Tage, glücklicher, zu denken wage, 'when I venture to think of past days, happy ones.'

c. An adjective clause, containing a verb and its subject, and introduced by a relative pronoun or conjunction: as, der Ring, den sie mir gab, 'the ring which she gave to me;' die Hütte, wo der alte Bergmann wohnt, 'the cottage where the old miner lives' (see **437**).

2. Sometimes an adverb, by an elliptical construction (as representing the predicate of an adjective clause), stands as adjunct to a noun: as, der Mann hier, 'tho man here;' der Himmel dort oben, 'heaven above'—that is, 'the man who is here,' etc.

111. A noun is very often limited by another noun.

1. By a noun dependent on it, and placed either before or after it.

a. Usually in the genitive case, and expressing a great variety of relations (**216**).

b. Very rarely, in the dative case (**225**).

2. By an appositive noun, following it, and agreeing with it in case (but not necessarily in gender or number): as, er hat den Kaiser Friedrich, seinen Herrn, verrathen, 'he has betrayed the Emperor Frederick, his master;' den sie, meine Geliebte, mir gab, 'which she, my beloved, gave me.'

The appositive noun is sometimes connected with its subject by the conjunction als, 'as:' thus, zieht, als der letzte Dichter, der letzte Mensch hinaus, 'the last man marches out as last poet.'

3. The other parts of speech used as substantives (**113**), of course, may take the place of the limiting noun.

112. A noun is limited by a prepositional phrase: that is, by a noun whose relation to it is defined by a preposition: as, der Schlüssel zu Hamlets Betragen, 'the key to Hamlet's behavior.'

This construction is especially frequent, and most organic, with verbal derivatives retaining something of the verbal force: thus, Erziehung zur Freiheit, 'education to freedom;' die Hoffnung auf eine Einigung mit dem Kaiser, 'the hoping for an understanding with the emperor.'

In other cases, the prepositional phrase is virtually the adverbial predicate of an adjective clause: as, der Mann im Osten, 'the man [who was. or lived] in the East.'

EQUIVALENTS OF THE NOUN.

113. 1. Other parts of speech are habitually or occasionally used as substantives, and may be substituted for the noun in a part or all of its constructions. These are

a. The substantive pronouns and numerals: as, ich, 'I;' dich, 'thee;' sie, 'she, her, they, them;' wer, 'who;' sechs der Männer, 'six of the men.'

b. Infinitives of verbs (which are properly verbal nouns): see **339** etc.

c. Adjectives (including pronominal and numeral adjectives and participles) are often converted into nouns (see **129**).

2. Any word or phrase, viewed in itself, as concrete representative of what it signifies, may be used as a neuter substantive: thus, sein eigen Ich, 'his own "I";' ohne Wenn oder Aber, 'without "if" or "but";' jedes Für und Wider, 'every pro and con.'

3. A substantive clause, containing a verb and its subject, and introduced generally by daß, 'that,' ob, 'whether,' or a compound relative word, takes the place of a noun in some constructions (see **436**).

For a fuller definition of the relations and constructions in which the various equivalents of the noun may be used, see the several parts of speech concerned.

ADJECTIVES.

114. The Adjective, in German, is declined only when used attributively or substantively.

115. 1. The attributive adjective always precedes the noun which it qualifies; it is varied for number and case, and (in the singular only) for gender, and agrees in all these particulars with its noun.

But the noun to which the adjective relates is often omitted: the latter, in such case, has the same form as if followed by the noun: as, er hat weiße Häuser, und wir haben braune, 'he has white houses, and we have *brown;*' geben Sie mir zweierlei Tuch, rothes und schwarzes, 'give me two kinds of cloth, *red* and *black.*'

2. For the adjective used as a substantive, see below, **129.**

116. The adjective remains uninflected when used predicatively, appositively, or adverbially.

1. The predicate adjective is used,—*a.* as *simple predicate*, after verbs that signify being, becoming, continuing, seeming, and the like: as, sein Haus war schön und weiß, wird aber jetzt alt, und sieht häßlich aus, 'his house was *white* and *handsome*, but is now growing *old*, and looks *ugly;*'—*b.* as *adverbial predicate*, defining more nearly the condition or action designated by the verb: as, todt und starr liegt die Wüste hingestreckt, 'the steppe lies *stretched out dead* and *stiff;*'—*c.* as *factitive predicate*, to express a condition effected in or ascribed to an object by the action of a transitive verb: as, sich halb todt lachen, 'to laugh one's self *half dead;*' er malt das Haus weiß, 'he paints the house *white;*' ich will meine Augen offen behalten, 'I will keep my eyes *open;*' die lang' ich vergessen geglaubt, 'which I had long believed *forgotten*'—whence, of course, also as simple predicate in the corresponding passive expression: as, das Haus wird weiß gemalt, 'the house is painted *white.*'

2. The appositive adjective usually follows the noun: as, wir waren zwei Kinder, klein und froh, 'we were two children, *small* and *merry;*' Worte süß wie Mondlicht, 'words *sweet* as moonlight.'

3. For the adjective used as adverb, see below, **130.**

4. The uses of the adjective in apposition, as predicate, and as adverb, pass into one another by insensible gradations, and the same word often admits of more than one understanding. The appositive adjective, also, is sometimes distinguished from the attributive rather formally than logically; as, bei einem Wirthe wundermild, 'with a host wondrous *kind;*' einen Blick zum Himmel hoch, 'a look to Heaven *high.*' The attributive adjective was formerly permitted after the noun as well as before, and was declined in that position; as was also the adjective used predicatively.

117. A few adjectives are always used predicatively, and are therefore never declined; others are used only attributively, and are therefore always declined.

a. Of the first class, some of the most common are bereit, 'ready,' feind, 'hostile,' kund, 'known,' gewahr, 'aware,' eingedenk, 'mindful,' theilhaft, 'participating.'

b. To the second class belong many adjectives expressing formal relations—viz., certain pronominal adjectives, as jener, 'yon,' jeder, 'every,' meinig, 'mine,' selbig, 'self-same;' some adjectives of number, time, and place, as zweit, 'second,' heutig, 'of to-day,' dortig, 'there situated;' and the adjectives of material in en, ern, for which, in predicate construction, prepositional phrases are usually substituted.

DECLENSIONS OF THE ADJECTIVE.

118. Each adjective, in its attributive use, is subject to two different modes of declension, according as it is or is not preceded by certain limiting words. These we shall call the FIRST and SECOND declensions (see **132**).

119. 1. The endings of the FIRST DECLENSION are the same with those of the definite article, already given (**63**).

Excepting that the nom. and acc. sing. neuter have es instead of as, and the nom. and acc. plural and fem. singular have e instead of ie: that is, the final and characteristic letter is the same, but differently preceded.

2. The SECOND DECLENSION has only two endings, e and en: e belongs to the nominative singular of all genders, and hence also (see **72.1**), to the accusative of the feminine and neuter; en is found in all the other cases. Thus

Adjective Endings of Declension.

	FIRST DECLENSION.				SECOND DECLENSION.			
	Singular.			*Plural.*	*Singular.*			*Plural.*
	m.	f.	n.	m. f. n.	m.	f.	n.	m. f. n.
N.	-er	-e	-es	-e	-e	-e	-e	-en
G.	-es	-er	-es	-er	-en	-en	-en	-en
D.	-em	-er	-em	-en	-en	-en	-en	-en
A.	-en	-e	-es	-e	-en	-e	-e	-en

3. It will be noticed that the first declension has more than twice as many distinct endings as the second, and that it therefore makes a correspondingly superior, though a far from complete, distinction of genders and cases.

120. 1. The endings as given are appended throughout to the theme of the adjective, or to the adjective in its simple predicative form.

Thus, from gut, 'good,' are formed, in the first declension, guter, gute, gutes, gutem, guten; in the second, gute, guten.

2. But adjectives ending in e reject this e in every case before taking the ending (or, what is the same thing, reject the e of every ending).

Thus, from träge, 'lazy,' come träger, träge, träges, trägem, trägen.

3. Adjectives ending in the unaccented terminational syllables el, en, er, also usually reject the e either of those syllables or of the declensional ending.

Thus, from edel, 'noble,' come edler, edle, edles, and generally edlem and edlen, less often edelm, edeln; from heiter, 'cheerful,' come usually heitrer, heitre, heitres, and heiterm and heitern, or heitrem and heitren; from eben, 'even,' come ebner, ebne, ebnes, ebnem, ebnen. The full forms of these words, however—as ebener, heiterer, and, less often, edeles—are also in good use, especially in a more stately or solemn style.

4. Hoch, 'high,' loses its c when declined: thus, hoher, hohe, hohes, etc.

121. 1. The adjective, now, takes the more distinctive endings of the first declension, unless preceded by a limiting word of a higher order (an article, pronoun, or pronominal adjective: see **123**) which itself has those endings.

Thus, as we say der Mann, 'the man,' so also guter Mann, 'good man,' but der gute Mann, 'the good man;' as die Frauen, 'the women,' so gute Frauen, and gute schöne Frauen, but die guten schönen Frauen, 'the good handsome women;' as dem Kinde, 'to the child,' so gutem Kinde, and gutem, schönem, artigem Kinde, but dem guten, schönen, artigen Kinde, 'to the good, handsome, well-behaved child.'

2. Or, in other words, a pronominal limiting word before the adjective, if it have itself the more distinctive adjective ending characteristic of the case and gender of the qualified noun, takes that ending away from the adjective, reducing the latter from the first to the second declension: the distinctive ending does not need to be, and is not, repeated upon both words.

Note that certain cases—the acc. sing. masculine, the nom. and acc. sing feminine, and the dat. plural—have the same ending in the one declension as in the other, and are therefore not altered, whatever the situation in which the adjective is placed.

3. By an irregular extension of this tendency to avoid the unnecessary repetition of a distinctive ending, a gen. sing. masculine or neuter ending in s (not a masculine ending in n) takes before it usually the second form of the adjective (in en), instead of the first (in es).

Thus, kalten Wassers, 'of cold water,' frohen Muthes, 'with joyous spirit,' großen Theils, 'in great part,' and so on, are much more common than kaltes Wassers, frohes Muthes, etc., although the latter are not incorrect.

122. Examples:—

1. Complete declension of an adjective, gut, 'good,' in both forms.

FIRST DECLENSION.

	Singular. m.	f.	n.	*Plural.* m. f. n.
N.	guter	gute	gutes	gute
G.	gutes	guter	gutes	guter
D.	gutem	guter	gutem	guten
A.	guten	gute	gutes	gute

SECOND DECLENSION.

	Singular. m.	f.	n.	*Plural.* m. f. n.
N.	der gute	die gute	das gute	die guten
G.	des guten	der guten	des guten	der guten
D.	dem guten	der guten	dem guten	den guten
A.	den guten	die gute	das gute	die guten

2. Declension of noun and accompanying adjective: rother Wein, 'red wine,' große Freude, 'great joy,' schlechtes Geld, 'bad money.'

	FIRST DECLENSION. *Singular.* m.	SECOND DECLENSION. m.
N.	rother Wein	der rothe Wein
G.	rothes or rothen Weines	des rothen Weines
D.	rothem Weine	dem rothen Weine
A.	rothen Wein	den rothen Wein

Singular.

	f.	f.
N.	große Freude	die große Freude
G.	großer Freude	der großen Freude
D.	großer Freude	der großen Freude
A.	große Freude	die große Freude
	n.	n.
N.	schlechtes Geld	das schlechte Geld
G.	schlechtes or -ten Geldes	des schlechten Geldes
D.	schlechtem Gelde	dem schlechten Gelde
A.	schlechtes Geld	das schlechte Geld

Plural.

	m. f. n.	m. f. n.
N.	rothe Weine ꝛc.	die rothen Weine ꝛc.
G.	großer Freuden ꝛc.	der großen Freuden ꝛc.
D.	schlechten Geldern ꝛc.	den schlechten Geldern ꝛc.
A.	große Freuden ꝛc.	die großen Freuden ꝛc.

123. The words which, when placed before an adjective, take away its distinctive ending, or reduce it from the first to the second declension, are

1. The two articles, der and ein, with kein (**195.2**), the negative of the latter.

2. The possessive adjectives, mein, dein, sein, unser, euer, ihr (**157** etc.).

3. The demonstrative, interrogative, and relative pronominal adjectives der, dies and jen (**163**), and welch (**174**).

4. The indefinite pronominal adjectives and numeral adjectives jed, jeglich, solch, manch, ander, einig, etlich, all, viel, wenig, mehr, mehrer (**170**, **184–194**).

But solch after ein is treated as a simple adjective, and does not affect a following adjective: thus, ein solcher guter Mann.

5. A few proper adjectives: namely, verschiedene, pl, 'sundry' (nearly equivalent with einige and mehrere), and folgend, erwähnt, obig, and their like, used idiomatically without the article (**66.6**) to indicate things which have been specified or are to be specified.

124. 1. Since, however, a part of these words—namely, ein, kein, and the possessive adjectives—lack the distinctive ending in three of their cases, the nom. sing. masculine and the nom. and acc. sing. neuter, the adjective following those cases retains the ending.

Thus, as we say guter Mann, gutes Kind, so also ein guter Mann, ein gutes Kind (as opposed to der gute Mann, das gute Kind), because there is nothing about the ein which should render the full ending upon the adjective unnecessary.

2. In this way arises what is sometimes reckoned as a "third" or "mixed" declension, composed of three forms taken from the first declension, and the rest from the second. For example, ein guter, 'a good,' keine gute, 'no good,' sein gutes, 'his good,' ihre guten, 'their good,' are declined

	Singular.			*Plural.*
	m.	f.	n.	m. f. n.
N.	ein guter	keine gute	sein gutes	ihre guten
G.	eines guten	keiner guten	seines guten	ihrer guten
D.	einem guten	keiner guten	seinem guten	ihren guten
A.	einen guten	keine gute	sein gutes	ihre guten

There is neither propriety nor advantage in treating this as a separate declension. For each gender and case, there are two forms of the adjective, and only two, and the learner should be taught to distinguish between them, and to note, in every case, the reason of their respective use—which reason is the same in the "mixed" declension as elsewhere.

3. In like manner, when manch, welch, and solch are used without an ending of declension (see **170, 174, 191**), the succeeding adjective takes the full ending of the first declension.

Thus, welch reicher Himmel, 'what a rich sky!' but welcher reiche Himmel; manch bunte Blumen, but manche bunten Blumen, 'many variegated flowers.'

4. The same is true after all, viel, wenig, and mehr, when they are undeclined: thus, viel gutes Obst, 'much good fruit;' mehr offene Wagen, 'more open carriages.'

125. 1. The adjective follows the first declension not only when it has no other limiting word, or only another adjective, before it, but also when preceded by an indeclinable word, such as etwas, genug, allerlei, and the numerals.

2. After the personal pronouns (which do not take the endings of adjective declension), the adjective ought, by analogy, to be of the first declension; and this is not absolutely forbidden; but in common usage the adjective takes the distinctive endings only in the nominative singular (with the accusative neuter), and follows in the other cases the second declension.—That is to say, the ad

jective after a personal pronoun is declined as after ein, or by the "mixed" declension (**124**.2).

Thus, ich armer Thor, 'I poor fool,' du liebes Kind, 'thou dear child; but wir armen Thoren, 'we poor fools,' ihr süßen Lieder, 'ye sweet songs.

126. The ending es of the nom. and acc. neuter in the first declension is sometimes dropped: this omission is especially frequent in poetry.

Thus, schön Wetter, 'fine weather,' falsch Geld, 'false money,' ein ander Fest, 'a different festival,' der Völker heilig Recht, 'the sacred law of nations.'

127. After a part of the pronominal adjectives mentioned above, **123**.4, it is allowable, and even usual, to use the ending of the first declension instead of the second in the nom. and acc. plural.

Thus, einige große Kasten, 'sundry big boxes,' manche glückliche Völker, 'many fortunate races,' mehrere lange Straßen, 'several long streets.'

Hardly any two authorities agree in their statement of the words after which this inconsistency is permitted, and it is better avoided altogether.

128. 1. When two or more adjectives precede and qualify the same noun, unless the first be one of those mentioned in **123**, all regularly and usually take the same ending.

2. Rarely, however, when the following adjective stands in a closer relation to the substantive, as forming with it a kind of compound idea, to which the preceding adjective is then added as a more adventitious determinative, the second is allowed to be of the second declension, though the first is of the first: but only in the genitive and dative cases.

Thus, hohe schattige Bäume, 'high shady trees;' mit frohem leichtem Sinn, 'with light joyous mind;' guter alter kostbarer Wein, 'good old costly wine;'—but von schönem rothen Tuche, 'of handsome red cloth;' frischer holländischen Häringe, 'of fresh Dutch herrings;' mit eignem inneren Organismus, 'with peculiar internal organization.'

3. Occasionally, what is more properly an adjective qualifying the noun is treated in German as an adverb limiting a following adjective before the noun, and so (**130**) is left undeclined: thus, die Wolken, die formlos grauen Töchter der Luft, 'the clouds, the gray shapeless (shapelessly gray) daughters of the air;' die unglückselig traurige Begegnung, 'the unhappy, sad meeting;' die Königlich Bayrische Akademie, 'the Royal Bavarian Academy.'

Exercise VI.

Adjectives of the first declension.

1. Man thut neuen Wein in neue Fässer. 2. Schlechte Männer verkaufen kaltes frisches Wasser als echte Milch. 3. Weißes Brod ist gut, aber schwarzes ist auch gut. 4. Ich habe harten Stahl und weiches Blei. 5. Meines Bruders blauer Rock ist von feinem Tuche. 6.

Gieb mir blaues oder weißes Papier; ich habe nur rothes. 7. Hohe schattige Bäume sind jetzt angenehm. 8. Der Ochse hat einen dicken Kopf, zwei lange Hörner, große runde Augen, und vier starke Beine.

Exercise VII.

Adjectives of the second declension.

1. Dieser neue Wein hält sich gut in dem neuen Fasse. 2. Ich habe das rothe Papier, und der alte Mann giebt mir das blaue. 3. Der blaue Rock meines lieben Bruders ist von dem feinen Tuche. 4. Der junge Schüler schreibt seinem alten Lehrer einen langen Brief. 5. Wir lieben das weiße Brod, aber wir kaufen das schwarze. 6. Im warmen Sommer sitzt man unter den schattigen Bäumen. 7. Die langen Hörner des starken Ochsen stehen über den runden Augen in seinem dicken Kopfe.

Exercise VIII.

Adjectives of various declension.

1. Dieser alte Mann war ein guter Soldat; er diente mit großem Ruhm im letzten Kriege. 2. Alle Kriege, die großen und die kleinen, bringen großes Unglück. 3. Ich schreibe auf dem dicken weißen Papier mit dünner rother Tinte. 4. Wir tragen leichte Kleider, denn der Sommer ist warm. 5. Mein lieber Bruder ist der gute Freund des armen Schülers. 5. Man pflückt reife Aepfel, und läßt die unreifen auf den Bäumen hangen. 7. Die guten reifen Aepfel sind nicht zu haben, denn sie hangen hoch auf den hohen Bäumen. 8. Im neuen Faß meines alten Nachbars ist kostbarer alter rother Wein.

129. *The Adjective used as Substantive.*

1. In German, as in other languages, adjectives are very often used as substantives, either with or without an article or other determining word.

2. When so used, the adjective is written with a capital letter, like any other substantive; but it retains its proper declension as an adjective, taking the endings of the first or of the second declension according to the rules already given.

3. An adjective used as a substantive in the masculine or feminine gender usually denotes a person; in the neuter (singular

only), a concrete abstract—a thing which, or that in general which, possesses the quality designated by the adjective.

Thus, der Gute räumt den Platz dem Bösen, 'the good (man) gives place to the wicked;' daß hie und da ein Glücklicher gewesen, 'that here and there has been one happy person;' eine Schöne, 'a beauty;' meine Geliebte, 'my beloved;' Ihre Rechte, 'your right hand;'—wo das Strenge mit dem Zarten, wo Starkes sich und Mildes paarten, 'where the hard has united with the tender, where what is strong and what is gentle have combined;' durch Kleineres zum Größern mich gewöhnen, 'accustom me by the less to the greater.'

4. Some adjectives are so constantly used in this way as to have quite acquired the character of substantives. From these are to be distinguished certain neuters derived from adjectives without a suffix, and declined as nouns of the first declension: as, Gut, 'property,' Recht, 'right,' Roth, 'red,' Deutsch, 'German (language).'

5. After etwas, 'something,' was, 'what, something,' nichts, 'nothing,' an adjective is treated neither as attributive nor as appositive, but as an adjective used as substantive, in apposition: it is therefore of the first declension, and (regularly and usually) written with a capital initial.

Thus, es muß noch etwas Größeres, noch etwas Herrlicheres kommen, 'there must be coming something more that is greater and more splendid;' was ich Grausames erlitt, 'what that was dreadful I endured;' es ist nichts Neues, 'it is nothing new.'

6. There is no strict and definite limit between the adjective belonging to a noun understood, and the adjective used as a noun, and many cases admit of interpretation as either the one or the other.

130. *The Adjective used as Adverb.*

Any adjective, in German, may be used in its predicative or uninflected form as an adverb.

Thus, ein ganzes Haus, 'a whole house;' but ein ganz schönes Haus, 'a wholly beautiful house,' and ein ganz schön gebautes Haus, 'a quite beautifully built house;' er schreibt gut, 'he writes well; er lachte noch viel dummer, 'he laughed yet much more foolishly.'

See further **363**; and, for the adjective with adverbial form, **128.3**.

Exercise IX.

Adjectives used as Substantives and as Adverbs.

1. Ein Guter liebt das Gute, aber die Schlechten wollen nur Schlechtes. 2. Diese Schöne hat eine schön rothe Rose in ihrer schönen Linken. 3. Der ehrliche fleißige Arme ist glücklicher als der faule Reiche. 4. Dieser Deutsche spricht sehr gelehrt; denn er hat recht fleißig studirt. 5. Nicht jeder Gelehrte ist ein Weiser. 6. Gieb dem

Kleinen etwas Süßes in seine Rechte. 7. Der Gute wählt immer das Bessere, und arbeitet für das Beste des Vaterlandes. 8. Vergeltet nicht Böses mit Bösem. 9. Der Blinde trägt den Lahmen, und der Lahme führt den Blinden.

131. *Participles as Adjectives.*—Participles, being verbal adjectives, are treated in nearly all respects as adjectives—as regards their various use, their mode of declension, and their comparison. See further **349** etc.

132. The double declension of the adjective is in some respects analogous with the two-fold mode of declension of nouns, and is often, like the latter, called "strong" and "weak" declension. The second or "weak" declension of adjectives, like that of nouns, is made upon the model of a theme ending in n. But the other shares in the peculiarities of the old pronominal inflection; being originally formed, it is assumed, by the composition of a declined pronoun (long since lost in separate use) with the adjective theme. The principle on which the distinction in the use of the two is now based—namely, the economical avoidance of unnecessary explicitness—is of comparatively recent introduction. The first declension was formerly used when the logical emphasis rested on the attribute; the second, when it rested on the person or thing to which the attribute related; the "strong" adjective qualified an indefinite or abstract object; the "weak," one definite or individualized.

COMPARISON OF ADJECTIVES.

133. Although the subject of comparison, or formation of derivative adjectives of the comparative and superlative degrees, comes more properly under the head of derivation or word-formation, it will be, for the sake of practical convenience, treated here.

134. The German adjective, like the English, is subject to variation by termination in order to express degree of quality indicated; a COMPARATIVE and a SUPERLATIVE degree are thus formed from the simple adjective, which, with reference to them, is called POSITIVE.

135. 1. The endings forming the comparative and superlative are the same as in English, namely, er and est. But

2. Adjectives ending in e add only r for the comparative; and those in el, en, er usually (before the endings of declension, always) reject the e of those terminations before er.

3. Except after a sibilant letter (z, s, ß, sch), and a d or t usually (especially when preceded by another consonant: and excepting the nd of the present participle), the e of the superlative ending

eſt is regularly omitted, and the ending reduced to simple ſt. After a vowel, except e, the e may be either omitted or retained.

136. Monosyllabic adjectives whose vowel is a, o, or u (not au) more usually modify those vowels in the comparative and superlative: but there are many (about fifty, including several which may follow either method) that leave the vowel unchanged.

Examples of these are bunt, 'variegated,' falſch, 'false,' froh, 'joyous,' lahm, 'lame,' nackt, 'naked,' raſch, 'quick,' rund, 'round,' ſanft, 'gentle,' ſtolz, 'proud,' voll, 'full,' wahr, 'true.'

137. The formation of comparatives and superlatives by the endings er and eſt is not, as in English, limited to monosyllabic adjectives. But the superlative in eſt is avoided in cases of harsh combination; nor are adjectives compared which (see **117***a*) are used only predicatively, and are incapable of declension.

Of course, as in English, some adjectives are by their signification excluded from comparison: e. g., ganz, 'entire,' todt, 'dead,' irden, 'earthen.'

138. Examples:—

Positive.	*Comparative.*	*Superlative.*
ſchön, 'beautiful'	ſchöner	ſchönſt
reich, 'rich'	reicher	reichſt
heiß, 'hot'	heißer	heißeſt
träge, 'lazy'	träger	trägſt
frei, 'free'	freier	freiſt, freieſt
alt, 'old'	älter	älteſt
fromm, 'pious'	frömmer	frömmſt
kurz, 'short'	kürzer	kürzeſt
froh, 'joyous'	froher	froheſt
ſanft, 'gentle'	ſanfter	ſanfteſt
dunkel, 'dark'	dunkler	dunkelſt
mager, 'thin'	magrer, magerer	magerſt
offen, 'open'	offner, offener	offenſt
verworfen, 'abandoned'	verworfener	verworfenſt
bedeutend, 'significant'	bedeutender	bedeutendſt

139. *Irregular and Defective Comparison.*

1. A few adjectives are irregular in the comparative, or in the superlative, or in both: namely

gut, 'good'	besser	best
viel, 'much'	mehr, mehrer	meist
hoch, 'high'	höher	höchst
nah, 'nigh'	näher	nächst
groß, 'great'	größer	größt (rarely größest)

2. A few are defective, lacking a positive,

——— 'little'	minder	mindest
——— 'mid'	mittler	mittelst

especially, a class derived from prepositions,

[in, 'in']	inner	innerst
[aus, 'out']	äußer	äußerst

or from adverbs or prepositions in er (itself really a comparative ending), having a quasi-comparative adjective of the same form,

[ober, 'above']	ober	oberst
[unter, 'below']	unter	unterst
[vorder, 'in front']	vorder	vorderst
[hinter, 'behind']	hinter	hinterst

This class is further irregular in forming its superlatives by adding the superlative ending to the comparative (which has not a proper comparative meaning).

3. Two lack (as adjectives) both comparative and superlative:

[ehe, 'ere']	[eher, 'sooner']	erst, 'first'
——— 'late'	———	letzt, 'last'

From these two superlatives are then irregularly formed new comparatives, erster, 'former,' and letzter, 'latter.'

140. *Declension of Comparatives and Superlatives.*

1. In general, comparatives and superlatives are subject to the same rules of declension as their positives, the simple adjectives.

That is to say, they are uninflected when used in apposition, as predicate, or as adverb (with the exceptions noted just below), and declined when used attributively or substantively; and they have the same double declension as simple adjectives, determined by the same circumstances The comparative presents no irregularities, but

2. *a.* The superlative does not often occur without an article or other limiting word before it, and is therefore more usually of the second declension.

It occurs of the first declension especially in the vocative, after a limiting genitive, and in phrases which omit the article: thus, liebster Bruder, 'dearest brother!' auf des Meeres tiefunterstem Grunde, 'on the sea's very lowest bottom;' in höchster Eile, 'in extreme (highest) haste.'

b. What is of much more importance, the superlative is not, like the positive and comparative, used predicatively in its uninflected form; but for this is substituted an adverbial expression, formed with the preposition an and the definite article dem (dat. sing. neuter), contracted into am.

Thus, er ist mir am liebsten, 'he is *dearest* to me;' im Sommer sind die Tage zu kurz; im Herbste, noch kürzer; aber am kürzesten im Winter, 'in summer the days are too short; in autumn yet shorter; but shortest in winter.'

This expression means literally 'at the dearest,' 'at the shortest,' and so on, but is employed as general predicate in many cases where we could not substitute such a phrase for it. Its sphere of use borders close upon that of the superlative with preceding article, agreeing with a noun understood; and it is often inaccurately used in place of the latter: e. g., er ist am fleißigsten unter allen Schülern, 'he is most diligent of all the scholars,' for er ist der fleißigste ꝛc., 'he is the most industrious,' etc. Thus, we ought to say, dieser Sturm war gestern am heftigsten, 'this storm was most violent yesterday,' but der gestrige Sturm war der heftigste, 'the storm of yesterday was the most violent' (e. g., of the year).

Only allerliebst is used directly as predicate: das war allerliebst, 'that was charming.'

c. For the superlative as adverb are also generally substituted adverbial phrases formed with am, aufs, and zum (see **363**.2).

141. *Comparison with Adverbs.*

1. Adjectives not admitting of comparison in the usual manner, by er and est (**137**), may be compared, as in English, with help of the adverbs mehr, 'more,' and am meisten, 'most.'

Thus, er ist am meisten knechtisch, 'he is most slavish;' er ist mir mehr feind, als ich ihm, 'he is more unfriendly to me than I to him.'

2. When, of two qualities belonging to the same object, one is declared to be in excess of the other, the comparison is usually and more properly made with mehr.

Thus, er war mehr tapfer als klug, 'he was more bold than prudent:'—but, wahrer, als klug und fromm, 'more true, than prudent and dutiful (Goethe).

142. *Additional Remarks.*

1. The superlative has, as in other languages, a twofold meaning and use: one implying direct comparison and eminence above others (superlative relative); the other, general eminence, or possession of the designated quality in a high degree (superlative absolute).

Thus, schönste Blumen, 'most beautiful (exceedingly beautiful) flowers;' die schönsten Blumen, 'the most beautiful flowers' (of all those had in view).

This distinction appears especially in adverbial superlatives: see **363**.2*c*.

2. To a superlative is often prefixed aller, in order further to intensify its meaning: thus, der allerschönste, 'the most beautiful of all.'

Aller is the gen. pl. of all, 'all,' and so is used in its literal sense, only combined with the adjective, and in connections where its introduction as an independent adjunct of the adjective would be impossible.

Exercise X.

Comparative and Superlative of Adjectives.

1. Wann haben wir die längsten Tage? 2. Die Tage sind länger im Sommer; im Winter sind sie am kürzesten und am kältesten. 3. Liebster Freund! schreibe mir bessere Briefe, und mit schwärzerer Tinte, auf deines Vaters weißestem Papier. 4. Die höchsten Bäume tragen nicht bessere Aepfel als die niedrigern. 5. Die Armen sind oft froher als die Reicheren. 6. Man ist am reichsten, wenn man am zufriedensten ist. 7. Das Gold ist das kostbarste Metall, aber das Eisen ist das nützlichste, und der Stahl ist das allerhärteste.

MODIFYING ADJUNCTS OF THE ADJECTIVE.

143. The adjective, in all its uses as adjective and as substantive (for its adverbial use, see under Adverbs, **363**), is liable to be limited by modifying adjuncts of various kinds.

144. 1. The customary adjunct of an adjective is an adverb: as, sehr gut, 'very good;' herzlich froh, 'heartily glad.'

2. An adjective may be limited by an adverbial clause, containing a verb and its subject, and introduced by a conjunction (see **438**.3*b*).

Thus, er ist so gut, daß ich ihn nur lieben kann, 'he is so good, that I can not but love him;' kränker als man glaubte, 'sicker than was supposed.'

An adverbial clause can hardly qualify an adjective, except as a specification of degree, where a comparison is made.

145. An adjective is often limited by a noun (or pronoun) dependent on it.

1. By a noun in the genitive case: thus, ledig aller Pflicht, 'free from all obligation;' ihrer Beute gewiß, 'sure of its prey:' see **217**.

2. By a noun in the dative case: thus, ihm eigen, 'peculiar to him; gleich einer Leiche, 'like a corpse:' see **223**.

3. By a noun in the accusative case, but only very rarely, and in predicative construction: thus, ich bin es müde, 'I am tired of it:' see **229**.

4. By an infinitive, with its sign zu, 'to:' thus, leicht zu verschaffen, 'easy to procure:' see **344**.

146. An adjective is limited by a prepositional phrase; that is, by a noun whose relation to it is defined by a preposition: thus, vom Schaume rein, 'free from scum;' angenehm von Gestalt, 'agreeable in figure.'

147. 1. An adverbial adjunct to an adjective always precedes it—except the adverb genug, 'enough.'

2. An adjective used attributively must be preceded by all its modifying adjuncts: thus, aller von dem deutschen Reiche abhängigen, oder dazu gehörigen Völkerstämme, 'of all the races dependent on the German empire, or belonging to it.'

3. Adjectives used in the predicate or in apposition may take the limiting noun, with or without a preposition, either before or after them: but the adjective more usually follows; and necessarily, if the limiting word be a pronoun without a preposition.

148. Participles, as verbal adjectives, share in most of the constructions of the adjective: see **349** etc.

PRONOUNS.

149. In German, as in English, substantive pronouns and pronominal adjectives are for the most part not distinguished from one another (as they are distinguished in French) by different forms, but the same word is used, according to circumstances, with either value. It will be convenient, therefore, to treat both classes together, explaining under each word its own proper use or uses.

150. The principal classes of pronouns are

1. The personal;

2. The possessive;

3. The demonstrative (including the determinative);

4. The interrogative;

5. The relative (all of which are also either demonstrative or interrogative);

6. The indefinite, with the indefinite numerals.

The determinative, indefinite, and numeral pronouns are in part of ambiguous character, being intermediate classes through which the pronouns shade off into ordinary adjectives and numerals.

PERSONAL PRONOUNS.

151. The personal pronouns are

FIRST PERSON.

	Singular.		*Plural.*	
N.	ich	'I'	wir	'we'
G.	meiner, mein	'of me'	unser	'of us'
D.	mir	'to me'	uns	'to us'
A.	mich	'me'	uns	'us'

SECOND PERSON.

N.	du	'thou'	ihr	'ye'
G.	deiner, dein	'of thee'	euer	'of you'
D.	dir	'to thee'	euch	'to you'
A.	dich	'thee'	euch	'you'

THIRD PERSON, *Singular.*

	masc.		fem.		neut.	
N.	er	'he'	sie	'she'	es	'it'
G.	seiner, sein	'of him'	ihrer	'of her'	seiner, sein	'of it'
D.	ihm	'to him'	ihr	'to her'	ihm	'to it'
A.	ihn	'him'	sie	'her'	es	'it'

Plural.

m. f. n.

N.	sie	'they'
G.	ihrer	'of them'
D.	ihnen	'to them'
A.	sie	'them'

Sich, the special reflexive of the third person (see **155.3**), is also a member of this class, a personal pronoun.

152. 1. Mein, dein, sein are older forms of the gen. singular, now antiquated, but occasionally met with; ihr, for ihrer, does not occur: unserer, for unser, and eurer, for euer, are not unknown, but rare.

Examples are ihr Instrumente spottet mein, 'ye instruments mock me' (R. 142.33); was bedarf man sein, 'what do they require of him?'

2. These genitives, in composition with halben, wegen, and willen, add a wholly anomalous et; and unser and euer, in like manner, add a t: thus meinethalben, deinetwegen, um seinetwillen, unsertwegen, euerthalben, etc.

3. Genitives of the personal pronouns are everywhere of rare occurrence, and only as objects of verbs (**219**) and adjectives (**217**). For the genitive limiting a noun is substituted a possessive adjective (**158**.2).

153. *Use of the Personal Pronouns in address.*

1. In German, as in English, the pronoun of the second pers. singular, du, 'thou,' is no longer used in address, in the ordinary intercourse of life.

It is retained (as in English) in the language of worship and of poetry: and further, in that of familiarity—the familiarity of intimacy, between equals, as between husband and wife, near relations, or particular friends, also among children;—the familiarity toward inferior age or station, as on the part of any one toward young children, or on the part of teachers or employers toward youthful pupils or servants;—and even, sometimes, the familiarity of insult or contempt.

2. The pronoun of the second pers. plural—ihr, 'ye,' etc.—was at one time generally current in Germany for the singular (like our *you*), and is yet met with in poetry or narrative: but modern use authorizes it only in addressing more than one of such persons as may, singly, be addressed with du.

3. The singular pronouns of the third person—er, 'he,' sie, 'she,' etc.—were also once used in customary address, but soon sank to the condition of address by an acknowledged superior to an inferior—as by a monarch to a subject, a master to a servant, and the like—with which value they are still retained, but are going out of vogue.

Employed in this way, er and sie and their cases are usually and properly written with a capital.

4. At present, the pronoun of the third pers. plural—sie, 'they'—and its possessive, ihr, 'their,' are alone allowed, in the sense of 'you, your,' in common life, in addressing either one person, or more than one. When thus used, they are, for distinction, written with capital letters, Sie, Ihnen, Ihr, etc. (but the reflexive sich is not so written).

Thus, ich danke Ihnen für Ihre Gefälligkeit, daß Sie sich die Mühe gegeben haben, 'I thank *you* for *your* kindness, in that *you* have given *yourself* the trouble.'

The verb with Sie is always in the plural, whether one person or more be intended. But a following adjective is either singular or plural, according to the sense: thus, Sie unglücklicher, 'you unhappy man!' but Sie unglücklichen, 'you unhappy ones!'

The use of Sie in address is quite modern, not having become generally established till about the middle of the last century.

5. Some authorities write all the pronouns of address with a capital, even Du, Dich, Euch, etc.: but this is not to be approved, except in such documents as letters, where the words are to reach the person addressed through the eye.

154. *Peculiarities in the use of Pronouns of the third person.*

1. As a general rule, the pronoun of the third person, in the singular, takes the gender of the noun to which it relates.

Thus, when speaking of a hat (der Hut), we use er and ihn; of a pen (die Feder), sie; of bread (das Brod), es.

Excepted from this rule are such words as Weib, 'woman, which are neuter, though designating female persons; also diminutives (neuter) of personal appellations, such as Mädchen, 'girl.' Fräulein, 'young lady,' Knäblein, 'little boy:' a pronoun referring to one of these usually follows the natural gender, instead of the grammatical. Kind, 'child,' is represented by es, 'it,' as with us.

2. But these pronouns are seldom used in the genitive or dative for things without life. For the genitive is substituted the genitive of a demonstrative, der or derselbe; for the dative, the dative of the same; or, if governed by a preposition, a combination of that preposition with the adverb da (or dar), 'there.'

Thus, damit, 'therewith,' davon, 'thereof,' darin, 'therein,' darnach, 'thereafter,' and so on, are used instead of mit ihm or ihr, 'with it,' etc. Dar is put instead of da before a vowel or n.

Similar substitutions of the demonstratives are often made also in other cases where we employ the personal pronouns: see below, **171**.

3. The neuter accusative es is, in like manner, almost never allowed after a preposition, but is replaced by da before the preposition: thus, dafür, darum, for für es, 'for it,' um es, 'about it.'

4. The neuter es has certain special uses.

a. It is, as in English, the indefinite and impersonal subject of a **verb**: thus, es regnet, 'it rains;' es ist sein Bruder, 'it is his brother;' es freut mich, Sie zu sehen, 'it rejoices me to see you.'

b. In this use, it often answers to our *there* before a verb: as, es war ein Kern darin, 'there was a kernel in it;' es wird Niemand kommen, 'there will no one come.'

c. Yet more often, it serves the purpose of a mere grammatical device for shifting the true subject to a position after the verb, and is itself untranslatable: as, es sperren die Riesen den einsamen Weg, 'the giants bar the lonely way;' es fürchte die Götter das Menschengeschlecht, 'let the human race fear the gods.'

d. In all these uses, the verb agrees in number with the following noun, the logical subject or the predicate: thus, es waren die allerschönsten, 'it was (or, they were) the very finest ones.'

e. Es also stands as indefinite object; also, as predicate, representing another word or phrase already used, and of which the repetition is avoided (to be rendered, then, by 'so,' 'be so,' 'do so,' or the like): thus, ich selber bin es nicht mehr, 'I myself am *so* [what I was] no longer;' als ich es noch konnte, 'when I was still able *to do so*.'

f. Instead of *it is I*, and the like, the German reverses the expression, and says ich bin es, 'I am it,' Sie waren es, 'you were it' (i. e., 'it was you'), etc.

g. Es, in all situations, is liable to be abbreviated to 's: the apostrophe should in such case always be written, but is sometimes omitted.

155. *Reflexive use of the Personal Pronouns.*

1. A reflexive pronoun is one which represents the same person or thing as the subject of a sentence, but in the relation of object—namely, as object, direct or indirect, of the verb in the sentence; or (less properly) in a prepositional adjunct to that verb.

It is usually to be rendered by a personal pronoun with the word *self* added: thus, ich wasche mich, 'I wash myself;' ich schmeichle mir, 'I flatter myself;' ich schone meiner, 'I spare myself;' ich stoße sie von mir, 'I thrust them from myself (or, from me).'

2. In the first and second persons, singular and plural, the reflexive pronoun is the same with the personal in every case, the latter being used in a reflexive sense, without any adjunct corresponding to our *self* (but compare 5, below).

The same is the case with the genitive of the third person—as, er schont seiner, 'he spares himself'—but

3. In the third person, there is a special reflexive pronoun, sich, which must always be used instead of the dative or accusative of a personal pronoun, after either verb or preposition, when the subject of the sentence is referred to. It has the value of both accusative and dative, of either number, and of any gender.

Thus, er, sie, es wascht sich, schmeichelt sich, 'he, she, or it washes or flatters himself, herself, or itself;' sie waschen sich, schmeicheln sich, 'they wash themselves, or flatter themselves;' das ist an und für sich gut, 'that is good in and by itself.'

The reflexive sich, when representing Sie, 'you' (**153**.4), is not written with a capital, except in letters and the like.

4. In German, as in French (there is no corresponding usage in English), the reflexive pronoun in the plural is not seldom employed in what is called a "reciprocal" sense, answering to our *one another*.

Thus, wir hätten u n s nie sehen sollen, 'we ought never to have seen *one another;*' ihr hasset e u ch, 'ye hate *each other;*' sie (Sie) geben s i ch das Zeichen, 'they (you) give *one another* the signal.'

Instead of the reciprocal reflexive (or, rarely and redundantly, along with it), the word einander, 'one another,' is often employed.

Only the connection and the requirement of the sense can show in any case whether the pronoun has its directly or its reciprocally reflexive value.

5. Selbst (or selber), 'self,' may be added to any reflexive pronoun, for greater emphasis; or, in the plural, to exclude the reciprocal sense.

It may also be added for emphasis to any pronoun, or noun, answering to our *myself*, *thyself*, *itself*, etc.

156. The dative of a personal pronoun is sometimes introduced into a clause expletively, for liveliness of expression: as, laß m i r herein den Alten, 'let the old man in here (*for me*):' compare **222**. III. *c*.

POSSESSIVE PRONOMINAL ADJECTIVES.

157. The personal pronouns are always substantive; their corresponding adjectives are the possessives: namely

mein, 'my'	unser, 'our'
dein, 'thy'	euer, 'your'
sein, 'his, its'	ihr, 'their'
ihr, 'her'	[Ihr, 'your']

The possessives of the masc. and neut. singular are the same, ſein. The possessive of the fem. singular and that of the plural of all genders also agree in form; and, as the latter (see **153.4**) is used in the sense of a second person, ihr has three meanings, 'her,' 'their,' and 'your' (the last of which is distinguished to the eye by the capital initial).

158. 1. It will be noticed that the possessives correspond closely in form with the genitives of the personal pronouns, being, in fact, the same words in a different condition.

2. The office, also, of the possessive, agrees with that of the genitive of a noun. The genitive of the pronoun is very seldom used to limit a noun, but for it is substituted a possessive in the form of an adjective, qualifying the noun (**216**.3).

Thus, die Arme des Mannes, 'the man's arms;' but ſeine Arme, 'his arms,' not die Arme ſeiner, 'the arms of him.'

Opinions differ as to whether the possessive is derived from the genitive, or the genitive from the possessive. Probably the latter opinion is correct; the history of language shows that a genitive is often, or usually, a stereotyped and invariable case of an adjective of relation.

159. As regards their declension, possessives are treated in the same manner as other adjectives.

1. They are used predicatively in their simple or thematic form.

Thus, der Becher iſt dein, 'the goblet is thine;' die Braut ſei mein, 'be the bride mine!'

2. When used attributively (their regular and ordinary office), they are declined, not like der, 'the,' but like ein, 'a' (63). Thus, mein, 'my,' is declined

	Singular. m.	f.	n.	*Plural.* m. f. n.
N.	mein	meine	mein	meine
G.	meines	meiner	meines	meiner
D.	meinem	meiner	meinem	meinen
A.	meinen	meine	mein	meine

and unſer, 'our,'

	m.	f.	n.	m. f. n.
N.	unſer	unſere	unſer	unſere
G.	unſeres	unſerer	unſeres	unſerer
D.	unſerem	unſerer	unſerem	unſeren
A.	unſeren	unſere	unſer	unſere

Unſer and euer follow the same rules as other adjectives (**120**.3) respecting the contraction of their endings: thus, we may have unſere or unſre, unſeres, unſers, or unſres, and so on.

3. The possessive is also often used substantively, or with the value of a pronoun (not qualifying a noun expressed, but representing one understood); in that case, it is declined in full like an adjective of the first declension: thus, nominatives meiner, meine, meines, meine.

For example, das ist nicht dein Becher; es ist meiner, 'that is not thy goblet; it is mine (i. e., my goblet);' sein Hirn, wie meines, 'his brain, like my own.'

4. In the same substantive use, the possessive may be preceded by the definite article; and it is then declined like any other adjective in like circumstances, or by the second adjective declension (119.2): thus, nom. der, die, das meine, gen. des, der, des meinen, etc.

For example, sein Richterstuhl ist nicht der meine, 'his judgment-seat is not *mine;*' löst mir das Herz, daß ich das eure rühre, 'set my heart free, that I may touch *yours.*'

5. Again, for the simple possessive, in its absolute or pronominal use after the definite article, is substituted a derivative in ig: thus, meinig, unsrig, etc. These are never used except with the article, and therefore always follow the second adjective declension. The nominatives of the whole series are

Singular.			*Plural.*
m.	f.	n.	m. f. n.
der meinige,	die meinige,	das meinige	die meinigen, 'mine'
der deinige,	die deinige,	das deinige	die deinigen, 'thine'
der seinige,	die seinige,	das seinige	die seinigen, 'his, its'
der ihrige,	die ihrige,	das ihrige	die ihrigen, 'hers'
der unsrige,	die unsrige,	das unsrige	die unsrigen, 'ours'
der eurige,	die eurige,	das eurige	die eurigen, 'yours'
der ihrige,	die ihrige,	das ihrige	die ihrigen, 'theirs'
[der Ihrige,	die Ihrige,	das Ihrige	die Ihrigen, 'yours']

Neither the derivatives in ig, nor the simple possessives preceded by the article, are ever used attributively, qualifying a noun expressed.

Mein etc. used predicatively, assert ownership pure and simple: thus, der Hut ist mein, 'the hat belongs to me, and to no one else.' Meiner, der meine, and der meinige are nearly equivalent expressions, combining with the idea of property an implication of the character of the thing owned: thus, er ist meiner etc., 'it is my hat, and no one else's.' Der meinige etc. are most common in colloquial use; der meine etc. are preferred in higher styles.

160. The absolute possessives preceded by the article (der meine, der meinige, etc.) are sometimes used substantively (like other adjectives: see **129**); the neuter singular denoting 'what belongs to one' (his property, his duty, or the like); the plural 'those who belong to one' (as his family, his friends).

Thus, unsere Pflicht ist, auf das Unsrige zu sehen, und für die Unsrigen zu sorgen, 'our duty is to attend to our business and take care of our dependents;' er ermunterte die Seinen, 'he encouraged his men.'

161. The German, like the French, avoids the use of the possessives in many situations where we employ them; either putting in their stead the definite article only, where the possessor is sufficiently pointed out by the connection; or, along with the article (or even without it), using the dative of the corresponding personal pronoun, where it can be construed as indirect object of the verb in the sentence (see **222.** III. *b*).

Thus, er schüttelte den Kopf, 'he shook *his* head;' der Frost dringt mir durch alle Knochen, 'the frost penetrates through all *my* bones;' er fiel ihr um den Hals, 'he fell upon *her* neck;' es kam mir in Sinn, 'it came into *my* mind.'

162. Dero and Ihro are old-style expressions, used in ceremonious address, before titles, etc.: thus, Ihro Majestät, 'your majesty;' Dero Befehle, 'your commands.'

Before titles, seine and seiner are often abbreviated to Se. and Sr.; and for euer, eure, is written Ew.

Exercise XI.

Personal, Reflexive, and Possessive Pronouns.

1. Meine Frau und ich kommen heute mit unsern Kindern zu Ihnen; finden wir Sie in Ihrem neuen Hause? 2. Wir sehen ihren Hut, und er gefällt uns nicht. 3. Erkennst du mich als deinen Freund? 4. Sie hat schöne Federn, denn ich gab sie ihr. 5. Er beträgt sich gut, und ich freue mich es zu hören. 6. Eure Pferde sind besser als die unsrigen und die seinigen. 7. Hier ist ihr Buch; sie schickte es mir, und ich leihe es Ihnen. 8. Ihr Apfel ist gut; meiner ist schlecht.

DEMONSTRATIVES.

163. The proper demonstratives are der, 'this, that,' dies, 'this, that,' and jen, 'yon, that.' Their original value is that of adjectives; but they are now with equal freedom used adjectively, qualifying a noun expressed, and absolutely, or as pronouns, standing for a noun understood.

Der is historically the same word with our *the*, *that*, and *they;* dies is our *this, these, those;* jen is our *yon*, and may by this correspondence be conveniently distinguished from jed (jeder), 'every' (see 190), with which it is apt to be confounded by learners.

164. 1. Der when used adjectively is declined like the article der (63); being, in fact, the same word, and distinguished from it only by greater distinctness, of meaning and of utterance.

Thus, der Ort ist übel regieret, '*that* place is ill governed;' der eine hat die, die anderen andere, Gaben, 'one has *these* gifts, others have other.'

2. Der when used absolutely, or as pronoun, has peculiar forms in a part of its cases—namely, the genitives singular and plural and the dative plural—where it adds en to the adjective forms, at the same time doubling their final s: thus,

	Singular.			*Plural.*
	m.	f.	n.	m. f. n.
N.	der	die	das	die
G.	dessen, (deß)	deren, (der)	dessen, (deß)	deren, (derer)
D.	dem	der	dem	denen
A.	den	die	das	die

The genitives singular deß, der, deß are also allowed, but very rarely used, except the neuter in certain compounds, as deßwegen, deßhalb (also written deswegen, deshalb).

In the genitive plural, derer is used instead of deren when a limiting addition, usually a relative clause, follows: thus, derer, die mich lieben, 'of those who love me;' derer von Paris, 'of them of Paris (people from Paris).

165. Dies and jen are declined as adjectives of the first declension, or like the definite article (only with es instead of as in the nom. and acc. neuter); and without any difference, whether they are used as adjectives or as pronouns. Thus,

	Singular.			*Plural.*
	m.	f.	n.	m. f. n.
N.	dieser	diese	dieses	diese
G.	dieses	dieser	dieses	dieser
D.	diesem	dieser	diesem	diesen
A.	diesen	diese	dieses	diese

The nom. and acc. neuter dieses is often abbreviated to dies (or dieß), especially when the word is used as a pronoun.

166. *Use of the Demonstratives.*

1. Dieser is a general demonstrative, answering to both *this* and *that*. If, however, the idea of remoteness in place or time is at all emphasized, either by the antithesis of *this* and *that*, or in any other way, *that* must be represented by jener. Often, dieser and jener are to be rendered 'the latter' (dieser, the one last mentioned, the nearer) and 'the former' (jener, the one mentioned earlier, the remoter). Dies and das are also sometimes contrasted as 'this' and 'that.'

2. Der has a great range of meaning, from the faint indefiniteness of the article to the determinateness of dieser—depending mainly on the emphasis with which it is uttered. Special uses worthy of note are as follows:

a. Der is the demonstrative employed in such phrases as unsere Pferde und d i e der Fremden, 'our horses and *those* of the strangers,' d e r mit den hellen Augen, '*he* (the one) with the sharp eyes.'

Rarely, derjenige (**168**) is used in the same sense.

b. It takes the place of the pronoun of the third person used emphatically: thus, d i e muß recht dumm sein, '*she* must be right stupid;' d e r füttre Kräh'n, 'may *he* be food for crows.'

3. The neuters singular, das, dies (or dieß, dieses), and (rarely) jenes, are used, like es (**154.4**), as indefinite subjects of verbs; and, if a plural predicate noun follows the verb, the latter agrees with the noun: thus, d a s ist mein Vater, 'that is my father;' d a s sind die Reizungen, 'those are the charms;' d i e s ist der Kampf der Pferde und Fische, 'this is the combat of horses and fishes.'

4. Compounds of the adverbs da and hier with prepositions are very frequently used instead of cases of the demonstratives with governing prepositions: thus, damit, 'therewith,' darin, 'therein,' for mit dem, in dem; hiermit, 'herewith,' hierin, 'herein,' for mit diesem, in diesem.

5. For the demonstratives as substitutes for the personal pronoun, see below, **171**.

Determinatives.

167. Certain pronominal words, connected with the demonstratives in derivation or meaning, or in both, are ordinarily called determinatives.

168. Derjenige.—1. This is made up of the definite article der, and jenig, a derivative from jen, 'yon, that' (like meinig from mein, etc., 159.5). The latter part never occurs without the former, and they are written together as a single word, although each is separately declined, the one as the article, the other as an adjective of the second declension. Thus,

	Singular. m.	f.	n.	*Plural.* m. f. n.
N.	derjenige	diejenige	dasjenige	diejenigen
G.	desjenigen	derjenigen	desjenigen	derjenigen
D.	demjenigen	derjenigen	demjenigen	denjenigen
A.	denjenigen	diejenige	dasjenige	diejenigen

2. Derjenige is used with equal frequency as adjective and as pronoun. Its specific office is that of antecedent to a following relative; in this office it is interchangeable with the demonstrative der, as the latter's more prosaic and colloquial substitute: thus, derjenige, or derjenige Mann, welcher weise ist, ist zufrieden, 'he (that man) who is wise is contented.'

169. Derselbe.—1. This word is composed of the definite article and the adjective selb. Both its parts are declined, after the manner of derjenige (168.1).

2. Derselbe is both adjective and pronoun, and means literally the same.' But it also interchanges with the demonstratives as substitute for the pronoun of the third person (see 171).

3. For derselbe are sometimes used derselbige and selbiger, which, however, are antiquated expressions. Der nämliche is its equivalent in the full sense of 'the same.'

Selber and selbst (155.5) are indeclinable forms of the same adjective selb, always following, appositively, the noun or pronoun which they qualify, often at a distance from it. Selbst is also used adverbially, meaning 'even,' and as substantive in the phrase von selbst, 'of its own accord.'

Selb is also, rarely, declined after dieser as after der. The genitive of derselbe is written either desselben or desselben: the former is theoretically preferable (3.1), the latter more usual (likewise dasselbe, neuter).

170. Solch.—1. Solch is the English 'such,' and is used, both as adjective and as pronoun, in nearly the same manner. It is declined like dieser (165); or, when preceded by ein, as any other adjective would be in the same situation (124).

2. *Such a* is either solch ein, or ein solcher, the adjective being undeclined when placed before the article. For *as*, when used after *such* with the value

of a relative pronoun, the German uses the relative· thus, solchen, die ihn kannten, 'to such as knew him.'

171. *The Demonstratives and Determinatives as Substitutes.*

The pronouns of these classes are often used where we put the third personal pronoun or its possessive:

1. For the emphatic pronoun (**166.**2*b.*), and the antecedent of a relative clause (**168.**2), as already explained.

2. Where the demonstrative meaning helps avoid an ambiguity: as, er ging mit meinem Vetter und dessen Sohn, or dem Sohne desselben, 'he went with my cousin and *his* (the latter's) son:'—or an awkward repetition: as, er hat eine Schwester: kennen Sie dieselbe (for kennen Sie sie)? 'he has a sister; do you know *her?*'

3. In the oblique cases, where things and not persons are intended: as, ich bin dessen benöthigt, 'I am in need of *it*' (seiner would mean 'of him,' rather). In like manner, with prepositions, instead of the adverbial compounds with da (**154.**2,3): as, ich habe einen Garten, und gehe oft in demselben (or darin) spazieren, 'I have a garden, and often go to walk in *it.*'

4. The substitution, especially of derselbe, is often made, in popular use, in cases where no reason can be assigned, and where the personal pronoun would be preferable.

INTERROGATIVES.

172. The interrogatives are wer, 'who,' was, 'what,' and welcher, 'what, which.' Wer and was are pronouns only; welcher is primarily adjective, but also frequently used as pronoun.

173. 1. Wer and was are peculiar in having no plural; also, in conveying no idea of gender, but being distinguished precisely as our *who* and *what*, the one denoting persons, the other things. They are declined as follows:

N.	wer	'who'	was	'what'
G.	wessen, (weß)	'whose'	wessen, (weß)	'of what'
D.	wem	'to whom'	——	
A.	wen	'whom'	was	'what'

2. Weß as genitive of wer is antiquated and out of use, and as genitive of was is hardly met with except in compounds like weßwegen, weßhalb (or weswegen, weshalb). Was has no dative: for both its dative and accusative as governed by prepositions are substituted compounds of those prepositions with the adverb wo or wor, 'where:' thus, womit, 'wherewith, with what,' worin, 'wherein, in what,' wofür, 'wherefore, for what' (like damit, hiermit, etc.: see **154.**2, **166.**4).

3. Popular colloquial usage sometimes puts was, both as accusative and as dative, after prepositions: thus, mit was, 'with what,' für was, 'for what.

4. Weß is, quite rarely, used adjectively: as, weß Sinnes der Herr sei, of what disposition the master is' (R. 92.7).

174. 1. Welch is declined like dies (**165**), or as an adjective of the first declension. As an adjective, qualifying a noun expressed, it means either 'what' or 'which;' used absolutely, it is our 'which.'

2. Before ein or an adjective, especially when used in an exclamatory way, welch generally loses its declensional endings, and appears in its simple thematic form.

Thus, welches Buch, 'what (or which) book;' welches von diesen Büchern, 'which of these books:'—welch tiefes Summen, welch ein heller Ton, 'what deep murmur, what a clear tone!' welch schlechte Sitten, 'what bad manners!'

175. Was with the preposition für, 'for,' after it (sometimes separated from it by intervening words), is used in the sense of 'what sort of, what kind of.' It is then invariable, and the words to which it is prefixed have the same construction as if they stood by themselves.

Thus, Was hast du für einen Fisch gefangen, 'what sort of a fish have you caught?' von was für Zeugen, und mit was für einem Werkzeuge, machen Sie das, 'of what kind of stuffs, and with what sort of an instrument, do you make that?'

176. 1. All the interrogatives are used also as relatives (see **177**).

2. Was stands often for etwas, 'something:' wer, in the sense of 'some one,' is quite rare; welch, as pronoun only, is familiarly, but not elegantly, used to signify 'some.'

Thus, noch was werth, 'still worth something;' ich möchte was profitiren, 'I would fain profit somewhat;' meinte wer aus der Gesellschaft, 'remarked some one in the company;' haben Sie Pflaumen? geben Sie mir welche, 'have you plums? give me some.'

3. Was is used not rarely for um was, or warum, 'why?' thus, was birgst du dein Gesicht, 'why hidest thou thy face?'

RELATIVES.

177. The demonstrative pronoun (not adjective) der, and the interrogatives wer, was, was für, and welcher (both adjective and pronoun), are used also as relatives; they are declined, as such, in the same manner as when having their more original and proper value.

178. Der and welcher are the ordinary simple relatives following an antecedent. In the nominative and accusative, they are used interchangeably, according to the arbitrary choice of speaker or writer. In the dative (except after prepositions) the cases of der are rather preferred to those of welcher; and, in the genitive (as pronouns), only dessen and deren are ever met with.

179. 1. Wer and was, was für, and welcher used adjectively (also absolutely, when meaning 'which'), like *who* and *what* in English, are properly compound relatives, or antecedent and relative combined.

Thus, wer bei Nacht vorbeifuhr, sah die Flammen, 'he who (whoever) went by at night, saw the flames;' was im Menschen nicht ist, kommt auch nicht aus ihm, 'what (whatever) is not in a man does not come out of him;' ich will vergessen, wer ich bin, und was ich litt, 'I will forget who I am and what I have suffered;' mit ihr wandelt, wem sie die Weihe lieh, 'with her walks he on whom she has bestowed consecration;' man suchte zu vergessen, welche Noth überall herrschte, 'one sought to forget what distress was everywhere prevailing;' wer weiß, was für eine List dahinter steckt, 'who knows what sort of a trick is hidden in that?'

2. But the demonstrative is repeated, for distinctness, after the compound relative, much more often in German than in English:

Thus, wer nicht vorwärts geht, der kommt zurücke, '*who* (whoever) does not advance, *he* falls back;' was du nie verlierst, das mußt du beweinen, '*what* you never lose, *that* you have to bewail;' was ich für Herrlichkeit geschaut, das steht nicht in der Worte Macht, '*what* kind of magnificence I saw, *that* is not in the power of words to tell.'

3. As occasional irregular variations of the mode of relative expression may be noticed the use of the personal pronoun instead of der as antecedent after wer (e. g., R. 67.20), of der instead of wer as preceding relative (e. g., R. 77.3), of wer instead of welcher after der (e. g., R. 52.22), etc.

4. The examples show that wer and was are sometimes to be translated by 'whoever' and 'whatever.' To give them more distinctly this indefinite sense, they may be followed (either immediately, or, more often, after one or more interposed words) by auch, 'even,' nur, 'only,' or immer, 'ever,' especially the first: thus, was er auch thue, '*whatever* he may do.'

5. After a neuter pronoun, personal, demonstrative, or indefinite (as es, das, alles, etwas, nichts, manches, viel, wenig), also after an adjective (especially a superlative) taken in a general sense, and

not referring to some definite object, the compound relative was is used, instead of the simple relative das or welches.

Thus, über das, was er selbst erzählte, 'about that which he was himself relating;' alles was von dir mir kam, 'all that came to me from thee; nichts was meine Meinung störte, 'nothing that should shake my opinion' das erste was sie hörten, 'the first thing which they heard.'

That is to say, for an adjective clause qualifying the antecedent is substituted a substantive clause in apposition with it.

180. For the dative or accusative case of a relative (either simple or compound) governed by a preposition, is usually substituted, when things and not persons are referred to, the compound of the preposition with an adverb (as in the case of the demonstratives and interrogatives: see **166.4**, **173.2**). But the compounds of da (davon, daraus, etc.) are only rarely used relatively, those of wo (wovon, woraus, etc.) being preferred.

181. A verb agreeing with a relative is put in the third person even when the antecedent of the relative was a pronoun of the first or second person (or a vocative), unless that pronoun be repeated after the relative.

Thus, um mich, der sich rettet zu dir, 'about me, who *am* taking refuge with thee;' bist du es der so zittert, 'is it thou who *art* trembling thus?'—but um mich, der ich mich rette; bist du es, der du so zitterst;—glückseliger Alexander, der du Italien nicht sahest, 'fortunate Alexander, that didst never see Italy!'

182. 1. In antiquated or archaic style, so is used as indeclinable relative, representing the nominative and accusative cases of der and welcher: thus, der Mann, so es sagte, 'the man who said it.'

2. In a like style, da is appended to a relative, der or welcher, in a manner wholly expletive, and unrepresentable by anything in English: thus, wer da athmet im rosigen Licht, 'whoever breathes in the rosy light.'

183. The relative, often omitted in English, must always be expressed in German: thus, die Freunde, die ich liebe, 'the friends I love.'

Exercise XII.

Demonstrative, Interrogative, and Relative Pronouns.

1. Wer sind Sie, und was wissen Sie? 2. Dies ist der Mann den Sie kennen, und von dem wir sprachen. 3. Welchen Mann meinen Sie? 4. Wer sind die Leute deren Bücher wir hatten, und denen wir sie wiedergaben? 5. Ich weiß weder was für Bücher es waren, noch von wem wir sie hatten. 6. Wer das nicht weiß ist ein Thor.

7. Wessen Hut und was für einen Rock trägt jener Knabe? 8. Liebet die, welche euch verfolgen; segnet diejenigen, die euch hassen. 9. Der ist glücklich, dessen Herz zufrieden ist; nicht derjenige, welcher nur reich ist.

INDEFINITE PRONOUNS AND INDEFINITE NUMERALS.

184. A class of words needs some attention under the above head, in connection with the pronouns, as being more or less related with the latter, and differing from ordinary nouns and adjectives, in derivation or in office, or both.

185. Man, 'one.'—Man (originally the same word with Mann, 'man') is employed as wholly indefinite subject to a verb, like the French *on*, our *one*, *they*, *people*, *we*, taken indefinitely. Thus, man sagt, 'one says, they say, it is said.' If any other case than a nominative is required, einer (**195**) is used instead.

186. Jemand, 'some one,' Niemand, 'no one.'—These are compounds of Mann, 'man,' with the adverbs je, 'ever,' and nie, 'never.' They ought, therefore, to be declinable only as substantives of the first declension: and it is proper always so to treat them, adding s in the genitive, and leaving the other cases like the nominative. But in the dative and accusative (especially where the phrase would otherwise be ambiguous or indistinct), they are allowed to take the endings em or en (R. 168.28; 171.19) in the dative, and en in the accusative.

Niemand, 'no one,' must be used instead of nicht Jemand, 'not any one,' except in an interrogative sentence.

187. Jedermann, 'every one.'—This word is made up of jeder, 'every' (**190**), and Mann, 'man,' but is used without distinction of gender. Its first part is undeclined, and it is varied only by adding s to form the genitive.

188. Etwas, 'something,' nichts, 'nothing.'—These words are invariable in form, and always have a substantive value. A following limiting adjective is treated as a substantive in apposition with them (**129.5**): and the same construction is usual with a noun after etwas; thus, etwas Geld, 'some money.'

For was in the sense of etwas, see **176.2**.

Nichts is usually and regularly used instead of nicht etwas, 'not anything,' except when the sentence is interrogative as well as negative.

189. Einig, etlich, 'some.'—These are used chiefly in the plural, and declined like dies (**165**). They are employed both adjectively and substantively.

Etwelch is a word, now antiquated, having the same meaning: for this, welcher is often used colloquially (**176**.2), as was for etwas.

190. Jed, jeglich, jedwed, 'each, every.'—Only the first of these is in familiar use. All are declined like dies; or, the first two as adjectives of the "mixed" declension (**124**.2) when preceded by ein, the only limiting word which can stand before them. They are used either adjectively or substantively.

The original themes are jeder and jedweder, and their er has not until modern times been treated as ending of declension only. For Jedermann, see above, **187**.

191. Manch, 'many.'—In the singular, manch means 'many a;' in the plural, 'many.' It is usually declined like dies (**165**), but, before an adjective, may be left uninflected: thus, manch bunte Blumen, 'many variegated flowers;' manch gülden Gewand, 'many a golden garment.' It is also used substantively.

192. Viel, 'much,' wenig, 'little.'—1. After another limiting word, viel and wenig are declined as any other adjectives would be in the same situation—except in ein wenig, 'a little.' If they precede the noun which they qualify (or another adjective qualifying it), they are sometimes declined and sometimes left unvaried —and the former more when the meaning is distributive, the latter more when collective: thus, viel Wein, 'a great quantity of wine,' but vieler Wein, 'wine of many kinds;' viel leicht beschwingte Gäste, 'a number of light-winged guests,' but viele andere Thiergestalten, 'many other animal shapes (individual)'—but this distinction is by no means closely observed. Both words are used substantively as well as adjectively, and may govern a partitive genitive: as, viele der Fußgänger, 'many of the pedestrians.'

2. Mehr, 'more,' and weniger, 'less,' comparatives of viel and wenig, are generally invariable. But mehr has a plural, mehre, or (irregularly, but much more commonly) mehrere, meaning 'several, many.'

193. All, 'all.'—1. When it directly precedes the noun it qualifies, all is fully declined (like dies, **165**): but before a pronominal word (adjectively or substantively used) it may remain unvaried (with a tendency toward the same distinction of collective and distributive meaning that appears in viel: see **192**.1).

Thus, aller Wetteifer, 'all zeal:'—alle deine hohen Werke, 'all thy lofty works;' alle die Tage des Festes, 'all the days of the festival;' von all dem

Glanze, 'by all the splendor; bei all diesen Verhältnissen, 'in view of all these circumstances.'

2. In certain phrases, alle is used instead of all undeclined: thus, bei alle dem, 'in spite of all that.'

3. The neuter singular alles (like the corresponding case of other pronominal words; as jedes, R. 170.11), is employed in an indefinite way of persons, meaning 'every one:' thus, alles nähert sich einander, 'all draw near to one another.'

4. The plural of all is sometimes used distributively: as alle Wochen, 'every week.'

194. Ander, 'other,' is a pronominal word, but not distinguished in its uses from an ordinary adjective.

For noch ein in place of ander, see **198.3***c*; for ander as ordinal, **203.1***a*.

195. Ein, 'one, an, a,' kein, 'not one, none, no.'—1. The numeral ein, 'one,' is also used as indefinite pronoun (see **198.2**), and as article (**63**).

2. Kein is the negative of ein, and is everywhere declined as the latter would be in the same situation. Like Niemand (**186**) and nichts (**188**), it often requires to be taken apart in translating into ein and nicht, 'not.'

NUMERALS.

196. Although the numerals do not form in the proper sense a separate part of speech, their peculiarities of form and use are such that they require to be treated as a class by themselves.

197. 1. The fundamental words denoting number, the CARDINAL numerals, are as follows:

1. ein	11. elf	21. ein und zwanzig
2. zwei	12. zwölf	22. zwei und zwanzig
3. drei	13. dreizehn	30. dreißig
4. vier	14. vierzehn	40. vierzig
5. fünf	15. fünfzehn	50. fünfzig
6. sechs	16. sechzehn	60. sechzig
7. sieben	17. siebzehn	70. siebzig
8. acht	18. achtzehn	80. achtzig
9. neun	19. neunzehn	90. neunzig
10. zehn	20. zwanzig	100. hundert

1000. tausend 1,000,000. Million

2. An older form of elf, 11, now nearly out of use, is eilf. For fünfzehn, 15, and fünfzig, 50, the less regularly derived forms funfzehn and funfzig are also in good and approved use. Siebenzehn, 17, and siebenzig, 70, instead of the contracted siebzehn and siebzig, are not infrequent. Sechzehn, 16, and sechzig, 60, are abbreviated, for ease of pronunciation, from sechszehn and sechszig, which may likewise be employed.

3. The odd numbers, between twenty and a hundred, are formed always by prefixing the name of the unit to that of the ten, with und, 'and,' interposed: thus, drei und zwanzig, 'three and twenty' (not zwanzig-drei, 'twenty-three'). With the higher numbers, the odd numbers follow, as in English: thus, hundert und sieben, 107; tausend und drei und vierzig, 1043; and the und, 'and,' may be dropped, especially when more than two numbers are put together: as, ein tausend acht hundert neun und sechzig, or achtzehn hundert neun und sechzig, 1869.

4. The higher numbers, hundert, tausend, million, are multiplied by prefixed numbers, as in English: thus, sechs hundert, 600; drei und achtzig tausend, 83,000. The German says eine Million, '*a* million,' as we do; but simply hundert, '*a* hundred,' tausend, '*a* thousand:' ein hundert, ein tausend, mean '*one* hundred,' '*one* thousand.'

198. Ein is the only cardinal number that is fully inflected.

1. If used adjectively, or qualifying a noun expressed, it is (unless preceded by another qualifying word: see 3) declined when numeral in the same manner as when indefinite article (**63**).

Thus, ein Mann, 'one man' or 'a man;' ein Kind, 'one child' or 'a child.'

2. When used absolutely, or pronominally, standing for a noun understood, it is declined like dies (**165**), or an adjective of the first declension (but eines is usually contracted to eins in the nom. and acc. neuter).

Thus, um ein Glied, und dann um noch eins länger, 'longer by one joint, and then by one more;' einer von euch, 'one of you;' einer der auf ein Abenteuer ausgeht, 'one who goes out upon an adventure;' von sich zu jagen, was einem lieb ist, 'to drive away from one's self what is dear to one!'

3. When preceded by another limiting word (usually the definite article), it is declined as any adjective would be after the same word.

Thus, der eine sprach, 'the one spoke;' mit dieser einen Irrung, 'with this one error;' auf seinem einen Beine, 'on his one leg.'

a. Der eine is often employed where we should say 'one' simply: occasionally it forms a plural, die einen, 'the ones, some.'

b. In numeration, the pronominal neuter, eins, is used: thus, eins, zwei, drei, 'one, two, three;' einmal eins ist eins, 'once one is one.'

c. Noch ein, 'one more,' is employed instead of ein ander, 'another,' where simple addition, not difference, is signified: thus, nimm noch ein Goldstück, 'take another gold piece' (i. e. in addition to the one you have); but nimm ein anderes, 'take another' (i. e. in place of the one you have).

d. In the compound numbers, ein und zwanzig, 21, etc., ein is invariable: also, usually, in ein und derselbe, ein Paar, ein wenig, etc.

e. In order to distinguish to the eye ein used as pronoun or numeral from the same word as article, some write it with a capital, Ein; others, with the letters spaced, e i n (the ordinary German equivalent of our *italics*); others, with an accent upon the e, éin: others leave the difference of value to be pointed out by the connection.

199. Zwei, 2, and drei, 3, are generally unvaried, but have gen. and dat. plural forms—zweier, zweien; dreier, dreien—which may be used where the case would otherwise be doubtful.

a. For zwei, the old masculine zween (*twain*) and feminine zwo are antiquated, but still occasionally met with: thus, waren mit mir zween Genossen, 'were with me two comrades;' zwo Schwalben sangen um die Wette, 'two swallows were singing in emulation'

b. Beide, 'both,' is often used where we say *two:* thus, meine beiden Brüder, 'my two brothers.'

200. 1. From the other units and tens, only a dative in en is occasionally formed, when the words are used substantively; or, yet more rarely, from all the units, a nom. and acc. in e (a relic of a former fuller declension) —namely, in certain special uses, as alle Viere, 'all fours;' or in poetry, to make an additional syllable; or in colloquial and low style.

2. Hundert, 100, and tausend, 1000, are frequently construed and declined as (neuter) collective substantives. Million (fem.) is regularly and usually so treated.

3. As names of the figures designating them, the numerals are treated as feminine nouns (Zahl, f. 'number,' being understood), and take the plural ending en, and sometimes e in the singular: ein forms die Eins, die Einsen.

201. 1. The cardinal numerals are used in general with equal freedom as substantives and as adjectives: thus, ein Kind, 'a child,' eins der Kinder, 'one of the children;' vier oder fünf solcher Mädchen, 'four or five of such girls' (R. 161.18); wir drei Freunde. 'we three friends;' unser drei, 'three of us,' etc.

2. For the use of a singular instead of a plural noun of measure after numerals, see 211.2.

202. From the cardinals come, by derivation or composition, all the other classes of numerals, the most important of which are explained below.

203. *Ordinals.* 1. The ordinals are a series of adjective derivatives, formed from the cardinals by the suffixes t and ſt : from the numbers 2–19, by adding t ; from the higher numbers by adding ſt.

Thus, zweit, 'second,' neunt, 'ninth,' ſechzehnt, 'sixteenth,' zwanzigſt, 'twentieth,' hundertſt, 'hundredth,' tauſendſt, 'thousandth.'

a. But the ordinal of ein is erſt, 'first;' drei forms irregularly dritt; and acht, acht (instead of achtt): ander, 'other,' is sometimes used instead of zweit, 'second.'

b. Compound numbers add, as in English, the ordinal ending only to their last member: thus, der zwei und zwanzigſte, 22d, der hundert und erſte, 101st, im achtzehn hundert neun und ſechzigſten Jahre, 'in the 1869th year.'

2. The ordinals are never used predicatively or adverbially, and consequently never appear (except in composition) in their simple thematic form. They are declined in all respects like other adjectives.

Exercise XIII.

Cardinal and Ordinal Numerals.

The numerals to be read out of figures into words.

1. Wir ſind 3 Brüder, Söhne eines Vaters; der 1ſte iſt 20 Jahre alt; der 2te iſt älter um 4 Jahre und 7 Monate; der 3te iſt geboren im Jahre 1835, und iſt alſo im 34ſten Jahr ſeines Alters. 2. In meiner Bibliothek ſind 35 Bücherbretter in 5 Reihen; das 4te Brett in jeder Reihe hält ſpaniſche Bücher, und das 7te hält deutſche; auf allen zuſammen ſind 678 Werke, in 1317 Bänden. 3. Was geſchah im Jahr 1492? und was, 284 Jahre ſpäter, im Jahre 1776? 4. Der Januar hat 31 Tage; der Februar, 28 oder 29. 5. Die Sanct Petri Kirche zu Rom hat 602 Fuß Länge, und 445 Fuß Breite; und das Kreuz auf dem Dome ſteht 430 Fuß über dem Pflaſter: ſie wurde geweiht im 1626ſten Jahre nach Chriſti Geburt.

204. *Multiplicatives.* These are formed by compounding the cardinals with the words fach or fältig: thus, einfach or einfältig, 'simple;' zweifach or zweifältig, 'double;' zehnfach or zehnfältig, 'ten-fold.' They are adjectives, and are treated in all respects like other adjectives.

205. *Variatives.* These add erlei to the cardinals: thus, einerlei, 'of one sort,' dreierlei, 'of three sorts;' vielerlei, 'of many sorts.' They are adjectives, but incapable of declension.

206. *Iteratives.* These are adverbs, formed by compounding the numeral with mal (literally 'mark;' hence 'repetition, time'): thus, einmal, 'once,' zehnmal, 'ten times,' manchmal, 'many times, often.'

a. The word mal is often written apart from the numeral, sometimes with a capital, as an independent word.

b. As the examples have shown, derivative words of these three classes are formed also from the indefinite numerals.

207. *Derivatives from the Ordinals.*

1. *Dimidiatives* are formed by adding halb, 'half,' to the ordinal as ending in te (or t), and denote a quantity half a unit less than the corresponding cardinal. Thus, viertehalb, 'four less a half,' or 'three and a half.' They are construed as invariable adjectives.

The implied meaning is, ['the first, second, and third, complete; but] the fourth, [only] half.' Instead of zweitehalb, 1½, anderthalb, irregularly formed from ander, 'other,' in the sense of 'second' (**203**.1*a*), is in use.

2. *Fractionals* are originally compounds of the ordinals with Theil, 'part;' but are abbreviated by the contraction of the latter into tel, before which the final t of the ordinal is dropped: thus, drittel (dritt-tel, dritt' Theil), 'third;' viertel, 'quarter;' zwanzigstel, 'twentieth part.'

Instead of zweitel, 'second part,' is used only halb, Hälfte, 'half.'

3. *Ordinal Adverbs* add the ending ens to the ordinal theme: thus, erstens, 'firstly;' zwanzigstens, 'in the twentieth place.'

208. Other derivative numeral words it belongs rather to the dictionary than to the grammar to explain.

USES OF THE FORMS OF DECLENSION.

209. The following rules apply only to nouns and to words (pronouns, numerals, adjectives, infinitives: see **113**) used as nouns; since the declension of all adjectives and words used adjectively (articles, pronominal adjectives, and participles) is determined by that of the nouns to which they belong, and with which they are made to agree in number, case, and gender.

Numbers.

210. The value and use of the numbers are, in general, the same in German as in English.

211. 1. This does not exclude minor differences in regard to particular words, which the one language may, in general or in certain connections, use as singular and the other as plural: for example, Zange (sing.), 'tongs' (pl.); Blattern (pl.), 'small-pox' (sing.); auf dem Arm (sing.), 'in the arms;' Sie (lit. 'they,' pl.), 'you' (meaning one or more: see **153**.4), etc.

2. Masculine and neuter nouns used to express measurement, of extent, quantity, weight, or number, generally stand in the singular instead of the plural after numerals (whether cardinal or indefinite).

Thus, sie haben sieben bis acht Fuß Länge, 'they have seven or eight *feet* of length'; zehn Faß Bier, 'ten *casks* of beer;' wieviel Pfund Zucker, 'how many *pounds* of sugar?' ein Hülfsheer von zehn tausend Mann, 'an auxiliary army of 10,000 *men;*' zwanzig Kopf Rinder, 'twenty *head* of cattle;' drei Zoll breit, 'three *inches* broad.'

But drei Ellen (f.) Tuch, 'three yards of cloth'; fünf Meilen (f.) weit, 'five miles distant';—and also tausend Schritte (m.) lang, '1000 paces long' (R. 155.26). Respecting the form of the noun expressing the thing measured, see below, **216**.5*a*.

3. In the familiar expressions for the time of day, Uhr, 'hour' is also unvaried after a numeral: thus, neun Uhr, 'nine o'clock.'

Cases.

Nominative.

212. The proper office of the nominative is to stand as the subject of the sentence: as, der Mensch denkt, Gott lenkt, 'man proposes, God disposes.'

Of course, also, a noun in apposition with a subject nominative is put in the nominative; since (**111**.2) an appositive noun always agrees in case with the noun it explains.

213. With the verb sein, 'to be,' and a few others, of kindred meaning—such as werden, 'become,' bleiben, 'continue,' heißen, 'be called,' scheinen, 'appear'—also, with the passive of verbs that govern a second accusative as factitive predicate (**227**.3*b*), a noun may be used as predicate in the nominative.

Thus, mein Bruder ist der Lehrer dieses Knaben, 'my brother is this boy's teacher;' der bleibt ein Narr sein Leben lang, 'he remains a fool his whole life long;' er wird ein Geizhals gescholten, 'he is called reproachfully a miser.'

a. With werden, however, the noun is often put in the dative, after the preposition zu: as, da werden Weiber zu Hyänen, 'then women become hyenas (turn to hyenas).'

214. The nominative is used in address (as a "vocative").

Thus, holder Friede, süße Eintracht, weilet über dieser Stadt, 'lovely Peace! sweet Concord! linger over this city.'

Genitive.

215. The genitive in German, as in the other related languages, is primarily and especially the adjective or adnominal casé, denoting by a form of the noun a variety of relations such as might be expressed by a derivative adjective. As was remarked above (under **158.2**), it is in part traceably of adjective origin. But its later uses arise also in part from its being merged with other primitive cases—particularly the ablative, the case representing the *from* relation, of origin or removal—and assuming their office. To trace all these uses to their origin would require vastly too much of detailed historical discussion, and will not be attempted here.

216. *The Genitive with Nouns.*

1. The German genitive, like the English possessive, is especially the case of a noun that is added to another noun in order to limit or define its meaning.

2. It is used, accordingly, in all the senses in which we use the possessive case of a noun, or a pronominal possessive (*my*, *your*, *his*, etc.); also, in most of the senses belonging to a noun connected with another noun by the preposition *of:* thus,

a. As genitive of proper possession or appurtenance: das Haus meines Vaters, 'the house of my father;' des Mannes Kopf, 'the man's head.'

b. As genitive of origin or cause: in des Schreckens Wahn, 'in the madness of terror;' der Trieb der Großmuth, 'the impulse of magnanimity.'

c. As complement of relation (designating that toward which the relation expressed by the governing noun is sustained): der Vater des Sohnes, 'the father of the son;' des Vaters Sohn, 'the father's son;' König dieses Reichs, 'king of this realm'

d. As partitive genitive (expressing a whole of which the governing noun is a part), in all its varieties: der Schrecklichste der Schrecken, 'the most terrible of terrors;' eins der kleinsten Kinder, 'one of the smallest children;' jedes dieser Bedürfnisse, 'each of these needs;' allzuviel des Spaßes, 'quite too much of the joke.'

e. As genitive of material, constitution, or equivalence: ein Dach schattender Buchen, 'a roof of shady beeches;' der Zweige laubiges Gitter, 'the leafy trellis-work of the branches;' eine Anzahl schreiender Knaben, 'a number of shouting boys;' des Goldes Ströme, 'streams of gold.'

f. As genitive of characteristic: ein Mann hohen Rangs und großer Tugend, 'a man of high rank and great virtue;' ein Hirtenstamm türkischer Abkunft, 'a shepherd-race of Turkish descent.'

g. As subjective genitive (implying an action of which the thing designated by the genitive is the subject): des Sturmes Sausen, 'the roaring of the storm;' der Magnete Hassen und Lieben, 'the hating and loving (attraction and repulsion) of magnets.'

h. As objective genitive (implying an action of which the thing designated by the genitive is the object): dein Wunsch des Guten, 'thy desire of good;' Verbesserer der Welt und des Gesetzes, 'Improver of the World and of the Law.'

The relation of the genitive to its governing noun is so infinitely various, that neither the above classification nor any other is exhaustive or peremptory.

3. In these relations, the genitive of a personal pronoun is rarely admitted; but for it is usually substituted a possessive pronominal adjective, qualifying the noun to be limited (158.2).

Exceptions: certain cases of partitives, of genitives followed by a qualifying word, and a few others: as, unser einer, 'one of us;' ihrer beiden Eindrücke, 'the impressions of them both;' ihrer Meister werden, 'to get the better of them.'

4. For the genitive, in all these uses, may be substituted a dative with the preposition von, 'of,' as in English.

The substitution is made, especially, when the expression would otherwise be ambiguous or unclear, from the want of a distinct ending to the genitive, or of a limiting word showing its character: thus, die Einwohner von Paris, 'the inhabitants of Paris;' Vater von sechs Kindern, 'father of six children;' but die Einwohner Berlins, 'the inhabitants of Berlin;' Vater dieser sechs Kinder, 'father of these six children':—or, to avoid a succession of several genitives: as, der Sohn von dem Oheime Kaiser Emanuels, 'the son of the uncle of Emperor Emanuel.' But it is made also without special assignable reason—most often for the partitive genitive, and the genitive of material and of characteristic, more seldom for the possessive and complement of relation, least often for the objective genitive.

5. *a.* After nouns signifying measure, of extent, quantity, weight, or number, the noun designating the substance measured, if not preceded by an adjective, is usually put neither in the genitive (partitive genitive), nor in the dative with von, 'of,' but is treated as indeclinable.

Thus, ein Glas Wein, 'a glass of wine' (i. e., wine, to the extent of one glass); zwei Pfund Thee, 'two pounds of tea;' drei Ellen Tuch, 'three yards of cloth;' einige Buch Papier, 'a few quires of paper;' große Blätter Rauschgold, 'great sheets of gold-tinsel;'—but, ein Glas dieses Weins, or von diesem Weine, 'a glass of this wine;' zwei Pfund guten Thees, 'two pounds of good tea.'

Exceptions are occasionally met with: thus, den besten Becher Weins, 'the best goblet of wine' (R. 62.2); 300 Zentner Goldes, '300 cwt. of gold (R. 189.18).

b. By abbreviation, the name of the month is left unvaried after a numeral designating the day: thus, den neunten Mai, 'the ninth of May.'

6. The genitive, in any of its senses, may be placed either before or after the noun which it limits (as is shown by the examples given). But its position before the noun, especially if limited by any other word than an article, belongs rather to a higher or poetic style; in plain colloquial prose, the genitive ordinarily follows the noun that governs it. An objective genitive most rarely precedes; and never, if another genitive be dependent on the same noun: thus, des Königs Wahl eines Ministers, 'the king's choice of a minister.'

217. *The Genitive with Adjectives.*

About thirty adjectives (with their corresponding negatives) are followed by a genitive, denoting that in respect of which the action or quality they express is exerted.

Thus, des Singens müde, 'weary of singing;' würdiger des Rings, 'more worthy of the ring;' eines Sultans unwürdig, 'unworthy of a Sultan;' süßer Erinnerung voll, 'full of sweet memories.'

These adjectives are mostly such as are followed by *of* in English, although some admit a different construction. Among the commonest of them (besides those already instanced) are bewußt, 'conscious,' fähig, 'capable,' gewiß, 'sure,' schuldig, 'guilty,' satt, 'sated,' überdrüssig, 'tired.' Some of them also are construed with prepositions, and a few (**229**) even govern an accusative, when used with the verbs sein and werden.

218. *The Genitive with Prepositions.*

About twenty prepositions govern the genitive.

Thus, wegen seiner Sünde, 'on account of his sin;' während meiner tollen Jagd, 'during my mad chase;' ungeachtet dieser Erklärung, 'notwithstanding this explanation;' statt duftiger Gärten, 'instead of fragrant gardens.'

The prepositions governing the genitive are mostly of recent derivation from nouns and adjectives. For a list of them, see below, under Prepositions (**373**).

219. *The Genitive as Object of Verbs.*

1. A genitive immediately dependent upon a verb has generally the office of a remoter impersonal object, further qualifying the action of the verb upon its nearer personal object.

2. About twenty-five transitive verbs govern a genitive in addition to their direct object, the accusative.

These are verbs of removing, depriving, accusing, convicting, admonishing, assuring, and the like, and one or two others (würdigen, 'esteem worthy,' vertröſten, 'console').

Thus, er klagt den Diener des Diebſtahls an, 'he accuses the servant of theft;' er hat uns einer großen Furcht entledigt, 'he has rid us of a great fear;' er beraubt den Unglücklichen der Hoffnung, 'he robs the wretched of hope.'

3. About forty reflexive verbs admit a genitive in addition to their reflexive object.

These verbs are of too various meaning to admit of classification. Some of them may be rendered in English either by a construction resembling the German, or as simple transitive verbs taking a genitive as direct object: thus, freue dich deiner Jugend, 'rejoice thyself of (enjoy) thy youth;' er entſinnt ſich jedes Wortes, 'he bethinks himself of (recollects) every word;' ſich gefährlicher Waffen bedienen, 'to serve one's self with (employ) dangerous weapons;'—others, only in the latter method: thus, mit Eifer hab' ich mich der Studien befliſſen, 'zealously have I pursued my studies;' deiner heiligen Zeichen, o Wahrheit, hat der Betrug ſich angemaßt, 'thy holy signs, oh Truth! has deceit usurped.'

4. A few impersonal verbs take a genitive of the object, with an accusative of the subject, of the feeling they represent.

They are erbarmen, 'pity,' gelüſten, 'long,' jammern, 'grieve,' reuen or gereuen, 'rue:' thus, mich erbarmt ſeines Elends, 'I pity his misery.'

5. About thirty verbs may take a genitive only, after the manner of a direct object.

Thus, er achtete nicht der warmen Sonne, 'he heeded not the warm sun;' es bedarf der Annahme nicht, 'it needs not the assumption;' andrer Frevel nicht zu gedenken, 'not to mention other atrocities;' laß mich der neuen Freiheit genießen, 'let me enjoy the new freedom;' jedes Leiden vergeſſend, 'forgetting every trial;' ihr ſpottet mein, 'ye mock me;' wo ich deiner warte, 'where I wait for thee.'

6. Many of the verbs in these various classes may take instead of the genitive an accusative, or else a noun governed by a preposition: for example, all the impersonals, and all but two (ermangeln and geſchweigen) of the last class. The construction with the genitive is an older one, which has for some time been going gradually out of use: thus, dieſe Freiheit, die ich jetzt genieße, 'this liberty which I now enjoy;' denen, auf die die ewige Freiheit wartet, 'to those for whom eternal freedom is waiting;' er freut ſich über ſein Glück, 'he rejoices at his good fortune.'

220. *Other uses of the Genitive.*

1. The genitive of a noun is often used in an adverbial sense; especially (with or without a limiting adjective) to denote time; also (with adjective) not infrequently manner, more rarely place.

Thus, eines Tages im Lenze, 'one day in spring;' des Winters ſind wir wie vergraben in dem Schnee, 'in the winter we are, as it were, buried up in the snow;' die Wolken, die Morgens und Abends über ihn hin segelten, 'the clouds which sailed along over him of a morning and evening;' er schlürft langen Halses, 'he sips with outstretched neck:' hörst du's klingen mächtigen Rufes, 'dost thou hear it ring with mighty sound?' ich ermahnte ihn alles Ernstes, 'I admonished him in all seriousness;' sachte schleich' ich meines Wege, 'I softly steal off on my way.'

A large number of adverbs are, by origin, genitives of nouns or adjectives, or of a noun and a limiting word which have grown together by familiar use: see **363–5**.

2. A genitive is sometimes used with a verb (especially sein and werden) in the sense of a predicative adjective: thus, sie waren munter und guter Dinge, 'they were merry and of good cheer;' die waren oft nicht so groß, oder gleichen Alters mit ihm, 'they were often not so big, or of equal age with him;' alle werden auf einmal eines Sinnes, 'all become suddenly of one mind;' ich bin Willens, 'I am of a mind.'

The genitive in this construction is allied with the genitive of characteristic (**216.2*f***).

3. By a construction formerly not rare, but now nearly obsolete, a partitive genitive is used with verbs: thus, er trank des Baches, 'he drank of the brook;' sie brachte des klaren herrlichen Weines, 'she brought of the clear excellent wine.'

4. Yet more unusual are cases of the occurrence of a possessive genitive and of a genitive of origin with verbs: thus, thue was deines Amtes ist, 'do what belongs to (is of) thy office;' Hungers sterben, 'to die of hunger.'

5. A genitive is sometimes used with an interjection, to signify the thing which is the occasion of the exclamation: thus, ach des Unglücks, 'alas for the mishap' (see **392**).

Dative.

221. 1. The dative is originally and properly the case of the indirect personal object, designating the person or persons with reference to whom, or as affecting whom, anything is or is done—a relation ordinarily expressed in English by the preposition *to* or *for*. In this sense, the dative in German is usually the adjunct of a verb, much less often of an adjective, very rarely of a noun.

2. The dative has also inherited the offices of primitive cases, now lost; especially of the instrumental, expressing the *with* or *by* relation, and the locative, expressing the *in* relation. In these senses, it is ordinarily governed by prepositions.

222. *The Dative with Verbs.*

The dative, in German, is most often the indirect personal object of a verb.

a. It is thus doubly contrasted in office with the genitive: the latter usually limits a noun; and, as indirect object, it is prevailingly impersonal: thus, ich versichere ihn einer Sache, 'I assure him of a matter,' but ich versichere ihm eine Sache, 'I assure (vouch for) a matter to him;' ich beraube ihn seines Geldes, 'I rob him of his money,' but ich raube ihm sein Geld, 'I steal from him his money.'

b. The connection of the dative with the action of the verb is of every degree of closeness, from constituting its essential or necessary complement to indicating a mere incidental interest in its action: thus, er bot mir die Hand, 'he offered me his hand;' ich legte es ihm auf den Tisch, 'I laid it on the table for him.'

I. 1. A large number of transitive verbs take, along with the accusative, a dative as more or less necessary complement of their action. Such are

a. Many simple verbs, especially such as denote a bringing near or removing, a giving or taking, imparting, commanding, permitting or refusing, and the like.

Thus, er brachte den Ring der Alten, 'he brought the ring to the old woman;' ich schreibe meinem Vater einen Brief, 'I write my father a letter;' man erlaubt alles einem Freunde, 'one permits a friend anything.'

b. Many verbs compounded with inseparable or separable prefixes, especially ent, er, ver, and an, auf, ab, bei, nach, vor, zu.

Thus, er vermacht den Ring dem liebsten seiner Söhne, 'he makes over the ring to the dearest of his sons;' er wollte ihm die Krone aufsetzen, 'he wished to set the crown on his head;' sie mußte ihm die Jungfrau zusagen, 'she had to promise him the girl.'

c. A few verbs that require a reflexive object in the dative, forming a class of improper reflexives (**290**): thus, ich habe mir Beifall verdient, 'I have earned myself applause.'

d. A few verbs compounded with adjectives, or verbal phrases akin with such: e. g., wahrsagen, 'prophesy;' kund machen, 'make known.'

2. In the passive of these verbs, where the object-accusative becomes a subject-nominative, the dative remains as sole object: thus, der Ring wurde der Alten gebracht, 'the ring was brought to the old woman;' es wird mir kund gemacht, 'it is made known to me.'

3. As the examples have shown, the English also often uses its objective without a preposition (when placed next the verb) in a dative sense. In other cases, it expresses the dative relation by prepositions, especially *to.* But, where the verb implies removal, the dative frequently answers to our objective with *from.*

Thus, nimm meiner Rede jeden Stachel, 'take *from* my words all sting; es stahl mir das Leben, 'it stole my life *from* me;' es deinem Mitleid zu entziehen, 'to withdraw it *from* thy compassion.'

The same is true of the dative after intransitive verbs: see below.

4. Either the direct or the indirect object may often be omitted, and the verb used with the other alone: thus, einem ein Buch vorlesen, 'to read a book aloud to some one;' ein Buch vorlesen, 'to read a book aloud;' einem vorlesen, 'to read aloud to some one;' also, simply vorlesen, 'to read aloud, lecture.'

II. 1. **Many verbs take a dative as their sole object.**

These, as not admitting an accusative, are reckoned as intransitive; but many of them correspond to verbs which in English are looked upon as transitive.

a. About thirty-five simple verbs, together with a few that have the inseparable prefixes be, ge, er; also, the contraries of several of them, formed with the prefix miß.

Thus, seid ihr ihnen nicht begegnet, 'did you not meet them?' folgt durch den Aether dem Strahl, 'follows the beam of light through the ether;' wie's ihnen gefällt, 'as it pleases them;' wenn es mir nicht mißfiele, 'if it did not displease me;' kann es dir nicht schaden, 'can it not harm thee?' helft mir, 'help me!' den Räumen und Zeiten zu trotzen, 'to defy space and time.'

b. A large number of verbs compounded with the inseparable prefix ent, and with the prepositions ab, an, auf, aus, bei, ein, entgegen, nach, unter, vor, wider, zu; deriving their power to take the dative object from the modification of meaning given by the prefix.

Thus, die Schwerter entfliegen der Scheide, 'the swords leap from the scabbard;' viele stimmten dieser Ansicht bei, 'many acceded to this view;' kommt einer ihm entgegen, 'if one comes to meet him;' um ähnlichen Ereignissen vorzubeugen, 'in order to avoid such occurrences;' welcher den Gefechten zusah, 'who was looking on at the contests.'

The meaning added by the prefix is, as the examples show, to be very variously rendered in English.

c. A number of verbs compounded with nouns, adverbs, and adjectives; also, of verbal phrases akin with such.

Thus, daß sein Gesang seinem Kleide gleichkommen müsse, 'that his song must correspond with his attire;' er eilte seinem Vater zu Hülfe, 'he hastened to the help of his father;' es thut mir leid, 'it pains me;' er macht dieser Dame den Hof, 'he is paying court to this lady;' es ward ihm zu Theil, 'it was granted him (fell to his share).'

d. Werden, 'become,' is sometimes used alone with a (possessive) dative in the sense of zu Theil werden: thus, dazu ward dem Menschen der Verstand, 'for that end was understanding given to man (became his).' Quite rarely, such a possessive dative follows sein: as, es ist ihm, 'it is his (belongs to him).'

e. A few impersonal verbs, or verbs used impersonally, take a dative designating the subject of the feeling or condition they express: thus, es graut mir, 'I am horrified;' ihm schwindelt, 'he turns giddy.' Some of these take also the accusative.

f. Also sein, werden, and gehen or ergehen, with adverbial adjuncts, are frequently thus used impersonally with the dative (**292.4**): thus, ihm war bange, 'he was in anxiety;' mir wird so wohl, 'so pleasant a feeling is coming over me;' wie ist mir denn, 'how is it then with me?' dem ist so, 'the case is thus (it is thus with regard to that).'

2. Of the intransitive verbs governing the dative, a part—especially those that denote an action proceeding from a person—may form an impersonal passive governing the same case (see **279.2**).

Thus, es ward mir hart begegnet, 'I have been harshly dealt with (met); es wurde ihm geholfen, 'he was helped.'

III. In a looser and less strictly dependent construction—as denoting the person (or thing) in behalf of whom, or as affecting whom, anything is or is done, the dative ("dative of interest") is used so freely, and with so many verbs, that to attempt giving rules for its occurrence would be useless. Only one or two points call for special notice.

a. A dative grammatically dependent on the verb takes the place of a possessive genitive qualifying a noun in the sentence: thus, der Amme um den Hals fallend, 'falling upon her nurse's neck;' leget den Miöllner der Maid in den Schooß, 'lay Miöllner in the maid's lap.'

b. This is especially common with the personal pronouns: thus, es blitzt aus den Augen ihm kühn, 'a daring look beams from his eyes' (see **161**).

c. The personal pronoun is sometimes thus used in a manner that is expletive: thus, sieh mir ob sie kommen, 'see (for me) whether they are coming' (compare **156**).

IV. For the dative dependent upon a verb, in all its varieties (but not with all verbs: especially not with those which take the dative after the manner of a direct object, II.1*a*), is sometimes substituted a case governed by a preposition (as zu, 'to,' für, 'for,' von, 'from'). This substitution is notably more frequent with a noun than with a personal pronoun; a dative of the latter is often used where one of the former would make a harsh or forced construction.

223. *The Dative with Adjectives.*

1. The construction of the dative with adjectives is analogous with its construction with verbs. Some adjectives call for the case as their essential or natural defining complement; others admit it in a looser relation, after the manner of a "dative of interest" (above, **222.**III.).

2. Adjectives taking the dative as their more essential complement are especially those that signify nearness or remoteness, likeness or unlikeness, suitableness, property, inclination, advantage or disadvantage, and the like. Usually, they require in English the preposition *to* before a noun limiting them.

Thus, wie nah fühl' ich mich dir, 'how near I feel myself to thee!' dem Ackerbau fremd, 'strangers to agriculture;' Wolken gleich Fittigen, 'clouds like wings;' einen ihm eigenen Werth, 'a value peculiar to it;' eine Seele, die der That nicht gewachsen ist, 'a soul that is not equal to the deed;' ein mir unverhofftes Glück, 'a happiness unhoped for by me.'

3. Participles of verbs governing the dative admit a complement in the same case, in analogy with the uses of the verbs from which they come, and according to their own character as active, passive, or neuter participles.

4. Verbal derivatives in bar and lich, signifying possibility, take a dative of the person whom the possibility concerns: thus, mir begreiflich, 'comprehensible to me;' dem Menschen unbewohnbar, 'uninhabitable by man.'

5. Almost any adjective qualified by zu, 'too,' or genug, 'sufficiently, enough,' admits an adjunct in the dative: thus, das Kleid ist mir zu lang, ihm aber nicht lang genug, 'the garment is too long for me, but not long enough for him.'

6. Many adjectives admit a dative adjunct more readily, or only, when used with a verb, either predicatively, or forming a more or less closely compounded verbal phrase: thus, das ist mir recht, 'that suits me (seems to me right);' das wird dem Knaben schwer, 'that grows hard for the boy.'

For such phrases, with transitive, intransitive, and impersonal verbs, see above, **222**.I.1*d*, II.1*c*,*f*.

7. For the dative with an adjective, also, is often used a case governed by a preposition (especially von, 'from,' für, 'for').

224. *The Dative with Prepositions.*

1. About twenty prepositions govern the dative.

For the list of them, see under Prepositions (**374**).

2. Nine prepositions govern the dative when the relation expressed is that of situation or locality; but the accusative, when motion or tendency toward anything is implied.

These are an, auf, hinter, in, neben, über, unter, vor, zwischen (see **376**).

225. *The Dative in other constructions.*

1. The use of the dative as a virtual possessive genitive, grammatically dependent on a verb, but logically qualifying a noun, has been explained above (**222**.III.*a*,*b*). Rarely, the dative is found having the same value with a noun alone: as, dem Riesen zur Lust, 'for the giant's pleasure (for a pleasure to the giant);' er gab, ihm zu Ehren, manche Feste, 'he gave many festivals in his honor.' Yet more rarely, it occurs with a noun in other relations usually expressed by a genitive, or with the aid of a preposition: as, ein Muster Bürgern und Bauern, 'a model for citizens and peasants;' Gewißheit einem neuen Bunde, 'assurance of a new covenant.'

2. The dative sometimes follows a noun in exclamatory phrases (as if the imperative of sein, 'to be,' were understood): thus, dem Buben und dem Knecht die Acht, 'outlawry to the villain and flunkey!' Freude dem Sterblichen, 'joy to the mortal!' Some words habitually employed as exclamations are also followed by a dative signifying the person toward whom the feeling expressed by the exclamation is directed: such are wohl, Heil, Weh and the like (see **392**).

Accusative.

226. The relations of the accusative are more simple than those of the other oblique cases. Its proper office is to stand as direct object of a verbal action; and also, in that relation, most nearly akin with the former, which we ordinarily express by *to:* but this it has in German only in part. The German uses it also as the case absolute.

227. *The Accusative with Verbs.*

1. The accusative is especially the case belonging to the direct object of a transitive verb: as, ich sehe den Mann; er trägt einen Hut, 'I see the man; he wears a hat.'

a. And a transitive verb, on the other hand, is one that takes a direct object in the accusative. The classification of verbs as transitive and intransitive is in part formal rather than logical, and

b. Some verbs which in English are regarded as transitive take in German the genitive (**219.**5) or the dative (**222.** II.1), and therefore belong to the class of intransitives. Again, some verbs which to us are intransitive are in German, uniformly or occasionally, transitive: as, ihr habt mich sprechen wollen, 'you have desired to speak *to me*.'

2. The accusative is also sometimes used as the object of a verb properly intransitive.

a. Some verbs may be followed by an accusative of meaning akin with their own, or signifying a substantive idea which they themselves virtually involve ("cognate accusative").

Thus, wir sterben hier den Tod der Freien, 'we die here the death of the free;' betet einen frommen Spruch, 'pray a pious phrase;' sie schläft den letzten Schlaf, 'she sleeps the last sleep.'

b. By a pregnant construction, an intransitive may be followed by an accusative of that which is effected or made to appear by the action it designates: thus, tönt die Glocke Grabgesang, 'the bell tolls a funeral hymn;' was grinsest du mir her, 'what grinnest thou at me (what does thy grinning signify)?'—or by an accusative and an adjective or other equivalent expression as factitive predicate, signifying the condition into which that which is designated by the accusative is brought by the action described by the verb: thus, sich halb todt lachen, 'to laugh one's self half dead; ich träum' als Kind mich zurücke, 'I dream myself back into childhood (as child);' du wirst die Wächter aus dem Schlafe schreien, 'thou wilt scream the guards out of sleep.'

c. Some impersonal verbs, denoting a personal condition or state of feeling, take an accusative signifying the person affected thus, es lüstet keinen, euer Mann zu werden, 'no one desires to become your husband;' mich hungert, 'I am hungry.' See **294.**

With these are included also dünken, däuchten, 'seem' (the only verbs in which a like construction still appears in English): thus, mich dünkt, 'me thinks;' mich däuchte, 'me thought.' These (and some of the others also) admit a dative instead of an accusative object (**222**.II.1*e*).

d. For the accusative after sein or werden with certain adjectives, see below (**229**).

3. A few transitive verbs govern two accusatives: these are

a. Fragen, 'ask,' lehren, 'teach,' and (rarely) bitten, 'beg,' which add to their personal object another denoting the thing to which their action relates: thus, er fragte mich manches, 'he asked me many a thing;' ich lehre ihn die Musik, 'I teach him music;' ich bitte dich nur dies, 'I beg of thee only this' (R.150.2).

b. Heißen and nennen, 'call, name,' schimpfen and schelten, 'call by way of reproach,' and taufen, 'christen,' which add to their personal object a second accusative as factitive predicate, denoting the name or title given: thus, ich will alles eine Schickung nennen, 'I will call the whole a work of destiny;' er schimpfte seinen Gegner einen Narren, 'he reviled his adversary as a fool.'

c. A noun in the accusative as factitive predicate now and then appears with other verbs—as, so glaube jeder seinen Ring den echten, 'then let each believe his own ring the genuine one:' but this construction is generally avoided by the use of a different expression: as, man macht or wählt ihn zum König, 'they make, or choose, him king (for king)'; ich halte ihn für meinen Freund, 'I deem him my friend;' ich kenne ihn als einen Ehrenmann, 'I know him a man of honor.'

228. *The Accusative with Prepositions.*

1. Eight prepositions always govern the accusative.

They are bis, durch, für, gegen or gen, ohne, sonder, um, wider (see **375**).

2. Nine prepositions are followed by the accusative when they indicate motion or tendency toward; otherwise, by the dative.

They are an, auf, hinter, in, neben, über, unter, vor, zwischen (see **376**).

229. *The Accusative with Adjectives.*

A few adjectives, when used predicatively with sein or werden (especially the latter), may take an object in the accusative.

They are ansichtig, bewußt, gewahr, gewohnt, los, müde, satt, überdrüssig, zufrieden: thus, die Geister werd' ich nun nicht los, 'I cannot now get rid of the spirits;' ich wär' es zufrieden, 'I should be content with it;' wenn wir nicht sein Eingreifen gewahr würden, 'if we did not feel its taking hold.'

This anomalous construction is of quite modern origin. The governing force belongs to the combination of adjective and verb (compare **223**.6).

230. *The Accusative in absolute construction.*

1. The accusative is used absolutely (that is, as adverbial adjunct of a verb or adjective, but not properly governed by them) to express measure—whether of duration of time, of extent of space, of weight, of value, or of number.

Thus, er horchte einen Augenblick, 'he listened for a moment'; an die ich viele Jahre nicht gedacht, 'of which I have not thought for many years; man hatte sie nur wenige Tage vorher gesehen, 'they had been seen only a few days before;' zwanzig Jahre her, 'twenty years since;' als sie eine gute Strecke fortgegangen waren, 'when they had gone on a good piece;' eine halbe Stunde vor dem Schloß, 'half a league outside the castle;' acht Morgen tief, 'eight furlongs deep;' es wiegt ein Pfund, 'it weighs a pound;' das kostet zwei Thaler, 'that costs two dollars;' ein Heer 300,000 Mann stark, 'an army 300,000 men strong.'

a. To an accusative expressing duration of time is often added the adverb lang, 'long:' as, er lag sieben Jahre lang, 'he lay for seven years;' den ganzen Tag lang, 'the whole day long:'—less often other adverbs: as, das ganze Jahr durch, 'the whole year through;' diese Zeit über, 'all this time.'

b. By a similar construction, an adverb of direction or motion is very frequently added to an accusative of space, in such way as almost to have the value of a preposition governing it: thus, die Treppen herunter, 'down the stairs;' den Berg hinan, 'up the mountain;' den Weg am Bach hinauf, 'up the path by the brook;' den ganzen Corso hin und wieder, 'through the whole Corso and back.'

2. The accusative is also used to express the time of occurrence ("time when").

Thus, das geschah jedes Jahr, 'that happened every year;' den Abend beim Tanze, 'that evening, at the dance;' er sieht die Welt kaum einen Feiertag, 'he sees the world only on a holiday.'

This use of the accusative borders on that of the adverbial genitive (**220.**1), and the two are to some extent interchangeable: but the accusative has the more definite meaning, and cannot be used without a defining adjunct: thus, Abends, des Abends, 'of an evening, in the evening' (now and then, or habitually); but diesen Abend, 'this evening,' letzten Abend, 'last evening,' and so on.

3. *a.* A noun in the accusative is sometimes used absolutely, with an adjunct (prepositional or adjective), to express an accompanying or characterizing circumstance—as if governed by *with* or *having* understood.

Thus, die Mütter erschienen, den Säugling im Arme, 'the mothers appeared, (with) their infants in their arms;' andere fliehen, wilde Angst im funkelnden Auge, 'others fly, wild terror in their flashing eyes.'

b. This is especially usual with a participle as adjunct of the noun: thus, winkt uns, die Fackel umgewandt, 'beckons to us, with torch inverted;' man gewöhnt es, den Kopf gegen den Corso gerichtet, still zu stehen, 'it is trained to stand still, having the head directed toward the Corso;' selbst Kranke nicht ausgenommen, 'even the sick not excepted.'

c. Allied with this is the so-called imperative use of the participle (see **359.**3).

CONJUGATION.

231. Conjugation is variation for mood, tense, number, and person.

Only verbs are conjugated: hence, the subject of conjugation is coincident with that of verbal inflection.

VERBS.

232. The essential characteristic of a verb is that it predicates or asserts something of a subject: that is to say, it ascribes some action, or state, or quality, to some being or thing expressed by a noun or pronoun.

This predication or ascription is not always direct and positive; it may be contingent, inquiring, or optative: compare **427**.

233. Verbs are variously classified.

1. They are divided into TRANSITIVE and INTRANSITIVE, according to the nature of the relation they sustain to a noun representing the object of their action: a verb that admits an object in the accusative is called transitive; otherwise, intransitive.

Thus, transitive verbs, ich lobe ihn, 'I praise him;' er schlägt mich, 'he strikes me:'—intransitive, ich stehe, er fällt, 'I stand, he falls;' er schonet seines Feindes, 'he spares his enemy;' ich danke Ihnen, 'I thank you.'

a. That the distinction of transitive and intransitive is in part formal rather than essential, has been pointed out above (**227.**1*a*,*b*): practically, however, it is one of importance.

2. Under these classes are distinguished

a. REFLEXIVE verbs, which take an object designating the same person or thing with their subject.

b. IMPERSONAL verbs, used only in the third person singular, and either with an indefinite subject or without an expressed subject.

3. Transitive verbs, again, form by the help of an auxiliary verb a PASSIVE VOICE, denoting the suffering of an action, and taking as its subject what was the object of the simple verb: which latter, by contrast with the other, is said to be of the ACTIVE VOICE.

4. Nearly all verbs, moreover, admit of being compounded

with certain prefixes, of a prepositional character: with reference to such composition, therefore, they are distinguished as SIMPLE and COMPOUND.

234. The general rules of conjugation apply alike to all verbs, of whatever class they may be. They will be first stated and illustrated in their application to simple personal verbs in the active voice.

SIMPLE FORMS OF THE VERB.

235. The German verb has the same simple forms as the English, namely:

1. Two *tenses*, the PRESENT, and the PRETERIT, or indefinite past.

The value and use of these tenses nearly correspond in the two languages. But the present is sometimes employed in place of our perfect, or our future; and the limits of the preterit and the perfect are also not precisely the same in both: see **324** etc.

2. These tenses are formed each in two *moods*, the INDICATIVE and the SUBJUNCTIVE.

The subjunctive is nearly extinct in English: the German subjunctive is employed sometimes for our potential and conditional; others of its uses have no correspondent in English: see **329** etc.

The rendering of the subjunctive tenses in the paradigms, therefore, by 'may' and 'might' is only conventional, and for the sake of uniformity; such rendering gives but one of their various meanings.

3. Each tense is declined in two *numbers*, with three *persons* in each number, as in English.

4. Of an IMPERATIVE mood there are two persons, the second singular and the second plural.

5. An INFINITIVE, or verbal noun.

6. Two PARTICIPLES, or verbal adjectives, one present and active; the other past, and prevailingly passive.

The infinitive and participles are not proper verbal forms, since they contain no idea of predication. They present the verbal idea in the condition of noun and of adjective respectively; but, as regards their adjuncts, they share in the construction of their corresponding verbal forms: see **348** and **357**.

236. Examples:

1. lieben, 'love' (root, lieb).

Pers.	Indicative		Subjunctive	
	Present.			
	Singular.		*Singular.*	
1	ich liebe	'I love'	ich liebe	'I may love'
2	du liebst	'thou lovest'	du liebest	'thou mayest love
3	er liebt	'he loves'	er liebe	'he may love'
	Plural.		*Plural.*	
1	wir lieben	'we love'	wir lieben	'we may love'
2	ihr liebt	'ye love'	ihr liebet	'ye may love'
3	sie lieben	'they love'	sie lieben	'they may love'
	Preterit.			
	Singular.		*Singular.*	
1	ich liebte	'I loved'	ich liebte, -bete	'I might love'
2	du liebtest	'thou lovedst'	du liebtest, -betest	'thou mightest love
3	er liebte	'he loved'	er liebte, -bete	'he might love'
	Plural.		*Plural.*	
1	wir liebten	'we loved'	wir liebten, -beten	'we might love'
2	ihr liebtet	'ye loved'	ihr liebtet, -betet	'ye might love'
3	sie liebten	'they loved'	sie liebten, -beten	'they might love'

IMPERATIVE.

	Singular.		*Plural.*	
2	liebe, liebe du	'love thou'	liebt, liebt ihr	'love ye

INFINITIVE.

lieben 'to love'

PARTICIPLES.

Present.		*Past.*	
liebend	'loving'	geliebt	'loved'

Remarks. 1. This verb illustrates the mode of inflection of verbs of the New conjugation, corresponding with what we call "regular verbs" in English. The special rules concerning the inflection of such verbs are given below: see **246** etc.

2. The forms liebest and liebet may be used also in the present indicative and the imperative, as well as liebete etc. in the preterit indicative, and geliebet in the past participle: see below, **237.3**.

2. geben, 'give' (root, geb).

	INDICATIVE.		SUBJUNCTIVE.	
		Present.		
	Singular.		*Singular.*	
1	ich gebe	'I give'	ich gebe	'I may give'
2	du giebst, gibst	'thou givest'	du gebest	'thou mayest give'
3	er giebt, gibt	'he gives'	er gebe	'he may give'
	Plural.		*Plural.*	
1	wir geben	'we give'	wir geben	'we may give'
2	ihr gebt	'ye give'	ihr gebet	'ye may give'
3	sie geben	'they give'	sie geben	'they may give'
		Preterit.		
	Singular.		*Singular.*	
1	ich gab	'I gave'	ich gäbe	'I might give'
2	du gabst	'thou gavest'	du gäbest	'thou mightest give
3	er gab	'he gave'	er gäbe	'he might give'
	Plural.		*Plural.*	
1	wir gaben	'we gave'	wir gäben	'we might give'
2	ihr gabt	'ye gave'	ihr gäbet	'ye might give'
3	sie gaben	'they gave'	sie gäben	'they might give'

IMPERATIVE.

	Singular.		*Plural.*	
2	gieb, gib du	'give thou'	gebt, gebt ihr	'give ye

INFINITIVE.

geben 'to give'

PARTICIPLES.

Present.		*Past.*	
gebend	'giving'	gegeben	'given'

Remarks. 1. This verb illustrates the mode of inflection of verbs of the Old conjugation, corresponding with what we call "irregular verbs" in English. The special rules concerning the inflection of such verbs are giver below: see **261** etc.

2. The forms gebet, gabest, gabet (for gebt, gabst, gabt) are occasionally met with; also gäbst, gäbt (for gäbest, gäbet). For the double forms giebst. gibst, etc., see **268.1*b*.**

237. *General Rules respecting the Simple Forms of the Verb.*

1. Of the forms thus given, three are called the PRINCIPAL PARTS, because, when they are known, all the others can be inferred from them: these are the *infinitive*, the 1st pers. sing. *preterit*, and the past *participle:* thus, lieben, liebte, geliebt; geben, gab, gegeben.

a. The infinitive always ends in n, and almost always in en. The rejection of this n or en gives us the ROOT of the verb.

Not ending in en are only sein, 'be,' thun, 'do,' and infinitives from roots of more than one syllable ending in l or r, as wandeln, 'walk,' wandern, 'wander.'

b. There are, as the examples show, two ways of forming the preterit and past participle: the preterit adding ete or te to the root, or else adding nothing, but changing the radical vowel; the participle taking the ending et or t, or else en or n. According to these differences, verbs are divided into two conjugations (see below, **245**).

2. The endings of tense inflection are

first pers. singular,	e, —	first pers. plural,	en, n
second pers. "	est, st, e, —	second pers. "	et, t
third pers. "	et, t, e, —	third pers. "	en, n

The rules for their use are as follows:

a. The first persons pres. indicative and subjunctive are the same, and formed by adding e to the simple root.

Exceptions are only bin, 'am,' sei, 'may be,' and the pres. indicative of the modal auxiliaries (see **251.**3).

b. The first (and third) pers. singular of the preterit subjunctive, and of the preterit indicative except in verbs of the Old conjugation (**269.**I.1), also end in e.

3. *a.* The third pers. sing. pres. indicative has the ending t or et (our *th*, *s* in *loveth*, *loves*): in all the other tenses, the third person is like the first.

Exceptions, without the ending t are only the modal auxiliaries (see **251.**3), and a few other verbs (**268.**5).

b. The ending of all second persons singular (except in the imperative) is st or est (our *st* in *lovest*); of all first and third persons plural (excepting only sind, 'are'), en or n; of all second persons plural (with the single exception ſeid, 'are') et or t.

c. The retention or rejection of the vowel e of the endings eſt, et (also of e before the te forming the preterit of one conjugation) depends partly on euphony, partly on arbitrary choice. The e must always be used when the final letter of the root is such that the consonant of the ending would not otherwise be distinctly heard —thus, we may say liebeſt or liebſt, but only lieſeſt, 'readest,' tanzeſt, 'dancest;' liebt or liebet, but only bittet, 'begs,' redet, 'talks'—also, when a harsh or unpronounceable combination of consonants would otherwise occur—thus, only athmeſt, athmet, 'breathest, breathes;' ſegneſt, ſegnet, 'blessest, blesses.' In other cases, the writer or speaker is allowed to choose between the fuller and the briefer form; the latter being more familiar or colloquial, the former more used in stately and solemn styles. But the e is generally retained in the subjunctive, especially when the distinction of subjunctive and indicative depends upon it.

The e of the ending en of the first and third persons plural is rarely dropped except after unaccented er or el, in the indicative.

Special rules affecting some of the forms of the Old conjugation will be given below (**268–9**).

d. The final unaccented e of all verbal forms (as of all other words in the language) is not unfrequently cut off, especially in poetry, and in colloquial style. An apostrophe should always be used, to show the omission; but this is sometimes neglected.

4. The inflection of the tenses is always regular, except in the second and third persons singular of the pres. indicative, which often show a difference of vowel or of consonant, or both, from the other persons of the tense. The same irregularities appear also in the imperative singular (see **268**, **270**).

5. The imperative singular ends in e in nearly all verbs (for exceptions, see **270**.2); the plural is the same with the second pers. pl. indic. present. Both numbers admit of use, as in English, either with or without a subject pronoun.

For the filling up of the imperative with subjunctive forms, see **243**.1.

6. The form of the present participle may always be found by adding d to the infinitive.

Only thun, 'do,' and ſein, 'be,' form thuend, ſeiend.

7. The past participle has usually the prefix ge. For exceptions, see **243**.3.

8. Notice that the third pers. plural of all verbal forms is used also in the sense of a second person, singular or plural (see 153.4), its subject sie being then written with a capital: thus, Sie lieben, 'you love;' Sie gaben, 'you gave.'

COMPOUND FORMS OF THE VERB.

238. As in the case of the English verb, again, the scheme of German conjugation is filled up with a large number of compound forms, made by the aid of auxiliary verbs.

239. *Conjugation of the Auxiliaries of Tense.*

The auxiliaries used in the formation of the tenses of ordinary conjugation are three, namely, haben, 'have,' sein, 'be,' werden, 'become.' The simple forms of these verbs are as follows:

1. Haben:—principal parts haben, hatte, gehabt.

	INDICATIVE.		SUBJUNCTIVE.	
		Present.		
	Singular.		*Singular.*	
1	ich habe	'I have'	ich habe	'I may have'
2	du hast	'thou hast'	du habest	'thou mayest have
3	er hat	'he has'	er habe	'he may have'
	Plural.		*Plural.*	
1	wir haben	'we have'	wir haben	'we may have'
2	ihr habt	'ye have'	ihr habet	'ye may have'
3	sie haben	'they have'	sie haben	'they may have'
		Preterit.		
	Singular.		*Singular.*	
1	ich hatte	'I had'	ich hätte	'I might have'
2	du hattest	'thou hadst'	du hättest	'thou mightest have
3	er hatte	'he had'	er hätte	'he might have'
	Plural.		*Plural.*	
1	wir hatten	'we had'	wir hätten	'we might have'
2	ihr hattet	'ye had'	ihr hättet	'ye might have'
3	sie hatten	'they had'	sie hätten	'they might have

IMPERATIVE.

	Singular.		*Plural.*	
2	habe	'have thou'	habt	'have ye'

INFINITIVE.

haben 'to have'

PARTICIPLES.

Present.		*Past.*	
habend	'having'	gehabt	'had'

2. Sein, 'be:'—principal parts ſein, war, geweſen.

	INDICATIVE.		SUBJUNCTIVE.	
		Present.		
	Singular.		*Singular.*	
1	ich bin	'I am'	ich ſei	'I may be'
2	du biſt	'thou art'	du ſeieſt	'thou mayest be'
3	er iſt	'he is'	er ſei	'he may be'
	Plural.		*Plural.*	
1	wir ſind	'we are'	wir ſeien	'we may be'
2	ihr ſeid	'ye are'	ihr ſeiet	'ye may be'
3	ſie ſind	'they are'	ſie ſeien	'they may be'
		Preterit.		
	Singular.		*Singular.*	
1	ich war	'I was'	ich wäre	'I might be'
2	du warſt	'thou wast'	du wäreſt	'thou mightest be
3	er war	'he was'	er wäre	'he might be'
	Plural.		*Plural.*	
1	wir waren	'we were'	wir wären	'we might be'
2	ihr waret	'ye were'	ihr wäret	'ye might be'
3	ſie waren	'they were'	ſie wären	'they might be

IMPERATIVE.

	Singular.		*Plural.*	
2	ſei	'be thou'	ſeid	'be ye

INFINITIVE.

ſein 'to be'

PARTICIPLES.

Present.		*Past.*	
ſeiend	'being'	geweſen	'been'

3. Werden, 'become:'—principal parts werden, ward or wurde, geworden.

	INDICATIVE.		SUBJUNCTIVE.	
		Present.		
	Singular.		*Singular.*	
1	ich werde	'I become'	ich werde	'I may become'
2	du wirst	'thou becomest'	du werdest	'thou mayest' etc.
3	er wird	'he becomes'	er werde	'he may become'
	Plural.		*Plural.*	
1	wir werden	'we become'	wir werden	'we may become'
2	ihr werdet	'ye become'	ihr werdet	'ye may become'
3	sie werden	'they become'	sie werden	'they may become
		Preterit.		
	Singular.		*Singular.*	
1	ich ward, wurde	'I became'	ich würde	'I might become'
2	du wardst, wurdest	'thou becamest'	du würdest	'thou mightest' etc.
3	er ward, wurde	'he became'	er würde	'he might become'
	Plural.		*Plural.*	
1	wir wurden	'we became'	wir würden	'we might become'
2	ihr wurdet	'ye became'	ihr würdet	'ye might become'
3	sie wurden	'they became'	sie würden	'they might become'

IMPERATIVE.

2	werde	'become thou'	werdet	'become ye'

INFINITIVE.

werden 'to become'

PARTICIPLES.

werdend 'becoming' geworden 'become'

4. *Irregularities in the Conjugation of these Verbs.*

a. Haben is analogous in its conjugation with lieben, above, but the frequency of its use has led to an abbreviation of a few of its forms. Thus, hast and hat are for older habst and habt, and hatte for habte. The modification of the vowel in hätte, pret. subj., is against the prevailing analogy of verbs of its class (see **250.2**).

b. Sein is of the same conjugation with geben, above. Its irregularity, which is far greater than that of any other verb in the language, comes mainly from its being made up of forms derived from three independent roots: bin and bist are from the same root as our *be, being, been* (original form *bhū; Lat. fui*, Greek *phüo*); the rest of the present from the same root as our pres. indicative *am* etc. (original form *as; Lat. sum*, etc., Greek *eimi*); while the preterit and past participle, gewesen, are from the root of our *was, were* (original form *was*, 'dwell, abide'). See the author's "Language and the Study of Language," p. 115.

Some authors still retain ey for ei (see **19**.3) in seyn, in order to distinguish it from the possessive sein (**157**).

c. Werden is a nearly regular verb of the same conjugation with geben. For its persons wirst and wird, see below, **268.5**. In the double form of its pret. ind. singular, it preserves a solitary relic of a condition once belonging to many verbs in the language, whose preterits had a different vowel in the singular and plural. Ward is the original form, and wurde is a quite modern and anomalous fabrication, made after the analogy of the plural wurden.

Exercise XIV.

Simple Forms of the Verb.

1. Der Vater liebt seine Kinder, und sie lieben ihn. 2. Wenn ich Ihnen gäbe was ich habe, hätte ich selber nichts. 3. Was hast du in der Tasche? 4. Er ist krank, aber er wird jetzt besser. 5. Derjenige, den ich liebte, ward mir jeden Tag lieber. 6. Wo sind Sie? und wo war sie als wir hier waren? 7. Gebt mir was ihr liebt, und ich bin zufrieden. 8. Es ist gut, reich zu sein; aber es wäre besser, zufrieden zu sein. 9. Alle Menschen sind Brüder, aber sie lieben einander nicht wie Brüder. 10. Er gebe was er will.

240. *Formation of the Compound Tenses.*

1. From haben or sein, with the past participle of any verb, are formed a perfect and a pluperfect tense, indicative and subjunctive, and a perfect infinitive.

a. The Perfect tense, indicative and subjunctive, is formed by adding the past participle to the present tense of haben or of sein: thus, ich habe geliebt, 'I have loved,' or 'I may have loved;' ich bin gekommen, 'I have (am) come,' ich sei gekommen, 'I may have come.'

b. The Pluperfect adds the participle to the preterit of the auxiliary: thus, ich hatte geliebt, 'I had loved,' ich hätte geliebt, 'I might have loved;' ich war gekommen, 'I had (was) come,' ich wäre gekommen, 'I might have come.'

c. But the modal auxiliaries (**251**) and a few other verbs (namely lassen, heißen, helfen, hören, sehen, lehren and lernen—the last two not uniformly), when construed with another verb in the infinitive, form their perfect and pluperfect tenses by adding the infinitive instead of the participle to the auxiliary (see **251**.4).

d. The PERFECT INFINITIVE prefixes the participle to the simple or present infinitive: thus, geliebt haben, 'to have loved;' gekommen sein, 'to have come.'

e. What verbs take haben and what take sein as their auxiliary, will be explained below (see **241**). For omission of the auxiliary, see **439**.3*a*.

2. From werden, with the infinitives, present and past, of the verb, are formed a future and a future perfect tense, indicative and subjunctive, and a conditional and conditional perfect

a. The FUTURE tense, indicative and subjunctive, is formed by prefixing to the present infinitive the present tense, indicative and subjunctive, of werden: thus, ich werde lieben or kommen, 'I shall love or come.'

b. The FUTURE PERFECT prefixes the same tenses to the perfect infinitive: thus, ich werde geliebt haben, 'I shall have loved;' ich werde gekommen sein, 'I shall have come.'

c. The CONDITIONAL and CONDITIONAL PERFECT are formed by prefixing to the present and perfect infinitive the preterit subjunctive of werden: thus, ich würde lieben or kommen, 'I should love' or 'come;' ich würde geliebt haben, 'I should have loved;' ich würde gekommen sein, 'I should have come.'

3. The uses of these tenses so nearly agree with those of the corresponding English phrases with which they are translated that they need no explanation here: for details, see **323** etc.

4. The German is the only one of the Germanic languages which, in its modern extension of the conjugational system by composition, has chosen werden as its auxiliary for forming the future tenses. Ich werde geben, literally 'I am becoming to give,' receives a future meaning through the idea of 'I am coming into a condition of giving,' or 'I am going to give.'

In the tenses formed with haben, the participle is originally one qualifying the object of the verb in the manner of a factitive predicate, or expressing the condition in which I 'have' ('possess, hold') the object. This, as being the constructive result of a previous action, is accepted as a description of that action, and ich habe die Arme ausgestreckt, for example, from meaning 'I have my arms stretched out,' comes to signify 'I have stretched out my arms.' (See the author's "Language and the Study of Language," p. 118).

On the other hand, in the tenses formed with sein, the participle is originally one qualifying the subject in the manner of a direct predicate, and defining a state or condition in which the subject exists. This, in English, has become (by a process quite analogous with that just above described) a passive, or an expression for the enduring of the action which produced that condition. But the German uses (see below, **275**) another auxiliary to form its passives, and, in its combination of sein with the participle, it only adds to the assertion of condition the less violent implication that the action leading to the condition is a past one: ich bin gekommen, 'I am here, being come;' i. e., 'my action of coming is a thing of the past;' or, 'I have come.'

In strictness, then, haben should form the past tenses only of transitive verbs, and when they take an object; and sein, only of intransitives which express a condition of their subject. But, as *have* in English has extended its use until it has become the auxiliary of all verbs without exception, so, in German, haben has come to be used with transitive verbs even when they do not take an object, and with such intransitives as are in meaning most akin with these; until the rules for the employment of the two have become as stated in the next paragraph.

241. *Use of* haben *or* sein *as Auxiliary of Tense.*

1. Verbs which take haben as auxiliary are

a. All transitive verbs (including the reflexives and the modal auxiliaries).

b. Almost all intransitives which take an object in the genitive (**219.**5) or the dative (**222.**II.1*a*).

c. A large number of other intransitives, especially such as denote a simple activity, a lasting condition, or a mode of motion (including all the proper impersonal verbs).

2. Verbs which take sein for auxiliary, as exceptions under the above classes, are

a. Especially, many intransitives which signify a change of condition, or a movement of transition, from a point of departure or toward a point of arrival.

These intransitives are partly such as do not take an object—as, werden, 'become,' kommen, 'come,' fallen, 'fall,' sinken, 'sink,' wachsen, 'grow,' sterben, 'die,' bersten, 'burst,' erstarren, 'stiffen,' erlöschen, 'become extinguished,' einschlafen, 'fall asleep,' zurücktreten, 'retreat:'—partly such as may take a dative object in virtue of the meaning given them by a prefix: as, entlaufen, 'run away from,' widerfahren, 'happen to,' entgegengehen, 'go to meet,' auffallen, 'strike the attention of.'

b. A few others, without reference to their meaning: namely, of verbs that take an objective dative, begegnen, 'meet,' folgen, 'follow,' weichen, 'give way,' gelingen and glücken, 'turn out successfully' (with their opposites, mißlingen and mißglücken): also sein, 'be,' bleiben, 'remain,' gehen, 'go.'

3. A small number of verbs may take either auxiliary.

a. Some that are used with different meanings: as, der Deckel hat aufgestanden, 'the cover has stood open;' mein Bruder ist aufgestanden, 'my brother has got up.'

b. About twenty verbs of motion, which take haben, when the act of motion or its kind are had in view (as in answer to the questions *how, how long, when, where?*), but sein when reference is had to a starting-point or an end of motion (as in answer to the questions *whence, whither, how far?*): thus, der Knabe hat gesprungen, 'the boy has jumped,' but er ist vom Baume gesprungen, 'he has jumped from the tree;' sie haben viel gereist, 'they have travelled much,' but er ist nach England gereist, 'he has gone to England.'

c. Stehen, 'stand,' liegen, 'lie,' sitzen, 'sit' (especially the first), are sometimes conjugated with sein, but properly take haben under all circumstances.

242. *Other verbal Auxiliaries.*

Besides the three heretofore spoken of, there are a number of verbs, generally or often used with other verbs, to impress upon them modifications of meaning more or less analogous with those expressed by the forms of conjugation of some languages. Such are

1. The MODAL AUXILIARIES, of which there are six, können, 'can,' mögen, 'may,' dürfen, 'be permitted,' müssen, 'must,' sollen, 'shall,' wollen, 'will.' They have, however, a much more independent value and use in German than in English, and are not to be treated as bearing any part in the ordinary verbal conjugation. Their peculiarities of inflection and construction will be explained below (**251** etc.).

2. The CAUSATIVE AUXILIARY, lassen, which (as one among many uses) is often employed in a causal sense with the infinitive of another verb: as, einen Rock machen, 'to make a coat;' einen Rock machen lassen, 'to have a coat made (cause to make it):' see **343.I.5**.

3. Thun, 'do' (**267.5**), which we employ so freely as auxiliary in English, is not used as such in German. Some of the German dialects, indeed, make an auxiliary of it; and it is now and then found having that value even in the literary language: thus, und t h u' nicht mehr in Worten kramen, 'and *do* no longer peddle out words' (R. 134.23).

243. *Other points in general conjugation, affecting the Imperative, Infinitive, and Past Participle.*

1. The third pers. singular, and the first and third pers. plural, of the present subjunctive are very commonly used in an imperative sense (see **331**), and may be regarded as filling up the defective declension of that mood. Thus, for the two verbs first given,

IMPERATIVE.

	Singular.		*Plural.*	
1			lieben wir	'let us love'
2	liebe, liebe du	'love'	liebet, liebt ihr	'love'
3	liebe er	'let him love'	lieben sie	'let them love
1			geben wir	'let us give'
2	gieb, gib du	'give'	gebt, gebet ihr	'give'
3	gebe er	'let him give'	geben sie	'let them give

Of these forms, the third plural is in especially frequent use as substitute for the second person of either number (153.4): thus, geben Sie mir das Buch, 'give me the book.'

Other imperative phrases—as, er soll geben, 'he shall give,' laß uns geben, laßt uns geben, lassen Sie uns geben, 'let us give'—are more or less employed, but need no special remark.

2. The infinitive, as in English (though not so uniformly), takes often the preposition zu, 'to,' as its sign: this is always placed next before the simple infinitive form: thus, zu geben, gegeben zu haben.

For details respecting the use of zu, see **341** etc.

3. The past participle of nearly all verbs has the prefix ge. Exceptions are

a. Verbs that begin with an unaccented syllable, especially 1. Those ending in the infinitive in iren or ieren (being verbs derived from the French or Latin, or others formed after their model): as marschiren, 'march,' part. marschirt; studiren, 'study,' part. studirt. 2. Those compounded with an inseparable, and therefore unaccented, prefix: as, vergeben, 'forgive,' part. vergeben.

b. Werden, when used as passive auxiliary, forms worden instead of geworden (see **276**.1*a*).

c. The syllable ge was not originally an element of verbal inflection, but one of the class of inseparable prefixes (see **307.5**). It was formerly used or omitted as special prefix to the participle without any traceable rule, and has only in modern times become fixed as its nearly invariable accompaniment. Hence, in archaic style and in poetry, it is still now and then irregularly dropped. The same prefix was employed, in very much the same manner, in the oldest form of English, the Anglo-Saxon; and traces of its use survived even down to a time comparatively modern, in such participles as *y-clad*, *y-clept*, *y-drad* (dreaded).

244. *Synopsis of the complete conjugation of* haben *and* sein.

The synopsis of werden will be given later, in connection with that of the passive voice of the verb (**277**).

INDICATIVE.

Present, 'I have,' etc.	'I am,' etc.
s.1 habe	bin
Preterit, 'I had,' etc.	'I was,' etc.
s.1 hatte	war
Perfect, 'I have had,' etc.	'I have been,' etc.
s.1 habe gehabt	bin gewesen
Pluperfect, 'I had had,' etc.	'I had been,' etc.
s.1 hatte gehabt	war gewesen
Future, 'I shall have,' etc.	'I shall be,' etc.
s.1 werde haben	werde sein

Future Perfect, 'I shall have had,' etc.	'I shall have been,' etc.
S.1 werde gehabt haben	werde gewesen sein

SUBJUNCTIVE.

Present, 'I may have,' etc.	'I may be,' etc.
S.1 habe	sei
Preterit, 'I might have,' etc.	'I might be,' etc.
S.1 hätte	wäre
Perfect, 'I may have had,' etc.	'I may have been,' etc.
S.1 habe gehabt	sei gewesen
Pluperfect, 'I might have had,' etc.	'I might have been,' etc.
S.1 hätte gehabt	wäre gewesen
Future, 'I shall have,' etc.	'I shall be,' etc.
S.1 werde haben	werde sein
Future Perfect, 'I shall have had,' etc.	'I shall have been,' etc.
S.1 werde gehabt haben	werde gewesen sein

CONDITIONAL.

Conditional, 'I should have,' etc.	'I should be,' etc.
S.1 würde haben	würde sein
Cond'l Perfect, 'I should have had,' etc.	'I should have been,' etc.
S.1 würde gehabt haben	würde gewesen sein

IMPERATIVE.

have,' etc.	'be,' etc.
S.2 habe	sei

INFINITIVES.

Present, 'to have'	'to be'
haben	sein
Perfect, 'to have had'	'to have been'
gehabt haben	gewesen sein

PARTICIPLES.

Present, 'having'	'being'
habend	seiend
Past, 'had'	'been'
gehabt	gewesen

Exercise XV.

Simple and Compound Forms of the Verb.

1. Wo ist er gewesen, und was hat er gehabt? 2. Meine Kinder würden zufrieden sein, wenn sie Spielzeug hätten. 3. Er wird mir alles geben, denn er liebt mich, und ist immer mein Freund gewesen. 4. Ich würde mit ihm gewesen sein, aber ich war anderswo, und man ist nicht leicht an zwei Orten zugleich. 5. Waren Sie je wo er neulich gewesen ist? 6. Wir sind schwach; aber wann werden wir stärker werden? 7. Jedermann liebt seine Freunde; liebt ihr eure Feinde.

CONJUGATIONS OF VERBS.

245. Verbs are inflected in two modes, called respectively the Old and the New conjugations.

246. 1. Verbs of the Old conjugation form their preterit by a change of the vowel of the root, without any added ending, and their past participle by the ending en: thus, geben, gab, gegeben; singen, sang, gesungen.

2. Verbs of the New conjugation form their preterit by adding te or ete to the root, and their participle by the ending et or t: thus, lieben, liebte, geliebt; reden, redete, geredet.

3. The Old and New Conjugations correspond to what are generally called in English the "Irregular" and "Regular" verbs. The former, as the name implies, is the more primitive method of inflection; its preterit was originally a reduplicated tense, like the Greek and Latin perfects (as *dedōka, tetigi*); and, in the oldest Germanic languages, many verbs have retained the reduplication (as *haihald*, 'held,' from *haldan*, 'hold;' *saislep*, 'slept,' from *slepan*, 'sleep'). By phonetic corruption and abbreviation, however, this reduplication led to an alteration of the radical vowel, and then was itself dropped, in the great majority of verbs; producing phenomena of conjugation so various that there was left no prevailing and guiding analogy by which to inflect the new derivative verbs, that were brought in as needed, to supplement the old resources of expression. Hence the need of a new method of conjugation; which was obtained by adding the preterit of the verb *do* (*did*) to the theme of conjugation. The preterit-ending te of the New conjugation is the relic of this auxiliary (as, in English, *I loved* stands for an original *I love-did*). See the author's "Language and the Study of Language," pp. 60, 80.

The Old conjugation therefore includes the primitive verbs of the language; the New, all those of later origin. Only, as the latter have become the larger class, and their mode of conjugation the prevailing one, some of the old verbs (although to by no means such an extent as in English) have been changed, in part or altogether, to conform to it. See below, 272. They are often styled, like the declensions (73, 132), "strong" and "weak."

We shall take up first the New conjugation, as being simpler in its forms, and easiest to learn.

New Conjugation.

247 The characteristics of the New conjugation are that its preterit ends in te, and its participle in t.

248. Examples: reden, 'talk;' wandern, 'wander.'

PRINCIPAL PARTS.

reden, redete, geredet	wandern, wanderte, gewandert

INDICATIVE.

Present, 'I talk,' etc.	'I wander,' etc.
S.1 rede	wandere, wandre
2 redest	wanderst
3 redet	wandert
P.1 reden	wandern
2 redet	wandert
3 reden	wandern
Preterit, 'I talked,' etc.	'I wandered,' etc.
S.1 redete	wanderte
2 redetest	wandertest
3 redete	wanderte
P.1 redeten	wanderten
2 redetet	wandertet
3 redeten	wanderten
Perfect, 'I have talked,' etc.	'I have wandered,' etc.
S.1 habe geredet	bin gewandert
2 hast geredet	bist gewandert
3 hat geredet	ist gewandert
P.1 haben geredet	sind gewandert
2 habt geredet	seid gewandert
3 haben geredet	sind gewandert
Pluperfect, 'I had talked,' etc	'I had wandered,' etc.
S.1 hatte geredet	war gewandert
2 hattest geredet	warst gewandert
3 hatte geredet	war gewandert
P.1 hatten geredet	waren gewandert
2 hattet geredet	wart gewandert
3 hatten geredet	waren gewandert
Future, 'I shall talk,' etc.	'I shall wander,' etc.
S.1 werde reden	werde wandern
2 wirst reden	wirst wandern
3 wird reden	wird wandern

P. 1	werden reden	werden wandern
2	werdet reden	werdet wandern
3	werden reden	werden wandern

Future Perfect, 'I shall have talked,' etc. — 'I shall have wandered,' etc.

S. 1	werde geredet haben	werde gewandert sein
2	wirst geredet haben	wirst gewandert sein
3	wird geredet haben	wird gewandert sein
P. 1	werden geredet haben	werden gewandert sein
2	werdet geredet haben	werdet gewandert sein
3	werden geredet haben	werden gewandert sein

Subjunctive.

Present, 'I may talk,' etc. — 'I may wander,' etc.

S. 1	rede	wandere, wandre
2	redest	wanderest, wandrest
3	rede	wandere, wandre
P. 1	reden	wanderen, wandren
2	redet	wanderet, wandret
3	reden	wanderen, wandren

Preterit, 'I might talk,' etc. — 'I might wander,' etc.

S. 1	redete	wanderte
2	redetest	wandertest
3	redete	wanderte
P. 1	redeten	wanderten
2	redetet	wandertet
3	redeten	wanderten

Perfect, 'I may have talked,' etc. — 'I may have wandered,' etc.

S. 1	habe geredet	sei gewandert
2	habest geredet	seiest gewandert
3	habe geredet	sei gewandert
P. 1	haben geredet	seien gewandert
2	habet geredet	seiet gewandert
3	haben geredet	seien gewandert

Pluperfect, 'I might have talked,' etc.		'I might have wandered,' etc.
S. 1	hätte geredet	wäre gewandert
2	hättest geredet	wärest gewandert
3	hätte geredet	wäre gewandert
P. 1	hätten geredet	wären gewandert
2	hättet geredet	wäret gewandert
3	hätten geredet	wären gewandert

Future, 'I shall talk,' etc.		'I shall wander,' etc.
S. 1	werde reden	werde wandern
2	werdest reden	werdest wandern
3	werde reden	werde wandern
P. 1	werden reden	werden wandern
2	werdet reden	werdet wandern
3	werden reden	werden wandern

Future Perfect, 'I shall have talked,' etc.		'I shall have wandered,' etc.
S. 1	werde geredet haben	werde gewandert sein
2	werdest geredet haben	werdest gewandert sein
3	werde geredet haben	werde gewandert sein
P. 1	werden geredet haben	werden gewandert sein
2	werdet geredet haben	werdet gewandert sein
3	werden geredet haben	werden gewandert sein

Conditional.

Conditional, 'I should talk,' etc.		'I should wander,' etc.
S. 1	würde reden	würde wandern
2	würdest reden	würdest wandern
3	würde reden	würde wandern
P. 1	würden reden	würden wandern
2	würdet reden	würdet wandern
3	würden reden	würden wandern

Cond. Perf., 'I should have talked,' etc.		'I should have wandered,' etc.
S. 1	würde geredet haben	würde gewandert sein
2	würdest geredet haben	würdest gewandert sein
3	würde geredet haben	würde gewandert sein

P. 1	würden geredet haben	würden gewandert sein
2	würdet geredet haben	würdet gewandert sein
3	würden geredet haben	würden gewandert sein

Imperative.

	'talk,' etc.	'wander,' etc.
S. 2	rede, rede du	wandere, wandre du
3	rede er, er rede	wandere er, er wandre
P. 1	reden wir	wandern wir
2	redet, redet ihr	wandert, wandert ihr
3	reden sie	wandern sie

Infinitive.

Present, 'to talk'	'to wander'
reden, zu reden	wandern, zu wandern
Perfect, 'to have talked'	'to have wandered'
geredet haben, geredet zu haben	gewandert sein, gewandert zu sein

Participles.

Present, 'talking'	'wandering'
redend	wandernd
Past, 'talked'	'wandered'
geredet	gewandert

Remarks. The conjugation of reden exemplifies the necessity of retention of e of the endings et, ete after a consonant with which t would be confounded in pronunciation. Wandern is one of the verbs which (**241.3***b*) take sometimes haben and sometimes sein as auxiliary. It exemplifies the loss of e of the ending en, and other peculiarities of the combination of endings with verbal roots in el and er.

Exercise XVI.

Verbs of the New Conjugation.

1. Reden wir immer redlich, und unsere Freunde werden uns lieben. 2. Er wäre jetzt nicht hier, wäre er weiter gewandert. 3. Wo warst du, als wir von dir redeten? 4. Was wird er denjenigen schicken, die er so liebt? 5. Er hatte uns nichts geschickt, denn es hätte uns geschadet. 6. Was hat er geredet, und wohin ist er gewandert? 7. Er würde nichts gekauft haben, hätten wir es nicht gewünscht. 8. Hörten Sie, was die Schüler gesagt haben? 9. Kaufen Sie nur was Sie wünschen, und dann wandern Sie fort. 10. Wir lobten die Kinder,

denn sie waren fleißig gewesen, und hatten viel gearbeitet. 11. Ich sagte ihnen, er würde nichts kaufen.

Irregularities of the New Conjugation.

249. A few verbs, all of which have roots ending in nn or nd, change the radical vowel e to a in the preterit indicative (not the subjunctive also), and in the past participle. Thus,

Infinitive.		*Preterit* indicative.	subjunctive.	*Participle.*
brennen	'burn'	brannte	brennte	gebrannt
kennen,	'know'	kannte	kennte	gekannt
nennen,	'name'	nannte	nennte	genannt
rennen,	'run'	rannte	rennte	gerannt
senden,	'send'	sandte	sendete	gesandt
wenden,	'turn'	wandte	wendete	gewandt

a. The last two, senden and wenden, may also form the pret. indicative and the participle regularly: thus, sendete, gesendet; wendete, gewendet.

b. After the altered vowel, the e is always omitted before te and t: in other cases, the general rules are followed: thus, brennete or brennte, etc.

250. 1. Two verbs, bringen, 'bring,' and denken, 'think,' are still more irregular, and agree closely in their forms with the corresponding English verbs. Thus,

Infinitive.		*Preterit* indicative.	subjunctive.	*Participle.*
bringen,	'bring'	brachte	brächte	gebracht
denken,	'think'	dachte	dächte	gedacht

2. The irregularities of haben have been given in full above (**239.4***a*): bringen, denken, and haben, with some of the modal auxiliaries, are the only verbs of the New conjugation which modify in the preterit subj. the vowel of the indicative, like the verbs of the Old conjugation (**269.**II).

251. *Modal Auxiliaries.*

1. These are (as already noticed)

dürfen, 'be allowed'	müssen, 'must'
können, 'can'	sollen, 'shall'
mögen, 'may'	wollen, 'will'

2. While the corresponding verbs in English are both defective and irregular, these have in German a complete conjugation (only lacking, except in wollen, the imperative), but with the following irregularities:

a. For the singular of the present indicative are substituted forms which properly belong to a preterit of the Old conjugation.

These are, in fact, relics of an ancient preterit used in the sense of a present—thus, kann, 'can,' is literally 'I have learned how;' mag, 'may,' is 'I have gained the power;' will, 'will,' is 'I have chosen:'—and the rest of their conjugation is of more modern origin.

b. Those which have a modified vowel in the infinitive reject the modification in the preterit indicative and the past participle

c. All the rest of their inflection is regular, according to the rules of the New conjugation (except that mögen changes its g to ch before t in the preterit and participle).

3. Thus, the simple forms are

Indicative Present.						
S. 1	darf	kann	mag	muß	ſoll	will
2	darfſt	kannſt	magſt	mußt	ſollſt	willſt
3	darf	kann	mag	muß	ſoll	will
P. 1	dürfen	können	mögen	müſſen	ſollen	wollen
2	dürft	könnt	mögt	müßt	ſollt	wollt
3	dürfen	können	mögen	müſſen	ſollen	wollen
Indicative Preterit.						
S. 1	durfte	konnte	mochte	mußte	ſollte	wollte
	etc.	etc.	etc.	etc.	etc.	etc.
Subjunctive Present.						
S. 1	dürfe	könne	möge	müſſe	ſolle	wolle
	etc.	etc.	etc.	etc.	etc.	etc.
Subjunctive Preterit.						
S. 1	dürfte	könnte	möchte	müßte	ſollte	wollte
	etc.	etc.	etc.	etc.	etc.	etc.
Imperative.						
S. 2						wolle
P. 2						wollt
Participles.						
Pres.	dürfend	könnend	mögend	müſſend	ſollend	wollend
Past.	gedurft	gekonnt	gemocht	gemußt	geſollt	gewollt
Infinitive.						
	dürfen	können	mögen	müſſen	ſollen	wollen

4. The compound tenses are formed in the same manner as those of other verbs—with one important exception, namely

a. When used in connection with another verb (infinitive), the infinitive is substituted for the participle in the perfect and pluperfect tenses.

Thus, er hat es nicht gekonnt, but er hat es nicht thun können, 'he has not been able to do it;' was habt ihr gewollt, 'what have you wished?

but ihr habt mich sprechen wollen, 'you have wanted to speak to me;' wir haben warten müssen, 'we have been compelled to wait.'

This is a simple grammatical anomaly, an original blunder of construction, though now sanctioned by universal use; it was apparently caused by the influence of the other neighboring infinitive, which "attracted" the auxiliary into a correspondence of form with itself. A similar construction is usual with a number of independent verbs, which are frequently used along with the infinitive of another verb: see **240.1c.**

5. The compound tenses are, then, as follows:

Perfect (first person the same in both moods).
s.1 habe gedurft, gekonnt, 2c.
or habe dürfen, können, 2c.

Indicative Pluperfect.
s.1 hatte gedurft, gekonnt, 2c.
or hatte dürfen, können, 2c.

Subjunctive Pluperfect.
s.1 hätte gedurft, gekonnt, 2c.
or hätte dürfen, können, 2c.

Future (first person the same in both moods).
s.1 werde dürfen, können, 2c.

Future Perfect (first person the same in both moods).
s.1 werde gedurft haben, gekonnt haben, 2c.

Conditional.
s.1 würde dürfen, können, 2c.

Conditional Perfect.
s.1 würde gedurft haben, gekonnt haben, 2c.

Infinitive Perfect.
gedurft haben, gekonnt haben, 2c.

6. *a.* The absence of a complete conjugation of the corresponding auxiliaries in English makes it necessary for us often to render the German verb by a paraphrase: substituting, for example, *be able* for *can* (können); *be compelled, have to*, for *must* (müssen); *be willing, wish, desire*, for *will* (wollen), and so on: compare below, **253–9.**

b. The same absence has led to the use of certain idiomatic and not strictly logical constructions in English, in which the auxiliary of past time, *have*, is combined with the principal verb in the participle, instead of with the modal auxiliary; while the German, more correctly, combines it with the latter. Thus, *he would not have done it* is not, in German, er wollte es nicht gethan haben, unless it signifies 'he was not willing to have done it;' if, as usual, it means 'he would not have been willing to do it,' it is er hätte es nicht thun wollen. Thus also, *he might have come* (that is, 'he would have been able to come') is er hätte kommen können, not er konnte gekommen sein. The logical sense of the sentence may be tested, and the proper German expression found, by putting the corresponding verbal phrase in place of the simple auxiliary in the English.

Uses of the Modal Auxiliaries.

252. Although the exposition of the meaning of these auxiliaries belongs rather to the dictionary than to the grammar, such is the frequency of their use, and the intimacy of their relation to the verbs with which they are combined, that it is desirable to give here some account of their chief uses.

253. Dürfen.—1. This represents two separate verbs of the older language, the one meaning 'need, require,' the other '*dare*, venture, trust one's self.' The former sense is nearly lost, appearing only occasionally with nur and kaum, and in a few other phrases: thus, er darf nur befehlen, 'he needs only to command.' The other has been in modern use modified into 'be authorized, permitted,' and, even where it approaches nearest to 'dare,' means properly rather 'feel authorized,' 'allow one's self.' Thus, Niemand darf plündern, 'no one is permitted to plunder;' darf ich bitten, 'may I ask?' einem Kaiser darf die Milde nie fehlen, 'an emperor may never lack clemency;' er durfte ihn ins Angesicht preisen, 'he was allowed to praise him to his face.'

2. The preterit subjunctive dürfte signifies, by a quite special use, probable contingency: as, das **dürfte** wahr sein, 'that is likely to be true.

254. Können.—The original meaning of können, as of our *can*, is 'to know how;' but both have alike acquired the sense of 'be able,' and signify ability or possibility in the most general way, whether natural, conceded, or logical. Thus, ich kann lesen, 'I can read;' meinetwegen kann er gehen, 'he can (may) go, for all me;' jene Tage können wieder kommen, 'those days may return (their return is possible);' er kann schon gekommen sein, 'he may possibly have already arrived.'

255. Mögen.—This verb meant originally to have power, but its use in that sense is now antiquated and quite rare: thus, wenn keiner sie ergründen mag, 'though none is able to fathom them.' At present, it has two leading significations:

1. That of power or capability as the result of concession on the part of the speaker; and that, either a real permission—as er mag ihn behalten, 'he may keep it'—or as a logical concession or allowance, as das mag wohl zu Zeiten kommen, 'that may happen at times.'

2. That of choice, liking, desire: thus, was sie dir nicht offenbaren **mag**, 'what she does not choose to reveal to thee;' das **mochte** er gar nicht hören, 'he did not like to hear that at all.' This meaning is most frequent with the preterit subjunctive: thus, es **möchte** kein Hund so länger leben, 'no dog would care to live longer thus;' auch ich **möcht'** mit dir sterben, 'I too would like to die with thee.'

Mögen has other uses (akin with the above, but of less definite character), in which it approaches very near to equivalence with the subjunctive tenses: thus, in expressing a wish, möge nie der Tag erscheinen, 'may the day never appear;' möchte die ganze Welt uns hören, 'would that the whole world might hear us;' also, in clauses expressing design or purpose—damit sie nicht ausgleiten mögen, 'that they may not slip'—or after an indefinite pronoun, as, was er auch thun mag (or thue), 'whatever he may do.'

256. Müssen.—This, like mögen, has wandered far from its primitive meaning, which was 'find room or opportunity,' and now designates a general and indefinite necessity (as können a correspondingly indefinite possibility), either physical, moral, or logical. It is rendered by our 'be compelled to,' 'be obliged to,' 'have to,' 'cannot but,' and the like. Thus, alle Menschen müssen sterben, 'all men must die;' wir müssen treu sein, 'we must be faithful;' es muß in dieser Weise geschehen sein, 'it must have taken place in this way;' wir mußten umwenden, 'we had to turn back;' heute muß die Glocke werden, 'to-day the bell has to come into existence;' man mußte glauben, 'one could not but suppose;' ich mußte über die Leute lachen, 'I could not help laughing at the people.'

As *must* in English is present only, such phrases as those above given should always be used in translating the other tenses of müssen.

257. Sollen.—Its proper sense is originally that of *duty* or *obligation*, and in the past tenses, especially the preterit, it is often still used in that sense: thus, es sollte so, und nicht anders sein, 'it ought to be thus, and not otherwise;' er hätte kommen sollen, 'he ought to have come.'

But to this meaning has now become added, in prevailing use, the distinct implication of a personal authority, other than that of the subject, as creating or enforcing the obligation: either

1. Proceeding from the speaker; in which case the auxiliary intimates a command, a promise, a threat, or the like: as, du sollst Gott lieben, 'thou shalt love God;' meine Töchter sollen dich warten, 'my daughters shall wait on thee;' man droht, dieser oder jener König solle gegen ihn ziehen, 'it is threatened that this or that king shall take the field against him.'

2. Recognized by the speaker, but not proceeding from him; in which case sollen is to be rendered by 'to be to,' 'to be intended or destined to,' or other like expressions: as, wenn man zuletzt halten soll, will man lieber hier bleiben, 'if one is finally to stop, one will rather stay here;' was soll geschehen, 'what is to happen?' man zweifelte welchen Weg man einschlagen solle, 'they doubted which road they were to take;' was mag ich hier wohl hören sollen, 'what can I be meant to hear here?' darüber sollte er bitter enttäuscht werden, 'he was destined to be bitterly undeceived upon that point.'

3. A special form of this use of sollen is its employment to report something that rests on the authority of others, is asserted by them: thus, Verbrechen, die er begangen haben soll, 'crimes which he is claimed to have committed;' viele sollen an diesem Tage umgekommen sein, 'many are said to have lost their lives on that day.'

In conditional and hypothetical clauses, sollte is sometimes used like our *should*, nearly coinciding in meaning with the proper conditional tenses: thus, sollt' er auch straucheln überall, 'even should he everywhere stumble:' so, elliptically, in interrogation: sollte das wahr sein, '[is it possible that] that should be true?'

258. Wollen.—This signifies will, intent, choice, on the part of the subject of the verb: thus, ich will dich gleichfalls begleiten, 'I will accompany thee likewise;' keiner will den Becher gewinnen, 'no one wants to win the goblet;' was er Zierliches aufführen will, 'whatever he intends to bring forward that is pretty;' ich wollte ihn mit Schätzen beladen, 'I would load him with treasures.'

a. Occasionally it indicates a claim or assertion (compare the correlative use of sollen above, **257.3**): thus, er will dich gesehen haben, 'he claims to have seen you (will have it that he has done so).'

b. Not infrequently it implies the exhibition of intent, or impending action. and is to be rendered by 'be on the point of' and the like; thus, er will gehen, 'he is on the point of going;' ein Bauer, welcher sterben wollte, 'a peasant who was about to die;' Braten will verbrennen, 'the roast is on the brink of burning.'

259. *The Modal Auxiliaries without accompanying Verb.*

All these auxiliaries are sometimes met with unaccompanied by an infinitive dependent upon them. Thus,

1. When an infinitive is directly suggested by the context, and to be supplied in idea: thus, daß jeder so toll sein dürfe als er wolle, 'that every one may be as wild as he will (be);' ich thue, was ich kann, 'I do what I can (do).'

2. Very often, an adverb of direction with the auxiliary takes the place of an omitted verb of motion: thus, wir müssen auch daran, 'we must also [set] about it;' sie können nicht von der Stelle, 'they cannot [stir] from the place;' wohin sollen die, 'whither are they to [go]?' der immer davon wollte, 'who all the time wanted [to get] away;' er darf nicht weit genug hinaus, 'he may not venture [to go] far enough out.'

3. Other ellipses, of verbs familiarly used with these, or naturally suggested by the context, are not infrequent: thus, was soll ich, 'what am I to [do]?' was soll diese Rede, 'what is this talk intended to [signify]?' die falschen Ringe werden das nicht können, 'the false rings will not be able [to accomplish] that;' nicht Vergoldung will man mehr, 'one will no longer [have] gilding.'

4. The auxiliary is thus often left with an apparent direct object, really dependent on the omitted verb. In other cases the object may represent the omitted verb—as, hätte ich mich gefreut, als ich es noch konnte, 'had I enjoyed myself when I was still able *to do so*'—or be otherwise more really dependent on the auxiliary. Wollen is most often used thus as a proper transitive: thus, nicht er will euren Untergang, 'not he wishes your ruin;' was Gott gewollt, 'what God has willed'—also, mögen in the sense of 'like:' as, ich mag ihn nicht, 'I do not like him'—and können in the sense of 'know (a language):' as, können Sie Deutsch, 'do you know German?'

260. Wissen, 'know, know how,' has a conjugation nearly akin with that of the modal auxiliaries: namely

Pres. Indic.	weiß, weißt, weiß, wissen, wißt, wissen.		
Pres. Subj.	wisse, etc.		
Pret. Indic.	wußte, etc.	*Pret. Subj.*	wüßte, etc.
Past Partic.	gewußt.		

Its present indicative singular, like that of the modal auxiliaries, is an old preterit, meaning 'I have seen:' it is historically the same word with the Greek *oida* and Sanskrit *veda*—which have likewise a similar office.

Exercise XVII.

Modal Auxiliaries.

1. Können sie heute mit uns gehen? 2. Ich kann heute gehen, aber morgen werde ich weder können noch wollen. 3. Hat ihr Bruder kommen dürfen? 4. Er hat gedurft, aber er hat nicht gewollt. 5. Wer einen Brief schreiben will, muß Papier haben. 6. Ich habe nicht schreiben können, denn ich habe arbeiten müssen. 7. Darf ich fragen, welche Sprache Sie jetzt lernen wollen? 8. Ich sollte und wollte Deutsch lernen, denn ich kann es noch nicht. 9. Er soll hier sein; man will ihn gesehen haben; aber er muß sogleich fort. 10. Er wäre gewiß hier; hätte er kommen sollen. 11. Wir mögen nicht immer thun was wir sollten. 12. Ich mag das nicht haben; er mag es behalten. 13. Wolle nur was du kannst, und du wirst alles können was du willst.

Old Conjugation.

261. The characteristics of the Old conjugation are: the change of radical vowel in the preterit, and often in the past participle also; and the ending of the past participle in *en*.

With these are combined other peculiarities of inflection, of less consequence, which will be found stated in detail below.

For the reason of the name "Old" conjugation, see above, **246**.3.

Change of Radical Vowel.

262. The changes of the radical vowel in verbs of the Old conjugation are, in general, as follows:

1. The vowel of the infinitive and that of the present tense (indicative and subjunctive) are always the same.

But the vowel of the present is sometimes altered in the second and third persons singular indicative: see below, **268**.

2. The vowel of the preterit is always different from that of the infinitive and present.

3. The vowel of the past participle is sometimes the same with that of the infinitive and present, sometimes the same with that of the preterit, and sometimes different from either.

263. According to the varieties of this change, the verbs are divided into three principal classes, each with several subdivisions.

Class I. Verbs whose infinitive, preterit, and participle have each a different vowel.

Class II. Verbs in which the vowel of the participle is the same with that of the present.

Class III. Verbs in which the vowel of the participle is the same with that of the preterit.

This is merely a classification of convenience, founded upon the facts of the modern language. The latter have undergone too great and too various alteration to allow of our adopting, with practical advantage, a more thorough classification, founded on the character of the original radical vowel, and the nature of the changes it has suffered.

264. First Class. Verbs whose infinitive, preterit, and participle have each a different vowel.

I. 1. Verbs having the vowels i — a — u in the three forms specified.
Example: ſingen — ſang — geſungen (sing, sang, sung).

To this subdivision belong 16 verbs, all of them having roots ending in ng, nk, or nd.

2. Vowels i — a — o. 6 verbs: root ending in nn or mm.
Example: ſpinnen — ſpann — geſponnen (spin, span, spun).

3. Vowels e — a — o. 22 verbs.
Example: brechen — brach — gebrochen (break, brake, broken).

One verb, gebären, has irregularly ä for e in the infinitive.

4. Vowels i or ie — a — e. 3 verbs.
Examples: ſitzen — ſaß — geſeſſen (sit, sat, sat).
liegen — lag — gelegen (lie, lay, lain).

These are properly verbs belonging to the first division of the next class, II. 1, but have their vowel irregularly varied in the infinitive.

265. Second Class. Verbs having the same vowel in the infinitive and participle.

II. 1. Vowels e — a — e. 10 verbs.
Example: ſehen — ſah — geſehen (see, saw, seen).

Three verbs properly belonging to this division have changed their vowel to i or ie in the infinitive, and thus become a fourth division of the first class (see above).

2. Vowels a — u — a. 10 verbs.
Example: ſchlagen — ſchlug — geſchlagen (slay, slew, slain).

3. Vowels a — ie or i — a. 16 verbs.
Examples: fallen — fiel — gefallen (fall, fell, fallen).
hangen — hing — gehangen (hang, hung, hung).

4. Vowels au, u, or o — ie — au, u, or o. 4 verbs.
Examples: laufen — lief — gelaufen, (leap) 'run.'
rufen — rief — gerufen, 'cry.'
ſtoßen — ſtieß — geſtoßen, 'thrust.'

266. Third Class. Verbs having the same vowel in the preterit and participle.

III. 1. Vowels ei — i — i. 22 verbs.
Example: beißen — biß — gebissen (bite, bit, bitten).
2. Vowels ei — ie — ie. 16 verbs.
Example: treiben — trieb — getrieben (drive, drove, driven).

These two divisions differ only in the length of the vowel of the preterit and participle. One verb, heißen, has the participle geheißen (below, 267).

3. Vowels ie or ü — o — o. 24 verbs (only 3 with ü).
Examples: fliegen — flog — geflogen (fly, flew, flown).
lügen — log — gelogen, 'lie' (speak falsely).
4. Vowels au — o — o. 4 verbs.
Example: saugen — sog — gesogen, 'suck.'
5. Vowels i, e, ä, ö, or a — o — o. 20 verbs.
Examples: klimmen — klomm — geklommen, 'climb.'
weben — wob — gewoben (weave, wove, woven).
wägen — wog — gewogen, 'weigh.'
schwören — schwor — geschworen (swear, swore, sworn).
schallen — scholl — geschollen, 'sound.'

All the verbs in this division are stragglers, irregularly altered from other modes of conjugation. Of those having e in the infinitive (like weben) there are eleven; of the other forms, only one, two, or three each.

6. Vowels i — u — u. 2 verbs.
Example: schinden — schund — geschunden, 'flay.'

These, also, are stragglers, from I.1.

267. *Verbs with irregular change of vowel.*

1. kommen — kam — gekommen (come, came, come): an exception under I.3, the original vowel of the infinitive being e.

2. heißen — hieß — geheißen, 'be called:' an exception under III.2, as noted above.

3. gehen — ging — gegangen, 'go:' an exception under II.3, the original infinitive being gangan.

4. stehen — stand — gestanden, 'stand:' in Old High-German, belonging to II.2 (stantan — stuont — stantan).

5. thun — that — gethan (do, did, done).

In that (Old High-German *teta*) is preserved a solitary relic of the original reduplication of the preterit tense (as also in our corresponding word *did*): its final t is that of the root; its initial th (t) that of the reduplicating syllable. See the author's "Language and the Study of Language," p. 268.

Formation and Inflection of the Simple Verbal Forms.

268. *Present Tense.*

The first person singular and all the plural persons of the present indicative, together with the whole of the present subjunctive, are, without exception, regularly formed (see 237), and need no remark. But the second and third persons singular of the indicative are subject to various irregularities.

1. Verbs having e as radical vowel in the first person change it to ie or i in the second and third—short e becoming i, and long e becoming ie (that is, long i: see 18): thus, helfe, hilfst, hilft; stehle, stiehlst, stiehlt; essen, issest, ißt; sehen, siehst, sieht. But

a. A few verbs leave the e unchanged: namely, gehen, stehen, heben, weben, pflegen, bewegen, melken, genesen—besides a few which here, as in others of their forms, follow the New conjugation.

b. Two or three verbs that have long e in the first person shorten it to i in the second and third: namely, nehmen, nimmst, nimmt; treten, trittst, tritt. Geben makes either giebst, giebt, or gibst, gibt.

2. Verbs having a as radical vowel in the first person modify it (to ä) in the second and third: thus, trage, trägst, trägt; lassen, läßest, läßt. But

a. The a remains unchanged in schaffen and schallen, and in other verbs which substitute in part the forms of the New conjugation.

3. Laufen, saufen, and stoßen also modify the vowel in the same persons: kommen does so sometimes, but not according to the best usage: löschen forms lischest, lischt.

4. Fliegen and about a dozen other verbs of its class (III.3) have a second and third person in eu—as fliege, fleugst, fleugt; lüge, leugst, leugt—which are now antiquated and only met with in archaic and poetic style. One or two that have roots ending in h, change this letter to ch after eu.

5. The tendency to reject the e of the endings est and et is stronger in these persons with altered vowel than anywhere else in conjugation. The e of est is rarely retained except after a sibilant—as in erlischest, läßest, given above. The e of et is always omitted, even when preceded by t, th, d; hence, after these letters, the t, being no longer audible, is also dropped in writing.

The verbs which thus lose the ending of the third pers. sing. pres. indicative are fechten, ficht; bersten, birst; flechten, flicht; gelten, gilt; schelten, schilt; werden, wird; halten, hält; rathen, räth; braten, brät; bieten, beut. Only laden forms lädt.

269. *Preterit Tense.*

I. 1. The preterit indicative is formed by the change of radical vowel alone, without an added termination, and therefore ends in the final letter of the root, whatever that may be. But *a*. A few roots, ending in the infinitive with a double consonant, and lengthening their vowel in the preterit, reduce the double consonant to a single one: namely, schrecken, schrak; treffen, traf; bitten, bat; backen, buk; schaffen, schuf; fallen, fiel; kommen, kam.

b. A few others (fifteen), on the contrary, shortening their vowel in the preterit, double the following consonant; and three of them, ending in d, change it to tt: namely, leiden, litt; schneiden, schnitt; sieden, sott.

All of these save three (triefen and sieden, III.3; and saufen, III.4) are of division III.1: e. g., reiten, ritt, geritten (ride, rode, ridden).

c. More isolated cases are ziehen, zog; hauen, hieb; sitzen, saß. For gehen, ging; stehen, stand; thun, that, see **267**.

2. The second person singular strongly inclines to the abbreviated form of the ending, st instead of est, and in ordinary use rejects the e except after a sibilant or in order to avoid a very harsh combination of consonants.

3. Traces of an ending e in the first and third persons are, very rarely, met with; especially sahe, for sah, 'saw:' also hielte (R. 89.10). For wurde, from werden, see **239.4***c*.

4. A few verbs have a double form in the preterit, of which one is in more common use, the other archaic or provincial.

But schwor and schwur are of nearly equal authority: of the others, those most often met with are hub, for hob (heben, III.5), and stund, for stand (stehen).

This double form (as in like cases in English: e. g., *began* or *begun*) is due to the fact that in the ancient language many verbs had different vowels in the singular and plural of the preterit indicative, both of which, in the later usage, appear in either number of a few verbs. The vowel of the subjunctive preterit agreed with that of the indicative plural, not the singular: whence the double forms of the subjunctive, noted below.

II. 1. The preterit subjunctive is regularly formed from the indicative by adding e (in the first person), and modifying the vowel, if the latter be capable of modification: thus, sang, sänge; sah, sähe; schlug, schlüge; fiel, fiele; flog, flöge; schwor or schwur, schwöre or schwüre; that, thäte. But

a. Some verbs have a double form of the subjunctive, of which one differs in vowel from the indicative: thus, all in division I.2 have a second in ö—e. g., spann, spänne or spönne—which is as common as that in ä, or more so; and others (especially in I.3) have second forms in ö or ü: e. g., galt, gälte or gölte, warb, wärbe or würbe. All that have two indicative forms have the two corresponding subjunctives: thus, stände and stünde, höbe and hübe.

The reason of this has been explained above: the subjunctive has sometimes retained the old vowel of the indicative plural, instead of becoming assimilated, with the latter, to the indicative singular.

270. *Imperative.*

1. The imperative singular regularly ends in e, the plural in et or t, adding those endings respectively to the root of the verb as shown in the infinitive: thus, singen, singe; schlagen, schlage; rufen, rufe; kommen, komme; gehen, gehe. But

2. Verbs which in the second pers. sing. of the pres. indicative change e to i or ie (268.1) take the latter also in the imperative singular (not in the plural)—at the same time rejecting the e of the ending.

Thus, helfen, hilf; stehlen, stiehl; essen, iß; sehen, sieh.

So, also, verbs that have an archaic second person in eu (268.4), have a corresponding archaic imperative: thus, fliegen, fliege or fleug. Erlöschen (268.3) forms erlisch. But verbs that modify a, au, o to ä, äu, ö (268.2,3) retain in the imperative the unchanged vowel and the ending: thus, tragen, trage; laufen, laufe; stoßen, stoße.

a. Exceptions are: werden (wirst) has werde; sehen (siehst) has either siehe or sieh.

3. The e of the singular ending is dropped much more freely in the other verbs of this than in those of the New conjugation, and in some—as komm, laß—is almost never used.

271. *Past Participle.*

1. The ending of the participle is en.

The e of the ending is ordinarily retained in all cases, but may be occasionally dropped, especially after a vowel or h: thus, gesehen or gesehn. When, however, the participle is used as an adjective and declined, it is subject to the same abbreviation as other adjectives ending in en (120.3): thus, vergangner Tage, 'of past days;' verschwundner Pracht, 'of vanished splendor.'

2. A number of participles share in the irregular changes of a final radical consonant exhibited by the preterit: namely

a. All those that shorten in the preterit the vowel of the infinitive (269.I.1*b*): thus, reiten, ritt, geritten; leiden, litt, gelitten; saufen, soff, gesoffen.

b. Of those that lengthen the vowel (269.I.1*a*), only one, namely bitten, bat, gebeten;—but treffen, traf, getroffen; fallen, fiel, gefallen, etc.

c. Also, ziehen (zog), gezogen; sitzen (saß), gesessen; gehen (ging), gegangen; stehen (stand), gestanden; thun (that), gethan.

3. Essen, 'eat,' inserts g in the participle: thus gegessen (for ge-essen).

272. *Mixed Conjugation.*

The same tendency which has converted a large number of the "irregular" verbs in English into "regular" has been active though to a much less degree, in German also. Besides those verbs which have entirely changed their mode of inflection, and therefore no longer require to be made any account of under the Old conjugation, there are others which form a part of their inflection by the one method and a part by the other, or which have equivalent forms of either conjugation. Thus,

1. Some have a double series of forms through the whole or nearly the whole conjugation: the forms of the Old conjugation being then either poetic and unusual (as in weben), or else belonging to the verb in certain special meanings (as in wiegen) or in its intransitive use (as in bleichen).

2. Some have certain forms of either conjugation—especially the second and third pers. ind. present and second sing. imperative, with differences of use as above stated; most often with intransitive meaning for the old forms: such are schrecken, verderben, sieben, löschen, schmelzen, schwellen, and others.

3. Some have retained only a participle of the Old conjugation; and even that in special uses or connections. The participle is in general the form that has maintained itself most persistently.

These irregularities, as well as those which are explained in more detail above, will be best exhibited in a TABLE OF IRREGULAR VERBS, given at the end of this volume.

273. *Examples of Verbs of the Old Conjugation.*

Binden (I.1). Kommen (267.1).

PRINCIPAL PARTS.

binden, band, gebunden. kommen, kam, gekommen.

INDICATIVE.

	Present, 'I bind,' etc.	'I come,' etc.
S.1	binde	komme
2	bindest	kommst
3	bindet	kommt
P.1	binden	kommen
2	bindet	kommt
3	binden	kommen
	Preterit, I bound,' etc.	'I came,' etc.
S.1	band	kam
2	bandst	kamst
3	band	kam
P.1	banden	kamen
2	bandet	kamt
3	banden	kamen

	Perfect, 'I have bound,' etc.	I have come,' etc.
S. 1	habe gebunden	bin gekommen
	etc.	etc.
	Pluperfect, 'I had bound,' etc.	'I had come,' etc.
S 1	hatte gebunden	war gekommen
	etc.	etc.
	Future, 'I shall bind,' etc.	'I shall come,' etc.
S. 1	werde binden	werde kommen
	etc.	etc.
	Fut. Perf., 'I shall have bound,' etc.	'I shall have come,' etc.
S. 1	werde gebunden haben	werde gekommen sein
	etc.	etc.

Subjunctive.

	Present, 'I may bind,' etc.	'I may come,' etc.
S. 1	binde	komme
2	bindest	kommest
3	binde	komme
P. 1	binden	kommen
2	bindet	kommet
3	binden	kommen
	Preterit, 'I might bind,' etc.	'I might come,' etc.
S. 1	bände	käme
2	bändest	kämest
3	bände	käme
P. 1	bänden	kämen
2	bändet	kämet
3	bänden	kämen
	Perfect, 'I may have bound,' etc.	'I may have come,' etc.
S. 1	habe gebunden	sei gekommen
	etc.	etc.
	Pluperf., 'I might have bound,' etc.	'I might have come,' etc.
S. 1	hätte gebunden	wäre gekommen
	etc.	etc.

	Future, 'I shall bind,' etc.	'I shall come,' etc.
S.1	werde binden	werde kommen
	etc.	etc.
	Fut. Perf., 'I shall have bound,' etc.	'I shall have come,' etc.
S.1	werde gebunden haben	werde gekommen sein
	etc.	etc.

CONDITIONAL.

	Conditional, 'I should bind,' etc.	'I should come,' etc.
S.1	würde binden	würde kommen
	etc.	etc.
	Cond. Perf. 'I should have bound,' etc.	'I should have come,' etc.
S.1	würde gebunden haben	würde gekommen sein
	etc.	etc.

IMPERATIVE.

	'bind,' etc.	'come,' etc.
S.2	binde	komme, komm
3	binde er	komme er
P.1	binden wir	kommen wir
2	bindet	kommt
3	binden sie	kommen sie

INFINITIVE.

Present, 'to bind'	'to come'
binden	kommen
Perfect, 'to have bound'	'to have come'
gebunden haben	gekommen sein

PARTICIPLES.

Present, 'binding'	'coming'
bindend	kommend
Past, 'bound'	'come'
gebunden	gekommen

EXERCISE XVIII.

Verbs of the Old Conjugation.

1. Was haben sie in meinem Garten gethan? 2. Einige saßen auf den Bänken, andere lagen unter den Bäumen; wir sprachen zusammen, und sangen unsere Lieder. 3. Wären wir nicht gekommen, hätten sie

uns nie gefunden. 4. Er war vom Dache gefallen, und hatte sich ein Bein gebrochen; die Kleine sah es, hob ihn auf, und trug ihn ins Haus; jetzt liegt er im Bette, und muß viel leiden. 5. Hilf mir, und ich werde dir wieder helfen. 6. Der Vogel fliegt in der Luft, die Fische schwimmen im Wasser, und die Würmer kriechen auf der Erde. 7. Wir möchten hier bleiben und fleißig schreiben.

Passive Voice.

274. The passive voice is a derivative conjugation of a transitive verb, in which that person or thing which in the simple conjugation is the object of the transitive action, becomes a subject of the suffering of that action: thus, active, der Hund biß den Knaben, 'the dog bit the boy;' passive, der Knabe wurde vom Hunde gebissen, 'the boy was bitten by the dog.'

a. That a kind of passive is also formed from some intransitive verbs is pointed out below (**279**.2,3).

b. The passive is mainly a grammatical device for directing the principal attention to the recipient of the action, and the action as affecting him, and putting the actor in a subordinate position.

275. The German passive, like the English, is formed by the aid of an auxiliary verb—but by a different one, namely the verb werden, 'become.'

276. 1. To form the passive of any verb, its past participle is combined with werden, throughout the whole conjugation of the latter. In this combination,

a. The past participle of the auxiliary, wherever it occurs, is abbreviated from geworden to worden.

b. The participle of the main verb is put after the proper verbal forms (simple tenses) of the auxiliary, but before its infinitives or participles.

This is in accordance with the general rule for the position of any word limiting an infinitive or participle: see below, **348**.2,**358**.

2. Hence, to produce any given person, tense, and mood of the passive of a verb, combine its past participle with the corresponding person, tense, and mood of werden.

277. *Synopsis of the Forms of* werden *and of a Passive Verb.*

Indicative.

Present, 'I become,' etc.	'I am loved,' etc.
s.1 werde	werde geliebt
Preterit, 'I became,' etc.	'I was loved,' etc.
s.1 ward, wurde	ward, wurde geliebt
Perfect, 'I have become,' etc.	'I have been loved,' etc.
s 1 bin geworden	bin geliebt worden
Pluperfect, I had become,' etc.	'I had been loved,' etc.
s.1 war geworden	war geliebt worden
Future, 'I shall become,' etc.	'I shall be loved,' etc.
s.1 werde werden	werde geliebt werden
Fut. Perf., 'I shall have become,' etc.	'I shall have been loved,' etc.
s.1 werde geworden ſein	werde geliebt worden ſein

Subjunctive.

Present, 'I may become,' etc.	'I may be loved,' etc.
s.1 werde	werde geliebt
Preterit, 'I might become,' etc.	'I might be loved,' etc.
s.1 würde	würde geliebt
Perfect, 'I may have become,' etc.	'I may have been loved,' etc.
s.1 ſei geworden	ſei geliebt worden
Pluperfect, 'I might have become,' etc.	'I might have been loved,' etc
s.1 wäre geworden	wäre geliebt worden
Future, 'I shall become,' etc.	'I shall be loved,' etc.
s.1 werde werden	werde geliebt werden
Fut. Perf., 'I shall have become,' etc.	'I shall have been loved,' etc.
s.1 werde geworden ſein	werde geliebt worden ſein

Conditional.

Conditional, 'I should become,' etc.	'I should be loved,' etc.
s.1 würde werden	würde geliebt werden
Cond. Perf., 'I should have become,' etc.	'I should have been loved,' etc.
s.1 würde geworden ſein	würde geliebt worden ſein

Imperative.

'become,' etc.	'be loved,' etc.
s.2 werde	werde geliebt

INFINITIVES.

Present, 'to become'	'to be loved'
werden	geliebt werden
Perfect, 'to have become'	'to have been loved'
geworden sein	geliebt worden sein

PARTICIPLES.

Present, 'becoming'	'being loved'
werdend	geliebt werdend
Past, 'become'	'been loved'
geworden	geliebt worden

Remark: geliebt worden is used only in forming the compound tenses since the past participle of a transitive verb has by itself a passive value.

278. The passive voice of a transitive verb has one peculiar form, a kind of *future passive participle*, formed from the present active participle, by putting zu before it: thus, zu liebend. It implies a possibility or a necessity: thus, ein zu liebendes Kind, 'a child to be loved;' i. e., 'which may or should be loved.' It can only be used as an attributive adjective, and therefore hardly deserves to be called a participle; it is, rather, a participial adjective.

It is in reality a quite modern and anomalous derivative from the infinitive, answering attributively to the infinitive with zu taken predicatively (343.III.1*b*): as, das Kind ist zu lieben, 'the child is to be loved;' i. e., 'may or should be loved.'

279. 1. Transitive verbs, with hardly an exception, may form a passive voice, with a complete scheme of conjugation, as given above.

Haben, 'have,' is not used in the passive.

2. Many intransitives (especially such as denote a mode of action by a person) may form an impersonal passive—that is, a passive third person singular, with indefinite subject es, or with omitted subject.

Thus, es wurde gelacht und gesungen, 'there was laughing and singing; um Antwort wird gebeten, 'an answer is requested.'

a. These passives do not represent any subject as suffering an action, but simply represent the action, without reference to an actor.

3. Those intransitives which, by a pregnant construction (**227.2*b***), govern an accusative along with a factitive predicate, are also convertible into passives in corresponding phrases: thus, sie werden aus dem Schlafe geschrieen, 'they are screamed out of sleep; er wurde frei gesprochen, 'he was acquitted (declared free).'

280. 1. Verbs which govern two accusatives (**227.**3), except lehren, take in the passive the second accusative, either as object (fragen, etc.), or as predicate nominative (nennen, etc.).

2. Transitive verbs which, in addition to their direct object, govern a genitive (**219.**2) or a dative (**222.**I.1), retain the latter along with the passive thus, der Diener wurde des Diebstahls angeklagt, 'the servant was accused of robbery;' alles wird einem Freunde erlaubt, 'everything is permitted to a friend.'

3. Of the intransitives that form an impersonal passive, such as govern a genitive or dative take the same case in the passive: thus, es wird meiner geschont, 'I am spared;' ihm wurde geholfen, 'he was helped.'

281. The passive is very much less frequently used in German than in English, being replaced by other modes of speech. Sometimes a full active expression, with subject and object, is employed instead. Most often, the intent of the passive form of speech is attained by using an active verb with the indefinite subject man, 'one,' etc. (**185**): thus, man sagt, 'it is said;' ein Gesetz, welches man erließ, 'a law which was passed.' Not infrequently, a reflexive phrase is substituted, the return of the action upon the subject being accepted as signifying the latter's endurance of the action: thus, es fragt sich, 'it is questioned (asks itself);' der Schlüssel hat sich gefunden, 'the key has been found.'

282. 1. By its use of werden, 'become,' instead of sein, 'be,' as auxiliary forming the passive, the German is able clearly to distinguish between the actual endurance of an action, and existence in a state which is the result of such action. Thus, alle Fenster werden nach und nach mit Teppichen behängt, 'all windows are by degrees hung with tapestry;' and wie alle Fenster mit Teppichen behängt sind, 'as all the windows are hung with tapestry' (R. 158); eingeladen wurden sie, 'they were invited,' and eingeladen sind sie all', 'they are all invited' (R. 50)—the latter phrases, in either pair, signifying the condition to which the act described by the former led. As we use the same verb, *to be*, in both senses, of copula and of passive auxiliary (accepting the simple statement of the resulting condition as sufficiently implying the suffering of the action), our expression is liable to ambiguity—an ambiguity which we are sometimes forced into removing by the use of the clumsy and objectionable phrase '*to be being:*' thus distinguishing *it is being cleaned* (es wird gereinigt) from *it is cleaned* (es ist gereinigt). And our sense of the distinction is so obscured that the English pupil finds it one of his greatest difficulties to know when to translate *to be* before a participle by sein, and when by werden. Only assiduous practice in noting the distinction as made in German will remove this difficulty. A practical rule which will answer in a great number of cases is this: if, on turning the expression into an active form, the same tense (pres. or pret.) is required, it was passive and requires werden; if the tense has to be changed to a perfect (perf. or plup.), sein is the proper word. Thus *they were invited* is sie wurden eingeladen when it means 'I invited them,' but sie waren eingeladen when it means 'I *had* invited them;' and sind is used in eingeladen sind sie all', because it means, 'I *have* invited them.'

2. The German itself sometimes loosely accepts the statement of condition, with the pres. or pret. of sein, in lieu of the full passive expression in perf or pluperfect. Thus, der Fisch war gefangen, 'the fish had been caught

(for war gefangen worden); sie ist ermordet auf der Londner Straße, 'she has been murdered, in London street.'

REFLEXIVE VERBS.

283. A reflexive verb is one that represents the action as exerted by the subject upon itself.

1. Such verbs are grammatically transitive, since they take an object in the accusative: they all, then, take haben as their auxiliary.

2. Logically, they are rather to be regarded as intransitive, since they do not signify an action exerted by the subject upon any object outside of itself: thus ich fürchte mich (literally, 'I frighten myself'), 'I am afraid,' is in idea as much intransitive as ich zittere, 'I tremble.' And, as noticed above (**281**), a reflexive verb is often used even in a passive sense, the idea of the endurance of the action on the part of the subject being more conspicuous to the mind than that of its exertion of the action.

284. Such a verb, therefore, takes as its object a reflexive pronoun, of the same person and number with its subject.

1. The reflexive pronouns of the first and second persons are the same as the personal; that of the third person is sich, in both numbers (**155**).

2. The reflexive pronoun is placed where any other pronoun would be placed as object of the verb: namely, after the verb in the simple tenses, but before the infinitives and participles.

285. *Conjugation of a Reflexive Verb.*

Sich freuen, 'to rejoice' ('rejoice one's self').

PRINCIPAL PARTS.

Sich freuen, freute sich, gefreut.

	INDICATIVE.	SUBJUNCTIVE.
	Present.	
S. 1	ich freue mich	ich freue mich
2	du freuest dich	du freuest dich
3	er freut sich	er freue sich
P. 1	wir freuen uns	wir freuen uns
2	ihr freut euch	ihr freuet euch
3	sie freuen sich	sie freuen sich
	Preterit.	
S. 1	ich freute mich	ich freuete mich
	etc.	etc.

Perfect.

S. 1	ich habe mich gefreut	ich habe mich gefreut
2	du haſt dich gefreut	du habeſt dich gefreut
3	er hat ſich gefreut	er habe ſich gefreut
P. 1	wir haben uns gefreut	wir haben uns gefreut
2	ihr habt euch gefreut	ihr habet euch gefreut
3	ſie haben ſich gefreut	ſie haben ſich gefreut

Pluperfect.

S. 1	ich hatte mich gefreut	ich hätte mich gefreut
	etc.	etc.

Future.

S. 1	ich werde mich freuen	ich werde mich freuen
2	du wirſt dich freuen	du werdeſt dich freuen
3	er wird ſich freuen	er werde ſich freuen
P. 1	wir werden uns freuen	wir werden uns freuen
2	ihr werdet euch freuen	ihr werdet euch freuen
3	ſie werden ſich freuen	ſie werden ſich freuen

Future Perfect.

S. 1	ich werde mich gefreut haben	ich werde mich gefreut haben
	etc.	etc.

CONDITIONAL.

	Conditional.	*Conditional Perfect.*
S. 1	ich würde mich freuen	ich würde mich gefreut haben
	etc.	etc.

IMPERATIVE.

	Singular.	*Plural.*
1		freuen wir uns
2	freue dich, freue du dich	freut euch, freut ihr euch
3	freue er ſich	freuen ſie ſich

INFINITIVE.

Present.	*Perfect.*
ſich freuen	ſich gefreut haben

PARTICIPLES.

Present.	*Past.*
ſich freuend	ſich gefreut

Remarks. 1. The reflexive pronoun is not given with the participle in the principal parts, since, that participle being in transitive verbs of a passive character, it can take no object except as used with an auxiliary in forming the compound tenses.

2. The ſich given with the infinitives and participles is, of course, only representative of the whole body of reflexive pronouns, with all of which those forms, not being restricted to any one person or number, may be construed.

286. Any transitive verb in the language may be used reflexively, or take a reflexive pronoun as object; but none are properly regarded as reflexive verbs except

1. Those which are only used with a reflexive object: as, ſich ſchämen, 'be ashamed;' ſich ſehnen, 'long;' ſich widerſetzen, 'resist.'

2. Those which are usually or often used reflexively, and have a special meaning in that use, the object not maintaining its independence, but combining with the verb to form a single conception, the equivalent of an intransitive verb: as, ſich hüten, 'beware' (hüten, 'guard'); ſich ſtellen, 'make believe, pretend' (ſtellen, 'place'); ſich verlaſſen, 'rely' (verlaſſen, 'quit').

287. 1. A reflexive verb is thus often related to the simple verb as a corresponding intransitive to a transitive—thus, freuen, 'give pleasure to,' ſich freuen, 'feel pleasure;' fürchten, 'fear,' ſich fürchten, 'be afraid.' But

2. A few are intransitive, and of nearly the same meaning, both as simple verbs and as reflexives: thus, irren and ſich irren, 'be mistaken;' nahen and ſich nahen, 'draw nigh;' zanken and ſich zanken, 'quarrel.'

288. 1. An intransitive verb is much more often used transitively (**227.2*b***) with a reflexive object than with one of another character: thus, er arbeitet und läuft ſich todt, 'he works and runs himself to death;' du ſollſt dich einmal ſatt eſſen, 'thou shalt eat thyself to repletion for once.'

2. An intransitive reflexive is sometimes used impersonally instead of an intransitive passive (**279.2**), especially with adverbs of manner, to express the action itself, without reference to a subject: thus, es tanzt ſich hier gut, 'it is good dancing here;' lebhaft träumt ſich's unter dieſem Baum, 'it is lively dreaming under this tree;' es ſieht ſich gar artig in die Kutſchen hinein, 'it is very pretty looking into the carriages.'

289. 1. A considerable number of reflexive verbs take an additional remoter object (impersonal) in the genitive (**219.3**).

a. The construction of a reflexive verb with the genitive is notably easier than of the same verb used otherwise than reflexively—thus, ich erinnere mich meines Vergehens, 'I remember (remind myself of) my fault,' but ich erinnere ihn an ſein Vergehen, 'I remind him of his fault'—yet many of these also frequently make their construction by the aid of a preposition, and many others admit only a prepositional construction: thus, ich verlaſſe mich auf ihn, 'I rely on him.'

2. Only two or three reflexives take a remoter object in the dative: such are ſich nahen, 'approach,' ſich widerſetzen, 'oppose,' ſich bequemen, 'submit.

290. A small number of verbs are used with a reflexive object in the dative, in a manner quite analogous with the true reflexive verbs, and therefore form a class of improper reflexives.

a. Most of these require in addition a direct object in the accusative: thus, ich maße mir kein Unrecht an, 'I make no unjust claim;' ich bilde mir das nicht ein, 'I do not imagine that;' du getrauest dir viel, 'thou darest much. But sich schmeicheln, 'flatter one's self,' is intransitive.

IMPERSONAL VERBS.

291. 1. An impersonal verb, or a verb used impersonally, is one by means of which the action implied in the verb is represented as exerted, without reference to a subject or actor.

2. Such a verb stands always in the third person singular, and either without a subject, or, more usually, with the indefinite subject es, 'it.'

Thus, es regnet, 'it rains,' i. e. 'there is rain falling;' es klopft, 'it knocks,' i.e. 'there is a knocking;' am Ganges duftet's und leuchtet's, 'on the Ganges are sweet odors and shining sights;' mich dünkt, 'me seems,' i.e. 'it seems to me;' ihn hungerte, 'him hungered,' i.e. 'he was hungry.'

292. No verbs in German are absolutely and exclusively impersonal: verbs impersonally used may be classified as follows:

1. Verbs describing the phenomena of nature, which are almost invariably impersonal in virtue of their meaning: thus, es hagelt, 'it hails;' es hat geschneit, 'it has snowed;' es wird donnern und blitzen, 'it will thunder and lighten.'

2. Certain verbs which by the idiom of the language are ordinarily used in an impersonal form: as dünken and däuchten, 'seem;' gelüsten, 'desire;' gelingen, 'prove successful;' and a number of verbs signifying personal conditions and feelings, as hungern, 'hunger,' dürsten, 'thirst,' frieren, 'freeze,' schwindeln, 'be giddy,' grauen, 'be horror-struck,' etc.

a. All this class of impersonals take an object designating the person affected by their action, or the subject of the feeling or condition they describe: some take an accusative, others a dative, others either an accusative or dative (**222.**II.1*e*; **227.**2*c*): thus, mich gelüstete nicht nach dem theuren Lohn, 'I should not long for the costly prize;' dürstet deinen Feind, so tränke ihn, 'if thine enemy is thirsty, give him to drink;' mir grauet vor der Götter Neide, 'I dread the envy of the gods;' es dünkt mir or mich, 'it seems to me.

3. Almost any verb, transitive or intransitive, is liable to occur in impersonal use—if transitive, along with its ordinary object.

Thus, wie steht's mit den Göttern, 'how fares it with the gods?' ergeht's euch wohl, 'if it goes well with you;' es fehlte an Holz, 'there was lack of wood;' plötzlich regt es sich im Rohre, 'suddenly there is a rustling in the reeds;' es treibt ihn den Preis zu erwerben, 'he is impelled to gain the prize;' es erfordert eine Drehung, 'it requires a turning;' es bedarf der Annahme nicht, 'it needs not the assumption.'

a. The very common use of es giebt, 'it gives' (i. e. 'there are given or furnished'), in the sense of 'there is or are,' with following accusative, requires special notice: thus, da gab es Schaukelstühle, 'there were rocking-chairs there;' es giebt viele, die älter sind, 'there are many who are older;' daß es weniger Christen gäbe als Saracenen, 'that there were fewer Christians than Saracens.'

4. Impersonal phrases formed with the verbs sein and werden along with adverbial or adjective adjuncts, describing personal conditions or states of feeling, and always accompanied by a dative designating the person to whom such conditions belong, are very frequent.

Thus, mir ist ganz anders zu Muth, 'I feel quite otherwise (it is to me quite otherwise in mind);' ihm war so bange, 'he was so apprehensive;' wie mir wohl ist, 'how well I feel!' wie ist mir denn, 'how is it with me then?'—nun wird mir immer bänger, 'now I grow more and more anxious;' wie weh wird mir, 'how I am beginning to suffer!' je kälter es ist, desto heißer wird mir, 'the colder it is, the hotter I become;' ihm ist's, als ob's ihn hinüberrief', 'he feels as if he were invited across.'

5. Impersonal expressions are often made from intransitive verbs in a passive or reflexive form (see **279.2, 288.2**).

Thus, heute Abend wird getanzt werden, 'there will be dancing this evening;' es sitzt sich schlecht hier, 'it is disagreeable sitting here.'

293. The impersonal subject es is (as is abundantly shown by the examples already given) very often omitted—not, however, with the impersonals describing the phenomena of nature; nor, generally, with verbs which are not of common use in impersonal form: but, as a rule, with verbs which are of common impersonal use, whenever the es would, by the rules for the arrangement of the sentence, come elsewhere than in its natural place next before the verb.

That is, especially in the cases mentioned in sections 2, 4, and 5 of the last paragraph, whenever the object of the impersonal verb, or an adjunct qualifying the verb, is placed before it—and the putting of the object first, with consequent omission of es, is the more usual construction.

294. Since the impersonal verb represents the simple action without reference to an acting subject, such impersonals as take an object, direct or indirect, representing the person or thing affected by the action or condition, are virtually equivalent to passives or intransitives, having that person or thing as their subject—and they often may or must be so rendered in English.

Many of the examples given above have been so rendered, and those with sein or werden hardly admit of being treated otherwise: thus, further, es erfordert eine Drehung, 'a turning is required;' es bedarf der Annahme nicht, 'the assumption is not needed.'

295. A verb having the indefinite subject es, 'it,' is not always to be regarded as impersonal: the es sometimes represents indefinitely a subject which is contemplated by the mind, and admits of being definitely stated: yet more often, es is a grammatical subject only, standing for a logical subject which is to be stated later, whether a substantive clause, an infinitive clause, or a simple substantive: thus, es freut uns, daß Sie hier sind, 'it rejoices us that you are here;' es freut uns, Sie zu sehen, 'it rejoices us to see you;' es freut uns diese Nachricht, 'this news rejoices us'

Exercise XIX.

Passive, Reflexive, and Impersonal Verbs.

1. Der fleißige Schüler wird gelobt, aber man tadelt den trägen. 2. Der Brief wird bald geschrieben werden; und sobald er geschrieben ist, wird er von uns zur Post getragen werden. 3. Das Buch wird jetzt gedruckt, und wird bald vollendet sein. 4. Dieser Hut ist verkauft, und kann nicht gekauft werden. 5. Wir freuten uns, als er so gelobt wurde; man lobte ihn weil seine Aufgaben gut geschrieben waren. 6. Ich schäme mich, so oft davon gesprochen wird. 7. Du solltest dich schämen als die That gethan wurde; und jetzt wieder, weil sie gethan ist; nicht nur, wenn sie von andern besprochen wird. 8. Wer ist dieser Mann; ich erinnere mich seiner nicht.

COMPOUND VERBS.

296. Verbs, in German, admit of composition with various other parts of speech—with nouns, adjectives, and adverbs. The importance and frequent use of certain classes of these compounds render it necessary that they be treated here, rather than later, under the general subject of the composition of words.

297. Verbs are compounded especially with a class of elements called PREFIXES. These are all of kindred derivation, being originally adverbs, words signifying place or direction; but they have become divided in modern use into two well-marked classes:

1. Prefixes which are also employed as independent parts of speech, adverbs or prepositions. These form a less intimate union with the verb, being separable from it in many of its forms; they are therefore called SEPARABLE PREFIXES, and a verb in combination with them is said to be SEPARABLY COMPOUNDED.

2. Prefixes which, in their present form, occur only in combination with verbs, and never admit of separation from verbal forms (or verbal derivatives): they are called INSEPARABLE PREFIXES, and the verb with them is said to be INSEPARABLY COMPOUNDED. But

3. A few independent prefixes sometimes form with verbs combinations after the manner of the inseparable prefixes, and therefore require to be treated as a class by themselves.

VERBS SEPARABLY COMPOUNDED.

298. The class of separable prefixes is divided into two sub classes, *simple* and *compound.*

1. The simple separable prefixes (including those sometimes also used as inseparable—see **308** etc.) are:

ab, 'off, down'	fort, 'forth, away'	ob, 'over, on'
an, 'on, at'	gegen, 'against'	über, 'over'
auf, 'up, upon'	in, 'in'	um, 'around'
aus, 'out, from'	heim, 'home'	unter, 'under'
bei, 'by, beside, with'	her, 'toward one'	vor, 'before'
da or dar, 'there, at'	hin, 'from one'	wider or wieder, 'against' or 'again'
durch, 'through'	hinter, 'behind'	weg, 'away'
ein, 'in, into'	mit, 'with'	zu, 'to'
empor, 'up, aloft'	nach, 'after'	zurück, 'back'
entzwei, 'in two, apart'	nieder, 'down'	zusammen, 'together'

2. The compound separable prefixes are

a. Combinations of many of the above with one another, especially with the words of more general direction or place her, hin, da or dar, vor: as heran, hinan, daran, voran.

b. One or two combinations of the above with preceding inseparable prefixes: namely, bevor, 'before,' entgegen, 'against' (this, however, is really derived from in=gegen).

c. Dazwischen, 'between' (zwischen by itself is not used as a prefix), and hintan, 'behind' (contracted from hinten an).

Note that, of those given in the list above, several are really compound adverbs (empor, entzwei, zurück, zusammen), although not made up of two different prefixes.

299. *Conjugation of Verbs compounded with Separable Prefixes.*

The conjugation of a compound verb is in general the same with that of the simple verb: only one or two matters regarding the treatment of the prefix require notice:

1. The prefix stands before the verb in the infinitive and both participles, but after it in all the other simple forms.

a. In the former case, the prefix is written with the verb as a single word; in the latter case it is, of course, separated from it; and, if the verb be followed by other adjuncts—as objects, adverbs, etc.—the prefix usually and regularly stands last, at the end of the whole clause: thus, from anfangen, 'begin,' ich fange an, 'I begin;' ich fing diesen Morgen früh zu studiren an, 'I began early this morning to study.'

b. But if, by the rules for the arrangement of the sentence (**434**), the verb is transposed, or removed to the end, it comes, even in the simple forms, to stand after its prefix, and is then written as one word with it: thus, als ich diesen Morgen früh zu studiren anfing, 'as I began to study early this morning.'

2. The ordinary sign of the past participle, ge, is inserted between the separable prefix and the root; also the sign of the infinitive, zu, whenever used.

Thus, angefangen, 'begun;' anzufangen, 'to begin:' in the latter case, as the example shows, the verb is written along with its infinitive sign and prefix, as one word.

3. The prefix has the principal accent.

300. Examples: anfangen, 'begin' (II.3); herannahen, 'draw nigh.'

PRINCIPAL PARTS.

anfangen, fing an, angefangen **herannahen, nahte heran, herangenaht**

Indicative.

	Present, 'I begin,' etc.	'I draw nigh,' etc.
s.1	fange an	nahe heran
2	fängst an	nahst heran
3	fängt an	naht heran
p.1	fangen an	nahen heran
2	fangt an	naht heran
3	fangen an	nahen heran
	Preterit, 'I began,' etc.	'I drew nigh,' etc.
s.1	fing an	nahte heran
	Perfect, 'I have begun,' etc.	'I have drawn nigh,' etc.
s.1	habe angefangen	bin herangenaht
	Pluperfect, 'I had begun,' etc.	'I had drawn nigh,' etc.
s.1	hatte angefangen	war herangenaht
	Future, 'I shall begin,' etc.	'I shall draw nigh,' etc.
s.1	werde anfangen	werde herannahen
	Fut. Perf., 'I shall have begun,' etc.	'I shall have drawn nigh, etc
s.1	werde angefangen haben	werde herangenaht sein

Subjunctive.

	Present, 'I may begin,' etc.	'I may draw nigh,' etc.
s.1	fange an	nahe heran
	etc., etc.	etc., etc.

Conditional.

	Conditional, 'I should begin,' etc.	'I should draw nigh,' etc.
s.1	würde anfangen	würde herannahen
	etc., etc.	etc., etc.

Imperative.

	'begin,' etc.	'draw nigh,' etc.
s 2	fange an, fange du an	nahe heran, nahe du heran
3	fange er an	nahe er heran
	etc.	etc.

Infinitives.

Present, 'to begin'	'to draw nigh'
anfangen, anzufangen	herannahen, heranzunahen
Perfect, 'to have begun'	'to have drawn nigh'
angefangen haben	herangenaht sein

PARTICIPLES.

Present, 'beginning'	'drawing nigh'
anfangend	herannahend
Past, 'begun'	'drawn nigh'
angefangen	herangenaht

301. 1. The meaning of the simple verb is often greatly altered by its composition with a prefix, as in anfangen, 'begin,' literally 'take hold on:' in other cases, each member of the compound retains its independent meaning nearly unchanged.

2. When the combination is of the latter character, no absolute line is to be established dividing the employment of the prefix as prefix from its use as independent adverb: and there are many instances in which the prefix (especially a compound one) is treated in both ways indifferently, and either written with the verb or separated from it; thus, wo man mager hinein geht und fett heraus kommt (or, hineingeht, herauskommt), 'where one goes in lean and comes out fat.'

VERBS INSEPARABLY COMPOUNDED.

302. The inseparable prefixes are be, ent (or emp), er; ge, ver, and zer.

These prefixes are, most of them, traceably descended from those of the other class: their original form and present office will be explained below (**307**).

303. They remain in close combination with the verb to which they are attached, through its whole conjugation, forming with it, as their name denotes, an inseparable combination, of which the radical syllable, and not the prefix, receives the accent. Hence,

1. The sign of the infinitive, zu, is put before the combination (and separated in writing from it), as if it were a simple verb.

2. The sign of the participle, ge, is omitted altogether.

Since, as was pointed out above (**243.3***a*), this is never prefixed to an unaccented syllable. Moreover, the ge is itself an inseparable prefix, and no verbal form is ever allowed to have two inseparable prefixes.

304. Examples: beginnen, 'begin' (I.2), verreisen, 'journey away'

PRINCIPAL PARTS.

beginnen, begann, begonnen	verreisen, verreiste, verreist.

INDICATIVE.

beginne	verreise
begann	verreiste
habe begonnen	bin verreist
hatte begonnen	war verreist
werde beginnen	werde verreisen
werde begonnen haben	werde verreist sein

SUBJUNCTIVE.

beginne	verreise
begänne or begönne	verreisete
etc., etc.	etc., etc.

CONDITIONAL.

würde beginnen	würde verreisen
etc., etc.	etc., etc.

IMPERATIVE.

beginne	verreise

INFINITIVES.

beginnen, zu beginnen	verreisen, zu verreisen
begonnen haben	verreist sein

PARTICIPLES.

beginnend	verreisend
begonnen	verreist

305. A few inseparably compounded verbs are further compounded with a separable prefix. Such combine the peculiarities of both modes of conjugation, taking no ge in the participle, and interposing zu of the infinitive between the two prefixes: thus, anerkennen, 'recognize,' anzuerkennen, erkannte an, anerkannt.

a. Some of these, however—as anbetreffen, auferstehen, auserlesen, einverleiben, vorenthalten—are never used except in such verbal forms, or in such arrangements of the sentence, as require the separable prefix to stand before the verb: thus, als Christus auferstand, 'when Christ arose;' but not Christus erstand auf, 'Christ arose.'

306. No verb separably compounded is ever further compounded with an inseparable prefix.

The words sometimes given as examples of such composition are really derivatives from nouns: thus, verabscheuen, 'regard with horror,' is not

Prefixes Separable or Inseparable.

308. A few prefixes, belonging properly to the separable class (being all of them in use also as independent parts of speech), nevertheless sometimes form compounds after the manner of inseparables.

309. These prefixes are

durch, 'through'	über, 'over'	unter, 'under'
hinter, 'behind'	um, 'about'	wider 'against'
		wieder 'again'

Wider and wieder are the same word, but differently spelt, to indicate a difference of meaning. All verbs compounded with wider are inseparable; all but one or two compounded with wieder are separable.

310. In verbs separably compounded with these prefixes, both members of the compound have their own full meaning, hardly modified by the combination; the inseparable compounds often take an altered or figurative sense.

Thus, as separable compounds, durchdringen, 'crowd through,' hintergehen, 'go behind,' übersetzen, 'set across,' umgehen, 'go around, revolve,' unterwerfen, 'throw under,' wiederholen, 'fetch back;'—but, as inseparable compounds, durchdringen, 'penetrate, permeate,' hintergehen, 'deceive,' übersetzen, 'translate,' umgehen, 'evade,' unterwerfen, 'subjugate,' wiederholen, 'repeat.' Yet the difference is not often so marked as in these examples, and in a host of cases the two classes of compounds are distinguished by only a slight shade of meaning, if at all.

311. The compounds, of either class, are accented and conjugated according to the rules already given. That is to say,

1. The separable compounds are accented on the prefix; they put the prefix before the verbal form in the infinitive and participles, but after it in other cases; they take the signs of participle and infinitive between the prefix and the root.

Thus, from durch'dringen, 'crowd through,' come durch'zudringen, dringe durch, drang durch, bin durch'gedrungen, werde durch'dringen, durch'gedrungen.

2. The inseparable compounds are accented on the radical syllable, reject the ge of the participle, and put zu of the infinitive before the whole combination.

Thus, from durchdrin'gen, 'penetrate,' come zu durchdrin'gen, durchdrin'ge, durchdrang', habe durchdrun'gen, werde durchdrin'gen, durchdrun'gen.

Other Compound Verbs.

312. Verbs compounded with other adverbs than those already mentioned, or with nouns or adjectives, fall into two classes:

1. True or close compounds, in which the first member has become an integral part of the combination, and the whole is treated as a simple verb.

Thus, handhaben, 'handle, manage,' zu handhaben, handhabte, gehandhabt; wahrsagen, 'prophesy,' zu wahrsagen, wahrsagte, gewahrsagt; liebkosen, 'caress,' zu liebkosen, liebkoste, geliebkost.

2. Loose or false compounds, phrases, written together as one word, in which the first member is treated as any such word limiting the verb would be, and the combination is conjugated like a verb separably compounded.

Thus, stattfinden, 'take place,' stattzufinden, fand statt, stattgefunden; wohlthun, 'benefit,' wohlzuthun, that wohl, wohlgethan; fehlschlagen, 'miscarry,' fehlzuschlagen, schlug fehl, fehlgeschlagen; lossprechen, 'absolve,' loszusprechen, sprach los, losgesprochen.

a. If a verb of the former class has not the accent on its first syllable, it loses (**243.**3*a*) the ge of the past participle: thus, frohlock'en, frohlockt'.

b. From the same class are to be carefully distinguished certain verbs which have the aspect of compounds, but are in fact derivatives from compound nouns: such are frühstücken, 'to breakfast' (from Frühstück, 'breakfast'), rathschlagen, 'consult' (from Rathschlag, 'consultation').

313. Miß and voll are treated as proper prefixes, forming both separable and inseparable compounds, which are accented and conjugated like those made with durch, etc. (**308–11**).

But miß is very rarely treated as a separable. Voll forms five or six inseparable compounds, as vollbringen, 'accomplish,' vollziehen, 'execute,' and a number of loose separables, as vollgießen, 'pour full.'

Exercise XX.

Compound Verbs, Separable and Inseparable.

1. Wann fangen Sie an, Ihre Briefe abzuschreiben? 2. Ich begann gestern, und schrieb einige ab, sobald ich sie empfangen hatte. 3 Er versteht alles was man ihm vorliest, und spricht die deutschen Wörter deutlich aus; aber er übersetzt nicht gut. 4. Der Tag naht heran, und die Sonne wird bald aufgehen; stehen wir auch auf, und kleiden wir uns an. 5. Sie haben vergessen was Sie mir versprochen hatten. 6. Sie hat ihre Ueberschuhe angezogen, und ist ausgegangen; sie wird bald abgereist sein. 7. Wiederhole deine Bitte, und ich hole dir wieder was du verlangst. 8. Wir kaufen ihm gleich ab, was er uns verkaufen will. 9. Er war schon zurückgekommen, ehe ich fortging. 10. Der Knabe hat den Ball in die Stube hineingeworfen, und den Spiegel zerbrochen.

ADJUNCTS OF THE VERB.

314. A verb, in a proper verbal form (that is to say, excluding the infinitives and participles: see **339**, **349**), always stands as the simple predicate of a sentence; and all that constitutes the complete predicate is brought in in the way of modifying adjuncts to the verb, variously limiting and qualifying its action.

a. The proper verbal forms, those possessing the characteristic of *person*, are often called its "finite" forms: they might also be called its *personal* forms.

b Even in the compound tenses of the verb itself, the rank of *verb* belongs in strictness only to the personal auxiliary, the other parts being adjuncts of the latter: thus, in ich habe ihn gekränkt, 'I have pained him,' habe is the simple predicate, and gekränkt is an attribute of the object, as much as finde and krank, respectively, in ich finde ihn krank, 'I find him sick;' ich werde gekränkt, 'I am pained,' ich bin gegangen, 'I am (have) gone,' are analogous, in like manner, with ich werde krank, 'I become sick,' ich bin weg, 'I am away;' and ich werde gekränkt worden sein, 'I shall have been pained,' is made up by the addition of successive modifying adjuncts to werde, each adjunct after the first being (see **348**.2) regularly prefixed to the one which it further limits; the phrase means literally 'I am entering (werde) into a state of having (sein) become (worden) pained (gekränkt).' That the auxiliaries have more or less completely the inferior value of copulas, connecting the subject with the chiefly significant part of the predicate, does not alter their formal or grammatical character.

c. No personal form of a verb has the value of adjunct to another personal form; there are as many separate sentences as there are separate verbs. All the other parts of speech (excepting the conjunctions: see **382**.*a*) may enter, by connection with the verb as its adjuncts, into the relation of parts of the predicate of a sentence.

315. *Object of a Verb.* Most verbs may take an *object*—that is to say, may be followed by a noun (or its equivalent) in an oblique case, designating the person or thing upon which, or as affecting which, the action which it describes is exerted by the subject.

1. A "transitive" verb takes its object in the accusative case; and such is called a *direct object:* thus, er hat e i n e n H u t, und trägt i h n, 'he has a hat, and wears it:' see **227**.

a. A few transitive verbs are followed by two accusatives: see **227.3**.

2. Many "intransitive" verbs take an *indirect object* in the genitive or dative case: thus, ich schone m e i n e s F e i n d e s, 'I spare my enemy;' er folgt m i r, 'he follows me:' see **219**, **222.II**.

3. Many verbs, beside their direct object, take a *remoter object* in the dative or genitive, indicating the person or thing affected less immediately by the action of the subject upon the object, or further defining that action: thus, ich raube d i e s e m M a n n e das Geld, 'I steal the money from this man;' ich beraube ihn s e i n e s Geldes, 'I rob him of his money:' see **219**, **222**.I.

316. *Predicate Noun or Adjective.* A noun or adjective is called predicate, if it is brought by the verb into connection with a noun (either the subject or the direct object of the verb), as limiting or qualifying that noun.

1. *a.* A predicate noun stands in the nominative, relating to the subject of the verb, after sein, 'be,' werden, 'become,' bleiben, 'continue,' scheinen, dünken, and däuchten, 'seem,' and heißen, 'be called;' also, with the passive of the verbs that take a noun in the accusative as factitive predicate: see **213**.

These are verbs of incomplete predication, requiring a complement. Especially sein, 'be,' is the ordinary simple connective of a subject with its predicated quality, and is therefore called the *copula*.

b. After a few verbs—of calling, regarding, and the like—a predicate noun stands in the accusative, brought by the verb into relation with its object: this is called a *factitive predicate:* thus, er nannte mich seinen Freund, 'he called me his friend:' see **227**.3*b*,*c*.

2. *a.* A predicate adjective is used after the same verbs as a predicate noun: thus, er ist und bleibt mir treu, und wird nie untreu werden, 'he is and continues faithful to me, and will never become unfaithful.'

b. With verbs of more complete predication, or of full predicative force, an adjective is often used in a manner which it is convenient to distinguish as *adverbial predicate:* thus, die Kinder standen s t u m m, 'the children stood silent;' die Stimme strömte himmlisch h e l l e vor, 'the voice poured forth heavenly clear;' wird's auch s c h ö n zu Tage kommen, 'will it also come forth beautiful?'

c. Some verbs are followed by an adjective as *factitive predicate,* relating to their object: thus, sie ringen die Hände wund, 'they wring their hands sore;' die ich gerne d r e i f a c h biete, 'which I gladly offer threefold;' sie stellt sich ü b e r r a s c h t, 'she feigns herself surprised;' ich fühle meine Kräfte h ö h e r, 'I feel my powers higher;' er hält ihn w a r m, 'he holds him warm.'

This predicative construction is much more common with adjectives than with nouns, which generally require als, 'as,' für, 'for,' zu, 'to,' or the like, before them: compare **227**.3*c*.

317. *Adverb.* The verbal idea is limited by an adverb, or by more than one, in the most various manner, in respect to time, place, occasion, manner, end, and so on. See Adverbs, **361** etc.

Thus, ich gehe jetzt, 'I am going now;' er wohnt hier, 'he lives here; sie sprechen gut, 'they speak well;' du bist heute morgen sehr spät erwacht, 'you woke very late this morning.

318. *Prepositional Phrase.* A phrase composed of a preposition along with the word (generally a noun, with or without adjuncts) which it governs, and the nature of whose relation to the verbal action it defines, is a very frequent adjunct to the verb, taking the place of object, predicate, or adverb.

a. As direct object in place of an accusative, such a phrase can hardly stand: but it may be used for a genitive object—as, ich warte auf ihn, for ich warte seiner, 'I wait for him;' for a dative object—as, er folgt mir, or er folgt auf mich, 'he follows me;'—yet more freely for a remoter object along with a direct object—as, ich freue mich über dieses, for ich freue mich dessen, 'I rejoice at this:' ich schreibe einen Brief an ihn, for ihm einen Brief, 'I write a letter to him.'

b. Examples of prepositional phrases with predicate value are es war von entscheidender Wichtigkeit, 'it was of decisive importance;' die Kranken blieben in der Mitte, 'the sick remained in the midst;' sie erwählten ihn zum Kaiser, 'they chose him emperor;' dies wird zum Ausdruck der Seele, 'this becomes an expression of the soul.'

c. Adverbial prepositional phrases are der Vogel spielt im Laube, 'the bird plays in the foliage;' wir bergen den Samen in der Erde Schooß, 'we hide the seed in the earth's bosom;' er rief mit lauter Stimme, 'he cried with a loud voice.'

319. *Order of the verbal adjuncts.*

1. In the normal or regular arrangement of the sentence, all the adjuncts of a personal verb are placed after it.

a. For the *inverted* order of arrangement, in which one of the adjuncts is frequently placed before the verb it modifies, and for the *transposed* order, in which the personal verb is placed after all its adjuncts, see the rules given for the order of the sentence, below, **431, 434**.

2. When the verb is modified by two or more adjuncts, the general rule is, that one which is more closely combined in idea with the verb, and more essentially modifies its predicative meaning, is placed further from it than one of a more external and accessory character. Hence,

a. The infinitive or participle, in a compound verbal form, stands at the end of the sentence: thus, sie hatte ihre Zähne scharf in seine Finger gesetzt, 'she *had sunk* her teeth sharply into his fingers;' ihr werdet euch so blutig eurer Macht nicht überheben, 'you *will* not *presume* so cruelly upon your power.'

b. An infinitive dependent upon any verb, modal or causative auxiliary or other, stands in like manner at the end of the sentence: thus, ich will vor ihr mich niederwerfen, 'I *will humble* myself before her.'

c. A separable prefix belonging to the verb takes the same place: thus, sie sah dabei recht finster und unwillig aus, 'she *looked* at the same time right gloomy and out of humor.'

d. Any part of speech compounded with a verb after the manner of a separable prefix, or forming with it a verbal phrase analogous with such a compound, takes the same place: thus, ich nahm nichts mehr von der hinter mir liegenden Ebene wahr, 'I no longer *saw* anything of the plain that lay behind me.'

e. Of two cases governed by the same verb, the second accusative (**227**.3) is placed after that which is the more immediate object of the verb; the genitive (**219**.2,3) follows the accusative; the dative (**222**.I.1) rather more usually precedes the accusative.

f. Of more than one adverb qualifying the same verb, an adverb of time ordinarily precedes one of place, and both are placed before one of manner or degree: thus, er arbeitet immer fleißig, 'he always works industriously;' du wohnst hier sehr bequem, 'you live here very comfortably.' Hence, also, the adverb of negation, nicht, if it modifies the general assertion of the sentence, stands last; but if its negative force applies to some particular adjunct of the verb, it is placed next before that adjunct.

3. The rules as above stated are subject to various modification under the influence of accent or emphasis, or of euphony.

a. Any adjunct of the verb may be transferred to a position other than its proper one (usually later), for the purpose of being made more prominent.

b. Since a pronoun is, in general, a less significant and emphatic word than a noun, usage has established the rule that

A pronoun immediately dependent on the verb (not governed by a preposition), whether as direct or indirect object, comes first among the verbal adjuncts.

Among the pronouns, a personal pronoun comes before a demonstrative, the briefer personal pronouns, especially es, 'it,' before the longer, and the reflexives first of all.

4. Prepositional phrases take, in general, the position belonging to the part of speech whose equivalent they are; but they are more liable than single words to change place for euphonic reasons.

5. The natural connections of the different verbal adjuncts are regarded in the arrangement of the sentence; those which affect one another, and exert a combined influence upon the verbal action, being put together.

6. The above are only the leading principles of the arrangement of words in a sentence. To follow out their application in detail, and illustrate their joint and mutual action, and the more or less irregular and arbitrary modifications which they admit, cannot here be attempted.

USES OF THE FORMS OF CONJUGATION.

Person and Number.

320. In general, the verb is of the same person and number as its subject.

Being, of course, of the first or second person only when its subject is a personal pronoun of those persons respectively, since all other words are of the third person.

321. *Special Rules respecting Person.*

1 When the same verb has subjects of more than one person, it is of the first person (plural) if either of its subjects is of the first person; otherwise, of the second: thus, ich und du sind hier, 'I and thou are here;' du und er glaubt es beide nicht, 'you and he both disbelieve it.'

2. After a relative (der) referring to an antecedent of the first or second person, the verb is in the third, unless the personal pronoun is repeated after the relative (compare **181**): thus, du, der dem Basilisk den Mordblick gab, 'thou who gavest to the basilisk his deadly glance' (but du, der du . . . . . gabst).

322. *Special Rules respecting Number.*

1. A verb having for its subject more than one singular noun is put in the plural.

a. To this rule there are frequent exceptions, either as the several subjects are regarded as combined into a single idea; or as, when preceding or following an enumeration of single subjects, the verb, by a familiar license of speech, is suffered to agree with the one nearest it alone; or as the verb is in fact understood with other than the one subject with which it agrees: thus, hinter mir liegt nur Kummer und Elend, 'behind me *lies* only sorrow and misery;' Fels und Meer wird fortgerissen, 'rock and sea *are* hurried onward;' es begleite durch Leben und Sterben uns Lied und Liebe und Wein, 'may song and love and wine accompany us through life and death;' Lügen, Morden, Stehlen und Ehebrechen hat überhand genommen, 'lying, murder, theft, and adultery *have* become prevalent.'

2. A collective noun in the singular takes a verb in the singular much more strictly than in English.

a. Exceptions are only such expressions as ein Paar, 'two or three,' eine Menge, 'a number,' ein Dutzend, 'a dozen,' which are frequently used with plural nouns (ordinarily construed appositionally with them: see **216**.5*a*), and have gained a plural value by association: thus, in welchem ein Paar Vögel hin und wieder hüpfen, 'in which a couple of birds hop back and forth;' im Hofe spielten ein Paar der munteren Kinder, 'in the yard were playing two or three of the merry children;' ein Paar sind gewöhnlich vor aus, 'a couple are generally in front.'

3. After the impersonal and indefinite subjects es, dies, das, was, welches, etc., the verb is put in the plural if a following predicate noun is plural: thus, es sind unser zwei, 'there *are* two of us;' das sind meine Freunde, 'those *are* my friends.'—So also occasionally in a case like die Frucht dieses Baumes sind kleine Beeren, 'the fruit of this tree *is* small berries.'

4. Out of exaggerated respectfulness, the plural verb is sometimes (the usage is happily going out of vogue) construed with a singular title, or name and title: as, belieben der Herr diesen Seckel zu erproben, 'may the gentleman be pleased to try this purse;' Seine Majestät der König haben geruht, 'his majesty the king *has* been graciously pleased to . . . .'

Mood and Tense.

Indicative.

323. The use of the indicative mood, in its various tenses, corresponds upon the whole pretty closely in German and in English. The principal points of difference will be stated below.

324. *Indicative Present.* 1. The German present—e. g. ich liebe—answers to the three English forms of the present 'I love,' 'I do love,' and 'I am loving:' the shades of difference among these different values are either left to be inferred from the context, or are expressed or intimated by adjuncts to the verb or by verbal phrases.

2. In German, as in English and French, the present is often substituted for the preterit in lively narration: thus, ich hielt stille, und sah mich nach dem Stande der Sonne um. Indem ich nun so emporblicke, sehe ich 2c., 'I stopped, therefore, and looked about me for the position of the sun. While, now, I *am* thus looking upward, I *see*' etc.

3. In expressing a past action or state which is continued so as to be present also (or in signifying what has been and still is), the German, like the French, indicates the present part and leaves the past to be inferred, while the English does the contrary: thus, sind sie schon lange hier, '*have* you *been* (are you) here already a long time?' er schläft seit fünf Jahren unter dem Schnee, 'he *has been* (is) *sleeping* for five years beneath the snow.'

4. The German present, much more often than the English, is used in the sense of a future: thus, wie fang' ich's an? ich dreh' mich um, so ist's gethan, 'how *shall* I set about it? I *will* turn myself around; that *will* fetch it;' die Güter, die er dereinst erbt, 'the property which he will one day inherit.'

This future use of the present is a direct inheritance from a former condition of Germanic language (as represented to us by the oldest Germanic dialects), in which the present and future meanings were both habitually expressed by the present tense, the later auxiliary futures, as *I shall* or *will love*, ich werde lieben, not having been yet brought into use. See the author's "Language and the Study of Language," pp. 119, 269.

325. *Indicative Preterit.* 1. The preterit answers to our own simple past tense, in its three forms of 'I loved,' 'I did love,' 'I was loving'—all expressed, without distinction, by ich liebte.

2. As the present for the perfect (**324.**3), so the preterit is sometimes used for our pluperfect, to express what, at a given time, had been and was still: thus, waren Sie schon lange da, '*had* you *been* (were you) there long already?'

3. The distribution of the expression of past time between the preterit and perfect is not precisely the same in German as in English. As (**326.**2) the German perfect often stands where we should use the preterit, so the contrary is also sometimes the case: thus, ihr hörtet, welch schreckliches Gericht des Herrn über Jerusalem erging, 'ye *have heard* what a terrible judgment of the Lord *has come* upon Jerusalem.'

326. *Indicative Perfect.* 1. The perfect answers in the main to our perfect, expressing completed action, or action in the past with implied reference to the present, as no longer continuing: thus, ich habe geliebt, 'I have loved,' or 'have been loving.'

2. But the perfect is not infrequently used where we employ the preterit: the perfect is rather the tense by which something is simply asserted as true, while the preterit implies a connection with other past events in continuous narration, or a personal participation of the speaker, as spectator or joint actor.

Thus, Gott hat die Welt erschaffen, 'God created the world (it was God who etc.);' ich bin gestern in der Kirche gewesen, 'I was at church yesterday;' unser Freund ist neulich gestorben, 'our friend died lately:'—but Gott erschuf die Welt in sechs Tagen, und ruhte am siebenten, 'God created the world in six days, and rested on the seventh;' ich war in der Kirche, wo Herr N. eine vortreffliche Predigt hielt, 'I was at church, where Mr. N. preached an admirable sermon;' unser Vater starb gestern, 'our father died yesterday (in our presence).'

Something of the same distinction appears also in English usage, and it is impossible to explain fully the difference in idiom between the two languages without a great deal of detailed illustration. Moreover, there are many cases in either tongue where both tenses might be employed with equal propriety.

3. For the present in place of our perfect, see **324.**3; for the perfect in place of the future, see **328.**3*b*.

327. *Indicative Pluperfect.* The pluperfect in German, as in English, expresses action already finished at a time in the past either defined or contemplated by the speaker: thus, ich hatte geliebt, 'I had loved' or 'been loving.'

328. *Indicative Future and Future Perfect.* 1. These tenses ordinarily agree in use with their English correspondents: thus, ich werde lieben, 'I shall love' or 'be loving;' ich werde geliebt haben, 'I shall have loved' or 'been loving.'

They express simple futurity, that which is going to be; and are carefully to be distinguished from the modal auxiliary forms composed of the infinitive with wollen and sollen (**257–8**), which more or less distinctly imply an assent or intent, a propriety or obligation.

2. The futures are sometimes used to indicate a claimed probability, or express a conjecture: thus, das wird wohl Ihr Bruder sein, 'that is your brother, is it not?' er wird nicht lange dort geblieben sein, 'I presume he did not stay there long.'

3. *a.* In German, as in English, the perfect is often employed where the future perfect would be logically more correct, the implication of futurity being sufficiently made by the context: thus, ich werde kommen, sobald ich meinen Brief geschrieben habe, 'I shall come as soon as I have written my letter' (for werde geschrieben haben, 'shall have written').

b. A present or perfect is occasionally substituted for a future, by a figure of speech, to indicate the certainty of what is to take place: thus, jene hat gelebt, wenn ich dies Blatt aus meinen Händen gebe, 'she has ceased to live, if I let this paper go out of my hands;' steh', oder du bist des Todes, 'stand, or thou art a dead man!'

c. For the frequent use of a present instead of a future tense, see **324.4.**

Subjunctive.

329. The subjunctive mood, which has almost passed out of use in English, still continues in full currency in German, having, if the two "conditional" tenses be included with it (as they are in fact subjunctive, both in form and character), more than a corresponding tense for every tense of the indicative. In some of its offices (the optative, potential, conditional) it answers to what is left of our own subjunctive, and to the compounded tenses (with the auxiliaries *may*, *might*, *would*, and *should*) by which we have in part supplied the place of the latter; in other offices (especially in indirect statement, **333**) there is in English hardly anything analogous, though the classical tongues present similar constructions in abundance.

330. The subjunctive is the mood of possibility, contingency, subjectivity, in contradistinction from the indicative as the mode of actuality, direct assertion, objectiveness.

a. The subjunctive of the Germanic languages is by origin an optative, or mood expressing wish or desire, and there was another mood more properly known as subjunctive In the Greek, both still subsist together; but in German, as in Latin, the two have become one, which combines, with various modifications and restrictions, their several offices.

b. Not every statement of a hypothetical or contingent character requires the subjunctive: that character is often sufficiently intimated by the radical meaning of the verb used, or of the adverbs or conjunctions employed with it; the cases in which this mood is availed of are those to be explained below.

c. Even in the cases detailed, there is considerable freedom of choice between a subjunctive and an indicative expression, depending on the degree of contingency or reality of the implied conception; the difference being sometimes so slight as to be hardly definable: and an indicative is occasionally used where analogy would lead us to expect a subjunctive, as if, by a figure of speech, to give a character of actuality to what is in itself properly contingent. It is not possible to say, as in some other languages, that certain grammatical constructions, or certain particles, require or "govern" the subjunctive.

d. In the subjunctive, the distinctions of tense are of only subordinate value, and are even to some extent effaced. The tenses do not, therefore, require to be separately treated.

331. *The Subjunctive as Optative.*

1. The present subjunctive is frequently used in an *optative* sense, as expressing a wish, request, or direction on the part of the speaker.

Thus, gesegnet sei er allezeit, 'blessed be he ever;' lang lebe der König es freue sich, wer da . . . 'long live the king! let him rejoice, who . . .;' bräutliches Leinen legen wir dem Thor an, 'let us dress Thor in bridal vestments.'

a. This use is limited to the third persons of both numbers, and the first plural: for the second persons, the imperative is used; and for the first singular, möge, 'may,' is needed as auxiliary. The same auxiliary may also be employed in the other persons.

b. The subject is put after the verb, except in the third pers. singular, where it may have either position, and more usually stands before.

c. The optative subjunctive is used, as already noticed (**243.**1), to fill out the declension of the imperative, and is practically, in the third pers. plural, the most common imperative form, since the use of the second person in ordinary address is no longer approved (**153**.4).

d. This subjunctive sometimes becomes, in application, concessive, or expresses a supposition or assumption: thus, man begegne Jemanden im Haus; es sei eine Gesellschaft beisammen, 'let one meet anybody in the house; let a company be assembled (*i. e.* supposing such to be the case);' er thue, was er wolle, 'let him do what he please (*i. e.* though he do).'

e. Hence, with denn, it becomes, by an elliptical construction, equivalent to 'unless;' thus, er führe denn Freya zur Braut mir heim, 'unless he bring me home Freya as bride,' (*i. e.* '[if he would gain what he wishes] then let him bring,' etc.)

2. The preterit and pluperfect tenses are also employed in a kind

of optative sense, but only by elliptical construction, in abbreviated conditional and indirect phrases.

Thus, wäre es doch Abend, 'if it were only evening!' hätte ich mich doch gefreut, 'had I only enjoyed myself (while it was still in my power to do so)!' ach, daß meine Augen Thränenquellen wären, 'O that my eyes were fountains of tears!'

332. *The Subjunctive as Conditional and Potential.*

The conditional and potential uses of the subjunctive so pass into one another, that they can hardly be treated separately. We commence, for convenience, with the hypothetical period.

1. The *hypothetical period* consists of two parts or clauses, the one expressing a conclusion or result which would follow, if the condition were true which is expressed by the other—it being at the same time implied that the condition is not realized, and, generally, that the result is therefore also untrue. This, in its complete form, requires a past tense (preterit or pluperfect) of the subjunctive both in the condition and the result.

Thus, regierte Recht, so läget ihr vor mir im Staube, 'if right prevailed, you would lie in the dust before me;' wenn's länger gedauert hätte, wäre ich im Frost erstarrt, 'if it had lasted longer, I should have been stiffened with frost;' glücklicher wäre auch ich, wenn ich nach Asien gezogen wäre, 'I too should be happier, if I had marched to Asia.'

a. Either of the two clauses may stand first, and the idea of *if* in the clause of condition may be expressed either by a conjunction (wenn) or by the inverted arrangement (**433**)—as the examples show.

b. In the result or conclusion, the conditional tenses may be used instead of the proper subjunctive: see below, **335**.

c. The implication as to the result is liable to modification by various causes; for example, by its being put into the form of a question—as, was wäre aus mir geworden, hättet ihr mich nicht aufgenommen, 'what would have become of me, if you had not received me?'—or by an 'even' involved in the condition: as, und wären von Gold sie, ich gäbe sie dir, 'even were they of gold, I would give them to thee.'

d. If the condition be regarded as doubtful merely, and not contrary to reality, the verbs are put in the indicative mood: thus, always when the tense is present or perfect — as, wenn er kommt, gehe ich fort, 'if he comes, I shall go away;' wenn er gekommen ist, will ich ihn sehen, 'if he be arrived, I wish to see him;' and often when the tense is past: thus, wenn er schon gekommen war, muß er uns gesehen haben, 'if he had already come, he cannot have failed to see us.'

2. In the *incomplete hypothetical period*, either the condition or the conclusion is unexpressed, but is more or less distinctly intimated or implied.

a. The conclusion is wanting altogether, and the condition has the value of a wish or prayer (see **331.2**). In this case a doch or nur is more often introduced to help the optative expression, but is not indispensable: thus, wären wir nur den Berg vorbei, '[how happy I should be] if we were only past the hill!' könnt' ich mit, 'if I could but go along with you!

b. The conclusion may be intimated by als, 'as,' and the conditionality of the other clause expressed either by a conjunction, ob or wenn, or (more commonly) by the inverted arrangement (**433**) of the clause after als:

Thus, ihr eilet ja, als wenn ihr Flügel hättet, 'you are hurrying as [you would do] if you had wings;' er will die Wahrheit so, als ob sie Münze wäre, 'he demands truth in this way as [he would demand it] if it were cash;' der Boden klafft auf, als wäre er von Erdstößen erschüttert, 'the soil cleaves open, as if it were shaken by earthquakes.'

c. The analogy of this construction calls always for a past tense, but a present is sometimes met with, as if the phrase were one of indirect statement (**333**) instead of conditional: thus, da ward es mir als könne ich durch den Boden sehen, als sei er grünes Glas, 'then it seemed to me as if I could see through the ground as though it were green glass.' Occasionally, it really represents an indirect phrase: thus, ich dachte als sei es . . ., for ich dachte, es sei . . ., 'I thought as if it were,' for 'I thought it was' so and so.

d. The conclusion is expressed by some other and virtually equivalent means: thus, ich gedachte, dafern ich kein Abenteuer fände, den Heimweg zu suchen, 'I intended, in case I should meet with no further adventure, to seek the way homeward.'

e. On the other hand, the conclusion may be fully expressed and the condition intimated by some word or phrase which more or less distinctly implies it:

Thus, O wäre ich ein großer Baum! d a n n könnte ich meine Zweige ausbreiten, 'O that I were a big tree! then [if I were so] I might spread out my branches;' manches hätt' ich gethan; a l l e i n wer scheut nicht die Kosten, 'I would have done much—only, who does not fear the cost? [if I had not feared the cost];' sonst wär' er gefallen, 'otherwise [if this were not so] he would have fallen.'

3. A yet less explicit implication of a condition makes of the past subjunctive a proper *potential*, expressing what in general, under the circumstances, might, could, or would be:

Thus, das ginge noch, 'that might answer yet;' es hätte sich's keiner vermogen, 'no one would have presumed to do so;' es könnte mich retten, 'it might be able to rescue me;' nimm ihr jeden Stachel, der verwunden könnte, 'take from it every sting that should be able to wound.'

a. The potential subjunctive is sometimes used in place of an indicative, when it is desired to soften the positiveness of an assertion: thus, ich dächte, 'I should think,' for 'I think;' ich möchte, 'I should like' (**255.2**); ich wäre fast gegen Baumstämme angerannt, 'I came near running against trunks of trees'

4. Analogous, on the other hand, with the clause expressing the condition in the hypothetical period, are occasional phrases like es wird nachgeahmt, wäre es nur mit einigen Kutschen, 'it is imitated, were it only with a

few carriages;' besonders, wenn er sich verschossen haben sollte, 'especially if he should chance to have exhausted his ammunition.'

5. Akin with the potential and hypothetical uses of the subjunctive are the following more special cases:

a. The subjunctive present is used in a clause involving an indefinite relative pronoun or conjunction (*whoever*, *however*, etc.): thus, wie auch der Menschliche wanke, 'however human (will) may waver;' so klein sie auch sei, 'however small it be;' auf welche Art es sei, 'in whatever way it may be.'

b. The subjunctive, present or past, is used after daß, um daß, damit, 'in order that,' to express the end had in view, or sought to be attained: thus, löst mir das Herz, daß ich das eure rühre, 'relieve my heart, that I may move yours;' er wünschte zu regieren, nur damit der Gute ungehindert gut sein möchte, 'he desired to rule only in order that the good might be able to be good without hindrance.'

The tense is governed by the requirements of the sense, generally according with that of the preceding verb.

c. In these, as in other constructions, the indicative is also met with: thus, was auch die Sinnlichkeit zu thun gedrängt wird, 'whatever our sensuousness is impelled to do;' damit man diese Stadt einnehmen kann, 'that the city may be (wherewith it is able to be) captured;' daß jeder Quell versiegt, 'that every fountain may dry up (so that every fount shall dry up).'

d. A subjunctive is used in a dependent substantive clause (generally after daß, 'that') to denote something that is provided for or looked forward to, regarded as of probable, desirable, or suitable occurrence: thus, er mußte bleiben bis (or bis daß) die Fluthen sich verliefen, 'he had to remain till the flood should subside;' es lag ihm daran, daß der Friede nicht unterbrochen werde, 'he was anxious that the peace should not be broken;' es gehört sich, daß das Bedürfniß befriedigt werde, 'it is proper that the want be satisfied.'

In some of its forms, this construction passes over into that of the subjunctive of indirect statement (see the next paragraph), after verbs of wishing, anticipating, and the like.

333. *The Subjunctive of Indirect Statement.*

1. By a construction which has only partial analogies in English, the German subjunctive is often used to express a thought indirectly, as reported, recognized, or contemplated by some one.

Thus, er antwortete, er achte Friedrich und wünsche den Frieden, 'he answered that he esteemed Frederick and desired peace;' wir wissen kaum, was zu thun sei, 'we hardly know what is to be done;' denkt man er gehe weg, 'if one thinks he is going away;' man sieht gleich, weß Sinnes der Herr sei, 'one sees at once, of what mind the master is.'

2. Such a subjunctive stands always in a (logically) dependent substantive clause. The use of this mood more fully subordinates the clause to the action of the verb in the other clause, upon which it depends, relieving the speaker from responsibility for it or concern with it.

3. Verbs most often followed by the subjunctive of indirect statement are especially

a. Verbs that signify imparting, in every form, as statement, report assertion, confession, reminding, and the like.

b. Verbs that signify apprehension, as perceiving, knowing, feeling, calling to mind, imagining, concluding, and the like.

c. Verbs that signify contemplation with feelings of various kinds, as belief, doubt, dread, wonder, joy, sorrow, wish, hope.

Some of these verbs complicate the idea of indirectness with that of desire, doubt, or conditionality, as expressed by the subjunctive in its other uses.

d. The verb upon which the clause of indirect statement depends may sometimes be omitted altogether: thus, die Lateiner wurden hart verfolgt, weil jener sie zu sehr begünstigt h a b e, 'the Latins were severely persecuted, because [it was claimed that] he had favored them too much.'

e. Or, the clause is dependent on a noun of kindred meaning with the verbs above mentioned: thus, aus Besorgniß, daß er Unruhen erregen w e r d e, 'out of apprehension that he would stir up disorders;' unter dem Vorwand, er h a b e früher beschworen alles anzuzeigen, 'under the pretext that he had earlier taken oath to denounce everything;' die Nachricht, daß er sie ins Gefängniß geworfen h a b e, 'the news that he had thrown them into prison.'

4. *a.* Regularly and ordinarily, the verb in the indirect statement has the same tense as it would have if the statement were made directly, by the person and under the circumstances contemplated.

Thus, sie glaubten, daß es wahr s e i, 'they believed that it *was* true (since they would have said "we believe that it *is* true"); er antwortete, er s e i nicht gekommen, Christen feindlich anzugreifen, sondern w e r d e nur Gewalt mit Gewalt zurücktreiben, 'he answered, he *was* not ["I *am* not"] come to attack Christians, but *would* only ["I *shall* only"] repel violence with violence;' bald fragte man nicht mehr, wer mitgehe, sondern wer zurückbleibe, 'soon it was no longer asked who *was* going along ["who *is* going?"], but who *was* staying ["who *is* staying?"] behind;' ich habe gewünscht, er s o l l e sich auf Reisen begeben, 'I have wished that he *should* betake himself to journeying.'

b. Hence, the use of the present, perfect, and future subjunctive in indirect statement is much more frequent than that of the preterit and pluperfect and of the conditional. But

c. The past tenses are used, when they would have been used (either as indicative or as subjunctive) in the corresponding statement made directly: thus, er wünschte, daß er auf dem Boden geblieben wäre, 'he wished he had remained in the garret;' wer kann wissen, was nicht Jemand glaublich fände, 'who can tell what somebody might not think credible?' des Gefühles, daß nichts im Leben recht geschähe wenn es bloß geschähe, 'of the feeling that nothing in life would be done rightly if it should be just simply done.'

Rarely, on the other hand, a subjunctive of indirect statement is forced out of the past tense which it should have into the present, as the more usual tense belonging to the indirect construction (see R. 190.33).

d. Moreover, in a clause dependent on a verb of past tense, the subjunctive is quite often put in the past (as it always is in English), contrary to strict rule: thus, sie glaubten es wäre [for sei] Hahnengeschrei, 'they thought it *was* the crowing of cocks;' sie fragten ob sie recht wüßte [for wisse] wer ihr Mann wäre [for sei], 'they asked whether she really *knew* who her husband *was;*' ging bei mir zu Rath, ob ich sie weckte [for wecke], 'took counsel with myself, whether I *should* wake her.'

e. This assimilation of the subjunctive in tense to the verb on which it depends is, in general, much more common in the more careless and less dignified styles of writing, and in colloquial discourse, than in higher styles. But it is occasionally met with in every style, sometimes without special assignable cause, sometimes where a present subjunctive form would not be distinguishable from an indicative, or where a clause is dependent on another dependent clause, and needs to be distinguished from the latter in construction: thus, er bot durch Gesandte an, die Fürsten möchten [for mögen, which would be indicative as well] selbst entscheiden, was er rechtmäßig besäße, 'he offered through embassadors that the princes might themselves decide what he rightfully possessed.'

5. The indicative may also be used in phrases similar to those above cited, mostly with an implication of actuality, as recognized by the speaker also: thus, wer weiß, wo dir dein Glücke blüht, 'who knows where thy fortune is blooming for thee [as it surely is blooming somewhere]?' man mußte glauben, daß er völlig vergessen war, 'one could not but believe that he was wholly forgotten;' er verweilte, bis er sich überzeugt hatte, daß keiner von den seinen zurückblieb, 'he delayed till he was persuaded that none of his men was left behind.'

But the difference of implication is often very indistinct, and the choice between the two moods depends in part upon the style used: too nice a use of the subjunctive in easy or colloquial discourse would be thought finical and pedantic.

6. The elliptical use of the subjunctive of indirect statement with optative meaning, or to express a wish, has been referred to above (**331.2**): thus, o daß sie ewig grünen bliebe, 'O that it might ever continue to flourish!' (*i. e.* ich möchte, daß . . . , 'I should wish that' . . .).

7. A past subjunctive tense is (rarely) used interrogatively, by way of questioning or disputing something supposed to have been asserted: thus, du hättest es gesagt? du hast mir nichts gesagt, '[is it claimed that] you have said so? you have said nothing to me'

Conditional.

334. The conditional tenses are, in form, subjunctive preterits corresponding to the future as a present: thus, er wird lieben, 'he is about to love,' er werde lieben, 'he may be about to love,' er würde lieben, 'he might or would be about to love.'

Their proper significance, then, is that of a contingent futurity, such a potentiality as may be signified by a tense past in form. In this they coincide (as appears from the rules and examples given above, **332**) with the past subjunctive tenses, preterit and pluperfect. In fact,

335. 1. The conditional corresponds in meaning with the preterit and pluperfect subjunctive, being an admissible substitute for these tenses in some of their uses.

a. Especially, in the conclusion of a complete hypothetical period (**332.1**): thus, lebtest du noch, ich würde dich lieben von dieser Zeit, 'wert thou yet alive, I should love thee henceforth;' keines würde lenksam genug sein, wenn wir bloß sein Dasein in der Hand gewahr würden, 'none would be manageable enough, if we were merely aware of its presence in the hand.'

b. In a conclusion with condition only intimated (**332.**2*e*): thus, die Vögel würden dann Nester in meinen Zweigen bauen, 'in that case (if this were so) the birds would build nests in my branches;' prob' es lieber nicht, denn du würdest zerschellt werden, 'rather, do not try it; for [if thou didst try it] thou wouldst be dashed in pieces.'

c. In a more strictly potential construction (**332.**3): thus, sich ernstlich zu wehren würde sehr gefährlich sein, 'to defend one's self seriously would be very dangerous;' das würde uns zu weit führen, 'that would lead us too far.'

2. The use of the conditional is much less frequent than that of the past subjunctive tenses in the constructions above explained. While the two are so nearly equivalent that the subjunctive may usually be put in place of the conditional, they are not absolutely identical in sense; the conditional may sometimes be preferred where the idea of futurity is prominent (as in the first example above, under *a*)—as also, for formal reasons, where the subjunctive verb would not be plainly distinguished from an indicative (as in the first example under *b*).

336. Quite rarely, the conditional is employed in indirect statement in place of the future subjunctive, in the same manner as a preterit subjunctive for a present (**333.**4*d*)—that is to say, with the value of a past subjunctive to the future: thus, er wußte, daß diese Anerbietungen den Kreuzzug nicht aufhalten würden [for werden, which would not be distinguishable from an indicative], 'he knew that these offers would not detain the crusade.'

Imperative.

337. The use of the imperative requires no explanation, being the same in German as in English.

a. With the proper imperative persons (the second persons singular and plural) the subject pronouns, du and ihr, may be either expressed or omitted: if expressed, they follow the verb.

b. For the use of the present subjunctive as imperative in the third persons singular and plural and the first plural, see **331.**1*c*.

338. Besides the phrases mentioned at **243.**1 as employed imperatively, the present indicative sometimes intimates a peremptory order, as if from one whose simple word is equivalent to a command; the past participle has, elliptically (see **359.**3), a similar force; and the infinitive is used dialectically or colloquially, with the same meaning (**347.**2).

Infinitive.

339. The infinitive is properly the verbal noun, and all its uses grow out of its value as such.

340. 1. Any infinitive is capable of use directly as a noun, either with or without an article or other limiting words. Such a noun is always of the neuter gender (**61**.3*c*), and declined according to the first declension, first class (**76**); and, having the value of an abstract, it very seldom forms a plural.

Thus, Gotteslästern, Lügen, Morden und Stehlen hat überhand genommen, 'blasphemy, lying, murdering, and stealing have become prevalent;' welch ein Appetit zum Schmausen, 'what an appetite for feasting!' er fing wieder mit seinem häßlich höflichen Grüßen an, 'he began again with his odiously polite greeting.'

2. As the examples show, such a noun is more usually to be rendered by our verbal noun in *ing* (which we often call "participial infinitive," although in truth it is quite another word than the present participle); but also, not rarely, by other verbal derivatives.

3. There are some nouns, originally infinitives, which are in such constant use as to have won an independent value as nouns: such are Leben, 'life,' Entsetzen, 'horror,' Andenken, 'memorial,' and so on.

341. In German, as in English, the preposition zu, 'to,' which was originally used only in its proper prepositional sense with the infinitive, governing the latter as it would govern any other noun under similar circumstances, has now become attached as a kind of fixed accompaniment, or sign, to the infinitive in a great part of its uses; and therefore, in describing the different infinitive constructions, it becomes necessary to distinguish between the cases in which zu is employed and those in which it is omitted.

342. *The Infinitive as subject of a verb.*

The infinitive, either with or without zu, is often employed as the subject of a verb.

Thus, wachsen, groß und alt werden, das ist das einzig Schöne, 'to grow, to become big and old—that is the only fine thing;' wo getäuscht zu werden uns heilsamer war, 'where to be deceived was more advantageous for us;' mit solchen ist nicht gut in der Nähe kämpfen, 'fighting at close quarters with such men is not good;' gefährlich ist's den Leu zu wecken, 'it is dangerous to wake the lion.'

a. The infinitive as subject is in the great majority of cases accompanied by zu.

b. More usually (as the examples show), the infinitive stands as logical subject, the verb taking in addition es, 'it,' or das, 'that,' or the like (especially the first), as impersonal or indefinite grammatical subject.

343. *The Infinitive as object, or dependent on another verb.*

I. The infinitive without zu is directly dependent on

1. The various auxiliaries: as, werden, the auxiliary of the future and conditional tenses (**240.**2); haben, the auxiliary of the perfect and pluperfect tenses, in the cases where the infinitive is used instead of the past participle in forming those tenses (**240.**1*c*); the auxiliaries of mood (**242.**1); thun, when used as auxiliary in the sense of our *do* (**242.**3); lassen, as causative auxiliary (**242.**2): see below, 5.

2. Haben, 'have,' in certain phrases, with an adjective: thus, du hast gut reden, 'that is easy to say' (*i.e.* 'thou hast talking good, makest an easy thing of talking').

3. Thun, and a few other verbs, followed by nichts als, 'nothing [else] than, nothing but:' thus, er that nichts als sie anschauen, 'he did nothing but look at her;' es kostet nichts als die Gemeine sein für alle, 'it costs nothing but being the common one for all.'

4. Lernen, 'learn:' thus, er hatte das Gute würdigen gelernt, 'he had learned to value what was good.'

5. A number of verbs admit an infinitive in the manner of a second direct object, along with their ordinary object: these are heißen, 'call, bid,' nennen, 'call,' lehren, 'teach,' helfen, 'help,' machen, 'make,' lassen, 'allow, cause,' and a few that denote perception by the senses, namely sehen (and rarely schauen), 'see,' hören, 'hear,' fühlen, 'feel,' and finden, 'find.'

Thus, er heißt ihn weder Kosten noch Mühe sparen, 'he bids him spare neither expense nor labor;' was man so erkennen heißt (nennt), 'what people call knowing;' das lehrt uns beurtheilen ob . . . 'that teaches us to judge whether . . . ;' wir müssen ihm helfen hüten, 'we must help him tend his herd;' die Freiheit macht euch schwärmen, 'this freedom makes you rave;' der Gott, der Eisen wachsen ließ, 'the God who made iron grow;' er sieht sie erbleichen und sinken hin, 'he sees her turn pale and sink down;' ich finde sie auf dem Sopha liegen, 'I find her lying on the sofa.'

a. With most of the verbs under this head, the object taken along with the infinitive has the logical value of a *subject-accusative to the infinitive*—which is the nearest approach made in German to that construction, so familiar in the classical tongues, especially in the Latin: thus, ich höre das Gras wachsen, 'I hear the grass grow,' signifies that the grass grows, and that I perceive it so doing.

This construction, especially with sehen, hören, and lassen (and by far oftenest with the last), is followed out into a variety of other forms, some of them of a peculiar and idiomatic character: thus,

b. The proper object of the governing verb is frequently omitted, and the infinitive then designates its action without reference to any definite actor: thus, ich höre klopfen, 'I hear [some one] knock (hear a knocking);' laßt klingeln, 'cause to ring (let the bell be rung);' laß überall für das Kreuzheer in den Kirchen beten, 'cause to pray for the crusading army everywhere in the churches (let it be prayed for).'

c. If, then, the infinitive itself takes an object, the construction is equivalent to one in which that object is directly dependent upon the governing verb, and is the subject-accusative of the infinitive taken as an infinitive passive; and it is generally best so rendered: thus, ich höre euch jeden Tag preisen, 'I hear you to be praised every day (hear [them] praise you);' er ließ die drei Ringe für einen machen, 'he caused the three rings to be made in place of one (caused to make them).'

d. That the construction has in fact, in the apprehension of those who use the language, been virtually converted into a passive one, and the real object of the infinitive transferred to the governing verb, is shown by the circumstance that that object, when designating the same person or thing with the subject of the verb, is expressed by the reflexive instead of the personal pronoun: thus, er wollte s i c h nicht halten lassen, 'he would not let *himself* be held' (instead of 'would not allow [any one] to hold *him*'); das läßt s i c h hören, 'that lets itself be heard (*i. e.* is worth hearing);' als er s i c h etwas vorlesen ließ, 'as he was having something read aloud to himself;' er läßt oft von sich hören, 'he lets himself be often heard from (lets [us] often hear from him).' Occasionally, the logical object of lassen is even added in the form of a prepositional adjunct: thus, sie ließen sich d u r c h d i e W a c h e nicht abhalten, 'they did not suffer themselves to be restrained by the guards' —instead of sie ließen die Wache sie nicht abhalten, 'they did not suffer the guards to restrain them.'

6. Special and more anomalous cases are—an infinitive in the sense of a present participle after bleiben, 'remain:' thus, sie blieben im Wasser stecken, 'they remained sticking in the water;' and after haben with a direct object: thus, er hat Wein im Keller liegen, 'he has wine lying in his cellar:' —an infinitive of purpose (below, III.1) without zu in a few phrases; as, laß sie betteln gehn, 'let them go begging!' er legt sich schlafen, 'he lays himself down to sleep;'—and spazieren, 'to be out for pleasure or exercise (*expatiate*),' after a verb expressing the kind of motion: as, ich reite, fahre, gehe spazieren, 'I ride, drive, or walk out for pleasure.'

II. The infinitive with zu is often construed as a direct object.

1. As the sole object of a considerable number of verbs, especially of verbs whose action points forward to something as to be attained or done: for example, such as signify begin, undertake, endeavor, venture, plan, hope, desire, promise, refrain; and some others.

2. Along with an indirect personal object, with verbs signifying command, permit, impute, forbid, and the like.

Thus, er gebot mir zu schweigen, 'he commanded me to remain silent;' die Wache erlaubt Niemandem vorzutreten, 'the guard allows no one to step forward.'

III. The infinitive with zu is construed in the manner of an indirect object:

1. To express the purpose or design of an action: thus, ich bin nicht da Räthsel zu lösen, 'I am not here to solve riddles;' die Meere zu befreien, sollten alle Länder erobert werden, 'to free the seas, all lands were to be subdued.'

a. This comes nearest to the original and proper purpose of an infinitive with zu, 'to, in order to, for to.' The same meaning is conveyed more explicitly by prefixing **um** (see below, **346**.1).

b. The infinitive stands thus often after sein, 'to be,' and stehen, 'stand, with the logical value of an infinitive passive: thus, da war so vieles zu sehen, 'there was so much there to be seen (so much for seeing, as object for sight).'

This construction in itself evidently admits of either an active or a passive interpretation, according as the thing mentioned is put forward as subject or object of the verbal action conveyed by the infinitive. German usage merely adopts the latter alternative.

c. Haben, with a following infinitive and zu, also sometimes forms a phrase in which what is properly the object of haben is regarded and treated as if dependent on the other verb: thus, wir haben den Corso zu beschreiben, 'we have to describe the Corso (have the Corso for describing, or as theme for description);'—the object may even be omitted, or an intransitive infinitive employed, leaving to haben simply the idea of necessity: thus, er hat nicht mehr zu fürchten, 'he no longer has [aught] to fear.'

2. In other relations such as are ordinarily expressed by a remoter object, or a prepositional phrase having the value of such an object, after verbs intransitive or transitive: thus, als er kam zu sterben, 'when he came to die (to dying);' da treibt's ihn, den Preis zu erwerben, 'then he feels impelled to gain the prize;' man gewöhnt es still zu stehen, 'it is trained to stand still;' nicht darf ich dir zu gleichen mich vermessen, 'I may not presume to be like thee;' wir freuen uns, das zu hören, 'we rejoice at hearing that;' er ruht nicht die Stadt zu verzieren, 'he ceases (rests) not to adorn the city;' das Gedränge hindert ihn zu fliehen, 'the crowd forbids (hinders) him to fly.'

As the examples show, the infinitive in this construction, though it often has the value of a dative, which its governing preposition zu, 'to,' best fits it to fill, is also sometimes used in the manner of a genitive, or an "ablative" (expressing the *from* relation).

344. *The Infinitive as adjunct to an Adjective.*

1. The infinitive, always with its sign zu, is used as limiting adjunct especially to adjectives denoting possibility, ease or difficulty, obligation, desire, readiness, and the like—to such, in general, as point forward, to something to be attained or done.

Thus, bereit den Aether zu durchdringen, 'ready to penetrate the ether;' leicht zu schaffen, 'easy to obtain;' bange, seinen Schmuck zu verlieren, 'afraid of losing his adornment.'

2. Many adjectives when qualified by zu, 'too,' or genug, etc., 'enough, sufficiently,' become capable of taking an infinitive as adjunct: thus, mächtig genug, die größten Thiere zu tödten, 'powerful enough to kill the largest animals;' zu klein den Raum zu füllen, 'too small to fill the space.'

But after zu and an adjective, the infinitive governed by um (346.1), or an awkward and illogical construction with als daß, 'than that,' is more frequent.

Compare the power to govern a dative given to an adjective by the same qualifying words (223.5): the cases are plainly analogous, the zu in such combinations having its proper prepositional force.

345. *The Infinitive as adjunct to a Noun.*

The infinitive, always accompanied by zu, is often dependent upon a noun.

The cases of such infinitives may be classified under three heads:

1. The governing noun is one related in meaning to the verbs and adjectives already specified as admitting a dependent infinitive: thus, Erlaubniß den Baum zu plündern, 'permission to plunder the tree;' ohne Hoffnung aufzustehen, 'without hope to rise again (of rising);' die Begierde, sie zu wecken, 'the desire to awaken her;' den Vorschlag, seine Söhne abzusenden, 'the proposal to send off his sons.'

2. The preposition zu has nearly its proper meaning as connecting the infinitive with the noun: thus, Zeit, sich zu ergötzen, 'time to please one's self (for pleasing);' Muth, mich in die Welt zu wagen, 'courage for venturing into the world;' der Augenblick zu reden, 'the moment for talking.'

3. The infinitive represents a genitive, most often a genitive of equivalence (**216**.2*e*), or has the logical value of an added explanation of the governing noun: thus, die Schwachheit, jedem zu versprechen, 'the weakness of promising to each one;' ein Gefühl des Verdienstes, diese ganze Höhe auszufüllen, 'a feeling of the merit of filling out this whole height.'

These classes, however, variously cross and pass into each other.

346. *The Infinitive governed by a Preposition.*

1. Only three prepositions—namely, um, 'in order,' ohne, 'without,' statt or anstatt, 'instead'—are allowed in German to govern the infinitive directly.

They are placed at the beginning of the infinitive clause, preceding all the words dependent on or limiting the infinitive, which stands last, always with zu next before it, and which is ordinarily to be rendered (except after um) by our "participial infinitive," or verbal in *ing*: thus, jedermann kommt, um zu sehen oder gesehen zu werden, 'every one comes in order to see or to be seen;' ohne euch schwer zu verklagen, 'without accusing you sorely;' anstatt aber die hiedurch erzeugte günstige Stimmung zu benutzen, 'instead, however, of improving the favorable state of mind thus brought about.'

2. With other prepositions, when a similar expression is required, the infinitive clause is represented beforehand by a da or dar in composition with the preposition, and then itself follows, as if in apposition with this da.

Thus, sie waren nahe d a r a n, auf ihn zu treten, 'they were near to treading on him (near to this—viz. to tread on him);' bewahrte mich d a v o r, die Natter an den Busen selbst zu legen, 'saved me from laying the adder to my own bosom (from this—viz. to lay etc.);' sie drangen d a r a u f, sich rechts zu wenden, 'they insisted on turning to the right.

a. Such a phrase as 'they insisted on *his* turning to the right,' where the subject of the action signified by the participial infinitive is different from that of the verb with which this is connected by the preposition, cannot be expressed in German by an infinitive: for the infinitive clause is substituted a complete substantive clause (**436**.3*d*), with a personal verb and its subject: thus, sie drangen darauf, daß er sich rechts wenden sollte, 'they insisted on this—that he should turn to the right.'

347. *The Infinitive in Absolute Constructions.*

1. In various elliptical constructions, chiefly analogous with such as are usual in English also, the infinitive stands without being dependent on any other word: thus, warum mich wecken, 'why awaken me?' ach! auf das muthige Roß mich zu schwingen, 'oh, to leap upon a spirited horse!' o schönes Bild, zu sehen . . . , 'oh beautiful picture! to see . . .;' anderer Frevel nicht zu gedenken, 'not to mention other outrages:' and so on.

2. By a usage not authorized in good German style, an infinitive is colloquially used with an imperative meaning: thus, da bleiben, 'stay there!'

348. *Infinitive Clauses.*

1. The infinitive used as a noun has the construction of an ordinary noun. But in its proper use as infinitive, it shares in the construction of the verb of which it forms a part, taking the same adjuncts—whether predicate, object, adverb, or prepositional phrase—as the personal forms of the verb; thus forming often extended and intricate *infinitive clauses*, which have the logical value of full substantive clauses, and are exchangeable with such.

Thus, man ist beschäftigt, das schöne Pflaster, wo es abzuweichen scheint, wieder neu in Stand zu setzen, 'they are occupied with setting the nice pavement newly in order again, wherever it seems to be giving way;' or, man ist damit beschäftigt, daß man . . . . in Stand setzt.

2. As a rule, the infinitive stands last in such a clause; and, in general, whatever is dependent on an infinitive is placed before it.

a. See the examples already given. When two or three infinitives come to stand together, each precedes the one it depends on, in the reverse of the English order: thus, ihr habt mich ermorden lassen wollen, 'you have wanted to cause to murder me (have me murdered).' But an infinitive used as participle (**240.1***c*) allows nothing to follow it, and an auxiliary infinitive must be placed before it: thus, ihr werdet mich h a b e n ermorden lassen wollen, 'you will have wanted' etc. Compare **439.2**.

3. The order in which the various members of an infinitive clause stand is the same which would belong to them if the infinitive were a part of a compound verbal tense: see **319**.

Participles.

349. The participles are properly verbal adjectives, and all their uses and constructions are those of adjectives.

350. The present participle has active force, representing in adjective form the exerting of an action, or the continuing of a state or condition, in the same way as this is represented by the present tense of the verb.

Thus, der reisende Maler, 'the travelling painter (*i. e.* the painter who travels);' eine liebende Mutter, 'a loving mother.'

a. In rare cases, and by a license which is not approved, a present participle is used passively: thus, eine melkende Kuh (eine Kuh welche gemelkt wird), 'a milking cow (a cow that is milked);' die vorhabende Reise (die Reise die man vorhat), 'the intended journey (the journey which one has before him);' der betreffende Punkt, 'the point concerned.'

351. 1. The past participle of a transitive verb has passive meaning, without any distinct implication of past time.

Thus, das geliebte Kind, 'the beloved child,' *i. e.* the child whom one has loved, or loves, or will love, according to the connection in which the term is used.

a. But such a participle, from a verb denoting a single act rather than a continuous action, may sometimes be used with a past meaning: thus, das gestohlene Pferd, 'the stolen horse;' der getrunkene Wein, 'the imbibed wine.'

2. The past participle of an intransitive verb has active meaning, and is for the most part employed only in the formation of the compound tenses of the verb. But,

a. The past participle of a verb taking sein as its auxiliary (**241**.2) may be used adjectively, with a distinctly past meaning: thus, der gefallene Schnee (der Schnee, welcher gefallen ist), 'the fallen snow.'

3. Many words have the form of past participles, but the value of independent adjectives, either as having a meaning which would not belong to them as participles, or as being divorced from verbs both in form and meaning, or as derived from verbs which are no longer in use as verbs, or as seeming to imply verbs which have never been in use.

Thus, gelehrt, 'learned,' bekannt, 'known,' verdrossen, 'listless;'—erhaben, 'lofty' (erhoben, 'raised'), gediegen, 'pure, sterling' (gediehen, 'thriven');—verstohlen, 'furtive,' verschieden, 'different;'—gestirnt, 'starry,' bejahrt, 'aged.'

a. Such past participles have not rarely assumed the value of present participles: thus, verschwiegen, 'silent;' verdient, 'deserving;' besorgt, 'anxious;' pflichtvergessen, 'duty-forgetting.'

352. The future passive participle, as has been already noticed (**278**), is formed only from transitive verbs, and is not used otherwise than attributively.

Thus, die Rolle einer auf keine Weise zu beruhigenden Frau, 'the part of a woman who was in no way to be pacified;' die gleichzeitig anzutretenden Pilgerfahrten, 'the pilgrimages to be entered upon at the same time'—but die Frau ist auf keine Weise zu beruhigen, 'the woman is in no way to be pacified' (**343**.III.1*b*).

353. The present participle is used freely as an attributive and hence also, like other attributive adjectives, as a substantive but it is rarely employed as a simple predicate.

Thus, die spielenden Lüftchen, 'the sporting breezes;' er erweckte den Schlummernden, 'he awoke the sleeper (slumbering one);' das trügende Bild lebender Fülle, 'the deceiving show of living fulness;' in der Hand des Schreibenden oder Malenden, 'in the hand of the writer or painter.'

a. But there are a number of present participles which have assumed the value and character of adjectives, and admit of predicative use: for example, reizend, 'charming,' hinreißend, 'ravishing,' bedeutend, 'important.'

b. Such constructions as our *he is loving*, *they were going*, though not unknown in ancient German, are no longer in use.

354. The past participle (except of an intransitive having haben as auxiliary: see **351**.2) is commonly employed both attributively and predicatively, and may be used as a substantive, like any other adjective.

Thus, die verlorene Zeit, 'the lost time;' in ewig wiederholter Gestalt, 'in ever repeated form;' gebt den Gefangenen ledig, 'set free the prisoner (imprisoned one).'

355. Both participles admit of comparison, or form a comparative and superlative degree, only so far as they lay aside the special character of participles, and become adjectives.

Thus, bedeutendere Summen, 'more important sums;' das erhabenste Bild, 'the most majestic image.'

356. As adverbs they are used rather sparingly, except those which have assumed the value of adjectives.

Thus, ausgezeichnet gelehrt, 'exceedingly learned;' siedend heiß, 'boiling hot;' entzückend oft, 'ravishingly often;' ihre gesenkt schlummernden Blätter, 'their droopedly slumbering leaves.'

357. Both participles are, especially in higher styles of composition, very commonly used appositively (**110**.1*b*), either alone, or with limiting adjuncts such as are taken by the personal forms of the verb.

Thus, der Alte sah kopfschüttelnd nieder, 'the old man looked down, shaking his head;' schlafend hatte sie mir so gefallen, 'she had so pleased me sleeping;' herrliche Gaben bescherend erscheinen sie, 'bestowing splendid gifts, they appear;' dem Beispiele folgend, empfingen diese jetzt das Kreuz, 'following the example, these now took the cross;' das Heer hatte, durch fruchtbare Gegenden vorausziehend, und reichlich mit Lebensmitteln versorgt, die Drau erreicht, 'the army, moving on through fruitful regions and abundantly supplied with provisions, had reached the Drave;' ich bin ein Freund von Geschichten, gut erzählt, 'I am fond of stories, well told;' noch lesen umflort die Augen die Inschrift nicht, 'my eyes, dimmed with grief, do not yet read the inscription;' ich kniete nieder, von Lieb' und Andacht ganz durchstrahlet, 'I kneeled down, quite irradiated with love and devotion;' vom Meißel beseelt, redet der fühlende Stein, 'animated by the chisel, the feeling stone speaks.'

a. Such a participle or participial phrase is used only in the sense of an adjective clause, and expresses ordinarily an accompanying circumstance, or describes a state or condition; it may not be used, as in English, to signify a determining cause, or otherwise adverbially: in such phrases as "not finding him, I went away," "walking uprightly, we walk surely," "having saluted him, we retired," full adverbial clauses must be substituted for the participial phrases: thus, da ich ihn nicht fand; — wenn wir aufrichtig wandeln; — nachdem wir ihn begrüßt hatten.

b. Rarely, however, the participle approaches a causative force: thus, dies befürchtend, tödtete er den Beauftragten, 'fearing this, he slew the messenger.' Compare also **431.***d.*

358. The participial clause follows the same rule of arrangement as the infinitive clause (**348**.2,3)—namely, the participle regularly and usually stands last, being preceded by all that limits it or is dependent on it.

This rule is without exception, when the participle is used attributively (compare **147**.2); in the appositive clause, the participle not very rarely stands first: thus, der dritte, mit den frohesten Hoffnungen begonnene, mit seltener Klugheit geführte Kreuzzug, 'the third crusade, begun with the gladdest hopes, conducted with rare prudence:'—in den Ideen der französischen Umwälzung erwachsen, rein gehalten von ihren Verbrechen, begabt mit der Geistesstärke . . . , 'grown up in the ideas of the French revolution, kept free from its crimes, gifted with the strength of mind . . .' (R. 194. 8–12).

359. *Special Uses of Participles.* 1. The past participle is used in the sense of a present participle, after one or two verbs of motion, to express the mode of motion: thus, so kam häufig ein Hase angesprungen, 'a hare often came jumping along;' heulend kommt der Sturm geflogen, 'the howling storm comes flying.'

2. After a verb of calling, a past participle is occasionally used in an infinitive sense: thus, das heißt auch für die Zukunft gesorgt, 'that I call (is called) caring for the future also.'

3. By an elliptical construction, a past participle has sometimes the value of an imperative: thus, ins Feld, in die Freiheit gezogen, 'march forth (let there be marching) into the field, to freedom!' den Rappen gezäumt, '[have] the steed bridled!' See 230. 3*c*.

INDECLINABLES.

360. There are three classes of words not admitting inflection, or grammatical variation of form indicating change of relation to other words, and which are therefore called indeclinables or particles. These three are ADVERBS, PREPOSITIONS, and CONJUNCTIONS. They pass over into one another, to some extent, the same word having often more than one office.

a. Ja, 'yes,' and nein, 'no,' are particles which fall properly into no one of the classes mentioned, each being by itself a complete expression or intimation of a thought.

b. The indeclinables are, in great measure, traceably descended from declined words, being cases of nouns, adjectives, and pronouns; and the rest are with probability presumed to be of the same origin. See the author's "Language and the Study of Language," pp. 275–6.

ADVERBS.

361. Adverbs are words qualifying verbs and adjectives, as also other adverbs, and defining some mode or circumstance of the action or quality signified by those parts of speech.

In certain exceptional cases, adverbs qualify prepositions also: see **369.1.**

362. Adverbs may be classified according to their meaning as

1. Adverbs of manner and quality: as, blindlings, 'blindly,' treulich, 'faithfully,' vollends, 'completely,' anders, 'otherwise,' also, 'thus.'

2. Adverbs of measure and degree: as, beinahe, 'almost,' gänzlich, 'wholly,' kaum, 'scarcely,' zu, 'too,' sehr, 'very.'

3. Adverbs of place and motion: as, hier, 'here,' dort, 'yonder,' her, 'hither,' hin, 'hence,' empor, 'up,' rechts, 'to the right,' weg, 'away.'

4. Adverbs of time: as, dann, 'then,' einst, 'once,' oft, 'often, schon, 'already,' endlich, 'finally,' nie, 'never,' heute, 'to-day.'

5. Adverbs of modality; or such as limit not so much the thought itself as its relation to the speaker, or show the logical relation between one thought and another: thus, affirmative, fürwahr, 'assuredly,' allerdings, 'by all means;'—negative, nicht, 'not,' keineswegs, 'by no means;'—potential, vielleicht, 'perhaps,' wahrscheinlich, 'probably;'—causal, daher, 'therefore,' warum, 'for what reason.'

a. This last is a transition class between adverbs and conjunctions: see **385.**

b. These leading divisions may be very variously subdivided, nor are their own limits precise or absolute. The relations expressed by adverbs are almost as indefinitely various as those expressed by adjectives, and are in like manner incapable of distinct and exhaustive classification. Hence it is of equal or greater importance to note their various derivation, to which we next pass.

363. *Adverbs from Adjectives.*

1. Almost all adjectives in German admit of use also as adverbs, in their uninflected or thematic form (see **130**).

a. Exceptions are: the articles and pronominal and numeral adjectives (except erst); further, most participles having their proper participial meaning (356); and a few others, as arm, gram, wahr, from which derivative adverbs have been formed by means of endings (below, 3).

b. In an earlier condition of the language, the adjective when used as adverb had an ending of inflection. A relic of this ending is the e of lange, 'long' (adj. lang, 'long'), and that of gerne, ferne, sachte, stille, and a few others, which are now more commonly used without e.

2. Adjectives are thus used as adverbs both in the positive and the comparative degree; but only rarely in the superlative.

a. Superlatives that are employed as adverbs in their simple form are meist, längst, jüngst, nächst, höchst, äußerst, möglichst, innigst, freundlichst, herzlichst, gütigst, gefälligst, and a few others.

b. Instead of the simple adjective, is commonly used in the superlative an adverbial phrase, composed of the adjective with preceding definite article and governed by a preposition, an or auf; more rarely, in or zu (compare the similar treatment of the superlative as predicate, **140**.2*b*).

Thus, was am meisten in die Augen fiel, 'what most struck the eye;' das Pferd, das sich gestern am schlechtesten gehalten, 'the horse that behaved worst yesterday;'—man muß sie aufs beste erziehen, 'one must bring them up in the best possible manner;' er bot durch Gesandte aufs höflichste an, 'he offered most courteously through ambassadors;'—Herren nicht im mind'sten eitel, 'gentlemen not in the least vain;'—da traf er zum ersten Thrym, 'then he smote Thrym first (for the first).'

c. Of the phrases formed with am and aufs, respectively, the former are used when there is direct comparison made, and eminence of degree above others is signified (superlative relative); the latter, when general eminence of degree, without comparison, is intended (superlative absolute: compare **142**.1): im and zum are used with certain adjectives, in special phrases.

d. Many superlatives form a derivative adverb with the ending ens: see below, 3*c*.

3. A comparatively small number of adverbs are formed from adjectives by means of derivative endings:

a. Lich forms a number of derivative adjectives from adjectives, nouns, and participles; and of these a few (fifteen or twenty) are used only with adverbial meaning: examples are freilich, neulich, schwerlich, sicherlich, treulich, wahrlich, folglich, hoffentlich.

Lich is by origin the same with our *ly*, which was also at first exclusively an adjective suffix, and the same word with the adjective *like*: our use of it as distinctive adverbial suffix is only recent: see the author's "Language and the Study of Language," pp. 58-60.

b. Six or eight adverbs are formed from adjectives (or nouns) by the ending lings: thus, blindlings, 'blindly;' schrittlings, 'step by step.' The s of this suffix is a genitive ending.

c. The suffix ens forms adverbs from many superlatives, and from all the ordinal adjectives: thus, bestens, 'in the best manner;' erstens, 'firstly,' zehntens, 'tenthly;'—also from übrig, übrigens, 'moreover.'

The en of this suffix is an ending of adjective declension, to which a genitive s has become farther attached, irregularly.

d. The simple genitive ending s forms adverbs from a small number of adjectives and participles: thus, links, 'on the left;' bereits, 'already;' anders, 'otherwise;' eilends, 'hastily;' vergebens, 'vainly;' zusehends, 'visibly;'—vollends, 'completely,' is a corruption of vollens.

e. A few other derivatives are too irregular and isolated to require notice here.

364. *Adverbs from Nouns.*

1. Besides the few adverbs formed from nouns by the suffixes lich and lings (above, **363**.3*a*,*b*), there is also a small number formed by the simple genitive ending s, as anfangs, 'in the beginning,' flugs, 'in haste,' theils, 'in part,' nachts, 'in the night.'

With these are to be compared the adverbial genitives of nouns, either without or with a limiting word, noticed at **220**.1.

2. A considerable number of adverbs of direction are formed from nouns and prepositions by the suffix wärts (by origin, the genitive case of an adjective wärt, 'turned, directed'): thus, aufwärts, 'upward;' ostwärts, 'eastward;' himmelwärts, 'heavenward.'

365. *Adverbs by combination.*

1. Combinations of a noun and a limiting word (article, adjective, pronominal adjective—even adverb), which, from being adverbial phrases, have become fused together into one word.

a. Such are of every oblique case, most often genitives, least often datives, but not infrequently with irregular endings or inserted letters.

Examples are größtentheils, 'mostly,' keineswegs, 'in no wise,' dergestalt, 'in such wise,' allenthalben, 'everywhere,' allezeit, 'always,' jedenfalls, 'in any event,' einmal, 'once,' vielmals, 'often,' abermals, 'again.'

b. Certain nouns are thus used with especial frequency, forming classes of compound adverbs: such are Ding, Fall, Halbe, Mal, Maß, Seite, Theil, Weg, Weile, Weise.

2. Combinations of a preposition with a following or preceding noun, or with a following adjective. These are also fused adverbial phrases.

Examples are unterwegs, 'on the way,' abhanden, 'out of reach,' zuweilen, 'sometimes,' überhaupt, 'in general,' indessen, 'meanwhile;'— bergab, 'down hill;' stromauf, 'up stream;'— zuerst, 'at first,' fürwahr, 'verily.'

3. Combinations of adverbs with adverbs or prepositions—more proper compounds. These are very numerous, and various in kind: one or two classes require to be especially noticed:

a. Combinations with the words of general direction or motion, such as are also used as compound prefixes to verbs; see **298**.2.

b. Combinations of prepositions with the adverbs da or dar, wo or wor, and hie or hier, used commonly as equivalents for the cases of pronouns governed by those prepositions (see **154**.2,3; **166**.4; **173**.2; **180**), with a demonstrative, an interrogative, or a relative value.

366. *Adverbs of obscure derivation.*

Many adverbs which appear like simple words are traceable to combinations analogous with those explained above.

Examples are zwar, 'to be sure' (*zi wâre*, 'in truth'), nur, 'only' (*ni wâre*, 'were it not'), sonst, 'else' (*so ne ist*, 'so it be not'), heute, 'to-day' (*hiû tagû*, 'on this day'), nie, 'never' (*ne ie*, 'not ever'), nimmer, 'never' (nie mehr, 'never more'), nicht, 'not' (*ne-wiht*, 'no aught').

367. *Original Adverbs.*

Besides the classes already treated of, there remain a number of adverbs which, though in part demonstrably forms of inflection of pronominal and other words, may be practically regarded as original. The most important classes of these are

1. The simple adverbs of place or direction, ab, an, auf, aus, bei, durch, in or ein, ob, um, vor, zu; —these are all of them commonly employed as prepositions, but retain their adverbial value especially as prefixes to verbs (**298**.1).

2. Derivatives from pronominal roots: thus,

a. from the demonstrative root (in der) — da, dar, dann, denn, **dort**, desto, doch.

b. from the interrogative root (in wer) — wie, wo, wenn, wann.

c. from an obsolete demonstrative root *hi* — hie, hier, her, hin, hinter

3. Farther derivatives from these classes, with adverbial or prepositional meaning: thus, from in, inne and innen; from ob, ober and oben, über and üben; from dann, wann, and hin, dannen, wannen, and hinnen; and so on.

a. In several cases, forms in er and en stand related to one another as corresponding preposition and adverb; thus, über and üben, hinter and hinten, außer and außen, unter and unten.

368. *Comparison of Adverbs.*

Adverbs, as such, do not generally admit of comparison: comparative and superlative adverbs, so-called, are for the most part comparative and superlative adjectives used adverbially.

a. Only oft, 'often,' forms öfter and öftest; and ehe (itself used only as conjunction, 'ere,' or, in a few compounds, as ehedem, with prepositional force) forms eher and am ehesten.

b. A few words now used only as adverbs have corresponding forms of comparison from other words, adjectives: for example, gern, 'willingly,' has lieber, am liebsten, from lieb, 'dear.'

c Adverbs whose meaning calls for such treatment may, rarely, form a kind of degrees of comparison with mehr, 'more,' and am meisten, 'most,' or other qualifying adverbs of similar meaning: thus, mehr rechts, 'more to the right;' am meisten vorwärts, 'farthest forward.'

369. *Certain special uses of Adverbs.*

1. Some adverbs qualify prepositions—or, rather, prepositional phrases of adverbial meaning: thus, m i t t e n um den Leib, 'midway about the body;' daß er bestände bis auf's Blut, bis .n den Tod die Fehde, 'that he might maintain his quarrel even to blood, even unto death.'

2. Adverbs are not seldom governed by prepositions: see below, **378.**

3. Adverbs are used elliptically with the value of adjectives: thus, dieser Mann hier, 'this man here;' Gräber und die Cypressen dran, 'graves and the cypresses thereon;'—or, in predicative relations, nun war der Abend vorbei, 'now the evening was past;' die Jahre sind noch nicht um, 'the years are not yet over;' alles soll anders sein und geschmackvoll, everything is to be otherwise, and tasty;' ist kein Mörder mehr unterweges, 'is there no longer a murderer on the way?' aller Wetteifer wird vergebens, 'all emulation becomes futile;' ich sah Nebel weit umher, 'I saw mist far about.'

4. An adverb is often added after a preposition and its object, to complete or to make more distinct the relation expressed by the preposition: see below, **379.**

370. *Place of Adverbs.*

1. An adverb precedes the adjective or adverb which it qualifies.

a. Except genug, 'enough,' which, as in English, follows the word it limits.

2. An adverb qualifying a personal verb is put after it in the regular arrangement of the sentence: one qualifying an infinitive or participle is placed before it.

As to the place of the adverb in relation to other adjuncts of the verb, see **319**; as to certain adverbial words which have exceptional freedom of position, see **385.4.**

PREPOSITIONS.

371. A preposition is a word used to define the relation between some person or thing and an action, a quality, or another person or thing with which it stands connected.

a. The distinctive characteristic of a preposition is that it governs an oblique case of a noun (or of the equivalent of a noun); and by this it is separated from an adverb: it is a kind of *transitive adverb*, requiring an object in order to the completion of the idea which it signifies. Many words are either adverbs or prepositions, according as they are used without or with such object.

b. The oldest prepositions were originally adverbs, and the various mode of relation of a noun to the action or quality which they aided to define was expressed by means of a more complete scheme of cases: the reduction of this scheme (in German, from six oblique cases to three: see the author's "Language and the Study of Language," pp. 271–2, 276), and the conversion of adverbs to prepositions, are parallel processes of change in the history of our language. In the German, as a fuller system of declension is still preserved, a host of relations are signified by the use of cases alone where we require prepositions in English.

c. Many of the German prepositions are of late formation from nouns or adjectives, or from adverbial phrases containing such. Some examples of these will be noted below.

372. Prepositions are most conveniently classified according to the case they govern, as the genitive, the dative, the accusative, and the dative or accusative.

a. A few govern either the dative or genitive, but their difference of use in this respect is not of consequence enough to found a class upon.

b. Since what determines the relation is originally the case of the noun, prepositions ought to be followed by cases according to the kind of relation they signify—thus, those that denote motion *toward* or *to* should take the accusative; those that mean *for* (original *dative*), *with* or *by* (original *instrumental*), and *in* or *at* (original *locative*), should take the dative; those that mean *of*, *from*, and the like (original *genitive* and *ablative*) should take the genitive—and those prepositions that denote different relations should be followed by different cases to correspond. This latter is to a certain extent still the case (see **376**.*c*): but, on the one hand, the relations of each ancient case now lost have not been assigned in bulk to one of those yet remaining; and, on the other hand, many prepositions which have undergone a great change of meaning continue to take the case by which they were originally followed: for example, nach, which is historically the same word with nah, 'nigh to,' governs the dative, the case regularly following nah, though itself used in the sense of 'after' and of 'toward, to.'

373. Prepositions governing the genitive are anstatt or statt, 'instead of,' halber or halben, 'for the sake of'—with the compounds of halb, namely außerhalb, 'without, outside,' innerhalb, 'within,' oberhalb, 'above,' unterhalb, 'below'—kraft, 'in virtue of,' längs, 'along,' laut, 'according to,' trotz, 'in spite of,' um . . . willen, 'on account of,' ungeachtet (or ohngeachtet), 'notwithstanding,' unfern and unweit, 'not far from,' mittels or mittelst or vermittelst, 'by means of,' vermöge, 'by dint of,' während, 'during,' wegen, 'on account of,' zufolge, 'in consequence of,' and the compounds of seit, diesseit or diesseits, 'on this side of,' and jenseit or jenseits, 'on the further side of, beyond.'

Thus, statt der goldnen Lieder, 'instead of the golden songs;' um dieser fremden Zeugen willen, 'on account of these stranger witnesses;' Genugthuung wegen der getödteten Christen, 'satisfaction on account of the slain Christians;' jenseit des Forstes, 'beyond the forest.'

a. Of these prepositions, längs, trotz, and zufolge also not infrequently govern the dative; some others do so occasionally.

b. Halben or halber always follows the noun it governs; um . . . willen takes the noun between its two parts; ungeachtet, wegen, and zufolge may either precede or follow (zufolge precedes a genitive, but follows a dative).

c. These prepositions are of recent use as such, and all evidently derived from other parts of speech. Halb is a noun meaning originally 'side:' wegen was formerly von wegen, which is still in occasional use.

d. The adverbial genitives Angesichts, 'in presence,' and Behufs, 'in behalf,' the adverbs inmitten, 'in the midst,' abseits, 'aside,' and some of those formed with wärts, as seitwärts, 'sideways,' nordwärts, 'northwards, also entlang, 'along,' and a few others, antiquated or of rare occurrence. are sometimes used prepositionally with a genitive.

374. The prepositions governing the dative are, of more ancient and original words, aus, 'out,' bei, 'by,' mit, 'with,' ob, 'above, for,' von, 'of,' zu, 'to;' of recent and derivative or compound words, nach, 'after, to,' seit, 'since,' gleich, 'like,' sammt and nebst, 'along with,' nächst, 'next,' binnen, 'within,' außer, 'outside,' entgegen, 'against,' gegenüber, 'opposite,' gemäß, 'in accordance with,' zuwider, 'contrary to.'

a. For prepositions which more regularly and usually govern the genitive, but are sometimes construed with a dative, see above, **373.***a.* Of those here mentioned, ob (which is now antiquated), when meaning 'on account of,' is occasionally used with a genitive: außer governs a genitive in the single phrase außer Landes, 'out of the country.'

b. Nach, gleich, and gemäß either precede or follow the governed noun: thus, nach der Stadt, 'to the city;' der Natur nach, 'according to nature;' gemäß den Urgeschichten, 'according to the old stories;' der Zeit und den Umständen gemäß, 'in accordance with the time and the circumstances;' sie zieht sich gleich einem Meeresarme hin, 'it stretches along, after the manner of an arm of the sea;' sie flog, einer Sylphide gleich, 'she flew like a sylph.'—Entgegen, gegenüber, and zuwider follow the noun; but gegenüber is sometimes (by a usage no longer approved) divided, and takes the noun between its two parts: thus, zwei Damen sitzen gegen einander über, 'two ladies sit opposite one another.'

c. Occasionally, by a bold construction, a word which is properly adverb only is construed as if preposition: thus, voran den kühnen Reihen, 'in front of the brave ranks:' compare **373.***d.*

375. The prepositions governing the accusative only are durch, 'through,' für, 'for,' gegen or gen, 'against,' ohne, 'without,' um, 'about,' wider, 'against;' also sonder, 'without,' bis, 'unto, till.'

a. Gen is now nearly out of use, except in certain phrases, like gen Himmel, 'toward heaven,' gen Westen, 'toward the west.' Sonder is hardly employed except in a phrase or two, as sonder gleichen, 'without equal.' Bis usually stands adverbially before a preposition (see **369.**1), but also governs directly specifications of place and time: thus, bis Antiochien, 'as far as Antioch;' warte nur bis morgen, 'only wait till tomorrow.'

b. Um is very often followed by her after the noun: see **379.***a.*

c. From the case of an accusative governed by a preposition requires to be distinguished that of an absolute accusative of place followed by an adverb of direction, as den Berg hinauf, 'up the mountain' (see **230.**1*b*). This construction is interesting as illustrating an intermediate step in the process of conversion of adverbs into prepositions.

376. Nine prepositions govern sometimes the dative and sometimes the accusative—the dative, when they indicate locality or situation merely, or answer the question "where?" the accusative, when they imply motion or tendency toward, or answer the question "whither?" They are an, 'on, at,' auf, 'upon,' hinter, 'behind,' in, 'in, into,' neben, 'beside,' über, 'above, across,' unter, 'under,' vor, 'before,' zwischen, 'between.'

Thus, ich halte an den Schranken, und reiche den Helm an einen Knappen zurück, 'I stop at the barrier, and hand back my helmet to a squire;' er lag auf der Erde, und hatte das Ohr auf den Rasen gelegt, 'he lay on the ground, and had his ear laid on the turf;' sie brüten hinter dem Ofen, 'they brood behind the stove;' er legte sich hinter eine Tabacksdose, 'he laid himself behind a snuff-box;' er ging ins Haus, und blieb lange in demselben, 'he went into the house, and staid a long time in it;' dort liegt er neben einem Stein, 'there it lies, beside a stone;' sie setzten sich neben den Baum, 'they seated themselves beside the tree;' der Rachen schließt sich über dem Schwimmer, 'the abyss closes over the swimmer;' über diesen Strom bin ich einmal gefahren, 'I once crossed over this stream;' der Kahn trieb unter eine Brücke; unter dieser Brücke wohnte eine Ratte; 'the boat drove underneath a bridge; under this bridge lived a rat;' im Augenblick waren sie vor dem Felsen, 'in a moment they were before the rock;' er trat vor die Königin, 'he came before the queen;' das Gestrickte ruhte zwischen ihren Händen, 'the knitting-work lay between her hands;' sie schlüpften zwischen seine Zweige, 'they slipped in among its branches.'

a. The difference of meaning determining the use of the dative or accusative after these prepositions is not always an obvious one; sometimes a peculiar liveliness is given to an expression by the employment of the accusative: thus, er machte eine Oeffnung in die Erde, 'he made a hole in (into) the ground;' und küßte sie an den Mund, 'and kissed her on the mouth (impressed a kiss);' über den Rand der Tiefe gebogen, 'arched over (thrown as arch across) the edge of the abyss;'—or, the accusative implies a verb of motion which is not expressed: thus, er stieg in ein Wirthshaus ab, 'he got down (and entered) into an inn;' er rettete sich in die Burg, 'he saved himself (betook himself for safety) into the castle;' sie stehen in die Höhe, 'they stand up (rise to a standing posture);'—or, the action is a figurative one: thus, an ihn denken, 'think of him (turn one's thoughts on him);' er sah auf all die Pracht, 'he looked upon all the beauty;' sie freueten sich über die schönen Aepfel, 'they were delighted with the beautiful apples;'—or there are phrases, the implication of which seems arbitrarily determined: thus, auf die beste Weise, 'in the best manner;' über tausend Jahre, 'after a thousand years.'

b. It is only by its use of *in* and *into* (as also, in colloquial phrase, of *on* and *onto*), that the English makes a corresponding distinction; and even this does not agree in all particulars with the German distinction of in with the dative and with the accusative. Hence the ground of the difference of case is the less easily appreciated by us, and needs to be carefully noted at every instance that occurs.

c. The accusative and dative with these prepositions have each its own proper value, the one as the case of directest action, the other as representing the ancient locative (or case denoting the *in* relation).

377. 1. Some prepositions govern a substantive clause, introduced usually by daß, rarely by a compound relative (**179**): such are auf, außer, bis, ohne, statt or anstatt, um, ungeachtet, während: thus, auf daß es dir wohl gehe, 'in order that it may go well with thee;' außer wer seine Mitschuldigen seien, 'except who were his accomplices.'

a. This is closely akin with the office of a conjunction; and bis, ungeachtet, and während may be used without daß, as proper conjunctions: thus, während wir da blieben, 'while we continued there' (compare **439.**5*c*).

2. The prepositions um, ohne, and statt or anstatt may govern an infinitive and its adjuncts, as equivalent of a complete clause (compare **346.**1)

378. An adverb not infrequently takes the place of a noun as object of a preposition. Thus,

a. Many adverbs of time and place: as, nach oben, 'upward (toward above);' auf immer, 'for ever;' für jetzt, 'for now;' von fern, 'from afar: in wie fern, 'how far.'

b. The adverbs da or dar, wo or wor, and hier or hie, as substitutes for the oblique cases of pronouns. These are compounded with the governing preposition, forming a kind of compound adverb (see **365.**3*b*).

379. 1. After the noun governed by a preposition is often added an adverb, to emphasize, or to define more nearly, the relation expressed by the preposition. Thus,

a. The general adverbs of direction, hin and her: as, um uns her, um ihn her, 'round about us or him;' hinter ihm her, 'along after him;' nach einer Richtung hin, 'in a single direction;' über das Meer hin, 'across the sea;' von allen Seiten her, 'from all sides.'

In these combinations, the distinctive meaning of the adverb, as denoting motion *from* and *toward*, is apt to be effaced. Um . . . her is the commonest case, and a stereotyped expression for 'round about.'

b. The same adverbs, in combination with the preposition itself repeated: thus, um mich herum, 'round about me;' in den Forst hinein, 'into the forest;' aus dem Walde hinaus, 'out of the wood;' aus der Brust heraus, 'forth from the breast;' durch Gefahren hindurch, 'through dangers.'

c. Other adverbs of direction, simple or compound, often adding an essential complement to the meaning of the preposition: thus, von nun an, 'from now on;' von dort aus, 'forth from there;' von Jugend auf, 'from youth up;' nach der Mitte zu, 'toward the middle;' sie gingen auf ihn zu, 'they fell upon him;' er hört die Feinde hinter sich drein, 'he hears the enemy [coming on] after him;' hinter Bäumen hervor, 'forth from behind trees;' zur Kammer hinein, 'into the room;' zum Thore hinaus, 'out at the gate.'

2. It may sometimes be made a question whether the adverb of direction belongs to the prepositional phrase, or, rather, to the verb of the clause, as its prefix: the two cases pass into one another.

380. To what members of the sentence a prepositional phrase forms an adjunct has been pointed out already: namely,

1. To a verb, with very various value: see **318.**

2. To a noun: see **112.**

3. To an adjective: see **146**.

4. Hence, also, to an adverb, when an adjective is used as such

381. 1. The rules for the position of a preposition, whether before or after the noun that it governs, have been given above, in connection with the rules for government.

2. Between the preposition and its following governed noun may intervene the various limiting words which are wont to stand before a noun—as articles, adjective pronouns, adjectives and participles, with their adjuncts—often to an extent discordant with English usage: thus, aus kleinen, viereckig zugehauenen, ziemlich gleichen Basaltstücken, 'of small, squarely hewn, tolerably equal pieces of basalt;' für dem Kranken geleistete Hülfe, 'for help rendered to the sick man.'

Respecting the combination of the preposition with a following definite article into a single word, see **65**.

CONJUNCTIONS.

382. Conjunctions are words which connect the clauses or sentences composing a period or paragraph, and show their relation to one another.

a. We have hitherto had to do only with the elements which enter into the structure of individual clauses, and among which conjunctions play no part. When, however, clauses themselves are to be put in connection with one another, conjunctions are required.

b. If certain conjunctions—especially those meaning 'and' and 'or'—appear to connect words as well as clauses, it is as such words represent clauses, and may be expanded into them: thus, er und ich waren da — er war da, und ich war da, 'he was there and I was there;' er ist mächtiger als ich [bin], 'he is mightier than I [am].'

c. Conjunctions, as a class, are the words of latest development in the history of language, coming from other parts of speech, mainly through the medium of adverbial use. A word ceases to be an adverb and becomes a conjunction, when its qualifying influence extends over a whole clause instead of being limited to a particular word in it. Almost all conjunctions in German are also adverbs (or prepositions), and their uses as the one or the other part of speech shade off into one another.

383. Conjunctions are most conveniently classified according to the character of the relations they indicate, and their effect upon the arrangement of the clauses they introduce, as

1. *General connectives*, which do not alter the arrangement of the clause.

2. *Adverbial conjunctions*, causing the inversion of a clause (that is to say, causing its subject to follow, instead of preceding the verb).

3. *Subordinating conjunctions*, which make the clause dependent, and give it the transposed order (removing the verb to the end).

The first two classes, in contradistinction from the third, may be called *co-ordinating conjunctions.*

384. The general connectives are those signifying 'and,' 'but,' 'for,' and 'or' and 'either.'

Namely, und, 'and;'—aber, allein, sondern (and sometimes doch), 'but;' —denn, 'for;'—entweder, 'either,' and oder, 'or.'

a. Of the words meaning 'but,' sondern is more strongly adversative than aber, being used only after a negative, and introducing some word which has a like construction with the one on which the force of the negation falls, and which is placed in direct antithesis with it: thus, weil nicht eigene Macht, sondern Gott, die Könige errettet, 'because not their own might, but God, saves kings;' er genoß nicht lange seines Ruhms, sondern ward bezwungen, 'he did not long enjoy his fame, but was subdued;' mein Retter war kein Mann, sondern ein Bach, 'my preserver was no man, but a brook;'—the combination nicht nur (or bloß) . . . sondern auch, 'not only . . . but also,' is likewise common: thus, nicht bloß jene sündigten, sondern auch wir, 'not they alone have sinned, but also we.' Allein means literally 'only,' and is often best so rendered, being more restricted than aber to the introduction of a definite objection. For doch as 'but,' see below, **385.5c.**

b. These connectives stand always at the head of the clause whose connection they indicate; except aber, which has great freedom of position, and may be introduced at any later point—without any notable difference of meaning, although often to be conveniently rendered by 'however.'

385. 1. The adverbial conjunctions are originally and strictly adverbs, qualifying the verb of the clause which they introduce; and, like any other of the adjuncts of the verb (**431**), when placed at the head of the clause, they give it the *inverted* order, putting the subject after the verb.

2. No distinct boundary separates the conjunctional use of these words from their adverbial use: they are conjunctions when their effect is to determine the relations of clauses to one another, rather than to limit the action of a verb—and these two offices pass insensibly into each other.

3. They may be simply classified as

a. Copulative (related to the general connective 'and'), uniting different phrases with no other implication than that of continuation, order, or division: as, auch, 'also,' außerdem, 'besides,' dann, 'then,' ferner, 'further,' erstens, zweitens, drittens, 'firstly, secondly, thirdly,' and so on, schließlich, 'finally,' weder . . . noch, 'neither . . . nor,' theils . . . theils, 'partly . . partly,' bald . . . bald, 'now . . . now.'

b. Adversative (related to 'but'), implying more or less distinctly an opposition of idea, a denial or restriction: as, doch, jedoch, dennoch, 'yet, though,' gleichwohl, dessenungeachtet, 'nevertheless;' dagegen hingegen, 'on the contrary,' indessen, 'however,' vielmehr, 'rather,' zwar, 'to be sure, wohl, 'indeed.'

c. *Causative* (related to 'for'), implying a ground, reason, or occasion. as, daher, deswegen, deshalb, 'therefore,' also, 'accordingly,' folglich, mithin, 'consequently.'

d. Adverbs of *place* and *time*, particularly the latter, sometimes assume a conjunctional value: as, unterdessen, 'meanwhile,' vorher, 'previously,' darauf, 'thereupon.'

4. Although these words in their conjunctional office tend toward the head of the clause, they do not always take that place; nor are they always conjunctions rather than adverbs when they introduce the clause. Especially nämlich, 'namely,' and some of the adversative and causative conjunctions—as doch, jedoch, indessen, zwar, wohl, also —have a freedom of position like that of aber (**384**.*b*).

5. The clause sometimes maintains its normal order, instead of being inverted, after conjunctions of this class; especially

a. When the emphasis of the clause, or of the antithesis in two correlative clauses, rests on the subject, so that the conjunction becomes a kind of adjunct of the subject: thus, auch dein Bruder hat es gewünscht, 'thy brother also has wished it;' weder er, noch ich waren da, 'neither he nor I were there.'

b. When the conjunction represents a clause which is not fully expressed, or is thrown in, as it were parenthetically. Conjunctions most often so treated are zwar, überdieß, folglich, zudem, hingegen, and ordinals, as erstens, zweitens.

c. Doch sometimes has its adversative force weakened to a mere 'but,' and leaves the order of the clause unchanged, like the other words that have that meaning (**384**).

386. **1.** The subordinating conjunctions are such as give to the clause which they introduce a dependent (subordinate, accessory) value, making it enter, in the relation of substantive, adjective, or adverb, into the structure of some other clause. Such a dependent clause assumes the *transposed* order—that is to say, its personal verb is removed to the end of the clause (see **434** etc.).

2. The conjunctions that introduce a *substantive dependent clause* are daß, 'that,' ob, 'whether,' and those that have a compound relative value, namely wie, 'how,' wann, 'when,' wo, 'where,' and the compounds of wo, whether with adverbs of direction, as wohin, 'whither,' woher, 'whence,' or with prepositions, as representing cases of the compound relative pronoun wer (**180**), as wovon, 'whereof,' womit, 'wherewith.'

Thus, ich weiß, daß er hier war; ob er noch hier bleibt, ist mir unbekannt; fragen Sie nur nach, wohin er sich begeben hat, 'I know that he was here; whether he still remains here is unknown to me; only inquire whither he has betaken himself.'

3. The conjunctions that introduce an *adjective dependent clause* are

chiefly those made up of prepositions, with the adverbs da and wo, representing cases of the simple relative pronouns der and welcher (180), or of words of direction with the same adverbs. The simple conjunctions wo, wenn, wann, da, als, wie, following specifications of place, time, or manner, also sometimes perform the same office.

Thus, das Bett, worauf er lag, 'the bed on which he lay;' ihr Quellen, dahin die welke Brust sich drängt, 'ye fountains toward which the drooping breast presses;' das Land, wo die Citronen blühn, 'the land where the lemons blossom;' die Art, wie man den Krieg führt, 'the way in which the war is carried on.'

4. The conjunctions that introduce an *adverbial dependent clause* are of very various derivation, character, and meaning: namely,

a. Conjunctions indicating *place:* as, wo, da, 'where.'

b. Time: as, da, als, wenn, wie, wo, 'when,' indem, indessen or indeß, weil, während, 'while,' nachdem, 'after,' seitdem, 'since,' bis, 'until,' ehe, bevor, 'before.'

c. Manner: as, wie, 'as.'

d. Cause: as, weil, dieweil, 'because,' da, 'since,' nun, 'now that,' daß, that.'

e. Purpose: as, damit, daß, auf daß, um daß, 'in order that.'

f. Condition: as, wenn, 'if,' so, wo, wofern, dafern, falls, 'in case,' indem, 'while;'—and, with implication of objection, ungeachtet, obgleich, obwohl, obschon, ob zwar, ob auch, wenngleich, wennschon, wenn auch, wiewohl, 'although.'

The compounds of ob and wenn with gleich, wohl, and schon, meaning 'although,' are often separated by intervening words.

g. Degree: as, wie, 'as,' je, 'according as,' als, denn, 'than.'

h. Besides these, there are numerous conjunctional phrases, of kindred value, composed of conjunctions and other particles: as, als ob, 'as if,' in wie fern, 'so far as,' je nachdem, 'according as,' so bald, 'as soon as,' so lang, 'so long as,' etc.

i. So, especially, with following adverb, forms (as in the last two examples) a great number of conjunctional phrases or compounds, after which the conjunction als, 'as,' is sometimes expressed, but more often implied: thus, so lang als es nur möglich ist, or so lang es nur möglich ist, 'so long *as* it is in any way possible' (compare 438.3*d*).

5. Few of these words are exclusively conjunctions: many are adverbs also, or prepositions, or both; some, as während, ungeachtet, are participial forms; some, as falls, weil, are cases of nouns; many are combined phrases composed of a preposition and a governed case; as indem, nachdem, seitdem.

INTERJECTIONS.

387. The interjections have a character of their own, separate from the other parts of speech, in that they do not enter as elements into the structure of sentences or periods, but are independent outbursts of feeling, or intimations of will, the uttered equivalents of a tone, a grimace, or a gesture.

388. Nevertheless, they are not purely natural exclamations, but utterances akin with such, which are now assigned by usage to the expression of certain states of mind or will.

389. The interjections most commonly used are

1. Of those expressing feeling—o or oh, used in a great variety of meanings; ach, weh, expressing painful or disagreeable surprise or grief; pfui, fi, bah, expressing disgust or contempt; ei, joyful surprise; ha, ah, wonder, pleasure, and the like; heisa, juchhe, exultation; hem, hm, doubt, hesitation; hu, horror, shuddering.

2. Of those intimating will or desire—he, heda, holla, to call attention; pst, the same, or to command silence; husch, to command silence; topp, to signify the closing of a bargain.

3. Here may be best classed, also, the various imitations of the cries of animals and other natural sounds, directions and callwords for animals, and the more or less artificially composed and unintelligent words which are used as burdens of songs and the like: as, hopsasa, vivallera, tumtedum.

390. As, on the one hand, the interjections are employed with a degree of conventionality, like the other constituents of language, so, on the other hand, many words that are proper parts of speech are very commonly used in an exclamatory way, quite as if they were interjections. Such are heil, 'hail!' gottlob, 'praise God!' bewahr, 'God forbid!' fort, weg, 'away!' sieh, 'behold,' brav, 'well done!' etc.; and the whole series of oaths and adjurations.

a. The ordinary equivalent of our *alas*, leider, is an abbreviation of the phrase was mir noch l e i d e r ist, 'what is yet more painful to me' (or something equivalent to this), and is capable of being introduced, parenthetically, at almost any point in the phrase—even, when put first, sometimes causing inversion, like an adverb.

391. The exclamatory or interjectional mode of expression prevails to no small extent in the practical use of language, when emotion or eagerness causes the usual set framework of the sentence, the verb and its subject, to be thrown aside, and only the emphatic elements to be presented at all.

Thus, euch zur Erbin erklären! der verrätherische Fallstrick, 'declare you my heiress! the treacherous snare!' flieh'! auf! hinaus ins weite Land! 'flee! up! out into the wide country!' ich versteh' dich; weiter! 'I understand you: further!'

The grammatical forms most frequently thus used are the nominative of address (or "vocative:" **214**), and the imperative.

392. Some of the interjections are also brought into a kind of connection with the structure of the sentence, being followed by cases, or phrases, such as would suit a more complete expression of the feeling they intimate.

Thus, o, ach, pfui may stand before a genitive expressing the occasion of the exclamation: as in o des Thoren! pfui der Schande! 'oh the fool! fie on the shame!'—some may take a prepositional phrase or a substantive clause after them: as, ach daß du da liegst, 'alas that thou liest there!' pfui über den Feigen, 'fie on the coward!'—and nouns used interjectionally often admit a dative object, signifying that toward which the feeling is directed: thus, Heil, o Frühling, deinem Schein, 'hail to thy brilliancy, oh Spring!' weh mir, daß ich dir vertraut, 'woe to me, that I have trusted thee!'

WORD-FORMATION, DERIVATION.

Introductory Explanations.

393. The etymological part of grammar, as thus far treated, deals with the character and uses of the *parts of speech*, and of their *grammatical* or *inflectional forms*, which are made from simple *themes* (stems, bases), chiefly by inflectional endings, but in part also by internal change.

Such grammatical forms (along with the indeclinable particles, which are ultimately derived from them) constitute the most essential part of the grammatical apparatus of a language, its instrumentality for the expression of relations of ideas, the means by which its names of beings, qualities, acts, etc., are placed in connection with one another, in order to express the thoughts of the speaker.

394. Another, and only less important part of the same grammatical apparatus is the array of means by which themes of declension and conjugation are formed from roots and from each other. These means are of the same character with those already described, consisting chiefly of suffixes, along with a few prefixes, and supplemented by methods of internal change.

395. There is no fundamental diversity between the two instrumentalities. The suffixes and prefixes of inflection and of derivation are equally, by origin, independent words, which were first uttered in connection with other words, then combined with the latter, and finally made to lose their independence and converted into subordinate elements, designating the relations of other more substantial and significant elements.

a. The working-out of grammatical apparatus, by the reduction of words once independent to the condition of endings of inflection or derivation, has been a part of the history of inflective languages, from their beginning down to modern times. Of many of the affixes formed in this way, as well as of some that are much more ancient, the origin can still be distinctly traced: but their history is to a great extent obscured by the effects of linguistic change and corruption. Compare what is said above of the derivation of the ending te, forming the preterits of the New conjugation (**246.**3) and of the suffixes lich, wärts, etc. (**363–4**); and see the author's "Language and the Study of Language," pp. 55 etc., 250 etc.

b. The difference between the two classes of endings lies in their mode of application, and in the frequency and regularity of their use. Certain suffixes of derivation are so regularly applied to whole classes of themes, and produce derivatives so analogous with forms of inflection, that they are conveniently and properly treated along with the subject of inflection Such are the endings er and est of comparatives and superlatives (**133** etc.), and those which form the infinitives and participles of verbs.

396. Among modern languages commonly studied, the German is the one which most fully and clearly illustrates the processes of word-formation; and the subject ought therefore to receive the attention of every advanced German scholar.

397. But no known language (not even such exceptional ones as the Sanskrit) has preserved so much of its primitive structure that we can carry back the analysis of its vocabulary to the actual beginning. By the help, especially, of a careful and searching comparison of related languages, the processes of word-combination can be traced up until we discover of what sort are the ultimate elements of speech, although we are by no means certain of being able to point them out in their very form and substance.

Principles.

398. The words of German, as of other related languages, are believed to come ultimately from certain monosyllabic ROOTS, which were not themselves distinct parts of speech, but material out of which were developed verbs, nouns (nouns adjective and nouns substantive), and pronouns; and, through these, the other parts of speech.

a. Because the roots of language are usually seen in their simplest form in verbs, we are accustomed to call them *verbal roots;* and we also ordinarily call the theme of verbal inflection a "root" (**237.**1*a*), yet without at all intending to imply that it is an original or ultimate root.

399. The means of derivation, through the whole history of development, have been chiefly suffixes or derivational endings—with some aid from prefixes.

a. The almost exclusive use of suffixes rather than prefixes, as means both of inflection and of derivation, is a characteristic feature of the family of languages to which the German (with our own) belongs. The few prefixes employed have retained much more distinctly the character of independent words, forming proper compounds with those to which they are attached: that character has been lost only by the inseparable prefixes (**307**) and one or two others (see below, **411**.II). The negative un is the only German prefix of really ancient character and obscure derivation.

400. Besides this, there have come in in German two other specific auxiliary methods of internal change, affecting the vowel of the root or primitive word. These are

1. The modification of vowel (**14**), or change of a, o, u, au into ä, ö, ü, äu, respectively: thus, Mann, Männer, 'man, men;' Fuß, Füße, 'foot, feet;' Maus, Mäuse, 'mouse, mice;' alt, älter, ältest, 'old, elder, eldest;' Korn, Körnlein, 'corn, kernel;' hange, hängt, 'I hang, he hangs;' flog, flöge, 'I flew, I might fly;' roth, röthen, 'red, redden.' This modification is by the Germans called Umlaut, 'change of sound.'

a. This is a euphonic change, coming from the assimilation of a hard or guttural vowel to a soft or palatal one (e, i) closely following it—although finally applied by analogy, in many single cases, where no such cause had been present. It is of comparatively recent introduction, although, as the examples show, shared in part by the English. It is quite unknown in one branch of Germanic speech, the Mœso-Gothic; and, on the other hand, most highly developed in the Scandinavian tongues.

b. In the present condition of the language, the cause of the modification is generally no longer to be seen, the assimilating vowel having been lost.

c. Some derivative words having vowels which are really the effect of modification are now, usually or always, written with the simple vowels e (for ä or ö) or i (for ü). Again, some words show a modified vowel as the mere result of an irregular variation of utterance, without etymological reason.

2. The variation of radical vowel: as in singen, sang, gesungen, 'sing, sang, sung;' werde, wird, ward, wurden, geworden, from werden, 'become; breche, bricht, brach, gebrochen, Bruch, from brechen, 'break.' This variation is by the Germans called Ablaut, 'divergence of sound.'

a. This second mode of vowel change is also, like the other, originally of euphonic character, one of the accidents attending the phonetic development of language, under the combined influences of quantity, accent, combination, addition of suffixes, and the like. But it is much more ancient, being one of the characteristic peculiarities of all the Germanic languages; and its specific causes and mode of evolution are in great part obscure.

b. The sphere of action of the variation of radical vowel is in the inflection of the older verbs of the language, and the formation of their earliest derivatives.

401. The modes of consonantal change which accompany the processes of word-formation are too various and irregular to be systematically set forth here. Some of them will be noticed below, in connection with the derivatives whose formation especially calls them out.

402. To carry back the historical analysis of German words to the farthest point attained by the aid of the languages kindred with the German would take the pupil into regions where he is a stranger, and would be unprofitable. Such study requires a knowledge of the older dialects, and belongs to a higher stage of progress. Only the processes of derivation whose results are traceable in the existing language will be set forth; and those words will be treated as "primitive" which have no German etymons, or more original words whence they are derived, even though evidence from other languages may not only show them to be derivatives, but also exhibit the earlier forms from which they came.

Derivation of Verbs.

403. *Primitive Verbs.* Verbs to be regarded as primitive are

1. The verbs of the Old conjugation, nearly two hundred in number (**264–7**), which constitute the most important body of primitive roots in the language.

a. Several verbs of this conjugation, however, are demonstrably derivative: thus, schreiben (III.2), 'write,' from Latin *scribo;* preisen (III.2), 'praise,' from Preis, 'value' (which comes from Lat. *pretium*), etc. Others are doubtless of the same character; since, down to that period in the history of the language at which the mode of inflection of the New conjugation was introduced, all verbs, whether recent or older, were inflected according to the Old conjugation.

2. Many verbs of the New conjugation: as, haben, 'have,' sagen, 'say,' reden, 'talk,' lieben, 'love,' leben, 'live.'

a. A number of the verbs of the New conjugation formerly belonged to the Old, having changed their mode of inflection under the influence of the tendency to extend a prevailing analogy and reduce more irregular to more regular forms. Others, if originally derivative, have lost the evidence of it. To the root of some there is a corresponding noun, and it may admit of question which is the more original, verb or noun.

b. All verbs whose root, or theme of conjugation, is of more than one syllable are to be classed as derivative: even though, as in the case of schmeicheln, 'flatter,' klettern, 'climb,' the original from which they come is no longer to be traced.

404. *Verbs derived from Verbs.*

I. By internal change of the root itself:

1. By change (generally, modification) of the root vowel, a class of *causative* verbs are formed, taking as their direct object what was the subject of the simple verb: thus, fallen, 'fall,' fällen, 'cause to fall, *fell;*' trinken, 'drink,' tränken, 'cause to drink,' *drench;*' sitzen, 'sit,' setzen, 'set;' liegen, 'lie,' legen, 'lay;' saugen, 'suck,' säugen, 'suckle:' fahren, 'go,' führen, 'lead.'

a. As some of the examples show, this class of derivatives has its representatives in English also, but they are much more numerous in German.

2. By change of the final consonant, with or without accompanying change of vowel, a few verbs are made, with various modification of the meaning of the simple verb: thus, stehen, 'stand,' stellen, 'place;' hangen, 'hang,' henken, 'execute by hanging;' biegen, 'bend, bücken, 'bow; neigen, 'incline,' nicken, 'nod;' wachen, 'wake, watch,' wecken, 'awaken, arouse;' essen, 'eat,' ätzen, 'corrode, etch.'

II. By additions to the root:

1. The suffix el forms a few diminutives, as lachen, 'laugh,' lächeln, 'smile;' lieben, 'love,' liebeln, 'dally, flirt;' kranken, 'be sick,' kränkeln, 'be sickly or ailing.'

a. But most of the diminutive verbs in eln are derived from nouns and adjectives: see below, **405**.II.1.

2. The suffix er forms a few iterative, desiderative, or causative verbs. as klappen, 'flap,' klappern, 'rattle;' lachen, 'laugh,' lächern, 'make inclined to laugh;' folgen, 'follow,' folgern, 'infer, conclude.'

a. But most verbs in ern, as in eln, come from nouns and adjectives; and those which appear to come from verbs are rather to be regarded as formed in imitation of such, or after their analogy.

3. The addition of ch gives in a few cases intensive force: as in hören, 'hear,' horchen, 'hearken;' schnarren, 'rattle,' schnarchen, 'snore, snort.'

4. Ir or ier. This is properly a French ending, representing the *er* or *ir* of the infinitive of French verbs; and it forms German verbs from French or Latin roots: thus, studiren, 'study,' marschiren, 'march,' spazieren, 'expatiate, go abroad for pleasure or exercise,' regieren, 'rule.'

a. But a few verbs in iren are formed, in imitation of these, from German words: as buchstabiren, 'spell' (from Buchstabe, 'letter'), schattiren, 'shade' (from Schatten, 'shadow').

b. At a certain period, about the middle of the last century, the German language was well-nigh swamped by the introduction of a multitude of such foreign verbs in iren. The greater part of them have been cast out from dignified and literary use, but they are still rife in low colloquial and humorous styles.

c. The syllable ir or ier of these verbs receives the accent; and they therefore admit no prefix ge in the participle: see **243**.3*a*.

III. By prefixes to the root:

1. By the inseparable prefixes be, ent or emp, er, ge, ver, and zer.

For the derivative (or compound) verbs formed by means of these prefixes, see above, **302** etc.

2. By separable prefixes.

Verbs formed by means of such prefixes have no real right to be regarded as derivative: they are compounds, rather: see **296** etc.

Remark.—Derivative verbs in German coming from other verbs directly are quite rare; and, of those usually regarded as so derived, some admit of explanation as denominatives, or as coming from nouns and adjectives.

405. *Verbs derived from Nouns and Adjectives.*

Verbs from nouns and adjectives are commonly called *denominatives.* They constitute in German, as in the other related languages, the great mass of derivative verbs. The relation of the verbal idea to the meaning of the primitive word is of the most varied character. Verbs from adjectives usually signify either, as intransitives, to be in or to pass into the condition denoted by the adjective, or else, as transitives, to reduce something to that condition. Verbs from nouns signify either to supply with that which the noun denotes, or to deprive of it, or to use or apply it, or to treat with it, or to be like it, and so on: for examples, see below.

I. By the simple addition of the endings of conjugation:

1. From nouns, more usually without modification of the vowel of the primitive word: as, fußen, 'set foot, find footing' (Fuß, 'foot'); hausen, 'house, dwell' (Haus, 'house'); grasen, 'graze' (Gras, 'grass'); altern, 'grow old, age' (Alter, 'age'); buttern, 'make or turn to butter' (Butter, butter'); prunken, 'make a show' (Prunk, 'show'); arbeiten, 'work' (Arbeit, 'labor'):—sometimes with modification of the vowel: as, pflügen, 'plough' (Pflug, 'plough'); hämmern, 'hammer' (Hammer, 'hammer'); stürzen, 'fall or hurl headlong' (Sturz, 'fall').

a. Rarely, a verb is formed from a noun in the plural: as, blättern, 'turn over the leaves of,' etc. (Blätter, 'leaves,' from Blatt).

b. Nouns (and adjectives) ending in the unaccented syllable en reject the e of that syllable in the derivative verb: thus, regnen, 'rain' (Regen, 'rain'); öffnen, 'open' (offen, 'open').

2. From adjectives, usually with modification of the vowel: thus, röthen, 'redden' (roth, 'red'); stärken, 'strengthen' (stark, 'strong'); tödten, 'kill' (todt, 'dead'); genügen, 'suffice' (genug, 'enough'); ändern, 'alter' (ander, 'other'); äußern, 'utter' (außer, 'out');—rarely without modification: as, nahen, 'draw nigh' (nah, 'nigh'); alten, 'grow old' (alt, 'old').

a. A number of derivative verbs are formed from adjectives in the comparative degree: thus, nähern, 'come nearer' (näher, 'nearer,' from nah); mindern, 'diminish' (minder, 'less').

II. By derivative endings, forming themes of conjugation:

1. The ending el forms from both nouns and adjectives (with modification of their vowel) verbs which have a diminutive, disparaging, or reproachful meaning: thus, künsteln, 'treat in an artificial or affected manner' (Kunst, 'art'); alterthümeln, 'be foolishly or affectedly fond of antiquity' (Alterthum, 'antiquity'); klügeln, 'subtilize, be over-critical' (klug, 'knowing'); frömmeln, 'affect piety, cant' (fromm, 'pious').

a. Compare derivatives formed from verbs by the same ending, **404.**II.1

2. The endings sch, z, and enz form a few verbs: sch forms only herrschen, 'rule' (Herr, 'master'), and feilschen, 'chaffer' (feil, 'cheap'); z forms duzen, 'to thee and thou' (du, 'thou'), and one or two others; enz forms faulenzen, 'play the sluggard' (faul, 'lazy'), etc.

3. The ending ig is properly one forming adjectives (below, **415.**9); but it is sometimes attached both to adjectives and nouns in order to the formation of a special theme of conjugation, by analogy with the numerous verbs derived from adjectives ending in ig: thus, reinigen, 'purify' (rein, 'pure') endigen, 'end, terminate' (Ende, 'end').

4. The ending ir forms a few verbs from German nouns: see **404.II.4a**

III. By prefixes (either with or without derivative endings):

1. The inseparable prefixes (except ge) form a very large number of denominative verbs, generally without any accompanying derivative ending, but occasionally along with such. In these denominatives, the prefixes have a force analogous with that which belongs to them in composition (see **307**): thus,

a. Be forms transitives, denoting especially a furnishing, making, or treating: thus, beseelen, 'endow with a soul' (Seele, 'soul'); begeistern, 'inspirit' (Geister, 'spirits,' from Geist); befreien, 'free, liberate' (frei, 'free'); bereichern, 'enrich' (reicher, 'richer,' from reich); beschönigen, 'beautify' (schön, 'beautiful'); benachrichtigen, 'inform' (Nachricht, 'news').

b. Ent forms especially verbs signifying removal, deprivation, and the like: thus, entfernen, 'withdraw' (fern, '**far**'); entblößen, 'strip' (bloß, 'bare'); enthaupten, 'behead' (Haupt, 'head'); entkräften, 'enervate' (Kraft, 'power'); entheiligen, 'desecrate' (heilig, 'holy'); entwaffnen, 'disarm' (Waffen, 'weapon').

c. Er forms transitives, intransitives, and reflexives, chiefly from adjectives, and signifying a passing into, or a reduction to, the state signified by the adjective: thus, erharten, 'grow hard,' erhärten, 'make hard' (hart 'hard'); ermatten, 'tire' (matt, 'weary'); ergänzen, 'complete' (ganz, 'entire'); erniedrigen, 'humble' (niedrig, 'low'); erlösen, 'release' (los, 'loose'); erweitern, 'extend' (weiter, 'wider,' from weit); erklären, 'explain' (klar, 'clear'):—but sometimes with more irregular meaning, from adjectives or nouns: thus, erobern, 'conquer' (ober, 'superior'); erinnern, 'remind' (inner, 'interior'); ergründen, 'fathom, explore' (Grund, 'bottom').

d. Ver has nearly the same value and office as er, but is more prevailingly transitive in effect: thus, verändern, 'alter' (ander, 'other'); vereiteln, 'frustrate' (eitel, 'vain'); vergnügen, 'gratify' (genug, 'enough'); verlängern, 'lengthen' (länger, 'longer,' from lang); verglasen, 'vitrify, glaze' (Glas, 'glass'); versilbern, 'plate with silver' (Silber, 'silver'); veralten, 'become antiquated' (alt, 'old').

e. Zer forms a very few derivatives: as, zerfleischen, 'lacerate' (Fleisch, 'flesh'); zergliedern, 'dismember' (Glieder, 'limbs,' from Glied).

2. A small number of denominatives are formed with the separable prefixes: such are abdachen, 'unroof' (Dach, 'roof'); auskernen, 'remove the stone or kernel of' (Kern, 'kernel'); einkerkern, 'imprison' (Kerker, 'prison'); umarmen, 'embrace' (Arm, 'arm'); aufmuntern, 'cheer up' (munter, 'cheerful'); ausweiten, 'widen' (weit, 'wide').

406. *Verbs derived from Particles.*

A few verbs are derived from other parts of speech by the same means as from nouns and adjectives.

Such are empören, 'excite, arouse' (empor, 'aloft'); begegnen, 'meet (gegen, 'against'); erwiedern, 'answer' (wieder, 'again'); vernichten, zernichten, 'annihilate' (nicht, 'not'); verneinen, 'deny' (nein, 'no'); bejahen, 'affirm' (ja, 'yes'); ächzen, 'groan' (ach, 'ah!'); jauchzen, 'exult' (juch juchhe, 'hurrah!').

Derivation of Nouns.

407. *Primitive Nouns.*

1. Primitive nouns are in part monosyllabic words which contain no evident sign of their really derivative nature, and of which the original roots are no longer traceable in German.

Such are Mann, 'man,' Haus, 'house,' Baum, 'tree,' Kind, 'child, Volk, 'people,' Fuß, 'foot.'

2. In part they are words of more than one syllable, the evident products of composition or derivation, containing elements more or less closely analogous with those by which other recognizable derivatives are formed, but coming from roots of which they are the only remaining representatives.

Such are Name, name,' Knabe, 'boy.' Auge, 'eye,' Erde, 'earth,' Vater, father,' Tochter, 'daughter,' Wasser, 'water,' Vogel, 'bird,' Nadel, 'needle,' Segel, 'sail.'

a. Some of the words in both these classes are traceable by comparison of the kindred languages to earlier roots from which they are descended: thus, Mann is usually (though doubtfully) referred to a root *man*, 'think (the same with meinen, 'think, mean'); Kind comes from the root *gan*, 'generate;' Fuß is identical with Latin *pes*, Greek *pous*, coming from *pad*, 'walk;' Name goes back to *gnâ*, 'know;' Tochter to *duh*, 'draw the breast, milk,' and so on.

408. *Nouns derived from Verbs.*

I. By variation of vowel (Ablaut: see **400.**2) alone, without added ending.

Thus, Band, 'volume,' Bund, 'bond,' from binden, 'bind;' Sitz, 'seat,' Satz, 'sediment,' Saß, 'settler,' from sitzen, 'sit;' Zug, 'draft,' from ziehen, 'draw;' Tritt, 'step,' from treten, 'tread;' Spruch, 'speech,' from sprechen, 'speak;' Sprung, 'spring,' from springen, 'spring.'

a. All these words originally had endings of derivation, which have become lost by phonetic corruption. They are prevailingly masculine.

b. In words thus derived appear sometimes irregular alterations of the root, especially of its final consonant, as the examples in part show.

c. The relation of meaning of such derivatives to the idea of action, state, or quality expressed by the verbal root is very various: but they signify in general either the act or quality itself, or the result of the action, or the person or thing that acts, or to which the state or quality belongs.

II. By brief and obscure endings, relics of earlier fuller forms, and no longer producing distinct classes of derivatives, with definable modifications of the radical meaning. Such endings are

1. Te, de, t (ſt, ft), d: thus, Bürde, 'burden,' from bären, 'bear; Scharte, 'notch,' from scheren, 'shear;' Fahrt, 'passage,' from fahren, 'go; Schrift, 'document,' from schreiben, 'write;' Tracht, 'dress,' from tragen, 'wear;' Brunst, 'heat,' from brennen, 'burn;' Kunst, 'art,' from kennen, 'know;' Kunft, 'coming,' from kommen, 'come;' Brand, 'combustion, from brennen, 'burn.'

2. E, which forms a very large number of derivatives: thus, Binde, 'tie, from binden, 'bind;' Sprache, 'language,' from sprechen, 'speak,' Gabe, 'gift,' from geben, 'give;' Fliege, 'fly,' from fliegen, 'fly.'

a. The derivatives of this class also share in the variation of radical vowel, and in the irregular alterations of the final consonant of the root, which characterize the older words of the language. They are of as various meaning as those of the preceding class. Their gender is prevailingly feminine—exceptions being appellations of males (persons and animals), and a few that are of anomalous character.

III. By endings of more distinct form, and more uniform and definable meaning.

The most important of these we will take up in alphabetical order, for the sake of more convenient reference.

1. Ei. This suffix is of foreign origin, being derived from the Latin and French *ia, ie.* It was used originally only to form derivatives from nouns (see below, **410.**2), but has come also to form from verbs ending in eln and ern abstract nouns of action, often with a disparaging or contemptuous implication: thus, Schmeichelei, 'flattery,' from schmeicheln, 'flatter;' Tändelei, 'trifling,' from tändeln, 'trifle;' Plauderei, 'chit-chat,' from plaudern, 'chatter;' Zauberei, 'witchcraft,' from zaubern, 'practise magic.'

a. Words formed with ei are feminine, and take the accent upon this syllable, as is required by the derivation of the suffix.

2. El. This suffix forms a considerable class of masculine derivatives, denoting generally an instrument, quite rarely an actor: thus, Hebel, 'lever,' from heben, 'raise;' Deckel, 'cover,' from decken, 'cover;' Schlägel, 'mallet,' from schlagen, 'beat;' Schlüssel, 'key,' from schließen, 'lock;' Flügel, 'wing,' from fliegen, 'fly.'

a. But a great many nouns in the language ending in el are from lost or unknown roots, and therefore have the value of primitive words (**407.**2): some of these are feminine or neuter: as are also some others, whose gender is determined by their signification.

3. En. Besides forming the infinitives of all verbs (**237.**1*a*), which, when used as ordinary nouns, are neuter (**340**), en is the suffix of derivation of a considerable class of masculine nouns, as Bissen, 'bit,' from beißen, 'bite;' Graben, 'ditch,' from graben, 'dig;' Schaden, 'harm,' from schaden, 'injure.'

a. Of the numerous words of obscure etymology in en, a few are neuter, but none are feminine.

4. Er. This suffix forms numerous masculine nouns denoting an actor: thus, Reiter, 'rider,' from reiten, 'ride;' Maler, 'painter,' from malen, 'paint;' Tänzer, 'dancer,' from tanzen, 'dance;' Bäcker, 'baker,' from backen, 'bake.' With these are closely akin a few names of instruments, as Bohrer, 'auger,' from bohren, 'bore;' Zeiger, 'pointer,' from zeigen, 'point.'

a. Of the older words ending in er, and requiring to be reckoned as primitives (**407.**2), many are feminine or neuter.

b. Er also forms classes of derivative nouns from nouns: see **410.**3.

5. Ling forms from verbs chiefly masculine nouns denoting the recipient

of the verbal action thus, Findling, foundling,' from finden, 'find;' Lehrling, 'pupil,' from lehren, 'teach;' Säugling, 'suckling,' from säugen 'suckle.'

a. For the derivatives in ling from nouns and adjectives, see **409.**II.4, **410.6.**

6. Niß. This suffix is chiefly used in German to form abstract nouns from verbs: much less often, like the corresponding English *ness*, to produce similar derivatives from adjectives (see **409.**II.5). Such abstracts come especially from derivative verbs and those compounded with inseparable prefixes, as be, er, ver; sometimes seeming to be formed from the participle rather than the simple verbal root. Like all abstract nouns, they may admit of use also as concretes, or pass wholly over into such. Examples are Zeugniß, 'testimony,' from zeugen, 'testify;' Hinderniß, 'hindrance,' from hindern, 'hinder;' Begräbniß, 'burial,' from begraben, 'bury;' Ereigniß, 'occurrence,' from ereignen, 'occur;' Verhältniß, 'relation,' from verhalten, 'stand related;' Geständniß, 'confession,' from gestehen (gestanden), 'confess;' Gefängniß, 'prison,' from gefangen, 'imprisoned.'

a. The greater number of nouns in niß are neuter, but a score or more of them are feminine, especially such as have retained more fully their abstract meaning. A few, as Ersparniß, Erkenntniß, are feminine when used abstractly, but neuter as concretes.

7. Sal, sel. These are two different forms of the same original suffix, which at first and more properly formed nouns from nouns, but whose existing derivatives are to be referred almost exclusively to verbal roots, and are akin in meaning with those in niß. Sel is used only in concretes. Thus, Schicksal, 'fate,' from schicken, 'send;' Irrsal, 'error,' from irren, 'wander;' Ueberbleibsel, 'remnant,' from überbleiben, 'remain over;' Räthsel, 'riddle, from rathen, 'guess.'

a. Derivatives in sal and sel are neuter, excepting two or three in sal (Drangsal, Mühsal, Trübsal), which may also be used as feminine.

8. Ung. This suffix is nearly equivalent in meaning and application with our *ing* forming verbal nouns ("participial infinitives," not present participles), but is peculiar in that it is hardly used except with derivative and transitive verbs. The nouns it forms admit an object (objective genitive: **216.**2*h*) nearly as regularly as the verbs from which they come. Many of the nouns in ung, like other abstracts, pass over into concrete use; and such as come from reflexive verbs have an intransitive force. Examples are Führung, 'leading, conduct;' Belehrung, 'instruction;' Erfindung, 'invention;' Vergebung, 'forgiveness;' Bemerkung, 'remark;' Bedeutung, 'meaning;' Bewegung, 'motion;' Neigung, 'affection'—from führen 'lead,' belehren, 'instruct,' and so on.

a. The derivatives in ung are feminine without exception.

9. Besides the suffixes above detailed, there are a few of infrequent use such are and (properly the old participial ending), in Heiland, 'Savior, from heilen, 'heal;'—icht, in Kehricht, 'sweepings,' from kehren, 'sweep,' etc.;—ig in Essig, 'vinegar,' from essen, 'eat;'—ath in Zierath, 'ornament,' from zieren, 'decorate;'—end in Tugend, 'virtue,' from taugen, 'be of value;'—and one or two others, of too little consequence to be worth noting. Schaft (**410.7**) and thum (**410.8**) also form from verbal roots two or three derivatives, as Wanderschaft, Wachsthum.

409. *Nouns derived from Adjectives.*

I. 1. That the adjective, of either number and of any gender, is capable of use directly as a noun, still retaining its adjective declension, was pointed out above (at **129**), and needs no further notice.

2. A few nouns are derived from adjectives without a suffix, being identical with the adjective theme, but being declined as independent (neuter) substantives: such are Roth, 'red;' Grün, 'green;' Recht, 'right;' Gut, 'property, goods.'

II. Nouns derived by the aid of suffixes.

1. E. The suffix e forms feminine abstracts (convertible into concretes) from primitive adjectives, the vowel of which is always modified if capable of it. Thus, Größe, 'greatness,' Güte, 'goodness,' Treue, 'truth,' Tiefe, 'depth;' from groß, 'great,' etc.

2. Heit. This suffix is the same with our *head* and *hood* (in *Godhead*, *manhood*, etc.), and forms feminine abstracts both from nouns (see below, **410**.5) and from adjectives. Thus, Freiheit, 'freedom,' Blindheit, 'blindness,' Albernheit, 'stupidity;' from frei, 'free,' etc.

3. Keit is originally the same suffix with heit, taking the place of the latter after most primitive adjectives ending in el and er, and after all those formed by the suffixes bar, ig, lich, and sam. Thus, Eitelkeit, 'vanity,' Bitterkeit, 'bitterness,' Dankbarkeit, 'gratitude,' Billigkeit, 'cheapness,' Höflichkeit, 'courtesy,' Sparsamkeit, 'economy;' from eitel, 'vain,' etc. To many adjectives, the additional adjective suffix ig (**415**.9) is added, with keit after it, instead of, or along with, keit alone: thus, from klein, 'small,' we have both Kleinheit and Kleinigkeit; from süß, 'sweet,' Süßigkeit; from standhaft, 'steadfast,' Standhaftigkeit; from treulos, 'faithless,' Treulosigkeit.

4. Ling forms a few masculine personal nouns from adjectives: thus, Fremdling, 'stranger,' Jüngling, 'youth;' from fremd, 'strange,' jung, 'young.' For derivatives with ling from verbs and nouns, see **408**.III.5, **410**.6.

5. Niß (see **408**.III.6) forms only four nouns from adjectives: namely, Finsterniß, 'darkness,' Geheimniß, 'secrecy,' Wildniß, 'wilderness,' Gleichniß, 'likeness.'

6. Schaft is chiefly employed in forming nouns from nouns (see **410**.7); only a few adjectives admit it, as Gemeinschaft, 'community,' Gefangenschaft, 'imprisonment,' Eigenschaft, 'peculiarity;' from gemein, 'common, etc. For the derivation etc. of schaft see below, **410**.7.

7. Tel, from Theil, 'part,' forms fractional numerals from ordinals: see **207**.2.

8. Thum, like schaft, is a suffix applied chiefly to nouns: see below, **410**.8. A few adjectives take it, as Reichthum, 'wealth,' Eigenthum, 'property;' from reich, 'rich,' eigen, 'own.'

9. Yet rarer suffixes are ung (compare **408**.III.8, **410**.9) in Festung, 'fortress,' from fest, 'strong;'—icht in Dickicht, 'thicket,' from dick, 'thick;'—uth in Armuth, 'poverty,' from arm, 'poor;'—end in Jugend, 'youth, from jung, 'young.'

410. *Nouns derived from Nouns.*

1. Chen, lein. These are equivalent suffixes, forming from nouns (al

ways with modification of the vowel of the latter, if it be one admitting modification) neuter diminutives: thus, Häuschen, 'little house;' Männchen, 'little man, mannikin;' Knäblein, 'little boy;' Büchlein, 'little book.'

a These suffixes correspond to the English diminutive endings *kin* and *ling* (in *gosling*, *duckling*, etc.). Chen belongs more to the northern dialects of German, lein (often shortened in popular use to el or le) to the southern; but in the literary language their respective use is mainly determined by considerations of euphony, and many words admit the addition of either.

b. The words formed by these suffixes often add to their meaning as diminutives, or substitute for it, an implication of intimacy or tenderness. Some of them have a well-established value as independent words: such are Fräulein, 'young lady, Miss;' Mädchen, 'girl;' Männchen and Weibchen, 'male and female of an animal species.'

2. Ei. The foreign origin of the suffix ei was explained above (**408.** III.1). As added to nouns, it indicates especially the state, condition, or occupation of a person; also sometimes the place where an occupation is carried on: thus, Jägerei, 'sportsmanship,' from Jäger, 'hunter;' Druckerei, 'printing-establishment,' from Drucker, 'printer.' In a few words it has a collective force: thus, Reiterei, 'cavalry,' from Reiter, 'rider.'

a. As it is itself accented, this suffix was added most easily to unaccented terminational syllables, as el and er; and there are but few words —as Abtei, 'abbacy,' Vogtei, 'bailiwick'—in which it is appended to radical syllables. Being oftenest used after er, it has come to assume er in many cases as a prefix to itself, forming a kind of compound suffix erei, which is freely used with words accented on the final: thus, Sklaverei, 'slavery,' Kinderei, 'childishness,' Schelmerei, 'roguery;' from Sklav, 'slave,' etc.

b. Especially in its recent derivatives, ei is apt to convey a disparaging implication: for example, Juristerei, 'lawyer's doings,' as compared with Jurisprudenz, 'jurisprudence.'

3. Er. *a.* Besides the numerous derivatives which it forms from verbs (**408.**III.4), er makes many names of a personal agent from nouns expressing the thing dealt with or acted upon: as, Sänger, 'singer,' from Sang, 'song;' Schäfer, 'shepherd,' from Schaf, 'sheep;' Gärtner, 'gardener,' from Garten, 'garden.'

b. It is also added to names of countries and towns, to indicate a native or inhabitant of the same: thus, Schweizer, 'Switzer;' Berliner, 'inhabitant of Berlin;' Leipziger, 'man from Leipzig.'

These nouns are then frequently employed as uninflected adjectives: see **415.5.**

c. For the same purpose, it is sometimes combined with Latin endings, forming compound suffixes, as aner and enser: thus, Amerikaner, 'American,' Athenienser, 'Athenian.'

d. After nouns, as after verbs, it is in a few cases irregularly converted into ner: thus, Glöckner, 'bell-ringer,' from Glocke, 'bell;' Harfner, 'harper, from Harfe, 'harp.'

e. It forms a small number of masculines answering to feminines in e thus, Wittwer, 'widower,' from Wittwe, 'widow;' Tauber, 'cock-pigeon, from Taube, 'dove.'

4. Jn (sometimes spelt inn). This suffix forms feminine from masculine appellations: thus, Hirtin, 'shepherdess,' from Hirt, 'shepherd;' Königin, 'queen,' from König, 'king;' Freundin, 'female friend;' Köchin, 'female cook;' Löwin, 'lioness;' Französin, 'French woman;' Berlinerin, 'woman of Berlin.' It is also added to titles to signify the wife of the person to whom the title belongs: as, Pfarrerin, 'pastor's wife;' Professorin, 'Mrs. Professor.'

Jn usually requires modification of the radical vowel, but there are (as the examples show) numerous exceptions.

5. Heit, like our *head* and *hood*, forms abstracts, and a few collectives, from nouns as well as from adjectives (**409**.II.2): thus, Gottheit, 'Godhead;' Kindheit, 'childhood;' Thorheit, 'folly;' Menschheit, 'humanity;' Geistlichkeit, 'clergy.'

6. Ling forms a few masculine personal names from nouns, as from verbs (**408**.III.5) and adjectives (**409**.II.4): such are Jährling, 'yearling,' Flüchtling, 'fugitive,' Günstling, 'favorite.'

7. *a.* Schaft is the same with our *ship* (in *lordship*, *worship*, etc.), and is derived from schaffen, 'shape, create;' it signifies primarily the shape or make of anything, then its character, office, rank, and the like: thus, Freundschaft, 'friendship,' Bekanntschaft, 'acquaintance,' Vormundschaft, 'guardianship.' All its derivatives are of the feminine gender.

b. It forms also a number of collectives: as, Priesterschaft, 'priesthood, Dienerschaft, 'body of servants,' Gesellschaft, 'company,' Landschaft, 'landscape.'

8. Thum, our *dom* (in *kingdom*, *wisdom*, etc.) is also a noun, of obscure derivation, but of meaning and application as a suffix nearly akin with those of schaft (above, 7). Its derivatives are neuter, with only two or three exceptions (namely Irrthum, Reichthum, and, according to the usage of some, Beweisthum and Wachsthum), which are masculine. It forms nouns signifying character, rank, or authority, which then, in a few cases, come to mean that over which authority is exerted: thus, Ritterthum, 'chivalry,' Papstthum, 'papacy,' Christenthum, 'christendom,' Königthum, 'kingdom,' Fürstenthum, 'principality.'

9. Suffixes forming a few isolated words are rich in Gänserich, 'gander,' from Gans, 'goose,' Fähnrich, 'ensign,' from Fahne, 'banner,' etc.;—ung in one or two collective words like Waldung, 'woodland,' from Wald, 'forest;' —ath in Heimath, 'home,' from Heim, 'home.' Niß (**408**.III.6) appears to form a derivative or two from nouns, as in Bündniß, 'covenant,' from Bund, 'tie;'—also sal (**408**.III.7), as in Mühsal, 'distress,' from Mühe, 'toil.'

411. *Nouns formed by means of prefixes.*

I. A very large number of nouns contain as their initial elements the verbal prefixes, both separable and inseparable (**297**). For the most part, however, they are not formed as nouns by means of those prefixes, but are derivatives, according to the methods explained above (**408**), from verbs compounded separably or inseparably. The only exceptions are, a considerable class formed by ge (below, **II**.1), and an occasional anomalous case like Anhöhe, 'rising ground,' from Höhe, 'height.'

II. The proper prefixes forming nouns are very few in number namely as follows:

1. Ge. This common prefix forms a large number of derivative nouns, both from nouns and from verbs, having in general a collective or frequentative character. Thus,

a. Collectives from nouns, generally with modification of vowel, sometimes with other more irregular vowel changes: such are Gesträuch, 'shrubbery,' from Strauch, 'shrub;' Gewölk, 'cloud-mass,' from Wolke, 'cloud; Gebirg or Gebirge, 'mountain-range,' from Berg, 'mountain;' Gefieder, 'plumage,' from Feder, 'feather.'

b. A few collective or associative personal appellatives, from nouns or verbs, in which ge has nearly its original meaning (**307.5**) of 'with:' thus, Gespiele, 'playfellow,' from spielen, 'play;' Gefährte, 'companion,' from fahren, 'go;' Gevatter, 'godfather,' from Vater, 'father;' Geschwister, 'brothers and sisters,' from Schwester, 'sister.'

c. From verbs, nouns signifying either the means or the effect of the verbal action: thus, Gehör, 'sense of hearing,' from hören, 'hear;' Gewehr, 'weapon,' from wehren, 'defend;' Gebet, 'prayer,' from bitten, 'ask;' Gemälde, 'painting,' from malen, 'paint.'

d. From verbs, frequentative or intensive abstracts, or nouns significant of the verbal action: thus, Gespräch, 'conversation,' from sprechen, 'speak;' Gespött, 'mockery,' from spotten, 'mock;' Gepränge, 'pageantry,' from prangen, 'make a show;' Getöse, 'din,' from tosen, 'roar.'

Remarks. *e.* These are the leading uses of the prefix ge; but in not a few of the derivatives it forms, its effect is too indistinct or various to be brought under any classification.

f. As the examples show, the words formed with ge exhibit the variation as well as the modification of vowel, and are either without suffix, or take one of the simpler suffixes (**408.**II.), especially e. In many words, this e may be either added or omitted.

g. Excepting the class under *b*, above, which are masculine, the nouns formed with ge are nearly all neuter. Masculine are only about a dozen (Gebrauch, Gedanke, Gefallen, Gehalt, Genuß, Geruch, Gesang, Geschmack, Gestank, Gewinn, Gewinnst); feminine, the same number (Geberde, Gebühr, Geburt, Geduld, Gefahr, Gemeinde, Genüge, Geschichte, Geschwulst, Gestalt, Gewalt, Gewähr).

h. A few nouns, as Glück, 'luck, happiness,' Glaube, 'belief,' contain the prefix ge, abbreviated to a simple g.

2. Miß. This prefix is the same with the English *mis*, and has a similar office. Its value is rather that of a compounded element than of a prefix. It takes always the principal accent, and does not affect the gender of the nouns to which it is prefixed. Thus, Mißgriff, 'mistake; Missethat, 'misdeed;' Mißgunst, 'disfavor;' Mißbehagen, 'discomfort.'

3. Un is, as in English, the negative prefix. It is used with nouns more often than in our language, always taking the accent, without affecting the gender; it either signifies actual negation, or implies something unnatural, repugnant, or injurious. Thus, Unrecht, 'wrong,' Undank, 'ingratitude,' Unglück, 'misfortune,' Unsinn, 'nonsense;'—Unmensch, 'unnatural monster. Ungestalt, 'misshapen form,' Unthat, 'misdeed'

4. Ur. This is, as has been already pointed out (**307**.4), the same word originally with the inseparable prefix er, and ultimately identical with aus, 'out' In a few words it still has a meaning akin with that of er: thus, Urtheil, 'judgment' (ertheilen, 'assign'), Urlaub, 'leave' (erlauben, 'permit'), Urkunde, 'document,' Ursprung, 'origin,' and so on. But in most of the derivatives which it forms it has an intensive force, with the distinct implication of originality or primitiveness: thus, Ursache, 'cause (original or fundamental thing),' Urwelt, 'primitive world,' Urbild, 'archetype,' Urgroßvater, 'greatgrandfather.'

a. Ur always takes the accent, and it leaves unchanged the gender of the word to which it is prefixed.

5. Erz is identical in derivation and meaning with our prefix *arch*, and denotes what is eminent or superior in its kind. In respect to accent and gender, it is like the three prefixes last treated of. Thus, Erzengel, archangel;' Erzherzog, 'arch-duke;' Erzdieb, 'arch-thief.'

6. Ant, originally the same with the inseparable prefix ent (**307**.3), appears in the present language only in Antwort, 'answer' (from Wort, 'word'), and Antlitz, 'countenance.'

412. From other parts of speech than those treated above, nouns are only with the greatest rarity formed directly, or otherwise than through the medium of derivative adjectives or verbs. Such words as Niederung, 'lowland,' from nieder (adverb), 'down,' and Innung, 'guild,' from in, 'in,' are anomalies in the German system of word-derivation.

Derivation of Adjectives.

413. *Primitive Adjectives.*

Primitive adjectives, like primitive nouns (**407**), may be divided into two classes:

1. Simple monosyllabic adjectives, the evidences of whose originally derivative character are effaced: thus, gut, 'good,' lang, 'long,' arm, 'poor' hart, 'hard,' grün, 'green.'

2. Adjectives containing an evident element of derivation, and analogous with those derived from known primitives, but coming from roots which are now lost: thus, träge, 'lazy,' heiter, 'cheerful,' eben, 'even,' dunkel, 'dark.'

a. Some of these, as of the "primitive" nouns (**407**.*a*), admit of being traced to more primitive roots by the researches of comparative philology

414. *Adjectives derived without Suffix or Prefix.*

Adjectives coming from verbal roots by simple variation of the radical vowel, without a suffix (like nouns: see **408**.I.), are very few in German: examples are brach, 'fallow,' from brechen, 'break up;' glatt, 'smooth,' from gleiten, 'slip;' dick, 'thick,' from the root of gedeihen, 'thrive;' flück, 'fledged,' from fliegen, 'fly.'

415. *Adjectives derived by Suffix.*

As the various endings forming adjectives are, almost without exception, used in derivation from different parts of speech, it will be more convenient to treat all the uses of each one together, taking the suffixes up in their alphabetical order.

1. Bar. This suffix is regarded as a derivative from the verb bären, 'bear, carry.' It was of infrequent use in ancient German, and only as attached to nouns.

a. Examples of its use with nouns are dienstbar, 'serviceable (service-bringing);' fruchtbar, 'fruitful (fruit-bearing);' furchtbar, 'terrible;' gangbar, 'current;' sichtbar, 'visible.'

b. In modern usage, it forms a large class of derivatives from verbs (almost always transitive), having the meaning of our adjectives in *able*, or indicating capability to endure the action of the verb; thus, eßbar, 'eatable, genießbar, 'enjoyable,' theilbar, 'divisible,' unbewohnbar, 'uninhabitable;' —unfehlbar, 'incapable of failing.'

c. Very rarely, it is added to an adjective: thus, offenbar, 'evident,' from offen, 'open.'

2. En, ern. The suffix en forms (from nouns) adjectives denoting material or kind: thus, golden, 'golden,' wollen, 'woolen,' irden, 'earthen,' eichen, 'oaken.' To words ending in er, only n is added: thus, kupfern, 'of copper,' silbern, 'of silver,' ledern, 'leathern.' Out of the frequency of this combination has grown in recent use the form ern, which was perhaps at first applied only to nouns forming a plural in er—thus, hölzern, 'wooden,' from Holz (pl. Hölzer), 'wood'—but is now used indiscriminately, requiring modification of the vowel of its primitive: thus, bleiern, 'leaden,' thönern, 'of clay (Thon),' stählern, 'of steel (Stahl).'

3. En, end. These endings, forming respectively the past participle of verbs of the Old conjugation, and the present participle of all verbs, are proper adjective suffixes, but need only be mentioned here, as their uses form a part of the subject of verbal conjugation, and have been already explained (see **349** etc.).

4. Er, est. These are the endings by which are formed, from simple adjectives, adjective themes of the comparative and superlative degree (see **133** etc.): also, st forms ordinal numerals from cardinals (see **203**).

5. Er. The patronymic nouns formed by the suffix er from names of countries or towns (**410**.3*b*) are very commonly used also with the value of adjectives. When so used, they are not subject to declension, but are treated as if they were compounded with the noun which they qualify. Thus, Berliner Blau, 'Berlin blue;' das Straßburger Münster, 'the Strasburg cathedral;' der Leipziger Messe, 'of the Leipsic fair.'

6. Et forms the past participle of verbs of the New conjugation: see **246**, **349** etc.

7. Haft. This suffix is regarded as derived from haben, 'have,' or haften, 'cling,' indicating primarily the possession or adhesion of the quality designated by the words to which it is attached.

a. It forms derivative adjectives especially from nouns signifying quality: thus, tugendhaft, 'virtuous,' sündhaft, 'sinful,' schreckhaft, 'frightful,' standhaft, 'steadfast;'—but also, not infrequently, from names of persons and things: thus, mannhaft, 'manful,' meisterhaft, 'masterly,' leibhaft, 'bodily.'

b. It is added to only a few verbal roots: as in wohnhaft, 'resident, schwatzhaft, 'loquacious.'

c. Only three adjectives admit it, namely boshaft, 'malicious,' krankhaft, sickly,' wahrhaft, 'true.'

d. To haft is sometimes added the further ending ig, as in leibhaftig, wahrhaftig; and this addition is always made before the suffix keit, forming abstract nouns (**409**.II.3): thus, Tugendhaftigkeit, 'virtuousness.'

8. Icht forms adjectives only from concrete nouns, especially such as denote material: thus, steinicht, 'stony,' dornicht, 'thorny,' salzicht, 'salty.' Its office is hardly distinguishable from that of ig (below, 9); and, in present use, its derivatives are almost superseded by those in ig, and are but seldom met with. Only thöricht, 'foolish,' is in familiar use, and is also peculiar in exhibiting the modification of vowel, and in being formed from a personal appellation (Thor, 'fool').

9. Ig. This suffix is the same with our *y* (in *stony*, *holy*, *easy*, etc.), and forms, from every part of speech, a very large number of German adjectives, which are constantly increasing by new derivatives. Thus,

a. From nouns, of every class: thus, mächtig, 'mighty,' günstig, 'favorable,' schuldig, 'guilty,' durstig, 'thirsty,' blutig, 'bloody,' wässerig, 'watery,' dickköpfig, 'thickheaded,' langarmig, 'longarmed.'

b. From verbs: thus, säumig, 'dilatory,' nachgiebig, 'yielding,' gefällig, 'obliging.'

c. From adjectives, in a few cases only: thus, gütig, 'kind,' völlig, 'complete;'—and from the possessive and other pronominal adjectives, as meinig, 'mine,' etc. (**159**.5), selbig, 'self-same' (**169**.3), jenig, 'yon' (**168**), einig, 'only, some' (**189**).

d. From indeclinable words, namely prepositions, adverbs, and adverbial conjunctions of various kinds: thus, vorig, 'former,' from vor, 'before;' übrig, 'remaining,' from über, 'over;' jetzig, 'present,' from jetzt, 'now;' heutig, 'of to-day,' from heute, 'to-day;' dortig, 'of that place,' from dort, 'there;' abermalig, 'repeated,' from abermals, 'again;' deßfallsig, 'relating to the case in hand,' from deßfalls, 'in that case.'

e. The addition of ig to other adjective endings before the suffix keit has been noticed above (**409**.II.3); also to haft in forming adjectives (above, 7*d*); to adjectives and nouns in forming derivative verbs (**405**.II.3); and to certain nouns in forming derivative adjectives (below, 15*e,f*).

f. Ig added to the suffix sal of certain nouns (**408**.III.7), along with modification of the vowel (written e instead of ä), forms a combination having the aspect of a separate suffix, selig: thus, mühselig, 'painful,' from Mühsal, 'distress;' trübselig, 'afflictive,' from Trübsal, 'affliction.' And the combination is in fact treated as an independent suffix, by being added to words which do not form derivatives in sal: thus, glückselig, 'blissful,' from Glück, 'happiness;' feindselig, 'inimical,' from feind, 'hostile;' redselig, 'talkative,' from reden, 'talk.'

g. A number of adjectives in ig are from lost roots, and so have in the present language the value of primitive words: thus, ewig, 'eternal,' selig, 'happy,' üppig, 'luxuriant.'

10. Isch. This is the same with our English suffix *ish*, and is used in much the same way.

a. It forms adjectives from nouns of different classes: thus, especially from proper names of persons, places, and peoples: as, lutherisch, 'Lutheran,' preußisch, 'Prussian,' baierisch, 'Bavarian,' spanisch, 'Spanish;'—from appellations of places, persons, and animals: as, himmlisch, 'heavenly,' städtisch, 'townish,' kindisch, 'childish,' diebisch, 'thievish,' dichterisch, 'poetical,' hündisch, 'doggish;'—and from a few abstracts or verbal nouns: as, abergläubisch, 'superstitious,' argwöhnisch, 'suspicious,' neidisch, 'envious.'

b. It often takes, in adjectives derived from the classical languages, the place of our endings *ic*, *ical*, *al*, *ian*, etc.: as, historisch, 'historic' or 'historical,' kritisch, 'critical,' logisch, 'logical,' indisch, 'Indian.'

c. In a few words, isch has a somewhat disparaging sense as compared with lich, much as in the corresponding English adjectives: thus, kindisch, 'childish,' and kindlich, 'childlike;' weibisch, 'womanish,' and weiblich, feminine.'

d. The use of isch with proper names of places and with foreign words is attended with some irregularities of detail, in respect to the form of the theme to which the suffix is appended: these cannot be dwelt upon here.

11. Lei forms indeclinable adjectives from numerals and words related with numerals, which, before it, take the ending er: thus, einerlei, 'of one sort,' mancherlei, 'of many sorts,' allerlei, 'of all sorts.'

The lei is by origin the genitive of a feminine noun, meaning 'sort,' and the preceding er is the proper ending of the adjective qualifying it: hence the treatment of its derivatives as indeclinable words.

12. Lich. This suffix corresponds with our *like*, *ly* (in *godlike*, *godly*, etc.), and, like these, forms a very large number of derivatives. It is historically the same word with the adjective *like* (German gleich): compare 363.3*a*.

Licht is also added to adjectives, perhaps as a mere variation of lich.

a. It is added to nouns of various classes (usually with modification of their vowel): thus, männlich, 'manly,' väterlich, 'fatherly,' künstlich, 'artful,' herzlich, 'hearty,' glücklich, 'happy,' jährlich, 'yearly,' geistlich, 'spiritual.'

b. It forms from other adjectives (always with modified vowel) adjectives that have in general a diminutive meaning: thus, röthlich, 'reddish,' säuerlich, 'somewhat sour,' länglich, 'longish.' But some of its derivatives are free from the diminutive implication; and a considerable number (see 363.3*a*) are used only in an adverbial sense, the ending having the same value as the English *ly* in similar derivatives from adjectives.

In a few words—as solch, welch, our *such*, *which*—it is greatly corrupted.

c. It is appended to many verbal roots; and either in an active sense (especially with intransitive verbs)—thus, schädlich, 'harmful,' beharrlich, 'persistent,' sterblich, 'mortal,' erfreulich, 'agreeable'—or, yet more often, in a passive sense: as glaublich, 'to be believed, credible,' verächtlich, 'contemptible,' begreiflich, 'comprehensible,' unsäglich, 'unspeakable.' Of this class of passive derivatives, many are in use only with the prefix un: e. g. there is no säglich, 'speakable.' Lich, as thus used, is closely equivalent with bar (above, 1*b*), and it is in part a matter of arbitrary custom, or determined only by euphony, which suffix shall be employed; in other cases, derivatives are formed with both, with a more or less distinct difference of meaning.

13. Sam is our *some* (in *wholesome*, *noisome*, etc.), and is supposed to be ultimately the adjective *same* (now lost in German). It forms derivatives

a. From nouns, mostly of an abstract character: thus, furchtsam, 'fearful,' gewaltsam, 'violent,' mühsam, 'laborious.'

b. From verbal roots: thus, aufmerksam, 'attentive,' folgsam, 'docile,' lenksam, 'manageable.'

c. From a few adjectives: thus, einsam, 'lonely' gemeinsam, 'common,' langsam, 'slow.'

14. T, besides one or two isolated adjectives, like dicht, 'thick, close,' from the root of gedeihen, 'thrive,' forms the class of ordinal adjectives from numerals below twenty (**203**).

15. There are certain words forming classes of derivative adjectives which have not yet (like bar, lich, sam, above) lost their independence of form and meaning sufficiently to be reckoned as adjective-suffixes, although approaching very near in value to such. The most noticeable of them are

a. Los, 'loose,' our *less*, forming numerous adjectives of deprivation: thus, endlos, 'endless,' herzlos, 'heartless,' treulos, 'faithless.'
These adjectives, like those ending in haft, always add ig before keit: thus, Treulosigkeit, 'faithlessness.'

b. Voll, 'full,' our *ful*, in *thankful*, *fearful*, etc.: examples are leidvoll, 'sorrowful,' gedankenvoll, 'thoughtful.'

c. Reich, 'rich:' examples are liebreich, 'gracious' (Liebe, 'love'), geistreich, 'witty, full of *esprit*.'

d. Fach, 'compartment, division,' forms multiplicatives with numeral words, cardinal or indefinite (**204**): examples are zehnfach, 'tenfold,' vielfach, 'manifold.'

e. Falt, 'fold,' is used in the same manner with fach. But multiplicatives with falt simply are antiquated and unusual: they now regularly take the additional adjective ending ig (above, 9), before which the vowel of falt (except in two or three words, as mannigfaltig) is modified: thus, zehnfältig, 'ten-fold,' vielfältig, 'manifold.'

f. Artig is, like fältig, an extension of a noun, Art, 'manner, kind,' by the adjective suffix ig, and forms a considerable class of derivatives denoting sort or manner: thus, nebelartig, 'cloudlike,' fremdartig, 'of strange fashion.' Other similar formations are förmig, from the foreign noun Form, 'form' (Lat. *forma*): thus, inselförmig, 'island-shaped;'—müthig, from Muth, 'mood, disposition:' as, friedmüthig, 'disposed to peace;'—mäßig, from Maß, 'measure:' as, rechtmäßig, 'lawful;' etc.

416. *Adjectives derived by Prefix.*

The prefixes forming adjectives are, in general, the same with those forming nouns (**411**), namely ge, miß, un, ur, erz, together with be.

1. Be forms a very few adjectives, as bereit, 'ready,' bequem, 'convenient.'

2. *a.* Ge aids to form past participles, or verbal adjectives (**243**.3);—and sometimes from nouns which do not furnish any other of the parts of a derivative verb: thus, gestiefelt, 'booted (provided with boots),' gehörnt, 'horned,' gesittet, 'mannered,' gestirnt, 'starred.'

b. It also forms, either without suffix or with ig, a class of adjectives from verbs: thus, genehm, 'acceptable' (nehmen, 'take'), gewiß, 'certain' (wissen, '**know**'), geläufig, '**current**' (laufen, '**run**'), gewärtig, '**expectant** (warten, 'wait').

c. Ge is prefixed to a few simple adjectives without noteworthy change of their meaning: thus, gerecht, 'righteous,' getreu, 'faithful,' gestreng, 'severe.' Gleich is thus formed, with abbreviated prefix, from an earlier leich, 'like.'

The other prefixes have the same value in adjectives as in nouns: thus,

3. Miß forms such adjectives as mißgünstig, 'grudging,' mißtrauisch, 'distrustful.'

4. Un forms negative adjectives, as unklar, 'unclear,' unglücklich, 'unhappy.'

a. That some of the adjectives formed with un have no corresponding positives has been noticed above (**415.**12*c*).

b. According to some authorities, the words formed with un always have the principal accent on that prefix: others except compounds of participles, as unbelohnt, 'unrewarded,' and of verbal derivatives with the suffixes bar, lich, sam, as undenk'bar, 'inconceivable,' unend'lich, 'unending,' unduld'sam, 'intolerant.'

5. Ur forms directly only a very small number of adjectives, from other adjectives, adding to the latter an intensive meaning, or an implication of primitiveness: thus, urplötzlich, 'very sudden;' uralt, 'of primitive antiquity.'

6. Erz is prefixed, in a half-humorous way, to a few adjectives, with intensive force: thus, erzdumm, 'excessively stupid,' erzfaul, 'very lazy.

Derivation of the other Parts of Speech.

417. Of the remaining parts of speech, the adverbs are the only ones which are to any extent formed in classes, by means analogous with those above explained; and they have been already sufficiently treated (**363** etc.) under Adverbs.

The derivation of the rest, so far as it is capable of being shown, is a matter for the lexicon to deal with, under each separate word.

WORD-COMBINATION, COMPOSITION.

418. A *compound word* is one that is made up of two (or more) independent words, each of which maintains in the composition its separate form and meaning. It is made one word by constancy of combination in practical use, by the absence of inflection except in the last member, and by being placed under the dominion of a single principal accent.

a. Thus, Jungfrau is distinguished from junge Frau, 'young woman,' by the adjective jung being made indeclinable and receiving a marked accent. By this means a unity of form is given to the word, to which a unity of idea is then further added by attribution of the meaning 'virgin,' which naturally grows out of the other, but yet is not the same with it.

b. As will appear hereafter (**422.**2*b* etc.), other members of a compound than the final one sometimes take an ending of declension, but irregularly and superfluously, and without liability to further variation in the inflection of the compound. There are also a few words which are arbitrarily written together as if compounds, while both their parts are declined in full, and they are not in fact of a different character from many collocations of words which the language writes separately: such are derselbe and derjenige (**168**, **169**), Hoheprieſter, 'high-priest,' etc. (**422.**1*a*).

c. All derivation and inflection begin with composition. The compound becomes in practical use an integral representative of the idea signified by it, its origin is more and more lost sight of, and it becomes liable to such alterations of form as more or less disguise its derivation: thus, Jungfrau has been in popular use abbreviated to Jungfer; and Jungherr (junger Herr, 'young sir'), in like manner, to Junker. And if the final member of the compound happens to be one that in practice is added to a large number of words, forming a considerable class of composite words, it may be turned into an ending, of derivation or inflection. Thus, dritter Theil became the compound Dritttheil, 'third part,' and this was contracted into Drittel; and, the same being done with the other ordinal numerals, tel became a "suffix," forming fractionals from ordinals (**207.2**). The conjugational ending ten, in wir hatten, 'we had,' represents in like manner an originally independent conjugational form, *tâtumês* (yet older *dadâmasi*), 'we did,' which has gone through a like process of abbreviation. (See the author's "Language and the Study of Language," p. 55 etc.) Composition therefore forms, in the grammatical treatment of a language, an appropriate transitional subject between inflection and derivation on the one side, and collocation or arrangement on the other.

419. Compounds are very much more numerous in German than in English, and the liberty of forming new ones, after the model of those already in use, is much more freely conceded than with us. In making practical acquaintance with the language, therefore, we are constantly meeting with them, of every class—from those in which the final member has almost acquired the value of a suffix (see above, **415.**15), or in which the fact of composition is otherwise disguised (as in Jungfer and Junker; or in ſolch and welch, see above, **415.**12), to the chance combinations which each speaker or writer forms as occasion arises, and which are not to be found explained in any dictionary, however complete.

a. Compounds are often also formed in German of a length and complexity unknown in English: thus, Feuerverſicherungsgeſellſchaft, 'fire insurance company;' Nordſeeſchifffahrt, 'North Sea navigation;' Luftröhrenſchwindſucht, 'bronchial consumption;' Reichsoberpoſtamtszeitungsſchreiber, 'editor of the imperial general postoffice journal.' Such, however, are for the most part met with only in technical and official language.

b. The parts of a compound—especially if it be a long and cumbrous one, or liable to an incorrect division—are sometimes separated by hyphens: thus, Feuerverſicherungs-geſellſchaft, or Feuer-verſicherungs-geſellſchaft. No rules are to be definitely laid down respecting this division, it being mainly left to the taste and choice of individual writers. Usage is also much at variance as regards the employment of capital letters for the separated parts of a compound noun—some writing, for example, Feuer-Verſicherungs-Geſellſchaft. The preferable method is to avoid as much as possible the multiplication of capitals.

c. Where two or more compound words having the same final member would follow one another, it is the usage in German often to omit that member except in the last word, noting the omission in the other cases by a hyphen appended to the former member: thus, alle Sonn- und Festtage eines Jahres, 'on all the Sundays and holidays of a year;' in dieser baum- und quellenleeren Einöde, 'in this treeless and waterless desert;' von der sonn- und festtägigen Spazierfahrt 'of the promenade usual on Sundays and holidays.' A similar liberty is even taken with words of foreign origin: thus, als Of- und Defensivwaffe, 'as offensive and defensive weapon' (R. 161.13); but it is not to be approved or imitated.

Composition of Verbs.

420. The importance of compound verbs in the general grammatical system of German has rendered necessary their treatment under the head of verbal conjugation (**296-313**). Only a brief recapitulation of the different classes, therefore, is called for here.

1. Verbs are compounded with the inseparable prefixes be, ent or emp, er, ge, ver, zer; being conjugated, in general, in the same manner as when simple, but losing the prefix ge of the past participle; retaining, also, their proper accent. See **302-7**.

2. Verbs are compounded with a considerable number of separable prefixes, simple and compound—which prefixes, however, stand before the verbal form, and are written with it as one word, only in the infinitive and participles; or in the personal forms of the verb also, when the sentence has the transposed arrangement. The prefix always has the principal accent. See **298-301**.

a. A few of the separable prefixes, however—namely, durch, hinter, über, um, unter, and wider or wieder—form with some verbs inseparable compounds. See **308-11**.

3. Verbs are compounded with nouns, adjectives, and adverbs; either closely, forming compound themes which are conjugated like simple roots, or loosely, forming themes which are conjugated after the manner of verbs with separable prefixes. See **312-13**.

a. There is no fixed line separating compounds of the latter character from verbal phrases, and some combinations are treated indifferently as the one or the other: thus, Dank sagen or danksagen, 'express gratitude;' Statt finden or stattfinden, 'take place.'

Composition of Nouns.

421. With few exceptions (**422.**6*b* etc.), compound nouns are made up of a noun with a preceding limiting word. The final noun determines the gender and mode of declension of the compound; the preceding member of the compound has the accent.

1. Exceptions as regards gender are

a. Names of towns, which are neuter (**61**.2*c*), even when they are compounds whose final member is masculine or feminine: thus, das Wittenberg (der Berg); das Magdeburg (die Burg).

b. Many compounds of der Muth, 'mood, spirit,' which are feminine: for example, die Anmuth, 'grace,' die Demuth, 'humility,' die Wehmuth, 'sadness.'

These are, by origin, feminine abstracts from compound adjectives, which have lost their suffix of derivation.

c. A few special words: thus, die Antwort, 'answer' (das Wort, 'word'): der Mittwoch, 'Wednesday' (literally, 'mid-week,' from die Woche, 'week'), which has taken the gender of the other names of week-days (**61**.2*a*); die Neunauge, 'lamper-eel' (literally, 'nine-eyes,' from das Auge, 'eye'): and Abscheu, 'horror,' is masculine, and Gegentheil, 'opposite,' is neuter, while Scheu, 'fear,' and Theil, 'part,' are now respectively used in general as feminine and masculine.

422. The varieties of compound nouns are

1. Nouns made up of a noun and a preceding qualifying adjective: thus, Vollmond, 'full moon,' Edelstein, 'precious stone,' Hochzeit, 'wedding' (lit. 'high time'), Kurzweile, 'pastime' (lit. 'short while').

a. A very few nouns are written as compounds of this class, although the adjective is declined as an independent word: thus, Hoherpriester, 'high-priest,' Langeweile, 'tedium,' Geheimerrath, 'privy-counsellor' (also Langweile, Geheimrath, as proper compounds).

2. Nouns made up of a noun and a preceding limiting noun: thus, Buchdrucker, 'bookprinter,' Geschichtschreiber, 'historian' (lit. 'history-writer'), Schullehrer, 'school-teacher,' Handschuh, 'glove' (lit. 'hand-shoe'), Weinglas, 'wine-glass,' Baumwolle, 'cotton' (lit. 'tree-wool'), Jagdleben, 'life by hunting,' Eichbaum, 'oak-tree.'

a. The relation of the first noun to the second is oftenest that of a genitive dependent on it; but it may stand in various other relations, often such as could not be expressed by any simple case, without the use of words of relation: or, the two words may be in apposition with one another.

b. Often the first noun is put formally in the genitive case: thus, Königssohn, 'king's son,' Landsmann, 'countryman,' Wirthshaus, 'inn' (lit. 'host's house').

c. And even, by irregular imitation of such forms, the first noun takes an s or es which does not properly belong to it as an independent word: thus, Geburtstag, 'birthday,' Liebesbrief, 'loveletter.'

d. The first noun sometimes takes a plural ending: thus, Bilderbuch, 'picture-book' (lit. 'pictures-book'), Wörterbuch, 'dictionary' (lit. 'words-book'), Kleiderschrank, 'clothes-press,' Waisenhaus, 'orphan asylum' (lit. 'orphans' house'), Tagebuch, 'journal' (lit. 'days-book').

e. These endings of declension are introduced in part for their meaning, in part for euphonic reasons; and insertions of a similar kind are occasionally made quite arbitrarily: as, Aschermittwoch, 'Ash-Wednesday,' Heidelbeere, 'heath-berry.'

3. **Nouns** made up of a noun and a preceding verbal root, having the value of a qualifying noun or adjective: thus, Singvogel, 'singing-bird, Brennglas, 'burning-glass,' Schreibfeder, 'writing-pen,' Studirzimmer, 'study-room,' Habsucht, 'covetousness' (lit. 'desire of having').

4. Nouns made up of a noun and a preceding particle, with qualifying force: thus, Außenseite, 'outside,' Inland, 'inland,' Auslaut, 'final sound (of a word),' Mitmensch, 'fellow-creature,' Vortheil, 'advantage' (lit. excelling part').

5. Nouns made up of an infinitive and words dependent upon it: thus, das Fürsichsein, 'the being by one's self,' das Zuspätkommen, 'the ccming too late.' These are unusual cases, and not employed in dignified style.

6. Compounds of a different and peculiar character, which designate an object by describing some peculiarity belonging to it, and which may be called *possessive* or *characterizing* compounds. Such are

a. A noun with preceding limiting word: as, Kahlkopf, 'bald-head' (a person or thing having a bald head), Blaustrumpf, 'bluestocking' (person wearing such), Schreihals, 'bawler' (lit. 'scream-neck'), Viereck, 'square' (lit. 'four-corners').

b. An adjective with preceding qualifying word: as, der Nimmersatt, 'the greedy-gut' (lit. 'never satiated'), das Immergrün, 'the evergreen.'

c. A verb with a following object, or other limiting word or phrase: as, Taugenichts, 'good-for-nothing,' Störenfried, 'kill-joy' (lit. 'disturb-peace'), Stelldichein, 'rendezvous' (lit. 'make thine appearance'), Springinsfeld, 'romp' (lit. 'jump into the field'), Kehraus, 'closing dance' (lit. 'turn-out').

d. One or two more anomalous cases: as, Garaus, 'end' (lit. 'all over').

Composition of Adjectives.

423. Compound adjectives are always made up of an adjective with a preceding limiting or qualifying word. Their treatment, as regards declension, use as adverbs, and the like, is the same with that of simple adjectives. The first member of the compound takes the accent.

424. The varieties of compound adjectives are

1. Adjectives made up of two adjectives, of which the former either is co-ordinate with the latter—as in taubstumm, 'deaf and dumb,' kaiserlich-königlich, 'imperial-royal'—or, much more often, limits it in the manner of an adverb: as, hellblau, 'bright blue,' todtkrank, 'deadly sick.'

2. Adjectives made up of an adjective (usually a participle) and a preceding adverb: as, wohledel, 'right-noble, worshipful,' wohlmeinend, 'well-meaning,' sogenannt, 'so-called,' weitaussehend, 'far-looking.'

3. Adjectives made up of an adjective and a preceding limiting noun: as, schneeweiß, 'snow white,' trostbedürftig, needing consolation,' eiskalt, 'ice-cold.'

a. A very frequent form of this compound is made up of a participle and its dependent noun: as, heilbringend, 'salutary' (lit. 'health-bringing'), pflichtvergessen, 'duty-forgetting,' gottergeben, 'god-devoted.'

b. The noun in such compounds, as in compounds with a noun (**422.2b**-*e*), often takes the form of a genitive or a plural: thus, lebenssatt, 'tired of life,' lobenswürdig, 'praiseworthy,' hoffnungsvoll, 'hopeful,' riesengroß, 'gigantic' (lit. 'giant-great'), kinderlos, 'childless' (lit. 'children-less').

4. Adjectives made up of an adjective and a preceding verbal root, having the value of a dependent noun: thus, merkwürdig, 'remarkable' (lit. 'worthy of noticing').

This form of compound is rare and exceptional, the infinitive being generally used, instead of the simple verbal root.

5. Adjectives formed by appending a suffix of derivation, especially ig (**415.9**), to the combination of a noun with a preceding limiting word (which combination is not itself in use as a compound noun): thus, vierfüßig, 'four-footed,' großherzig, 'great-hearted,' hochnasig, 'supercilious' (lit. 'high-nosed').

Composition of Particles.

425. 1. The modes of formation of compound particles have been already sufficiently explained and illustrated, under the head of the different kinds of particles (see especially **365**). Such particles are, in part, cases of compound words, analogous with those just treated of; in part, phrases composed of independent and fully inflected words, which have simply run together into one by frequent usage; in part, they are combinations of particles.

2. *a.* Compound particles of the last class, and those of the second which are made up of a governing preposition and its governed case, are accented on the final member: thus, vorher', 'previously,' hervor', 'forth,' zudem', 'besides,' überhaupt', 'in general,' bergab', 'down hill.'

b. Such, on the other hand, as are originally cases of compound words, or phrases composed of a noun and a preceding limiting word, are accented on the first member: thus, him'melwärts, 'heavenwards,' viel'mals, 'often,' kei'neswegs, 'in no wise,' der'gestalt, 'in such wise.'

c. A few are accented on either the first or second member; and either indifferently, or according to a difference of meaning: thus, also' or al'so, 'accordingly,' et'wa or etwa', 'perchance,' ein'mal, when ein means distinctly 'one,' rather than 'a;' dar'um, war'um, hier'mit, when the emphasis rests on the pronominal element—and so on.

d. There are occasional irregular exceptions to these rules of accentuation, which may be left to the dictionary to point out.

CONSTRUCTION OF SENTENCES.

Introductory Explanations.

426. 1. A SENTENCE is a combination of words having completeness in itself as the expression of a thought.

2. It is composed of a SUBJECT, designating that of which something is asserted (inquired, desired), and a PREDICATE, expressing that which is asserted (inquired, desired) of the subject.

a. That a thought cannot be signified or communicated without the combination of a subject and a predicate is not claimed (compare **391**); but only that this combination is its full and regular mode of expression, the form to which all expressed thoughts may be reduced, or of which they are to be regarded as variations.

b. The division of the predicate, as above defined, into *predicate* and *copula* (the latter being always a person of the present tense of ſein, 'be:' compare **316.1***a*, remark)—for example, of er liebt, 'he loves,' into er iſt liebend, 'he *is* loving'—though of value in the logical analysis of expression, is unimportant in grammatical analysis, and has no bearing upon the construction of the sentence. All verbs except ſein, 'be' (and even that, in some of its uses), contain the copula combined with a more or less complete predication of some action, state, or quality: some require more than others a complement, to fill out their idea and make a significant predication: a few (**316.1**), so especially as to be called "verbs of incomplete predication;" a transitive verb is in itself less complete than an intransitive, and so on.

c. The completeness of a sentence composed of subject and predicate is a relative one—namely, as compared with a word, or a phrase not containing those two elements. A noun by itself suggests an object of thought; a noun with qualifying adjuncts *implies* certain things as standing in certain relations to one another, an object as invested with qualities: so also a verb by itself, or with adjuncts, calls up an intelligent conception in the mind; and either, in certain circumstances, has all the value of a complete expression, because the mind of the hearer or reader *understands*, or intelligently supplies, whatever is wanting. But we do not feel that anything is really *said* until a verb and its subject are combined, until something is predicated of something.

d. A sentence may signify only a small part of the thought which is in the mind of the speaker, and which he sets out to express; it may require to be set in connection with other sentences in order to perform its full office, as much as a word with other words to form a sentence. And, in the development of language, a means is found by which individual sentences are so combined as to form a higher unity—by which, instead of being merely set side by side, they are twined together into a complex sentence or period. This means is the conversion of independent sentences into *dependent clauses* having the formal as well as logical value of parts of a sentence (see below **435** etc.). For the simple sentence still remains the norm and unit of complete expression: the dependent clauses have value only as they enter into the structure of such a sentence, in the quality of adjuncts either to its subject or its predicate. They themselves, then, though containing a subject and a predicate, become incomplete, because they distinctly imply a relation to something else, which requires to be also expressed.

427. Sentences are of three fundamental kinds, *assertive*, *interrogative*, and *optative* (or imperative).

Thus, assertive, du liebst mich, 'thou lovest me;'—interrogative, liebst du mich, 'lovest thou me?'—optative, liebe du mich, 'love thou me!'

a. Of only the first of these can it be truly said that it involves the predication of something of a subject. The relations of the three to one another are best developed by reducing them to the common form of dependent clauses, expressing what is affirmed, inquired, or desired by some defined speaker. Thus, we say of another, er behauptet, daß du ihn liebst, 'he asserts that thou lovest him;' er fragt (will wissen), ob du ihn liebest, 'he asks (wants to know) whether thou lovest him;' er verlangt, daß du ihn liebest, 'he requires that thou love him.' When, now, we come to speak in our own persons, we change ich behaupte, daß du mich liebst, 'I maintain that thou lovest me,' into du liebst mich, 'thou lovest me,' the assertion of the assertion being usually a quite unnecessary formality; ich will wissen, ob du mich liebest, 'I wish to know whether thou lovest me,' becomes liebst du mich, 'lovest thou me?' the wish to know being intimated by arrangement and tone; and ich verlange, daß du mich liebest, 'I require that thou love me,' is changed into liebe du mich, 'love thou me!' the desire or demand being expressed by arrangement, tone, and appropriate verbal form. That is to say, the usage of language has established modes of expression by which the speaker can signify his desire to know, or his request or command, directly, without putting it necessarily, as he may do optionally, into the form of an assertion.

b. All these kinds of sentence alike consist of a subject and a predicate (save that the subject of the imperative sentence is often omitted as superfluous, when of the second person, or representing the individual to whom the request or command is directly addressed). And the assertive sentence is properly assumed as the norm or standard, of which the other two may be treated and explained as variations.

c. The formal construction and logical office of the three kinds of sentence do not always correspond. A variety of modes of expression (338) may be used as intimations of a command; a question may be expressed (432.1*b*) in the form of an assertive sentence; and an assertion may be implied in the asking of a question.

d. The direct assertive force of an assertive sentence may be variously and greatly modified, either by the mood and tense of the verb or by adjuncts, so that the statement is made uncertain or hypothetical to any degree—yet without affecting the grammatical character of the sentence. A negative sentence is only one variety of the assertive, in which, of two opposite and mutually exclusive things, one is affirmed by the denial of the other.

428. 1. The subject of a sentence is always a substantive word —that is to say, either a noun, or one of the equivalents of a noun (**113**)—along with such adjuncts (**109** etc.) as may be attached to it for its limitation and qualification.

2. The predicate of a sentence is always a personal form of a verb, since this alone has predicative force (**232, 314**): it may be accompanied by the various modifying adjuncts (**314** etc.) which it is capable of taking.

429. The arrangement of the sentence, as thus constituted, is subject to stricter and more intricate rules in German than in English: which rules will now be set forth.

a. The differences in construction between the two languages are in good part of comparatively modern growth; some of the peculiar rules which now domineer German sentences were only tendencies and preferences a few centuries ago.

b. Hence, in archaic style, as well as in poetry, the rules are much less strictly observed than in ordinary prose.

Regular or Normal order of the sentence.

430. 1. In its ordinary and normal arrangement, the German sentence, like the English, requires the subject to be stated first, and to be followed by the predicate.

a. This rule has reference to the simple assertive sentence; such a sentence, as explained above (**427.***b*), being taken as the standard from which the other forms are deduced. For the arrangement of the interrogative and optative sentences, see below, **432.**

b. Taken in connection with the rules already given as to the order in which the adjuncts of a noun and verb are respectively arranged (**110-12, 319**), this rule determines the whole order of the normal sentence; but it is desirable to call especial attention to the peculiarities which distinguish the German order.

2. No one of the adjuncts of the predicate is ever allowed to stand between the subject and the verb.

Thus, for English 'he truly loves justice, and never willingly commits a wrong,' the German must say er liebt treulich das Recht, und begeht nie willig ein Unrecht.

a. Rarely, a word or phrase is found inserted between the subject and the verb. Such a one, however, is never an adjunct of the predicate, but one of the conjunctions having exceptional freedom of position (**385.**4,5), or an asseverative particle, or a phrase of parenthetical force. The words oftenest met with in this position are aber, nämlich, also, indessen, and jedoch.

3. Since the infinitive (**348.**2) and the participle (**358**) are regularly preceded by whatever limits them, and since (**319.**2) the word most closely combined in idea with the verb as sharing in its predicative quality is put farthest from it, it results that

in sentences containing a compound tense, or a simple form of a separably compounded verb, the non-personal part of the verb (prefix, participle, or infinitive) stands at the end of the sentence: and the same place is taken by an infinitive dependent on the verb of the sentence, or by a word, other than a prefix, separably compounded with it, or forming with it a verbal phrase.

Thus, er blickte mit Wohlgefallen auf den emporschauenden Sohn der Erde hernieder, 'he *looked down* with complacency upon the upgazing son of earth;' du hast zwar nicht klug, aber doch natürlich und nach kindlicher Weise gehandelt, 'thou *hast acted*, not wisely, indeed, but yet naturally, and in childish fashion;' ihr werdet euch so blutig eurer Macht nicht überheben, you *will* not *presume* so cruelly upon your power;' ich will mein Leben als ein Geschenk aus eurer Hand empfangen, 'I *will receive* my life as a gift from your hand;' ich nahm nichts mehr von der hinter mir liegenden Ebene wahr, 'I *perceived* nothing more of the plain that lay behind me.'

a. Where there is more than one non-personal part of the verb in the sentence, the prefix stands before the participle, or the infinitive, or the participle and infinitive; and the participle stands before the infinitive: thus, ich gebe es auf, ich habe es aufgegeben, ich werde es aufgeben, ich werde es aufgegeben haben, es wird aufgegeben worden sein — since each element is prefixed to that to which it is added as a limitation (**314.***b*).

b. In the greater number of sentences, therefore, the two parts of the verb, the personal and non-personal, form as it were a frame within which are set all the verbal adjuncts, according to rules of arrangement (**319**) which are (except the one requiring the personal pronoun to come first) on the whole somewhat loosely observed, and liable to manifold variation. The three fixed points in the normal order of the sentence are the subject, the personal verb, and the non-personal part of the verb (if there be one present).

Inverted order of the sentence.

431. To arrange all sentences in the manner above described would result in an intolerable monotony. The German enjoys the same privilege as the English, and with even greater freedom, of putting at the head of the sentence any other member of it than the subject—for the general purpose of attaining a euphonious variety; or, more often, in order to lay an emphatic stress upon the member thus removed from its proper place. But, when any part of the predicate is thus put in the place of the subject, the latter is no longer allowed to stand before the verb, but is put next after it instead. This is called the *inversion* of the sentence.

Thus, in normal order, ein Landmann brachte seinen Kindern aus der Stadt fünf Pfirsiche, 'a countryman brought his children from the city five peaches:'—inverted, with no other change of meaning than as regards emphasis, fünf Pfirsiche brachte ein Landmann seinen Kindern aus der Stadt; or, again, aus der Stadt brachte ein Landmann seinen Kindern fünf Pfirsiche; or, seinen Kindern brachte ein Landmann aus der Stadt fünf Pfirsiche.

a. This arrangement is styled *inverted*, because, when the sentence consists of only three members, its effect is completely to invert their regular order: thus, er liebt mich, 'he loves me:' inverted, mich liebt er; er ist gut, 'he is good:' inverted, gut ist er. In all cases, too, the term is appropriate as denoting an inversion of the natural order of the two essential elements of the sentence, the personal verb and its subject.

b. The same inverted order, as occasioned by the same cause, is in English sentences also more or less usual, only not imperative, except in certain special phrases: thus, we say always "hardly had he gone, when . . .," but either "thus was it," or "thus it was;" and "slowly and sadly we laid him down," but "few and short were the prayers we said." In such phrases as "said I," "replied he," "added they," interjected in the midst of a quotation of some one's words, the inversion (made alike in English, German, and French) is best explained as falling under the principle here stated, since the part of the words already quoted is logically the object of the verb in the interjected phrase.

c. The only words (other than the subject) which are allowed to stand at the head of the sentence without causing its inversion are the *general connectives* (**384**), meaning 'and,' 'but,' 'for,' and 'either' or 'or.' Even the co-ordinating *adverbial conjunctions* (**385**) invert the sentence in their conjunctional use, as when proper adverbs.

d. As will appear below (**438.3*f***), an adverbial clause, if placed at the head of the sentence of which it forms a part, has the same inverting force as a simple adverb.

Even an adjective phrase belonging appositively to the subject, if placed at the head of the sentence, inverts it, being treated as if it were an adverbial adjunct of the predicate (as it often logically is so): thus, einstweilen beruhigt, zog nun das Heer Nikopolis vorüber, 'being for the time tranquillized (*i. e.* since it was so), the army now marched past Nikopolis;' zart und edel entsprossen, wuchs die königliche Blume hervor, 'the royal flower, having tenderly and nobly sprung forth, continued to grow (*i. e.* after springing forth).'

e. It is not usual, nor in good style, to remove to the head of the sentence more than a single connected member of the predicate—which may, however, consist of any number of words: thus, not seinen Kindern aus der Stadt brachte ein Landmann fünf Pfirsiche;—but dort, hinter diesen Fenstern, verträumt' ich den ersten Traum, 'yonder, behind those windows, I dreamed my first dream;' jetzt schnell, eh' die Brandung wiederkehrt, befiehlt der Jüngling sich Gott, 'now quickly, ere the surge returns, the youth commits himself to God.'

f. The members of the predicate most often placed at the head of the sentence for emphasis, with consequent inversion, are the object (direct, indirect, or remote), and the various adverbial adjuncts; less often a predicative adjunct (**316**); least often one of the non-personal parts of the verb. No part of the predicate, however, is exempt from such treatment, and even *g.* The personal verb itself is sometimes placed first in the sentence by inversion, with the effect of emphasizing the predication—that is to say, of strengthening the general force of the assertion made. In such an inversion, the verb is usually followed by doch, 'though;' much less often by ja, 'surely:' but neither of these particles is absolutely necessary.

Thus, sind doch ein wunderlich Volk die Weiber, 'surely women are a strange race of beings!' hab' ich dich doch mein' Tage nicht gesehen, 'surely I never saw you in my life!' Ja, so sind sie! schreckt sie alles gleich, was eine Tiefe hat! 'Yes, that is the way with them! everything that has any depth straightway terrifies them.'

h. In general, the inversion of the sentence affects the arrangement only of the personal verb and its subject. If, however, the subject be a noun and there be a personal pronoun in the sentence as object of the verb, the pronoun generally remains next the verb, and is put between it and the subject.

Thus, da verließ mich der Mann Gottes in tiefem Staunen, 'then the man of God left me in deep astonishment;' danach schlang sich der Lange um sie beide in einen Kreis, 'after that, the tall fellow twined himself round about both of them.'

The same thing is customary in the interrogative and the optative sentence (**432**): thus, wie haben euch die schönen Aepfel geschmeckt, 'how did the beautiful apples taste to you?' bewahre dich der Himmel, 'may Heaven preserve thee!'

A similar transfer of the pronoun from its proper place is usual also in transposed clauses: see **439**.1.

i. When, of two co-ordinate clauses following one another, the first is inverted, the second usually retains its normal order, even though the word or phrase which caused the inversion of the one logically forms a part of the other also: thus, darauf blieb er sitzen, und ich ging fort, 'thereupon he remained sitting and I went away.'

432. *Interrogative and Optative sentences.*

1. In German, as in English, an interrogative sentence is ordinarily arranged in the inverted order, or with the subject after the verb. In a direct question (one requiring "yes" or "no" as an answer), the verb comes first of all; in an indirect question, the interrogative word (pronoun, pronominal adjective, or particle), or phrase involving such a word, comes first.

Thus, wird die junge Schöpfung aufhören, 'will the young creation cease?' hält sie mich nicht mehr, 'does it no longer confine me?'—wo ist er, 'where is he?' was sucht ihr, 'what seek ye?' welches Buch hat er gelesen, 'what book has he read?' mit wessen Geld hat er es gekauft, 'with whose money has he bought it?'

a. When the interrogative word or phrase is itself the subject of the verb, the sentence necessarily retains its normal order: thus, wer hat mir das gethan, 'who has done that to me?' wessen Buch liegt hier, 'whose book lies here?'

b. Often, however (also as in English), a sentence is made interrogative by the tone with which it is uttered, while it has the construction of an assertive sentence: thus, ihr schweigt? die Ringe wirken nur zurück? 'you are silent? the rings only work backward?' das soll die Antwort sein auf meine Frage? 'that is to be the answer to my question?'

Often or usually, an interrogative sentence so constructed has a some what different force, implying "is it possible that . . .!" or "do you mean that . . .?" or the like.

c. An exclamatory sentence sometimes has the interrogative form: thus, wie schön ist der Morgen! wie scheint die Sonne so warm und mild! 'how beautiful the morning is! how warmly and gently the sun shines!'

2. The optative or imperative sentence takes, as in English, the inverted arrangement: that is to say, in the second persons, singular and plural, of the imperative, and in the various persons of the subjunctive used optatively or imperatively, the subject follows the verb, instead of preceding it.

Thus, sprich du, und wir hören, 'do thou speak, and we hear;' such' Er den redlichen Gewinn, 'seek thou (lit. 'let him seek') for honest gain!' möge nie der Tag erscheinen, 'may that day never appear!' wäre es hier nur nicht so dunkel, 'would that it only were not so dark here!' möcht' auch doch die ganze Welt uns hören, 'would that even the whole world might hear us!' o wär' ich nie geboren, 'O that I had never been born!' Compare **243.1, 331.**

a. But in the third person singular of the present subjunctive, the subject may also stand before the verb, and more frequently does so: thus, jeder komme wie er ist, 'let each one come as he is.'

433. *Conditional clauses.*

A clause of a sentence is very often inverted in German to express the conditionality of a statement—that is, to add the meaning of *if*.

Thus, hätte er gerufen, so hätten sie ihn gefunden, 'had he cried out (if he had cried out), they would have found him;' hat von euch jeder seinen Ring von seinem Vater, 'if each of you has his ring from his father;' erhebet ein Zwist sich, 'if a quarrel arises;' hat der Begrabene schon sich erhoben, 'if the buried one hath already arisen;' ließ er uns hier zurück, 'if he left us behind here.'

a. This mode of signifying the conditionality of a sentence is (as the first example shows) not unusual also in English, in the past subjunctive tenses *had* and *were*, in the conditional clause of a complete hypothetical period (**332.**1); and it is not wholly unknown under other circumstances: but in German the construction is a very common one, with all the different tenses of verbs of every class.

b. The same construction is frequent in the conditional clause of an incomplete hypothetical period, after an als representing the omitted conclusion (see **332.**2*b*): thus, er behandelte sie, als wären sie seine Unterthanen, 'he treated them as [he would treat them] if they were his own subjects;' er nickte mit dem Kopfe, als wolle er sagen: Schon recht, 'he nodded his head, as if he meant to say "quite right!"'

c. **Rarely, of two succeeding conditional clauses, only the first is inverted thus,** war es dann Winter, und der Schnee lag rings umher, 'if then it was winter, and the snow lay about:' compare 431.*i.*

Transposed order of the sentence.

434. The two modes of arrangement heretofore explained belong to independent or principal sentences or clauses (excepting only the inverted conditional clauses, treated in the last paragraph). The German construction, however, is most peculiar in that it has a special mode of arrangement for dependent (sometimes also called subordinate or accessory) clauses. In these, namely, while the other members of the sentence remain in their normal order, the personal verb is removed from its proper place to the end of the clause. This removal is called *transposition*, and the resulting arrangement is styled the *transposed.*

Thus, in normal order, der Tag **neigt** sich zu seinem Ende; but, transposed, wir sehen, daß der Tag sich zu seinem Ende **neigt**, 'we see that the day is drawing to its close;'— die Dämmerung **verhüllt** wie ein duftiger Schleier die Höhen und Thäler; but, die Dämmerung, welche wie ein duftiger Schleier die Höhen und Thäler **verhüllt**, 'the twilight which envelopes like a misty vail the heights and valleys;'— die Sonne **hatte** ihre Bahn vollendet; but, als die Sonne ihre Bahn vollendet **hatte**, 'when the sun had finished its course.'

a. The name "*transposed* order or arrangement" is abbreviated, for the sake of convenience, from "arrangement with transposed verb," which would be more fully and truly descriptive.

435. *Dependent clauses.*

1. A dependent clause is one which enters, with the value of a substantive, an adjective, or an adverb, into the structure of some other clause.

2. Dependent clauses are of three kinds, according to the parts of speech which they represent—namely, substantive clauses, adjective clauses, and adverbial clauses.

436. 1. A *substantive dependent clause* is one which has the logical value and construction of a noun.

2. Such a clause is introduced by daß, 'that,' ob, 'whether,' the compound relative pronouns and pronominal adjective wer, was, and welcher (179), or the compound relative conjunctions (385.2), wie, wann, wo and its compounds, etc.

3. A substantive clause stands in various constructions: thus,

a. As subject of a verb: as, **daß** er die Gesandten befreite, ist zwar gut, 'that he has released the ambassadors, is, to be sure, well;' **wann** diese

Erscheinung sich zutrug, **welche** Kraft den Einbruch bestimmte, ist tief in das Dunkel der Vorzeit gehüllt, 'when this event happened, what power determined the inroad, is deeply hidden in the darkness of antiquity.'

b. As object of a verb: thus, sie fragten, **ob** sie recht wüßte, **wer** ihr Mann wäre, 'they asked whether she really knew who her husband was;' ich will sehen, **wo** es liegt, 'I will see where it lies;' nichts kann ihm wieder ersetzen, **was** er verloren hat, 'nothing can make up to him what he has lost.'

c. In apposition with a noun or its equivalent: thus, mit der Entschuldigung, **daß** er zum Kriege beredet worden sei, 'with the excuse, that he had been persuaded into the war;' des Gefühles, **daß** nichts im Leben recht geschähe, wenn es bloß geschähe, 'of the feeling, that nothing in life was done properly, if it was just simply done;'—after es, as preceding indefinite subject (**154**.4): thus, zweifelhaft blieb es jetzt, **welchen** Weg man einschlagen solle, 'it remained doubtful now, which road one was to take;'—after other neuter indefinites, pronominal and adjective (see **179**.5): thus, allem, **was** da blüht, 'to everything that blossoms;'—explaining a preceding da, that represents the case of a relative pronoun governed by a preposition: thus, dies trug ohne Zweifel **dazu** bei, **daß** nur billiges verlangt wurde, 'this doubtless contributed to the result that nothing unreasonable was demanded;' sie dachte nur **darauf**, **wie** sie die Menschen ins Verderben locken könnte, 'she thought only of how she could entice men to destruction:' see below, *d.*

d. As governed by a preposition: thus, **ohne daß** er ein Glas nöthig hatte, 'without needing a glass;' harret ihr, **bis daß** der rechte Ring den Mund eröffne, 'are you waiting till [the time that] the right ring shall open its mouth?' außer wer seine Mitschuldigen seien, 'except whoever were his accomplices.'

Only a few prepositions thus govern a substantive clause directly, and some of these (**377**.1), the daß being omitted, have assumed the character of conjunctions: thus, **bis** die Fluthen sich verliefen, 'till the floods should run out:'—in general, if such a clause is to be placed under the government of a preposition, it is anticipated by a da in combination with the preposition, and itself follows, as if in apposition with the da: see just above, *c*; and compare **346**.2*a*.

e. As dependent on a noun: thus, dies waren die **Hauptursachen**, **daß** sie nirgends Freunde sahen oder gewannen, 'these were the chief reasons [of the fact] that they nowhere found or made friends.'

f. A substantive clause not infrequently stands in dependence upon a noun or a verb, by a pregnant construction, where a simple substantive could not stand without a preposition, or even sometimes more than that, to explain its relation to the noun or verb: thus, er erlag dem Schmerze, **daß** solch Unglück in seinen Tagen einträte, 'he broke down under his grief [at the fact] that such a misfortune should occur in his time;' ich danke Gott, **daß** ich meine Söhne wiedergefunden habe, 'I thank God that I have found my sons again;' sorgt, **daß** sie nicht aus meiner Kammer kommt, 'take care that she does not leave my room.'

g. A conditional clause after als (compare **433**.*b*) is sometimes used with the value of a substantive clause: thus, die anmuthige Täuschung, **als** sei es die eigene Existenz, die in allen diesen Anhängen mitschwebt, 'the pleasing illusion that (lit. 'as if') it 's our own personality which floats in all these appendages.'

437. 1. An *adjective dependent clause* is one which belongs to and qualifies a noun.

2. Such a clause is introduced by a relative pronoun, der or welcher (or a prepositional phrase containing such), or by a relative conjunction—namely, the compounds of da and wo with prepositions or with adverbs of direction, and the simple conjunctions wo, wenn, wann, da, als, wie (compare **386**.3).

Thus, ein Wunsch, den auch ich in meinen Jünglingsjahren hatte, 'a wish which I also had in the years of my youth;' das einzige Mährchen, welches er gehört hatte und zu erzählen wußte, 'the only story which he had heard and knew how to tell;' den Menschen, für dessen Vertheidigung ihre Stammväter kämpften, 'man, for whose defense their ancestors fought;' ihr Quellen, dahin die welke Brust sich drängt, 'ye fountains toward which the drooping breast presses;' einen Vertrag, wonach die Griechen einen friedlichen Durchzug erlaubten, 'a compact, by which the Greeks permitted a peaceable transit;' das Land, wo der Brunnquell des Glaubens entsprang, 'the land where the fountain of faith first sprang up;' in der Regenzeit, wenn das Delta überschwemmt ist, 'in the rainy season, when the delta is inundated.'

a. Any simple qualifying adjective may be converted by means of a relative pronoun into an adjective clause: thus, der gute Mann, 'the good man,' into der Mann, welcher gut ist, 'the man who is good:'—and, on the other hand, the German often puts into the form of an attributive adjective (especially a participle), with modifying adjuncts, what we more naturally express in English by an adjective clause: thus, er besiegte die zu unvorsichtig und in einzelnen Abtheilungen vordringenden Normannen, 'he vanquished the Normans, who were pressing on too incautiously and in isolated divisions.'

The order of the parts of such a compound adjective is the same with that of an adjective clause: thus, die Normannen, welche zu unvorsichtig und in einzelnen Abtheilungen vordrangen.

b. The German not infrequently uses an independent clause, introduced by a demonstrative pronoun, where our idiom requires an adjective clause, with a relative: thus, da ist einer, der kann mehr als ich, 'there is one—*he* can do more than I' (for der mehr als ich kann, '*who* can do more than I'). The difference of arrangement shows plainly enough what such a clause literally means.

c. An adjective clause is often employed, as in English, not so much to describe or qualify a noun, as to add to the sentence, in a more intimate way than by a simple connective, something relating to a noun: thus, die nationale Leidenschaft waffnete sich gegen ihn; der er unterlag, nachdem . . ., 'the national passion armed itself against him; to which he succumbed, after . . .'—instead of und dieser unterlag er, 'and to this he succumbed.' Or, what has logically a different value, as of a ground or reason, is cast into the shape of a descriptive clause: thus, deshalb beschloß der Kaiser, dem daran lag, schnell zu seinem Sohne zu kommen, 'accordingly the emperor, who was desirous of getting quickly to his son, resolved . . .'—instead of da es ihm daran lag, 'since he was desirous.'

438. 1. An *adverbial dependent clause* is one which performs the part of an adverb, by qualifying a verb, an adjective, or an other adverb.

2. It is introduced by one of the subordinating conjunction mentioned and classified above, under Conjunctions (386.4).

3. *a.* An adverbial clause, in most cases, qualifies a verb.

Thus, as adverb of *place*, wo in der Wildniß alles schwieg, vernahm ich das Geläute wieder, 'where in the wilderness all was silent, I heard the pealing again;'—of *time*, als nun die Morgendämmerung begann, berührte Eloah den Schlummernden, 'when now the morning twilight began, Eloah touched the slumberer;' eh' es zwölf schlug, saßen sie wie vorher, 'before it struck twelve, they sat as before;'—of *manner*, du magst alles schauen, wie ich dir gesagt habe, 'thou mayest behold everything as I have told it thee;' es raschelt mit den Aesten, daß mein Gaul toll wird, 'it rustles with the branches in such wise that my horse becomes frantic;'—of *cause*, ich blieb um sie, weil sie freundlich gegen mich war, 'I hung about her, because she was friendly toward me;'—of *purpose*, der muß mitgehen, damit wir den Felsen wegschaffen, 'he must go along, in order that we may get the rock out of the way;'—of *condition*, wenn du mir dienen willst, so komm mit, 'if you would like to serve me, then come along;' obgleich sie ihm nahe waren, konnten sie ihn doch nicht erblicken, 'although they were near him, they yet could not espy him;'—of *degree*, je heißer es ist, desto mehr frier' ich, 'the hotter it is (in proportion as it is hotter), so much the colder am I.'

b. An adverbial clause qualifying an adjective is usually one of degree or manner, introduced by wie or als, 'as' or 'than,' or by so daß: thus, solche Bedingungen, wie er sie vorzuschlagen gewagt hat, 'such conditions as he has dared to propose;' ein Stab, leicht umfaßt, so daß seine Bewegungen einigen Spielraum haben, 'a staff lightly grasped, so that its movements have some play;' ich habe so helle Augen daß ich durch die ganze Welt sehen kann, 'I have so clear eyes that I can see through the whole world;' das ist besser, als ich von ihm erwartet hatte, 'that is better than I had expected of him.'

. Where a so is present, it strictly qualifies the adjective as an adverb, and is itself qualified by the adverbial clause.

c. An adverbial clause qualifying an adverb is for the most part either introduced by daß as correlative to so, or it follows a demonstrative adverb of the same kind with that by which it is itself introduced, and correlative to the latter: thus, sie hob das eine Bein so hoch empor, daß er es durchaus nicht finden konnte, 'she lifted one leg so high up that he could not find it at all;' er konnte schon da, wo die Brücke aufhörte, den hellen Tag erblicken, 'he could already see the bright day at the point where the bridge ended;' nur darum, weil eine Seele vorhanden ist, 'only for the reason that a soul is present;' er spottete der Idee überall, wo sie nicht seines Sinnes war, 'he mocked at ideas in all cases in which they were not of his way of thinking;' ich kann sie erst dann stellen, wenn die Griechen andere ausliefern, 'I can only furnish them at the time when the Greeks deliver up others.'

In the latter class of cases, the preceding adverb is often superfluous, and the adverbial clause logically qualifies the verb.

d. Out of the frequent use of so with a following adverb in the principal clause, and limited by a succeeding adverbial clause introduced by als—for example, er ist so bald gekommen, als ich ihn rief, 'he came as soon as I called him'—has grown a very common construction in which the adverbial clause is itself introduced by so and the adverb (often combined into one word), and the als is usually omitted: thus, in Afrika, soweit wir es kennen, 'in Africa, so far *as* we know it;' sobald der Mensch sich dem Drucke der äußersten Noth entwunden hat, 'as soon *as* man has relieved himself of the pressure of extreme need;' so lang' ein Aug' noch weinen, ein Herz noch brechen kann, so lange wallt auf Erden die Göttin Poesie, 'so long *as* an eye can yet weep, a heart yet break—so long walks upon earth the goddess Poetry.'

e. A similar construction is sometimes made with an adjective, predicative or attributive: thus, aber so großen Ruhm dieser Sieg auch den Pilgern brachte, 'but, great as was the fame this victory brought to the pilgrims,' or 'however great fame this victory brought,' etc.—literally, 'so great fame *as* it even brought.'

In both these classes of cases, the implication of the omitted als is clearly shown by the transposed arrangement of the clause; and they are thus readily distinguished from the cases where sobald, so lange, etc., have simply their literal meaning.

f. If an adverbial clause, or an inverted conditional clause (**433**), be put at the head of the sentence, the principal clause takes the inverted arrangement, just as after a simple adverb (**431**): thus, wie er das hörte, stand er auf, 'when he heard that, he arose;' wenn die Grasdecke in Staub zerfallen ist, klafft der erhärtete Boden auf, 'when the covering of grass has fallen into dust, the hardened earth cleaves open;' ehe sie zur Natur zurückkehrt, kommt sie zur Manier, 'before it returns to nature, it becomes mannerism;' weil mir dieß sehr mißbehagte, dankte ich ihm ganz kurz, 'as this was very disagreeable to me, I thanked him quite curtly.'

g. After a prefixed adverbial clause, the principal clause is very often introduced by a particle—so, da, or the like; especially so—correlative to the conjunction of the former, and rendering easier the inversion: thus, wenn das ist, so kann ich dich brauchen, 'if that is the case, (then) I can make use of you;' als er die Hand zurückzog, da hob sich die Scholle, 'when he withdrew his hand, (then) the clod rose.'—A so stands in like manner as correlative to the implied wenn, 'if,' of an inverted conditional clause: thus, kann euch das nützen, so will ich euch gern dienen, 'if that can help you, (then) I will gladly serve you.'

And the inversion of the principal clause comes so to depend in appearance upon the correlative particle, that, when the particle is omitted, the clause not very infrequently retains (improperly) its normal order: thus, hätte er den Frieden gewünscht, es wäre seinem Reiche vortheilhaft gewesen (for wäre es, or so wäre es), 'had he wished peace, it would have been advantageous to his realm.'

h. An independent clause is often employed in German where our usage requires a dependent adverbial clause. Thus, for example, usually in a clause after one containing kaum, 'hardly:' as, kaum war der Vater todt, so kommt ein jeder mit seinem Ring, 'hardly was the father dead, *when* (lit., 'then') each one comes with his ring.'

i. An adverbial clause, like an adjective clause (**437**.*c*), is sometimes made use of to add something to the sentence—thus, doch plünderten einige aus Uebermuth; weshalb die Zufuhr aufhörte und Mangel entstand, 'yet some, out of wantonness, committed pillage: on which account the supply ceased and want arose'—or to make an antithesis—or for other purposes not wholly accordant with the office of a simple adverb.

439. *Additional rules respecting dependent clauses in general.*

1. In the transposed, as in the inverted (**431.***h*) order of the sentence, a personal pronoun as object of the verb not infrequently stands before the subject: thus, dafür, daß ihnen die christlichen Kirchen in Palästina eingeräumt werden sollten, 'on condition that the Christian churches in Palestine should be placed in their possession;' ein Land, wo sich alles in Fülle vorfindet, 'a land where everything is found in abundance;' als wenn sie ihm der Tod geraubt hätte, 'than if death had snatched her from him.'

2. When a clause ends with two or more infinitives, of which the last is used in place of a participle (**240.**1*c*), the transposed verb is put next before instead of after them: thus, weil ich nicht habe gehen können, 'because I have not been able to go;' denn ihr wißt, daß ihr mich habt ermorden lassen wollen, 'for you know that you have wanted to have me murdered.' Compare **348.2***a*.

By imitation of this construction, the transposed verb is also sometimes placed before a participle and infinitive, or two participles.

3. *a.* In a dependent clause, the transposed auxiliary (haben or sein) of a perfect or pluperfect tense is very frequently omitted: thus, früher als ihr gedacht [hattet], 'earlier than you *had* thought;' daß hie und da ein Glücklicher gewesen [ist], 'that here and there *has* been one happy man;' indem er zwei nicht [hat] drücken mögen, 'as he *has* not wished to do injustice to two;' was Feuers Wuth ihm auch geraubt [habe], 'whatever the fire's fury *may have* taken from him.'

b. Much more rarely, the transposed copula (a form of sein, 'be') is in like manner omitted: thus, daß mir es immer unerklärt [ist], 'that it *is* ever unaccountable to me;' wenn des Fragens ihr nicht müd' [seid], 'if ye *are* not weary of asking;' die Wege, auf welchen das Beste zu haben [ist], 'the ways in which the best *is* to be had.'

4. *a.* An exclamation often has the arrangement of a dependent clause: thus, wer mit euch wanderte, 'if one could but go with you!' (lit. '[how happy he] who should' etc.); wie er sich windet, 'how he twists himself!'

b. A question may be asked in the same manner: thus, ob sie wohl horcht, '[I wonder] whether she is perhaps listening?'

5. Whether a dependent clause shall be placed within the framework of the one upon which it depends, or outside that framework, is determined mainly by rhetorical or euphonic considerations: but it is much more usually placed outside: thus, das allererste, was sie in dieser Welt hörten, als der Deckel von der Schachtel genommen wurde, in der sie lagen, war das Wort: „Zinnsoldaten!" 'the very first thing that they heard in this world, when the cover was taken from the box in which they lay, was the word "tin soldiers!"'—not was sie in dieser Welt, als der Deckel von der Schachtel, in der sie lagen, genommen wurde, hörten, which would be excessively awkward. But, as the example shows, clauses qualifying the subject of a sentence have to be brought in before the predicate—unless, indeed, as is often done, the principal clause is inverted.

6. In general, no sentence in German takes the transposed arrangement, as a dependent clause, unless it be *grammatically* as well as logically dependent—that is to say, unless it be introduced by a word (conjunction or

relative pronoun) which gives it distinctly and formally a dependent character. Many a clause is logically dependent (especially as a substantive clause) without being so formally: thus, ich dächte, es wäre um desto göttlicher (or, daß es um desto göttlicher wäre), 'I should think it was so much the more divine' (or, 'that it was' etc.).

Exceptions are

a. A clause following another dependent clause, and implying the same subordinating word by which the former was introduced: thus, hiezu kam, daß die Könige von Sicilien mit Hofränken kämpfen mußten, der Norden zu fern lag, und Spanien sich kaum der näheren Feinde erwehren konnte, 'to this was added, that the kings of Sicily had to contend with court intrigues, [that] the north lay too far away, and [that] Spain could hardly defend herself against nearer enemies.'

b. The cases explained above (**438.**3*d,e*), where als is omitted after so followed by an adverb or adjective.

c. A number of words (adverbs, prepositions, and so on) which were formerly construed with substantive clauses introduced by daß, 'that'—or, in part, are sometimes still so construed—have now won the character of conjunctions, and themselves introduce a dependent clause directly, the daß being omitted: thus, bis, 'until' (for bis daß, 'as far as the time that'); ungeachtet, 'although' (for ungeachtet daß, 'it being disregarded that'); nun, 'now' (for nun daß, 'now that'), and others: compare **377.**1.

d. It may be remarked here that an inverted conditional clause (**433**) is really a dependent clause, both logically and formally—as much so as if it were introduced by wenn, 'if,' and had the transposed order of arrangement; only its dependence is shown in another and peculiar manner.

Summary of the Rules of Arrangement.

440. For the convenience of both teacher and learner, the leading rules respecting the arrangement of clauses, those which it is most important to commit to memory and keep constantly ready for application, are presented below in summary.

441. 1. There are three modes of arranging the sentence in German:

a. The *normal*, or *regular;*

b. The *inverted;*

c. The *transposed.*

2. The first two belong to independent clauses, the third to dependent.

3. Their character is determined by the position of the simple predicate, or the personal verb:

a. In the *normal* arrangement, the personal verb immediately follows the subject;

b. In the *inverted* arrangement, it precedes the subject

c. In the *transposed* arrangement, it is at the end of the clause.

442. The order of the *normal* sentence is

1. The subject;

2. The simple predicate, or personal verb;

3. The various modifying adjuncts of the predicate, as objects, adverbs, predicate noun or adjective;

4. Finally, the non-personal part of the verb (if there be one) —namely, prefix, participle, or infinitive: and, if more than one be present, they follow one another in their order as here mentioned.

Among the modifying adjuncts of the predicate, standing after the personal verb, or between it and the non-personal part of the verb,

a. A personal pronoun directly dependent on the verb regularly comes first;

b. An accusative object precedes a genitive, and more usually follows a dative;

c. An adverb of time ordinarily comes before one of place, and both before one of manner;

d. A predicate noun or adjective, especially a factitive predicate, usually comes last.

More special rules would be too liable to exceptions to be worth giving.

Examples of a normally arranged sentence:

1.	2.	3.	4.
er	schickt;		
er	schickt	das Buch;	
er	hat	mir das Buch	geschickt;
mein Freund	wird	mir das Buch bald nach Hause	zurückgeschickt haben:

that is, 'he sends;' 'he sends the book;' 'he has sent me the book; 'my friend will soon have sent the book back home to me.'

443. The order of the *inverted* sentence is the same with that of the normal sentence, except that the subject comes next after the personal verb, instead of next before.

The inverted order is followed

1. When any part or adjunct of the predicate is put in the place of the subject, at the head of the sentence;

2. Rarely, for impressiveness; with the personal verb first, and usually with doch or ja, 'surely,' somewhere after it;

3. In interrogative sentences, or when a question is asked;

4. In optative or imperative sentences—that is, when a command or desire is expressed;

5. Often in conditional sentences, or to give the meaning of *if*.

Special rules. *a.* The general connectives, meaning 'and,' 'but,' 'for,' or 'or,' are the only words which, save in rare and exceptional cases, are allowed to precede the subject without inverting the sentence.

b. In an inverted sentence, a personal pronoun as object is often put before the subject.

Examples of inverted sentences:

1 mir hat er das Buch geschickt;
das Buch hat er mir geschickt;
geschickt hat er mir das Buch:

that is, 'he has sent me the book'—with varying emphasis, first on 'me,' then on 'the book,' last on 'sent.'

2. hat er mir doch das Buch geschickt:

that is, 'surely he has sent me the book.'

3. hat er mir das Buch geschickt?
was hat er mir geschickt?
wem hat er das Buch geschickt?

that is, 'has he sent me the book?' 'what has he sent me?' 'to whom has he sent the book?'

4. schicke er mir das Buch!

that is, 'let him send me the book!'

5. schickt er mir das Buch, so thut er wohl:

that is, 'if he sends me the book, he does well.'

b. hat mir mein Freund das Buch geschickt?

that is, 'has my friend sent me the book?'

444. The order of the *transposed* clause is the same with that of the normal sentence, except that the personal verb is removed from its proper place to the very end of the clause.

The transposed order is followed in *dependent clauses*—that is to say, in such as, being introduced by a subordinating word (relative pronoun or conjunction), are made to enter as members into the structure of some other clause.

Such a clause has the value either of a noun, an adjective, or an adverb, and is accordingly reckoned as a *substantive*, *adjective*, or *adverbial* dependent clause.

1. A *substantive dependent clause* is either the subject or ob-

ject of a verb, or in apposition with or dependent upon a noun or governed by a preposition.

It is introduced by daß, 'that,' ob, 'whether,' or a compound relative pronoun or particle.

Example of a substantive dependent clause (objective):

ich weiß, daß er mir das Buch geschickt hat:

that is, 'I know that he has sent me the book.'

2. An *adjective dependent clause* belongs to and qualifies a noun. It is introduced by a relative pronoun or a relative particle.

Example of an adjective dependent clause:

das Buch, welches er mir geschickt hat:

that is, 'the book which he has sent to me.'

3. An *adverbial dependent clause* qualifies usually a verb, sometimes an adjective or an adverb.

It is introduced by a subordinating conjunction of place, time, manner, cause, purpose, condition, or degree.

Examples of an adverbial dependent clause:

als er mir das Buch schickte;

wenn er mir das Buch geschickt hat:

that is, 'when he sent me the book;' 'if he has sent me the book'

Special rules. *a.* In a transposed sentence, a personal pronoun as object is sometimes put before the subject (if the latter be a noun).

b. If the sentence ends with more than one infinitive, the transposed verb is put next before instead of after them.

Examples:

a. ob mir mein Freund das Buch geschickt hat;

b. weil er mir das Buch nicht hat schicken wollen:

that is, 'whether my friend has sent me the book;' 'because he has not wanted to send me the book.'

Concluding Remarks.

445. It must not be supposed that the rules of arrangement, as drawn out in the preceding pages, are always and everywhere strictly observed, even in prose. The demands of euphony, the suggestions of style, even sometimes the arbitrary and unexplainable choice of a writer, lead to their not infrequent violation. A few cases of such violation, of sufficiently prevalent occurrence to constitute exceptional classes, have been pointed out above; but to show in detail the different degree of obligatory force belonging to the different rules, and how and under what circumstances their neglect is permitted, would require a treatise.

446. The construction of sentences has been taken up and treated here only on its grammatical side. To treat it on its rhetorical or stylistic side—to explain how and to what extent clauses may be put together so as to form admissible or harmonious sentences and periods—is not the duty of a grammar. There is, in theory, no limitation to the expansion of a simple sentence; for both its subject and predicate may involve a variety of modifying adjuncts in the shape of words, phrases, and clauses; and each part of these clauses may take on further clauses as adjuncts—and so on, *ad infinitum.* The usages of the language, gradually established under the influence of a regard for euphony and for convenient intelligibility, practically set bounds to this indefinite expansion. But the bounds are very differently drawn in different styles of composition, in every language, and the variety in German is notably greater than in most other languages. Between the style of simple narration, and that excessive involution and intricacy in which many German writers love to indulge, there is an immense interval. It is because poetry is intolerant of involved periods that German poetry is, upon the whole, decidedly easier to the learner than German prose. No one, of course, can put together German periods which shall be tolerable—much less, elegant—after study of the rules of construction in a grammar: familiarity with the language as spoken and written, the acquisition of what seems an instinctive feeling for the harmony of construction, but is in fact an educated habit, the product of much reading and hearing, can alone enable one to compose such sentences as Germans compose.

RELATION OF GERMAN TO ENGLISH.

447. 1. A part, and the most essential part, of our English language—namely, that derived from the Anglo-Saxon—is of near kindred with the German.

a. That other and very important part of our language which is more directly akin with the French and Latin was brought in and grafted upon the Anglo-Saxon in consequence of the conquest of England by the Normans, in the 11th century. The Normans were of Germanic (Scandinavian) race, though they had been settled in France long enough to have substituted the French language for their own. Thus our Germanic blood is purer from intermixture than our Germanic speech.

2. This part akin with German includes, along with the most frequently used and familiar words in our vocabulary, nearly the whole of the *grammatical apparatus* of English—that is to say, all its *endings of inflection* (**393**), most of its *endings of derivation*, its suffixes and prefixes (**394-5**), and the larger part of its indeclinable particles, or words of relation.

448. Kindred in language, as elsewhere, implies descent from a common ancestor: the English and German are modern dialects of one original language.

a. That is to say, there was a time when the forefathers of the English-speakers and those of the German-speakers formed together a single community, of uniform speech. By its division, under historical causes, into separate and independent communities, and by the consequently discordant changes which these communities have wrought each upon its own speech, the various dialects now spoken have gradually come to exhibit the differences which characterize them. (See, for the causes affecting the growth of dialects, the author's "Language and the Study of Language," p. 153 etc.)

b. Thus, the Englishman and the German both use the words *sing*, *sang* (ſing', ſang) in the same sense, because each has received them with this sense by uninterrupted tradition—going down from father to son just as language goes nowadays—from ancestors who lived together and differed in their talk no more than we ourselves and our immediate neighbors. Thus, on the other hand, the one says *slay*, *slew*, and the other ſchlag', ſchlug ('strike, struck')—words originally identical in pronunciation and meaning, though now different in both—because these words have, in the course of their tradition, become differently altered in the one and the other line, in the same manner as words are altered nowadays.

449. The English and German are joint members of a group or sub-family of dialects called the GERMANIC (often also "Teutonic"); which, again, is a member of a larger family, called the INDO-EUROPEAN (also "Indo-Germanic," "Japhetic," or "Aryan").

450. The Indo-European family includes most of the languages of Europe and southwestern Asia. Its divisions are

1. The *Germanic* (**451**);

2. The *Slavic* (Russian, Polish, Bohemian, Servian, etc.) and *Lithuanic*;

3. The *Celtic* (Welsh, Irish, Gaelic, etc.);

4. The *Italic* (Latin, etc.; and, as modern representatives of the Latin, the Italian, French, Spanish, etc.);

5. The *Greek* (ancient and modern);

6. The *Persian* (Zend, Modern Persian, etc.);

7. The *Indian* (ancient Sanskrit, Pali, Prakrit; modern Hindi, Bengali, Marathi, etc.).

a. The resemblances and differences of these languages are of the same kind with those of the English and German, and due to the same causes If, where we say *six* and the German ſechs, the ancient Roman said *sex*, the ancient Greek *hex*, the ancient Hindu *shash*, and so on, it is all for the same reason for which the Germans and we say *sing* and *sang* (above, **448**.*b*). Only, in this wider family, of races whose separation is much more ancient, the remaining correspondences are proportionally fewer and less conspicuous, the discordances more numerous and deeper.

b. Although relationships for the languages here named have been surmised and are often claimed, on a yet wider scale (for example, with the Hebrew and the other "Semitic" languages), they have not been demonstrated. See, for the Indo-European family in general and in particular the author's "Language and the Study of Language," p. 186 etc.

451. The divisions of the Germanic branch of this great family are as follows:

1. The *Low-German*, occupying the lowlands of northern Germany. To this division belong—the *English*, as modern representative of the Anglo Saxon, which was carried into England, and made to displace the Celtic, by the invading tribes from the northern shores of Germany, in the fifth century; the *Dutch*, or literary language of the Netherlands; the ancient *Saxon* and *Frisian*, no longer cultivated; and the various dialects now spoken among the people in northern Germany, whose literary language is the cultivated High-German, or "German."

2. The *High-German*, occupying central and southern Germany. The only existing cultivated dialect of this division is the one which we know as "the German" language; its history will be given with a little more fulness farther on (**462** etc.).

3. The *Scandinavian*, occupying the peninsulas of Denmark and Sweden and Norway, with the island of Iceland (colonized from Norway in the ninth century). Its languages are the ancient Icelandic or *Old Norse*, and the modern *Norwegian*, *Swedish*, and *Danish*.

These are all the divisions represented by existing languages. Besides them, however, is to be noticed

4. The *Gothic*, represented by parts of a Gothic version of the Bible made in the fourth century of our era in the dialect of the Goths of Mœsia (generally called, therefore, the Mœso-Gothic), by their bishop Ulfilas. Of all the extant monuments of Germanic language, this is by two or three centuries the oldest, and therefore of the highest value in all inquiries into the history of the whole Germanic family of languages.

452. 1. The more immediate connection of English is thus seen to be with the Low-German languages; but its relation to the German is very near, as compared with that to the other European tongues, and the correspondences of word, grammatical form, and meaning, between the two are numerous and striking.

2. These correspondences—beside their intrinsic interest, and their value as historical evidences bearing upon the development of both languages, the relations of the races speaking them, and the growth of ideas and institutions among those races—have also a practical value, as a help to the scholar to whose attention they are brought in retaining the meaning of the German words he is endeavoring to learn.

3. It is the proper duty of a German-English dictionary to point out in detail the English words which are to be regarded as identical, or of kindred

elements, with German words (a duty sought to be fulfilled in the vocabulary to the author's German Reader). But no small part of the correspondences are readily to be discovered by the scholar himself, especially if his researches are guided at first by a judicious and enlightened teacher.

4. The varieties of difference, both of form and meaning, which distinguish German words from their English correspondents, are much too great to allow of their being set forth here. To exhibit with fulness even the more important among them, and explain their reasons (so far as these admit of explanation), would be the work of a professed comparative grammar of the Germanic languages. There is, however, one set of differences which are so regular in their occurrence, and which are of such prime importance for one who undertakes to compare German words with English, that they may not be passed without notice.

The Law of Progression of Mutes.

453. The law of progression of mutes (in German, the Lautverschiebung, 'pushing of sounds out of place:' generally called "Grimm's Law," after the great German grammarian Jacob Grimm, who was the first clearly to illustrate and establish it) is one of the most striking and characteristic features of the whole body of Germanic languages, affecting the original mutes of those languages with a regular but intricate system of changes.

454. The original mute letters of the Indo-European languages are nine in number, and of three classes—*lingual* or *t*-mutes, *palatal* or *k*-mutes, and *labial* or *p*-mutes: each class containing a surd mute (*t, k, p*), an aspirate (*th, kh, ph*—more originally *dh, gh, bh*), and a sonant (*d, g, b*). Thus,

	surd.	aspirate.	sonant.
lingual mutes	*t*	*dh* or *th*	*d*
palatal mutes	*k*	*gh* or *kh*	*g*
labial mutes	*p*	*bh* or *ph*	*b*

a. These aspirates are to be understood as uttered in the way they are written—that is to say, with an *h* or aspiration audibly following the mute letter which begins them: and not, for instance, as we are accustomed to pronounce our *th* and *ph*. These last are not aspirated mutes, but *spirants*, simple continuable sounds, which have grown out of the aspirates, but are phonetically of quite another character. Any aspirate in the Germanic languages which had become a spirant was no longer liable to the law of progression.

455. It is found now that, as a general rule, in the great body of the Germanic languages (Gothic, Scandinavian, Low-German), each of these mutes has been pushed forward one step in its own class, the surds having become aspirates, the aspirates sonants, and the sonants surds; while, in the High-German languages (including the "German"), each has been pushed forward two steps, the surds having become sonants, the aspirates surds, and the sonants aspirates.

456. 1. This rule would in strictness require that

	lingual	labial	palatal	
original	*t, th, d*	*p, ph, b*	*k, kh, g*	should have become
English	*th, d, t*	*ph, b, p*	*kh, g, k*	and
German	*d, t, th*	*b, p, ph*	*g, k, kh;*	

but to the regularity of this result there are many exceptions:

a. Original *p* and *k*, in whole classes of words, at their first change were converted into the spirants *f* and *h*, instead of the aspirated mutes *ph* and *kh*, and so remained unaltered by the second change.

b. The High-German dialects in general took the second step of progression less completely and less strictly in the labial and palatal than in the lingual series. In the two first, some dialects, at a certain period, were more faithful to the requirements of the rule than were others; but, in the modern German, the authority of the latter has prevailed. Thus, for bin, 'be,' the older monuments give *pim* (*p* for *b*)—and so in a great number of other cases.

c. In the lingual series, the German has converted the aspirate *th*, regularly required as the correspondent of English *t*, into a sibilant, ſ or ʒ.

2. Hence, the actual correspondence between English and German, so far as concerns the law of progression, is in general as follows:

	lingual	labial	palatal	
to English	*th, d, t*	*f, b, p*	*h, g, k*	correspond
German	d, t, ſ,ʒ	b,f, b, f,p	h, g, k.	

Even these correspondences, however, do not hold strictly in all cases: thus,

a. A mute is often protected from alteration by combination with another letter: thus, *d* by *n* or *l*: as in Land, *land*, wandern, *wander*; Gold, *gold*; —*t* by *s*, *h* (*ch*, *gh*), *f*: as in Stein, *stone*, Hast, *haste*; Nacht, *night*; Kraft, *craft*.

b. Even the oldest English and German (the Anglo-Saxon and the old High-German) have their irregular exceptions to the rules of correspondence; and these exceptions have become much more numerous in later times, as each language, in the course of its history, has suffered anomalous changes in some of its words and letters.

457. Below are given examples of the more important correspondences between German and English consonants—those which result from the law of progression, and a few others.

458. *Lingual series.*

1. D in German answers regularly to English *th*: thus, das, *that*, denken,

think, dick, *thick*, doch, *though*, Durst, *thirst*, drei, *three*, Bad, *bath*, Bruder, *brother*, Erde, *earth*.

a. The most important exception is that of a d after n or l, as noticed above (**456**.2*a*).

2. T (or th: see **37**) in German answers regularly to English *d*: thus, Tag, *day*, tief, *deep*, Tod, *death*, thun, *do*, liebte, *loved*, Gottheit, *godhead*, selten, *seldom*, Wort, *word*, unter, *under*.

a. Excepted especially is a t after s, ch, f, which (as noticed above, **456**.2*a*) usually corresponds to an English *t*.

3. The lingual sibilants in German, s, ss, ß, z, often correspond to English *t*: thus, das, daß, *that*, heiß, *hot*, es, *it*, aus, *out*, besser, *better*, Fuß, *foot*, zwei, *two*, zu, *to*, Zeit, *tide*, Zahl, *tale*, Zoll, *toll*.

a. But the sibilants are also in numberless cases the representatives of original sibilants, and are therefore found alike, or with but slight variations, in German and English: thus, sing, *sing*, so, *so*, dies, *this*, Stein, *stone*, Scham, *shame*, Schnee, *snow*, schelten, *scold*.

459. *Labial series.*

1. *a.* B, in German, when initial, regularly answers to English *b*: thus, Bad, *bath*, Bruder, *brother*, Blut, *blood*, geboren, *born*.

b. In the middle of a word, or as final, it is usually represented in English by *f* or *v*: thus, ab, *off*, *of*, halb, *half*, taub, *deaf*, Weib, *wife*, lieb, *lief*;—Taube, *dove*, sterben, *starve*, sieben, *seven*, Knabe, *knave*, über, *over*, Fieber, *fever*.

2. P in German answers, with very few exceptions, to English *p*: thus, passen, *pass*, Pech, *pitch*, Plage, *plague*, Spieß, *spit*, springen, *spring*.

3. *a.* F, like b, agrees with English *f* when initial: thus, fallen, *fall*, Fisch, *fish*, Fuß, *foot*, fliegen, *fly*, frei, *free*.

b. Elsewhere in a word, it usually corresponds to English *p*: thus, tief, *deep*, Schlaf, *sleep*, auf, *up*, reif, *ripe*, schaffen, *shape*, helfen, *help*, werfen, *warp*, offen, *open*.

4. Pf is a peculiar German combination, occurring with great frequency in words anciently derived from the Latin, as representing a Latin *p*: thus, Pflanze, *plant* (Lat. *planta*), Pforte, 'door' (Lat. *porta*), Pfeil, 'arrow' (Lat. *pilum*), Pfeffer, *pepper* (Lat. *piper*), Pfund, *pound* (Lat. *pondus*). But it is also found in a good many words of Germanic origin: thus, Apfel, *apple*, Pflicht, *plight*, Schnepfe, *snipe*, hüpfen, *hop*, Pfropf, *prop*.

460. *Palatal series.*

As a general rule, the letters of this series—namely, g, k, h, also nk and ng—are the same in German and English: thus, Gott, *god*, vergessen, *forget*, grün, *green*, Wagen, *wagon*;—kalt, *cold*, dick, *thick*, wirken, *work*, klar, *clear* Knabe, *knave*;—Haar, *hair*, Herz, *heart*;— sinken, *sink*, singen, *sing*.

Exceptions, however, of a more irregular kind, are very numerous. Thus,

a. English *ch* is found not infrequently where the German has k: thus, Kinn, *chin*, Strecke, *stretch*.

b. German ch is variously represented in English, by *k*, *gh*, *tch*, etc. thus, Buch, *book*, doch, *though*, leicht, *light*; Pech, *pitch*.

c. An original g, which the German has retained, has very often undergone manifold corruption or loss in English: thus, Tag, *day*, liege, lüge *lie*, mag, *may*, Weg, *way*;—Hügel, *hill*, Ziegel, *tile*, Vogel, *fowl*;—folgen, *follow*, Balg, *bellows*, Sorge, *sorrow*, borgen, *borrow*;—and so on.

d. H, as has been pointed out, is in German very often a mere orthographical device for signifying the long quantity of the neighboring vowel. Of course, where it has this character, nothing corresponding with it in English is to be looked for.

461. Into the discussion of the general tendencies and the special causes which have led to the harmonies and discrepancies of German and English words, and have produced either classes of correspondences or single and apparently anomalous cases of difference, we cannot here enter: such subjects would be in place in a historical grammar of German, or a comparative grammar of the Germanic languages in general.

BRIEF HISTORY OF THE GERMAN LANGUAGE.

462. The German language is, as has been seen, one of the dialects of the High-German sub-division of the Germanic division or branch of the Indo-European family of languages.

a. Every cultivated or literary language is, in the same way, by origin one of a group of more or less discordant dialects—one to which external circumstances have given prominence above the rest.

b. Since unity of speech cannot be maintained over a wide extent of country, or through a numerous community, except by aid of the unifying influences of high civilization and literature, it is only a matter of course that Germany, at the beginning of the historical era, was filled with a variety of dialects—many of which are yet far from being extinct.

c. Germany was first brought to the knowledge of the rest of the world by the Romans, whose attempts to conquer the country, as they had conquered Gaul (France), proved in vain, partly owing to the stubborn resistance of the German tribes, partly because of the remoteness of the country, and the decay of the aggressive force of the Roman empire. Later, nearly all the European provinces of the empire were overwhelmed, one after another, by roving hordes of Germans; but these nowhere established themselves in sufficient numbers to maintain their own speech. Thus the dialects of the Goths, the Vandals, and other noted German races, became extinct, by the absorption of those races into the communities of other speech among whom they settled.

d. The introduction of Roman Christianity, civilization, and letters into Germany (beginning in the fifth century), the establishment of the Frankish empire under Chlodowig over nearly all the German tribes (about the end of that century), and its yet more brilliant renewal under Charlemagne three centuries later (A. D. 742–814), produced in the country a state of things favorable to a unity of customs, institutions, and language. It remained then for circumstances to determine which of the many existing dialects should win such importance in the eyes of all the German peoples as to be accepted by them as their literary language.

463. The history of the High-German dialects falls into three periods:

1. The *Old High-German* period (Althochdeutsch), down to the twelfth century;

2. The *Middle High-German* period (Mittelhochdeutsch), covering four centuries, from the beginning of the twelfth to the time of Luther;

3. The *New High-German* period (Neuhochdeutsch), from the Reformation down to our own days.

464. 1. The Old High-German period commences with the eighth century; from which, however, only fragments have come down to us.

a. As the oldest of these is regarded the *Hildbrandslied*, a pre-Christian poem, in the alliterative verse which appears to have been the original form of poetic expression of the whole Germanic race.

2. The literature of this period is chiefly Christian, and consists of versions from the Latin, collections of words or glosses, paraphrases and comments of Scripture, and the like.

a. The most noteworthy productions of this class are Otfried's *Krist* (A. D. 868), a harmony of the four Gospels, in the first rhymed verse; a prose version of Tatian's harmony of the Gospels, of about the same period; the works of the monk Notker (about A. D. 1000) and his school, especially his prose version and explanation of the Psalms; Williram's (about A. D. 1075) prose paraphrase and explanation of Solomon's Song.

b. Besides these, there are a few songs, forms of imprecation, and other like remnants of a more popular and native class of productions.

3. The leading Old High-German dialect was the Frankish, as being the language of the ruling race and dynasty; but there was no prevailing literary dialect accepted through the whole country, each writer used his own native idiom.

a. Other dialects represented in this period are the Alemannic and Swabian, and the Bavarian and Austrian.

465. 1. In the Middle High-German period, the literary dialect was the Swabian.

a. Because it was the court-language of the empire under the Swabian emperors, Conrad and Frederick Barbarossa and their successors (A. D. 1138–1268).

b. The grand difference distinguishing the language of the Middle period from that of the Old, is the reduction of the former full and distinct vowels of the endings of words to the indifferent and monotonous e. Thus, gebe, 'I give,' was in the first period *gibu;* geben, 'to give,' was *gëban;* Fischen, 'to fishes,' was *viscum;* blindes, 'blind' (neut. sing.), was *blindaz;* blinden (gen.pl.) was *blindôno;* and so on. In this respect the Middle and New High-German stand nearly upon the same level.

2. The literature is abundant and various, and of a very high order of merit.

It may be divided into

a. The works of the *Minnesänger* ('love-singers'), of whom more than three hundred are more or less known. Some of the most eminent among them were Hartmann von der Aue, Wolfram von Eschenbach, Heinrich von Ofterdingen, Walther von der Vogelweide, and Gottfried von Strassburg. They wrote songs of love and chivalry, epics (chiefly founded on French and Provençal subjects), didactic poems, fables—almost everything excepting dramas.

b. The popular legendary epics, new workings-up of stories—half-mythical, half-historical—which had long been current among the German races, and even in part belonged to the whole Germanic race. Their authors are unknown. Chief among them is the Lay of the Nibelungen (*Nibelungenlied*), a magnificent poem; others are *Gudrun*, and the lesser tales which make up the *Heldenbuch* ('Book of Heroes').

c. The works of the *Meistersänger* ('master-singers'). These were poets by trade, organized into guilds, and carrying on their handicraft in a very regular and very uninteresting manner, in the fourteenth and fifteenth centuries (and later), after the decay of the national literature which had flourished under the Swabian emperors. Their productions have mostly gone into merited oblivion.

466. During the time of literary depression which occupied the last century or two of the Middle period, the foundations were laying for the New. The wearing-out of the feudal system; the rise of the cities to importance and wealth; the awakened sense for Art, both in architecture and in painting; the establishment of universities; the impulse given to classical learning through Europe in consequence of the capture of Constantinople by the Turks; the invention of printing, which put literature within the reach of a vastly increased class—all these circumstances prepared the way for a national culture which should be as much wider and deeper-reaching than that of the preceding period, as this than that of the first. And whereas in the Old period literature had been the property chiefly of the church and the priests, with complete diversity of dialects; and, in the Middle, the property of courts and the great, with acknowledged pre-eminence of the court-dialect; so now, it was to be shared in by the great body of the people, and to possess for its use something like a true national language.

467. The New High-German period begins with the grand

national movement of the Reformation, and especially with the writings of Luther.

a. The dialect which Luther used was not a continuation of the Swabian, which had long since sunk into insignificance, while each author had again begun to write in his own idiom; nor was it the precise spoken language of any part of the country: it was, as he himself states, the language of public affairs in Saxony, and used by the various courts throughout Germany. It had grown up in a measure on paper, in learned and literary use, and united in itself some discordant dialectic elements.

b. It was the nationality of Germany that created the possibility of a national language: it was the excited and receptive state of the national mind at the time of the Reformation, the inherent force and vigor of style in the writings of Luther and his coadjutors, the immense and immediate circulation which they won among all classes of the people, and the adoption of his version of the Bible as a household book through nearly the whole country, that gave to the particular form of speech used by him an impulse toward universality which nothing has since been able to check or interfere with. It has become more and more exclusively the language of education and learning, of the courts, the pulpit, the lecture-room, the school, the press; and in the large towns and cities it has to some extent extirpated or deeply affected the old popular dialects, which are now hardly met in purity except among the rude country population. Thus

468. The language of Luther, not a little modified in spelling, utterance, and construction, and greatly enriched by new formations and additions, is now the speech of the educated in all Germany (both High-Germany and Low-Germany), and therefore entitled to be called the GERMAN LANGUAGE.

a. To illustrate the alteration which it has undergone during the three centuries and a half of its existence, is here added Luther's version of the Lord's Prayer, as given in his first edition of the Gorman New Testament (1522): **Vnser Vater ynn dem Hymel, Deyn Name sey heylig; Deyn Reych kome; Deyn Wille geschehe auff Erden wie ynn dem Hymel; Unser teglich Brott gib unns heutt; Und vergib uns unsere Schulde, wie wyr unsernn Schuldigern vergeben; Unnd fure uns nitt ynn Versuchung; Sondern erlose uns von dem Vbel; Denn deyn ist das Reych, und die Krafft, unnd die Herlickeyt in Ewickeyt. Amen.**

b. The former dialects not only still subsist in Germany among the uneducated, but their influence more or less affects the literary speech, especially as regards its pronunciation, so that the educated even, from different parts of the country, do not speak precisely alike.

469. To give any history of the language, its cultivation, and its literature, during this its modern period, will not be attempted here: even to mention the names of the principal writers who have distinguished themselves by their contributions in German to literature and science would require pages. Such are their merits that to possess no knowledge of German is to be cut off from one of the most important sources of knowledge and culture within our reach.

GERMAN WRITTEN CHARACTER.

The German written letters are as follows:

Cap.	small.	equiv't.	Cap.	small.	equiv't.	Cap.	small.	equiv't.
		a			*j*			*s*
		b			*k*			*t*
		c			*l*			*u*
		d			*m*			*v*
		e			*n*			*w*
		f			*o*			*x*
		g			*p*			*y*
		h			*q*			*z*
		i			*r*	—		*sz*

The general peculiarity requiring especial notice in this character is the prevalence of angular instead of rounded strokes among the small letters. Owing to this, *i* is distinguished from *c* only by its dot; also *u* from *n* only by the round stroke above the former (which stroke, however, is omitted as unnecessary when the *u* is modified). Further, *e* is distinguished from *n* only by the strokes being made much closer together. For the same reason, the *a*, *g*, *o*, *q* are not entirely closed at the top.

The use of the two forms of small *s* corresponds precisely with that of the two forms of the same letter in printed text: the first is to be everywhere written for ſ, and the other for s.

For *sz* is written a peculiar character (as shown in the table), instead of a combination of those for *s* and *z*. Special forms of combination of *ss* and *st* are also sometimes made.

Examples:

Apfel. Bücherbrett. Christus. Deutsch. Erde. Fluß. Gebirge. Hammer. Ihr. Jedermann. Kreuz. Länge. Mädchen. Nachbar. Ochse. Preußen. Röcke. Spielzeug. Tochter. Ueberschuh. Vaterlandes. Wahrheit Xenien. Ypsilon. Zimmer.

Eile mit Weile. Aufgeschoben ist nicht aufgehoben. Jeder weiß am besten, wo der Schuh ihn drückt. Jeder ist sich selbst der Nächste. Morgenstund hat Gold im Mund. Neue Besen kehren scharf. Wovon das Herz voll ist, geht der Mund über. Allzuviel ist ungesund.

Du bist wie eine Blume,
So schön, und hold, und rein,
Ich schau' dich an, und Wehmuth
Schleicht mir ins Herz hinein.

Mir ist's, als ob ich die Hände
Aufs Haupt dir legen sollt',
Betend, daß Gott dich erhalte
So schön, und rein, und hold.

Heine.

Ueber allen Gipfeln — Ist Ruh;
In allen Wipfeln — Spürest du
Kaum einen Hauch;
Die Vögelein schweigen im Walde;
Warte nur, balde
Ruhest du auch.

Göthe.

ALPHABETICAL LIST OF

VERBS OF THE OLD CONJUGATION,

AND OF THE IRREGULAR VERBS OF THE NEW CONJUGATION

Explanations.—In the following table are given the principal parts of all the verbs of the Old conjugation, together with the preterit subjunctive; also the second and third singular indicative present and the second singular imperative, whenever these are otherwise formed than they would be in the New conjugation. Forms given in full-faced type (thus, **gebacken**) are those which are alone in use; for those in ordinary type (thus, bäckst, bäckt) the more regular forms, or those made after the manner of the New conjugation, are also allowed; forms enclosed in parenthesis are especially unusual, poetical, or dialectic: a subjoined remark gives additional explanation, if any is needed. The number of the class and division to which each verb belongs (see **263–6**) is added at the end.

For convenience, the forms of the modal auxiliaries and other irregular verbs of the New conjugation are included in the List, with reference at the end to the paragraph in the grammar where their conjugation is explained. They are distinguished by being put in ordinary type throughout.

No verb is given in the list as a compound. If found only in composition, hyphens are prefixed to all its forms, and an added note gives its compounds.

Infinitive.	pres't indic. sing.	pret. indic.	pret. subj.	imper.	past part.	class.
Backen, 'bake'	bäckst, bäckt	buk	büke	——	**gebacken**	II.2
often of New conj., especially when transitive; except the participle.						
-bären,	-bierst, -biert	**-bar**	**-bäre**	-bier	**-boren**	I.3
only in gebären, 'bear, bring forth' (formerly geberen).						
Beißen, 'bite'	—— ——	**biß**	**bisse**	——	**gebissen**	III.1
Bergen, 'hide'	**birgst, birgt**	**barg**	**bärge** **bürge**	**birg**	**geborgen**	I.3
Bersten, 'burst'	birstest, birst	barst borst	bärste börste	birst	geborsten	I.3
Biegen, 'bend'	—— ——	**bog**	**böge**	——	**gebogen**	III.3
Bieten, 'offer'	(beutst, beut)	**bot**	**böte**	(beut)	**geboten**	III.3
Binden, 'bind'	—— ——	**band**	**bände**	——	**gebunden**	I.1
Bitten, 'beg'	—— ——	**bat**	**bäte**	——	**gebeten**	I.4
Blasen, 'blow'	**bläsest, bläst**	**blies**	**bliese**	——	**geblasen**	II.3
Bleiben, 'remain'	—— ——	**blieb**	**bliebe**	——	**geblieben**	III 2
Bleichen, 'bleach'	—— ——	blich	bliche	——	geblichen	III.1
as intransitive, of either conj.; as transitive, of New only.						
Braten, 'roast'	brätst, brät	briet	briete	——	**gebraten**	II.3
Brechen, 'break'	**brichst, bricht**	**brach**	**bräche**	**brich**	**gebrochen**	I.3
Brennen, 'burn'	—— ——	brannte	brennte	——	gebrannt	249
Bringen, 'bring'	—— ——	brachte	brächte	——	gebracht	250
-deihen	—— ——	**-dieh**	**-diehe**	——	**-diehen**	III.2
obsolete except in gedeihen, 'thrive.'						

Infinitive	pres't indic. sing.	pret. indic.	pret. subj.	imper.	past part.	class.
Denken	—— ——	dachte	dächte	——	gedacht	250
-derben	-dirbst, -dirbt	-darb	-därbe -dürbe	-dirb	-dorben	I.3
only in verderben, 'perish;' which, as transitive, 'destroy,' is of New conj.						
Dingen, 'engage'	—— ——	dung (dang)	dünge	——	gedungen	III.6
Dreschen, 'thresh'	drischest, drischt	drasch drosch	dräsche drösche	drisch	gedroschen	I.3
-driessen	—— (-dreußt)	-droß	-drösse	(-dreuß)	-drossen	III.3
only in verdriessen, 'vex.'						
Dringen, 'press'	—— ——	drang	dränge	——	gedrungen	I.1
Dürfen, 'be permitted'	darf, darfst, darf	durfte	dürfte	wanting	gedurft	251
Essen, 'eat'	issest, ißt	aß	äße	iß	gegessen	II.1
Fahren, 'go'	fährst, fährt	fuhr	führe	——	gefahren	II.2
Fallen, 'fall'	fällst, fällt	fiel	fiele	——	gefallen	II.3
Fangen, 'catch'	fängst, fängt	fing fieng	finge fienge	——	gefangen	II.3
Fechten, 'fight'	fichtest, ficht	focht	föchte	ficht	gefochten	III.5
-fehlen	-fiehlst, -fiehlt	-fahl	-fähle -föhle	-fiehl	-fohlen	I.3
only in befehlen, 'command,' empfehlen, 'commend:' fehlen, 'fail,' is another word.						
Finden, 'find'	—— ——	fand	fände	——	gefunden	I.1
Flechten, 'twine'	flichtst, flicht	flocht	flöchte	flicht	geflochten	III.5
Fleißen, 'apply'	—— ——	fliß	flisse	——	geflissen	III.1
antiquated except in sich befleißen, 'exert one's self.'						
Fliegen, 'fly'	(fleugst, fleugt)	flog	flöge	(fleug)	geflogen	III.3
Fliehen, 'flee'	(fleuchst, fleucht)	floh	flöhe	(fleuch)	geflohen	III.3
Fließen, 'flow'	(fleußest, fleußt)	floß	flösse	(fleuß)	geflossen	III.3
Fragen, 'ask'	frägst, frägt	frug	früge	——	gefragt	II.2
properly a verb of the New conj. only.						
Fressen, 'devour'	frissest, frißt	fraß	fräße	friß	gefressen	II.1
Frieren, 'freeze'	—— ——	fror	fröre	——	gefroren	III.3
Gähren, 'ferment'	—— ——	gohr	göhre	——	gegohren	III.5
also spelt gären etc., without h.						
Geben, 'give'	giebst, giebt gibst, gibt	gab	gäbe	gieb gib	gegeben	II.1
Gehen, 'go'	—— ——	ging	ginge	——	gegangen	267
Gelten, 'be worth'	giltst, gilt	galt	gälte gölte	gilt	gegolten	I.3
-gessen	-gissest, gißt	-gaß	-gäße	-giß	-gessen	II.1
only in vergessen, 'forget.'						
Gießen	(geußest, geußt)	goß	gösse	(geuß)	gegossen	III.3
-ginnen	—— ——	-gann	-gänne -gönne	——	-gonnen	I.2
only in beginnen, 'begin.'						
Gleichen, 'resemble'	—— ——	glich	gliche	——	geglichen	III.1
usually of New conj. when transitive, 'make similar.'						
Gleiten, 'glide'	—— ——	glitt	glitte	——	geglitten	III.1
Glimmen, 'gleam'	—— ——	glomm	glömme	——	geglommen	III.5
Graben, 'dig'	gräbst, gräbt	grub	grübe	——	gegraben	II.2

Infinitive.	pres't indic. sing.	pret. indic.	pret. subj.	imper.	past part.	class.
Greifen, 'gripe'	—— ——	**griff**	**griffe**	——	**gegriffen**	III.1
Haben, 'have'	hast, hat	hatte	hätte	——	gehabt	239
Halten, 'hold'	**hältst, hält**	**hielt**	**hielte**	——	**gehalten**	II.3
Hangen, 'hang'	**hängst, hängt** (hangst, hangt)	**hing** **hieng**	**hinge** **hienge**	——	**gehangen**	II.3
sometimes confounded in its forms with hängen, 'hang' (trans.), New conj.						
Hauen, 'hew'	—— ——	hieb	hiebe	——	gehauen	II.4
Heben, 'raise'	—— ——	**hob** **hub**	**höbe** **hübe**	——	**gehoben**	III.5
Heißen, 'call'	—— ——	**hieß**	**hieße**	——	**geheißen**	III 2
Helfen, 'help'	**hilfst, hilft**	**half**	**hälfe** **hülfe**	**hilf**	**geholfen**	I 3
Keifen, 'chide'	—— ——	kiff	kiffe	——	gekiffen	III.1
Kennen, 'know'	—— ——	kannte	kennte	——	gekannt	249
Kiesen, 'choose'	—— ——	kos	köse	——	gekosen	III.3
antiquated, and most often met in erkiesen: küren is the same word.						
Klemmen, 'press'	—— ——	klomm	klömme	——	geklommen	III.5
forms of Old conj. very rare except from beklemmen.						
Klieben, 'cleave'	—— ——	klob	klöbe	——	gekloben	III.3
Klimmen, 'climb'	—— ——	klomm	klömme	——	geklommen	III.5
Klingen, 'sound'	—— ——	klang	klänge klünge	——	geklungen	I.1
rarely of New conj., especially when transitive.						
Kneifen, 'pinch'	—— ——	kniff	kniffe	——	gekniffen	III.1
Kneipen, 'pinch'	—— ——	knipp	knippe	——	geknippen	III.1
Kommen, 'come'	(kömmst, kömmt)	**kam**	**käme**	——	**gekommen**	267
Können, 'can'	kann, kannst, kann	konnte	könnte	wanting	gekonnt	251
Kriechen, 'creep'	(kreuchst, kreucht)	**kroch**	**kröche**	(kreuch)	**gekrochen**	III.2
Küren, 'choose'	—— ——	kor	köre	——	gekoren	III.3
Laden, 'load'	lädst, lädt	lud	lüde	——	**geladen**	II.2
Lassen, 'let'	**lässest, läßt**	**ließ**	**ließe**	——	**gelassen**	II.3
Laufen, 'run'	**läufst, läuft**	**lief**	**liefe**	——	**gelaufen**	II.4
Leiden, 'suffer'	—— ——	**litt**	**litte**	——	**gelitten**	III.1
Leihen, 'lend'	—— ——	**lieh**	**liehe**	——	**geliehen**	III.2
Lesen, 'read'	**liesest, liest**	**las**	**läse**	**lies**	**gelesen**	II.1
Liegen, 'lie'	—— ——	**lag**	**läge**	——	**gelegen**	I.4
-lieren	—— ——	**-lor**	**-löre**	——	**-loren**	III.3
only in verlieren, 'lose.'						
-lingen	—— ——	**-lang**	**-länge**	——	**-lungen**	I.1
only found in gelingen, 'succeed,' mißlingen, 'fail:' used in third person only.						
Löschen, 'extinguish'	lischest, lischt	losch	lösche	lisch	geloschen	III.5
the forms of New conj. preferably limited to transitive meaning.						
Lügen, 'lie'	(leugst, leugt)	**log**	**löge**	(leug)	**gelogen**	III.3
Mahlen, 'grind'	mählst, mählt	muhl	mühle	——	**gemahlen**	II.2
the forms of Old conj. now in use only in the participle.						
Meiden, 'shun'	—— ——	**mied**	**miede**	——	**gemieden**	III.2
Melken, 'milk'	(milkst, milkt)	**molk**	mölke	(milk)	gemolken	III.5
Messen, 'measure'	**missest, mißt**	**maß**	**mäße**	**miß**	**gemessen**	II.1
Mögen, 'may'	mag, magst, mag	mochte	möchte	wanting	**gemocht**	251

Infinitive.	pres't indic. sing.	pret. indic.	pret. subj.	imper.	past part.	class.
Müssen, 'must'	muß, mußt, muß	mußte	müßte	wanting	gemußt	251
Nehmen, 'take	nimmst, nimmt	nahm	nähme	nimm	genommen	I.3
Nennen, 'name'	—— ——	nannte	nennte	——	genannt	249
-nesen	—— ——	-nas	-näse	——	-nesen	II.1
only in genesen, 'recover, get well.'						
-nießen	(-neußest, -neußt)	-noß	-nöſſe	(-neuß)	-nossen	III.3
obsolete, except in genießen, 'enjoy.'						
Pfeifen, 'whistle'	—— ——	pfiff	pfiffe	——	gepfiffen	III.1
Pflegen, 'cherish'	—— ——	pflog pflag	pflöge	——	gepflogen	III.5
Preisen, 'praise'	—— ——	pries	priese	——	gepriesen	III.2
forms of the New conj. are occasionally met with.						
Quellen, 'gush'	quillst, quillt	quoll	quölle	quill	gequollen	III.5
of New conj. when transitive, 'swell, soak.'						
Rächen, 'avenge'	—— ——	(roch)	(röche)	——	gerochen	III.5
forms of Old conj. very rare, except the participle.						
Rathen, 'advise'	räthst, räth	rieth	riethe	——	gerathen	II.3
Reiben, 'rub'	—— ——	rieb	riebe	——	gerieben	III.2
Reißen, 'tear'	—— ——	riß	risse	——	gerissen	III.1
Reiten, 'ride'	—— ——	ritt	ritte	——	geritten	III.1
Rennen, 'run'	—— ——	rannte (rennte)	rennte	——	gerannt (gerennt)	249
Riechen, 'smell'	(reuchst, reucht)	roch	röche	(reuch)	gerochen	III.3
Ringen, 'wring'	—— ——	rang rung	ränge rünge	——	gerungen	I.1
Rinnen, 'run'	—— ——	rann	ränne rönne	——	geronnen	I.2
Rufen, 'call'	—— ——	rief	riefe	——	gerufen	II.4
rarely of New conj. in preterit.						
Saufen, 'drink'	säufst, säuft	soff	söffe	——	gesoffen	III.4
Saugen, 'suck'	—— ——	sog	söge	——	gesogen	III.4
forms of New conj. occasionally met: sometimes confounded with säugen, 'suckle.'						
Schaffen, 'create'	—— ——	schuf	schüfe	——	geschaffen	II.2
generally of New conj. when meaning 'be busy,' or 'procure.'						
Schallen, 'sound'	—— ——	scholl	schölle	——	geschollen	III.5
-schehen,	—— -schieht	-schah	-schähe	——	-schehen	II.1
only in geschehen, 'happen:' used in third person alone.						
Scheiden, 'part'	—— ——	schied	schiede	——	geschieden	III.2
of New conj. when transitive, 'disjoin.'						
Scheinen, 'appear'	—— ——	schien	schiene	——	geschienen	III.2
Schelten, 'scold'	schiltst, schilt	schalt	schälte schölte	schilt	gescholten	I.3
Scheren, 'shear'	schierst, schiert	schor	schöre	schier	geschoren	III.5
Schieben, 'shove'	—— ——	schob	schöbe	——	geschoben	III.3
Schießen, 'shoot'	(scheußest, scheußt)	schoß	schösse	(scheuß)	geschossen	III.3
Schinden, 'flay'	—— ——	schund	schünde	——	geschunden	III.6
Schlafen, 'sleep'	schläfst, schläft	schlief	schliefe	——	geschlafen	II.3
Schlagen, 'strike'	schlägst, schlägt	schlug	schlüge	——	geschlagen	II.2
Schleichen, 'sneak	—— ——	schlich	schliche	——	geschlichen	III.1

Infinitive.	pres't indic. sing.	pret. indic.	pret. subj.	imper.	past part.	class
Schleifen, 'whet'	—— ——	ſchliff	ſchliffe	——	geſchliffen	III 1
in other senses than 'whet, sharpen,' properly of New conj.						
Schleißen, 'slit'	—— ——	**ſchliß**	**ſchliſſe**	——	**geſchliſſen**	III.1
Schliefen, 'slip'	—— ——	**ſchloff**	**ſchlöffe**	——	**geſchloffen**	III.3
Schließen, 'shut'	(ſchleußeſt, ſchleußt)	**ſchloß**	**ſchlöſſe**	(ſchleuß)	**geſchloſſen**	III.3
Schlingen, 'sling'	—— ——	**ſchlang**	**ſchlänge**	——	**geſchlungen**	I.1
Schmeißen, 'smite'	—— ——	**ſchmiß**	**ſchmiſſe**	——	**geſchmiſſen**	III.1
Schmelzen, 'melt'	ſchmilzeſt, ſchmilzt	ſchmolz	ſchmölze	ſchmilz	geſchmolzen	III.5
usually and properly of New conj. when transitive.						
Schnauben, 'snort'	—— ——	ſchnob	ſchnöbe	——	geſchnoben	III.4
Schneiden, 'cut'	—— ——	**ſchnitt**	**ſchnitte**	——	**geſchnitten**	III.1
Schrauben, 'screw'	—— ——	ſchrob	ſchröbe	——	geſchroben	III.4
Schrecken, 'be afraid'	ſchrickſt, ſchrickt	ſchrak	ſchräke	ſchrick	geſchrocken	I.3
of New conj. as transitive, 'frighten.'						
Schreiben, 'write'	—— ——	**ſchrieb**	**ſchriebe**	——	**geſchrieben**	III.2
Schreien, 'cry'	—— ——	**ſchrie**	**ſchriee**	——	**geſchrieen**	III.2
Schreiten, 'stride'	—— ——	**ſchritt**	**ſchritte**	——	**geſchritten**	III.1
Schwären, 'suppurate'	(ſchwierſt, ſchwiert)	**ſchwor**	**ſchwöre**	——	**geſchworen**	III.5
Schweigen, 'be silent'	—— ——	**ſchwieg**	**ſchwiege**	——	**geſchwiegen**	III.2
sometimes of New conj. as transitive, 'silence.'						
Schwellen, 'swell'	ſchwillſt, ſchwillt	ſchwoll	ſchwölle	ſchwill	geſchwollen	III.5
of New conj. as transitive.						
Schwimmen, 'swim'	—— ——	**ſchwamm** **ſchwomm**	**ſchwämme** **ſchwömme**	——	**geſchwommen**	I.2
Schwinden, 'vanish'	—— ——	**ſchwand** **ſchwund**	**ſchwände** **ſchwünde**	——	**geſchwunden**	I.1
Schwingen, 'swing'	—— ——	**ſchwang** **ſchwung**	**ſchwänge** **ſchwünge**	——	**geſchwungen**	I.1
Schwören, 'swear'	—— ——	**ſchwor** **ſchwur**	**ſchwöre** **ſchwüre**	——	**geſchworen**	III.5
Sehen, 'see'	**ſiehſt, ſieht**	**ſah**	**ſähe**	**ſieh**	**geſehen**	II.1
Sein, 'be'	**bin, biſt, iſt** 2c.	**war**	**wäre**	**ſei**	**geweſen**	239.2
Senden, 'send'	—— ——	ſandte ſendete	ſendete	——	geſandt geſendet	249
Sieden, 'boil'	—— ——	ſott	ſiedete	——	geſotten	III.3
Singen, 'sing'	—— ——	**ſang**	**ſänge**	——	**geſungen**	I.1
Sinken, 'sink'	—— ——	**ſank**	**ſänke**	——	**geſunken**	I.1
Sinnen, 'think'	—— ——	**ſann**	**ſänne** **ſönne**	——	geſonnen	I.2
Sitzen, 'sit'	—— ——	**ſaß**	**ſäße**	——	**geſeſſen**	I.4
Sollen, 'shall'	ſoll, ſollſt, ſoll	ſollte	ſollte	wanting	geſollt	251
Speien, 'spit'	—— ——	ſpie	ſpiee	——	geſpieen	III.2
rarely, of the New conj.						
Spinnen, 'spin'	—— ——	**ſpann**	**ſpänne** **ſpönne**	——	**geſponnen**	I.2
Spleißen, 'split'	—— ——	ſpliß	ſpliſſe	——	geſpliſſen	III.1
Sprechen, 'speak'	**ſprichſt, ſpricht**	**ſprach**	**ſpräche**	**ſprich**	**geſprochen**	I.3
Sprießen, 'sprout'	(ſpreußeſt, ſpreußt)	**ſproß**	**ſpröſſe**	(ſpreuß)	**geſproſſen**	III.3
Springen, 'spring	—— ——	**ſprang**	**ſpränge**	——	**geſprungen**	I.1

Infinitive.	pres't indic. sing.	pret. indic.	pret. subj.	imper.	past part.	class.
Stechen, 'prick'	**stichst, sticht**	**stach**	**stäche**	**stich**	**gestochen**	I.3
Stecken, 'stick'	stickst, stickt	stak	stäke	stick	gestocken	I.2
usually of New conj., especially when transitive.						
Stehen, 'stand'	—— ——	**stand** **stund**	**stände** **stünde**	——	**gestanden**	267
Stehlen, 'steal'	**stiehlst, stiehlt**	**stahl** **stohl**	**stähle** **stöhle**	**stiehl**	**gestohlen**	I 3
Steigen, 'ascend'	—— ——	**stieg**	**stiege**	——	**gestiegen**	III.2
Sterben, 'die'	**stirbst, stirbt**	**starb**	**stärbe** **stürbe**	**stirb**	**gestorben**	I.3
Stieben, 'disperse'	—— ——	**stob**	**stöbe**	——	**gestoben**	III.3
Stinken, 'stink'	—— ——	**stank** **stunk**	**stänke** **stünke**	——	**gestunken**	I.1
Stoßen, 'push'	**stößest, stößt**	**stieß**	**stieße**	——	**gestoßen**	II.4
Streichen, 'stroke'	—— ——	**strich**	**striche**	——	**gestrichen**	III.1
Streiten, 'strive'	—— ——	**stritt**	**stritte**	——	**gestritten**	III.1
Thun, 'do'	—— ——	**that**	**thäte**	——	**gethan**	267
the pret. indic. thät is common in dialectic German, especially as auxiliary.						
Tragen, 'carry'	**trägst, trägt**	**trug**	**trüge**	——	**getragen**	II.2
Treffen, 'hit'	**triffst, trifft**	**traf**	**träfe**	**triff**	**getroffen**	I.3
Treiben, 'drive'	—— ——	**trieb**	**triebe**	——	**getrieben**	III.2
Treten, 'tread'	**trittst, tritt**	**trat**	**träte**	**tritt**	**getreten**	II.1
Triefen, 'drip'	(treufst, treuft)	troff	tröffe	(treuf)	getroffen	III.3
Trinken, 'drink'	—— ——	**trank** **trunk**	**tränke** **trünke**	——	**getrunken**	I.1
Trügen, 'deceive'	—— ——	**trog**	**tröge**	——	**getrogen**	III.3
Wachsen, 'grow'	wächsest, wächst	**wuchs**	**wüchse**	——	**gewachsen**	II.2
Wägen, 'weigh'	—— ——	wog	wöge	——	gewogen	III.5
sometimes of New conj.: compare =wegen and wiegen, which are the same word.						
Waschen, 'wash'	wäschest, wäscht	**wusch**	**wüsche**	——	**gewaschen**	II.2
Weben, 'weave'	—— ——	wob	wöbe	——	gewoben	III.5
=wegen	—— ——	=wog	=wöge	——	=wogen	III.5
only in bewegen, 'induce;' bewegen in other senses is of New conj.						
Weichen, 'yield'	—— ——	wich	wiche	——	gewichen	III.1
of New conj. when meaning 'soften' (as trans. or intrans.).						
Weisen, 'show'	—— ——	**wies**	**wiese**	——	**gewiesen**	III.2
Wenden, 'turn	—— ——	wandte wendete	wendete	——	gewandt gewendet	249
Werben, 'sue'	**wirbst, wirbt**	**warb**	**wärbe** **würbe**	**wirb**	**geworben**	I.3
Werden, 'become'	**wirst, wird**	**ward** etc.	**würde**	——	**geworden**	239.3
Werfen, 'throw'	**wirfst, wirft**	**warf**	**wärfe** **würfe**	**wirf**	**geworfen**	I.3
Wiegen, 'weigh'	—— ——	wog	wöge	——	gewogen	III.3
the same word with wägen and =wegen: wiegen, 'rock,' is of New conj.						
Winden, 'wind'	—— ——	**wand**	**wände**	——	**gewunden**	I.1
=winnen	—— ——	**=wann**	**=wänne** **=wönne**	——	**=wonnen**	I.2
only used in gewinnen, 'win.'						

Infinitive.	pres't indic sing.	pret. indic.	pret. subj.	imper.	past part.	class
Wissen, 'know'	weiß, weißt, weiß	wußte	wüßte	——	gewußt	250
Wollen, 'will'	will, willst, will	wollte	wollte	——	gewollt	251
Zeihen, 'accuse'	—— ——	**zieh**	**ziehe**	——	**geziehen**	III.2
Ziehen, 'draw'	(zeuchst, zeucht)	**zog**	**zöge**	(zeuch)	**gezogen**	III.3
Zwingen, 'force'	—— ——	zwang	**zwänge**	——	**gezwungen**	I 1

VOCABULARY TO THE EXERCISES.

Abbreviations.

adj. adjective.
adv. adverb.
art. article.
conj. conjunction.
f. feminine noun.
irreg. irregular.
m. masculine noun.
n. neuter noun.
N. New conjugation.
num. numeral.
O. Old conjugation.
prep. preposition.
pron. pronoun.
refl. reflexive.
v. verb.

In the case of verbs of the Old conjugation, their class and division (**263–6**) is added in parenthesis after *v. O.* References are frequently made to the Grammar, by paragraph and division, in the same manner as in the Grammar itself. Unusual meanings of a word are referred to the exercise and sentence where they occur.

To each noun is added the ending of the genitive singular (except in the case of feminines), and the nominative plural (**68**).

English words which are historically identical or nearly akin with the German translated by them are in **full-faced letter;** and, to help the recollection of the German word, its English correspondent is sometimes prefixed, in parenthesis, to its translation.

aber, *conj.* but.
abkaufen, *v. N.* buy from.
abreisen, *v. N.* journey off, depart.
abschreiben, *v. O*(III.2). copy.
Adler, *m.* =rs, =r. eagle.
Advokat, *m.* =ten, =ten. **advocate,** lawyer.
all, *pron.* (**193**). **all.**—**alle,** *nom. pl.*—**aller,** *gen. pl.*
allerhärtest, *from* **hart** (**142.2**).
als, *conj.* **as;** when; *after a comparative,* than.
also, *adv.* accordingly.
alt, *adj.* (ä *in comparison*). **old.**
Alter, *n.* =rs, =r. age.
am = an dem (**65**).
an, *prep.* at; **on;** in.
ander, *adj.* other.—**anderen,** *dat. sing. fem.*
anderswo, *adv.* elsewhere.
anfangen, *v. O*(II.3). begin.
angenehm, *adj.* pleasant.
ankleiden, *v. N. refl.* dress one's self.
anziehen, *v. O*(III.3). draw **on.**
Apfel, *m.* =ls. Aepfel. **apple.**
arbeiten, *v. N.* work.—**arbeitet,** works.
Arm, *m.* =mes, =me. **arm.**
arm, *adj.* (ä *in comparison*). poor.
auch, *conj.* also.
auf, *prep.* on, **upon;** at (Ex. 4.3).
Aufgabe, *f.* =ben. task, exercise.
aufgehen, *v. O.* (**267**). (**go up**) rise.
aufheben, *v. O*(III.5). (**heave up**) lift, raise.
aufstehen, *v. O.* (**267**). (**stand up**) get **up.**
Auge, *n.* =ges, =gen. **eye.**
aus, *prep.* **out** of; of (Ex. 5.1).
ausgehen, *v. O.* (**267**). **go out.**
aussprechen, *v. O*(I.3). (**speak out**) pronounce.
Bach, *m.* =ches, =äche. brook.
bald, *adv.* soon.
Ball, *m.* =lles, =älle. **ball.**
Band, *m.* =des, =ände. volume.
Bank, *f.* =änke. **bench.**
Baum, *m.* =mes, =äume. (**beam**) tree.
Bäumchen, *n.* =ns, =n. little tree.
beginnen, *v. O*(I.2). **begin.**
behalten, *v. O*(II.3). keep.
Bein, *n.* =nes, =ne. (**bone**) leg.
besprechen, *v. O*(I.3). **speak** of.
besser, *adj.* (**139.1**). **better.**
best, *adj.* (**139.1**). **best.**
bestehen, *v. O.* (**267**). consist.—**besteht,** consists
betragen, *v. O*(II.4). behave.—**beträgt,** behaves.
Bett, *n.* =ttes, =tten. **bed.**
Bibliothek, *f.* =ken. library.
Bild, *n.* =des, =der. picture.
Bitte, *f.* =tten. request.
Blatt, *n.* =ttes, =ätter (**blade**) leaf.
blau, *adj.* **blue.**
Blei, *n.* =eies. lead.
bleiben, *v. O*(III.2). remain.
blind, *adj.* **blind.**
bös, *adj.* bad.
Bote, *m.* =ten, =ten. messenger.
brechen, *v. O*(I.3). **break.**
Breite, *f.* =ten. **breadth**
Brett, *n.* =ttes, =tter. **board,** shelf.
Brief, *m.* =fes, =fe. letter.
bringen, *v. N. irreg.* (**250**). **bring.**—**bringe,** bring
Brod, *n.* =des, =de. **bread.**
Bruder, *m.* =ders, =üder. **brother.**

Buch, *n.* =ches, =ücher. **book.**
Bücherbrett *n.* =tts, =tter. **book**-shelf.

Chemie', *f.* **chem**istry.
Christus, *m.* =ti, — (**107**). **Christ.**

Dach, *n.* =ches, =ächer. roof.
dann, *adv.* **then.**
davon, *adv.* (**166.4**). thereof, of it.
dein, *poss. adj.* **thy.**— **deines,** of thy.
denn, *conj.* for.
der, die, das, *art.* the.— *demonstr. adj. and pron.* that, that one.— *rel. pron.* who, which, that.
derjenige *etc.*, *determ. adj. and pron.* (**168**). that one.
deutlich, *adj.* plain.
deutsch, *adj.* German.
Deutsch, *n. indecl.* German language.
dick, *adj.* **thick.**
dienen, *v. N.* serve.— **diente,** served.
dies, *demonstr. adj. and pron.* (**165**). **this,** that. — **dieses, dieser, diese,** *cases of* **dies.**
dir, *pron. from* **du.**
Dom, *m.* =mes, =me. **dome.**
dreißig, *num.* **thirty.**
drucken, *v. N.* print.
du, *pron.* (**151**). **thou.**
dünn, *adj.* **thin.**
dürfen, *v. N. irreg.* (**251**). be allowed.

echt, *adj.* genuine, real.
ehe, *conj.* before.
ehrlich, *adj.* honest.
ein, *art.* a, **an.**—*num.* **one.**
einander, *pron. indecl.* **one** another.
einig, *pron. adj.* —*pl.* **einige,** some.
Eisen, *n.* =ns, =n. iron.
empfangen, *v.* *O*(II.3). receive.

er, *pron.* (**151**). he, it.
Erde, *f.* =den. **earth.**
erinnern, *v. N. refl.* remember.
erkennen, *v. N. irreg.* (**249**). recognize.—**erkennst,** recognizest.
erst, *adj.* first.
es, *pron.* **it.**
essen, *v.* *O*(II.1). **eat.**
etwas, *pron.* (**188**). something.
euch, *pron.* (**151**). **you.**
euer, *poss. adj.* (**157**). **your.**

fallen, *v.* *O*(II.3). **fall.**
Familie, *f.* =lien. **family.**
fand, *from* **finden. found**
Faß, *n.* =sses, =ässer. cask.
faul, *adj.* lazy.
Februar', *m.* =res, =re. **February.**
Feder, *f.* =rn. (**feather**) pen.
fein, *adj.* **fine.**
Feind, *m.* =des, =de. (**fiend**) enemy.
Feld, *n.* =des, =der. **field.**
Fenster, *n.* =rs, =r. window.
finden, *v.* *O*(I.1). **find.**
Fisch, *m.* =sches, =sche. **fish.**
Fläche, *f.* =chen. surface.
fleißig, *adj.* industrious.
fliegen, *v.* *O*(III.3). **fly.**
Floß, *n.* =ßes, =öße. raft.
Flügel, *m.* =ls, =l. wing.
Fluß, *m.* =sses, =üsse. river.
fort, *adv.* **forth,** away.
fortgehen, *v.* *O*(**267**). **go** away.
fragen, *v. N.* ask.
Frau, *f.* =auen. woman, wife.
Fräulein, *n.* =ns, =n. young lady.
freuen, *v. N. refl.* rejoice. — **freue mich,** am glad.
Freund, *m.* =des, =de. **friend.**
frisch, *adj.* **fresh.**
froh, *adj.* cheerful.
Frosch, *m.* =sches, =ösche. **frog.**
führen, *v. N.* lead. — **führt,** leads.
für, *prep.* **for.**
Fuß, *m.* =ßes, =üße. **foot.** — **Füß,** feet (**211.2**).

gab, *from* **geben. gave**
Garten, *m.* =ns, =ärten. **garden.**
Gatte, *m.* =tten, =tten. husband.
Gebirge, *n.* =ges, =ge mountain range.
gebären, *v.* *O*(I.3). **bear.** — **geboren, born.**
geben, *v.* *O.* (**236.2**). **give** — **gebe,** (I) **give.**
geboren, *from* **gebären.**
gebrochen, *from* **brechen.**
Geburt, *f.* =ten. **birth.**
Gefahr, *f.* =ren. danger.
Gefährte, *m.* =ten, =ten. comrade.
gefallen, *v.* *O*(II.3). please. — **gefällt,** pleases.
gefunden, *from* **finden.**
gehen, *v.* *O.* (**267**). **go.** — **geht,** goes.
Geist, *m.* =tes, =ter. (**ghost**) spirit.
gelehrt, *adj.* learned.
geschehen, *v.* *O*(II.1). happen. — **geschah,** happened, took place.
gesehen, *from* **sehen. seen.**
gestern, *adv.* yesterday.
gethan, *from* **thun.**
geweiht, *part. of* **weihen.** — **wurde geweiht,** was consecrated.
gewiß, *adj.* sure, certain.
gieb, *from* **geben. give!**
giebt, *from* **geben. gives.**
gleich, *adv.* immediately.
glücklich, *adj.* happy.
Gold, *n.* =des. **gold.**
Gott, *m.* =ttes, =ötter. **god.**
Grab, *n.* =bes, =äber. **grave.**
Graf, *m.* =fen, =fen. count.
groß, *adj.* (ö *in comparison*). **great.**
gut, *adj.* **good.**

habe, *from* **haben. have.**
haben, *v. N. irreg.* (**239.1**). **have.**
halten, *v.* *O*(II.3). **hold.** —**hält sich,** holds, keeps itself.
Hammer, *m.* =rs, =ämmer. **hammer.**
Hand, *f.* =ände. **hand.**
hangen, *v.* *O*(II.3). **hang.**

hart, *adj.* (ä *in comparison*). **hard.**
hassen, *v. N.* **hate.**
hat, *from* **haben. has.**
hatten, *from* **haben, had.**
Haus, *n.* -ses, -äuser. **house.**
heben, *v.* *O* (III 5). (**heave**) raise, lift.
Held, *m.* -den, -den. hero.
helfen, *v.* *O*(I.3). **help.**
herannahen, *v. N.* draw **nigh.**
Herr, *m.* -rrn, -rren (**93**). master.
heute, *adv.* to-day.
Herz, *n.* -zens, -zen. **heart.**
hier, *adv.* **here.**
hilf, *from* **helfen** (**270.2**).
hineinwerfen, *v.* *O*(I.3). throw in.
hoch, *adj.* (**139.1**) (ö *in comparison*). **high.**
hohe, *from* **hoch.**
hören, *v. N.* **hear.**
Horn, *n.* -nes, -örner. **horn.**
Hut, *m.* -tes, -üte. **hat.**

ich, *pron.* (**151**). **I.**
ihnen, *pron.*, from **er.**
ihr, *poss. adj.* (**157**). her, its, their.—**ihre, ihrem, ihren, ihrer, ihres**, *cases of* **ihr.**
Ihr, *poss. adj.* (**157**). your.
im = **in dem** (**65**).
immer, *adv.* always.
in, *prep.* **in**, into.
ins = **in das** (**65**).
ist, *from* **sein** (**239.2**). **is.**

Jahr, *n.* -res, -re. **year.**
Januar, *m.* -rs, -re. **January.**
je, *adv.* ever.
jed, *pron. adj.* (**190**). each, every. — **jedem, jeder**, *cases of* **jed.**
Jedermann, *pron.* (**187**). every one.
jen, *pron. adj.* **yon**, that.
jetzt, *adv.* now.
jung, *adj.* (ü *in comparison*). **young.**
kalt, *adj.* (ä *in comparison*). **cold.**

kann, *from* **können.**
Käse, *m.* -ses, -se. **cheese.**
kaufen, *v. N.* buy.
kennen, *v. N. irreg.* (**249**). (**ken**) know.
Kind, *n.* -des, -der. **child.**
Kirche, *f.* -chen. **church.**
Kleid, *n.* -des, -der. garment.
klein, *adj.* small, little.
Knabe, *m.* -ben, -ben. boy.
kommen, *v.* *O*(**267**). **come.**
können, *v. N. irreg.* (**251**). **can.**
Kopf, *m.* -fes, -öpfe. head.
kostbar, *adj.* precious.
krank, *adj.* (ä *in comparison*). sick.
Kreuz, *n.* -zes, -ze. **cross.**
kriechen, *v.* *O*(III.3). crawl.
Krieg, *m.* -ges, -ge. war.
Kugel, *f.* -geln. ball.
kurz, *adj.* (ü *in comparison*). short.

lagen, *from* **liegen.**
lahm, *adj.* **lame.**
lang, *adj.* (ä *in comparison*). **long.**
Länge, *f.* -gen. **length.**
lassen, *v.* *O*(II.3). **let.** — **läßt**, lets.
leben, *v. N.* **live.**
Lehrer, *m.* -rs, -r. teacher.
Leib, *m.* -bes, -ber. body.
leicht, *adj.* **light**, easy.
leiden, *v.* *O*(III.1). suffer.
leihen, *v.* *O*(III.2). lend. — **leihe**, (I) lend.
lernen, *v. N.* **learn.**
letzt, *adj.* **last.**
Leute, *m. pl.* (**100.2**). people.
Licht, *n.* -tes, -ter. **light.**
lieb, *adj.* dear.
lieben, *v. N.* (**236.1**). **love.** — **liebt**, loves. — **liebet**, love ye!
Lied, *n.* -des, -der. song.
liegen, *v.* *O*(I.4). **lie.**
link, *adj.* left.
loben, *v. N.* praise.
Luft, *f.* -üfte. air.

machen, *v. N.* **make.** — **machte, made.**
Mädchen, *n.* -ns, -n. **maiden**, girl.

man, *pron.* (**185**). one.
Mann, *m.* -nnes, -änner. **man.**
mein, *poss. adj.* (**159.2**). **my.**—**meinem, meinen, meiner, meines**, *cases of* **mein.**
meinen, *v. N.* **mean.**
Mensch, *m.* -schen, -schen. **man.**
Messer, *n.* -rs, -r. knife.
Metall', *n.* -lles, -lle. **metal.**
mich, *from* **ich. me.**
Milch, *f.* **milk.**
mir, *from* **ich.** to **me.**
mit, *prep.* with.
möchten, *from* **mögen.**
mögen, *v. N. irreg.* (**251**). **may.**
Monarch, *m.* -chen, -chen. **monarch.**
Monat, *m.* -ts, -te. **month.**
morgen, *adv.* to-**morrow.**
Müller, *m.* -rs, -r. **miller.**
müssen, *v. N. irreg.* (**251**). **must.**
Mutter, *f.* -ütter. **mother.**

nach, *prep.* after.
Nachbar, *m.* -rs, -rn. **neighbor.**
Nation', *f.* -nen. **nation.**
Neffe, *m.* -fen, -fen. **nephew.**
neu, *adj.* **new.**
neulich, *adv.* recently.
nicht, *adv.* **not.**
nichts, *pron.* (**188**). nothing.
nie, *adv.* never.
niedrig, *adj.* low.
noch, *adv.* yet.
noch, *conj.* nor (*after* **weder**).
nur, *adv.* only.
nützlich, *adj.* useful.

Ochs, *m.* -sen, -sen. **ox.**
oder, *conj.* or.
oft, *adv.* **often.** — **so oft**, as often as.
Onkel, *m.* -ls, -l. **uncle.**
Ort, *m.* -tes, -te. place.

Papier', *n.* -rs, -re. **paper.**
Person', *f.* -nen. **person.**
Petrus, *m.* **Peter.**—**Petri**, Peter's (**107**).
Pferd, *n.* -des, -de. horse.
Pflaster, *n.* -rs, -r. pavement.
pflücken, *v. N.* **pluck.**—**pflückt**, plucks.
Pole, *m.* -len, -len. **Pole.**
Post, *f.* -ten. **post**, post-office.
Preuße, *m.* -ßen, -ßen. **Prussian.**
Pult, *n.* -tes, -te. desk.

reden, *v. N.* (**248**). talk.
redlich, *adj.* honest.
recht, *adj.* **right.**
reich, *adj.* **rich.**
reif, *adj.* **ripe.**
Reihe, *f.* -hen. **row.**
Rock, *m.* -kes, -öcke. coat.
Rom, *n.* -ms. Rome.
Rose, *f.* -sen. **rose.**
roth, *adj.* (ö *in comparison*). **red.**
Ruhm, *m.* -mes. fame, credit.
rund, *adj.* **round.**

sagen, *v. N.* **say.**
sah, *from* **sehen.** **saw.**
Sanct, *adj.* **Saint.**
sangen, *from* **singen.**
saßen, *from* **sitzen.**
schaden, *v. N.* (**scathe**) injure.
schämen, *v. N. refl.* be **ashamed.**
schattig, *adj.* **shady.**
schauen, *v. N.* look.
schicken, *v. N.* send.—**schickte**, sent.
schlecht, *adj.* bad.
Schnabel, *m.* -ls, -äbel. bill.
schon, *adv.* already.
schön, *adj.* beautiful.
schreiben, *v. O*(III.2). write.—**schreibt**, writes.—**schreibe**, (I) write; write!
Schuh, *m.* -hes, -he **shoe.**
Schüler, *m.* -rs, -r. **scholar.**
schwach, *adj.* (ä *in comparison*). weak.

schwarz, *adj.* (ä *in comparison*). (**swart**) black.
schwimmen, *v. O*(I.2). **swim.**
sechs, *num* **six.**
segnen, *v. N.* bless. — **segnet**, bless ye!
sehen, *v. O*(II.1). **see.**—**sehe**, (I) see.
sehr, *adv.* very.
sein, *poss. adj.* his, its. —**seine, seinem, seinen**, *cases of* **sein.**
sein, *v. O.* (**239.2**). be.
seinig, *poss. adj.* (**159.5**). his, its.
selber, *pron. adj.* (**155.5**). **self.**
sich, *refl. pron.* (**155.3**). himself *etc.*
sie, *pron.* (**151**). they, them, she.—**Sie**, you.
sieht, *from* **sehen** (**268.1**).
sind, *from* **sein**, *v.* are.
singen, *v. O*(I.1). **sing.** —**singt**, sings.
sitzen, *v. O*(I.4). **sit.**—**sitzt**, sits.
so, *adv.* **so.**—**so oft**, as often as.
sobald, *conj.* as soon as.
sogleich, *adv.* immediately.
Sohn, *m.* -nes, -öhne. **son.**
Soldat, *m.* -ten, -ten. **soldier.**
sollen, *v. N. irreg.* (**251**). **shall.**
Sommer, *m.* -rs, -r. **summer.**
Sonne, *f.* -nen. **sun.**
spanisch, *adj.* **Spanish.**
spät, *adj.* late.
Spiegel, *m.* -ls, -l. mirror.
Spielzeug, *n.* -gs, -ge. playthings.
Sprache, *f.* -chen. (**speech**) language.
sprachen, *from* **sprechen**, **spoke.**
sprechen, *v. O*(I.3). **speak.** — **spricht**, speaks. — **sprachen**, (they) spoke.
Stadt, *f.* -ädte. city.
Stahl, *m.* -les, -ähle. **steel.**
stark, *adj.* (ä *in comparison*). strong.
stehen, *v. O.* (**267**). **stand.** —**steht**, stands.

Storch, *m.* -ches, -örche **stork.**
Stube, *f.* -ben. room.
Student', *m.* -ten, -ten **student.**
studiren, *v. N.* **study.**—**studirt**, studied.
Stuhl, *m.* -les, -ühle. (**stool**) chair.
stützen, *v. N.* rest.—**stützt** rests.
süß, *adj.* **sweet.**

tadeln, *v. N.* blame.
Tag, *m.* -ges, -ge. **day.**
Tasche, *f.* -schen. pocket
Teller, *m.* -rs, -r. plate.
Thal, *n.* -les, -äler. **dale**, valley.
That, *f.* -ten. **deed.**
Thor, *n.* -res, -re. (**door**) gate.
Thor, *m.* -ren, -ren. fool.
thun, *v. O.* (**267**). **do**, put. —**thut**, puts.
Tinte, *f.* -ten. ink.
Tisch, *m.* -sches, -sche. table.
Tochter, *f.* -öchter. **daughter.**
tragen, *v. O*(II.2). carry; bear, wear. — **trägt** (**268.2**), carries, wears.
träge, *adj.* lazy.
Tuch, *n.* -ches, -che. cloth.
Tugend, *f.* -den. virtue.

über, *prep.* **over**, above.
Ueberschuh, *m.* -hs, -he. **overshoe.**
übersetz'en, *v. N.* translate.
um, *prep.* around, about; by (Ex. 13.1).
und, *conj.* **and.**
Ungar, *m.* -rn, -rn. **Hungarian.**
Unglück, *n.* -cks. misfortune.
Universität, *f.* -ten. **university.**
unreif, *adj.* **unripe.**
uns, *pron.* (**151**). **us.**
unser, *poss. adj.* (**159**). **our.**
unsrig, *poss. adj.* (**159.5**) our.
unter, *prep.* **under.**

Vater, *m.* -rs, -äter. **father.**

Vaterland, *n.* -des, -de. one's country.
verfolgen, *v. N.* persecute.
vergelten, *v. O*(I.3). reward. — **vergeltet**, reward ye!
vergessen, *v. O*(II.1). **forget.**
verkaufen, *v. N.* sell.
verlangen, *v. N.* require.
versprechen, *v. O*(I.3). promise.
verstehen, *v. O.* (**267**). understand.
viel, *pron.* (**192**). much, many.
vier, *num.* **four.**
Vogel, *m.* -ls, -ögel. (**fowl**) bird.
Volk, *n.* -kes, -ölker. (**folk**) people.
vollenden, *v. N.* finish.
von, *prep.* of, from.
vom = **von dem** (**65**).
vor, *prep.* be**fore**, outside (Ex. 2.6).
vorlesen, *v. O*(II.1). read to.—**vorliest** (**268**.1).

wählen, *v. N.* choose.—**wählt**, chooses.
Wahrheit, *f.* -ten. truth.
Wald, *m.* -des, -älder. forest, wood.
wann, *adv.* **when?**
wandern, *v. N.* **wander.**
war, *from* **sein**, *v.* **was.**
waren, *from* **sein**, *v.* **were.**
warm, *adj.* (ä, *in comparison*). **warm.**
was, *pron.* **what.**
was für, *pron.* **what** sort of.
Wasser, *n.* -rs, -r. **water.**
weder, *conj.* neither.
Weib, *n.* -bes, -ber. (**wife**) woman.
weich, *adj.* (**weak**) soft.
weihen, *v. N.* consecrate.
weil, *conj.* because.
Wein, *m.* -nes, -ne. **wine.**
weise, *adj.* **wise.**
weiß, *adj.* **white.**
weiß, *from* **wissen**, know, knows.
weit, *adj.* (**wide**) far.
welch, *pron.* who, **which.**
wenn, *conj.* **when**, if.
wer, *pron.* **who.**
werden, *v. O.* (**277**). become.
Werk, *n.* -kes, -ke. **work.**
wie, *conj.* as, like.
wieder, *adv.* again; in return.
wie'dergeben, *v. O*(II.1). **give** back.—**wiedergaben**, gave back.
wie'derholen, *v. N.* fetch back.
wiederho'len, *v. N.* repeat.
will, *from* **wollen.**
Winter, *m.* -rs, -r. **winter.**
wir, *pron.* (**151**). **we.**
wissen, *v. N. irreg.* (**260**) know. — **weiß**, know, knows.
wo, *adv.* where? where.
wohin, *adv.* whither.
wollen, *v. N. irreg.* (**251**) **will**, wish.
Wort, *n.* -tes, -te *or* -örter. **word.**
wünschen, *v. N.* **wish.**
Wurm, *m.* -mes, -ürmer. **worm.**

zerbrechen, *v. O*(I.3). **break** in pieces.
Ziege, *f.* -en. goat.
Zimmer, *n.* -rs, -r. room.
zu, *prep.* **to**; at (Ex. 13.5).—**zu haben**, to be had (**343**.III.1).
zufrieden, *adj.* contented.
zugleich, *adv.* at the same time, at once.
zur = **zu der** (**65**).
zurückkommen, *v. O.* (**267**) **come** back.
zusammen, *adv.* together.
zwei, *num.* **two.**
zwölf, *num.* **twelve.**

INDEX.

SUPPLEMENT

TO

WHITNEY'S GERMAN GRAMMAR.

EXERCISES FOR TRANSLATING FROM ENGLISH INTO GERMAN.

INTRODUCTORY NOTE.

THE Exercises here given form an appendix to the author's German Grammar, although also capable of being used independently of that work. Owing to other absorbing occupations, I have been obliged to put out of my own hands the preparation of the text of them, which has accordingly been done, under my detailed direction, by a gentleman well qualified for the task (Mr. B. G. Hosmer, of New York). They are divided, as will be noticed, into four Series. The first may be written through, if the instructor chooses, in connection with the pupils' first lessons in the Grammar; I should not myself, however, make use of them, preferring to let a class learn the whole body of essential principles of grammar, and read more or less, before beginning to turn English into German at all. The second Series is designed to help enforce the rules of construction of the sentence; it begins with the simplest elements of which the sentence is composed, and brings in, one after another, the other elements, ending with the most intricate and highly developed of them all, the dependent clause. I trust that it will be found upon the whole well adapted, and sufficiently full, to teach and impress the main peculiarities of German sentence-making. The third Series calls attention to the more important specialties of the grammar, etymological and syntactical. This, in particular, would admit of almost indefinite extension beyond the rather restricted limits to which I have confined it; but perhaps enough is given to prepare the pupil for dealing with sentences and paragraphs of a miscellaneous character, the difficulties and nicer points of which shall be explained as they occur. In an abbreviated course, indeed, the whole Series will admit of being passed over; or only the Exercises deemed more important may be written out, and in such order as the teacher shall prefer (that in which they are set down is simply the order of subjects in the Grammar). Material for general practice is offered in the fourth Series, the Exercises in which are founded on passages in the author's Reader. These passages are supposed to have been first thoroughly read, and their vocabulary and phraseology mastered by the pupil, who thus becomes responsible for the proper construction and grammatical correctness of his task, while his choice of expressions is guided or prescribed by the model passage. Of exercises of this character I have in my own teaching made especial use, and those here given are intended partly as examples of what each instructor may profitably do for his class, in connection with any text which they may be reading, devising either general illustrations of construction, or exemplifications of particular points—drilling exercises upon individual difficulties of German idiom which may from time to time present themselves.

A complete vocabulary (which, however, turns out of greater length than was anticipated) forms a necessary part of such a set of Exercises as this, which does not suppose in the pupil enough familiarity with the language to enable him to choose the right expression for himself in the larger English-German dictionaries. But that here given does not include those words and phrases in the fourth Series which occur in the foundation-passages; it being an essential part of the plan that the pupil master the passage and turn it into its new shape, with help only upon the new words and phrases which may have been introduced.

No one, I trust, will suppose me to assume that these Exercises, and such as these, are going to enable the scholar to write German idiomatically and freely. They are strictly auxiliaries to the grammar, helps to a thorough and practical comprehension of the rules of German construction, and will require to be supplemented by an indefinite amount of reading and writing, if one is to attain anything like a command of German style.

No given set of exercises can have a universal or a lasting usefulness. Each teacher really wants his own, adapted to his style of teaching and to the particular needs of his classes. I am not at all confident of having here met the precise wants of any very large number of instructors; I only hope to have furnished what will be of some service to many—enough, perhaps, to repay the labor which their preparation has cost, and furnishing ground for experiment and criticism which may lead to the substitution by and by of something fuller and better.

EXERCISES.

EXPLANATIONS.

English words in *Italics* are to be omitted altogether in rendering.

Words superfluous in the English, but requiring to be introduced in the German, are inserted in brackets.

Words connected below by the sign ‿ are to be rendered by a single German word.

Words numbered by "superior" figures are to be put in the order indicated by the figures; and, in a few cases, a single word so marked with 1 is to be put at the beginning of the clause.

Occasional suggestions and references are introduced in parenthesis.

SERIES I.

EXERCISES TO ACCOMPANY (IF DESIRED) THE FIRST LESSONS IN THE GERMAN GRAMMAR.

(INVOLVING ONLY WHAT IS IN THE LARGEST PRINT.)

EXERCISE 1.

Nouns, first declension, first class (75–9); *also articles* (63), *and present indicative of* sein (239.2).

1. The daughters are in the convents, and the mothers are in the gardens. 2. The cheeses are on the plate, the plate is on the cushion, and the cushion is on the floor. 3. The girl's father is an Englishman. 4. The brothers of the priest are here. 5. The owner of the little‿house is an American, but the tenants are Italians. 6. The birds are in the gardens on the mountain-range. 7. The young‿lady is in the garden with the gardener's spade. 8. In the garden *there* are little‿trees, and on the ground under the little‿trees *there* are apples.

EXERCISE 2.

Nouns, first declension, second class (81–5); *also present indicative of* haben (239.1).

1. September, October, and November are the autumn‿months. 2. On the river *there* are rafts and boats, and the boats have sails and oars. 3. The gardener's daughter has shoes, but the beggar's son has neither shoes nor stockings. 4. The axes are under the benches. 5. The savings (*sing.*) of the workmen are in the trunk yonder. 6. The horses have oats (*sing.*) and the dog has a bone. 7. The tree is not far from the little‿house, and the

little‿house is not far from the brooklet. 8. He has meetings with his friends. 9. The sons of the peasant are at the brook with a pail and a basket; in the pail is water, and in the basket are fish.

Exercise 3.

Nouns, first declension, third class (87–90); *also present indicative of* lieben (236.1).

1. [The 66.1] men love riches, [the] women love splendor. 2. God loves the man‿of‿honor, but not the villain. 3. The child's guardian has a house in the valley. 4. The trees in the field and in the forest have leaves. 5. [The 66.2] death and the grave are the termination of [the] life. 6. The artist loves pictures and books. 7. The little‿child has a song-book and loves the songs. 8. The girl has dresses and rings; the girl's brother has a horse and a little‿dog. 9. In the forests are trees, and leaves, and nuts. 10. The inhabitants of the village are robbers.

Exercise 4.

Nouns, second declension (91–4); *also present indicative of* geben (236.2).

1. The messenger gives the Frenchman a letter. 2. The Bavarians are in the house, the Hungarians in the yard. 3. God gives [the 66.1] man [the] speech, [the] virtue, and [the] reason. 4. The students of the university are Prussians, Saxons, and Poles. 5. [The 66.2] truth is a mark of the man‿of‿honor. 6. Cares are the companions of the monarch. 7. The lawyers give the students books. 8. The princes are in danger. 9. The hunter gives the soldier a musket.

Exercise 5.

Adjectives, of both declensions, in attributive and predicative use (114–24).

1. The old wine-bottles are upon the wooden table in the large room. 2. The good doctor gives the child the medicine; for the child has a bad cough, and is very ill. 3. The spirited horse is in the stable with the quiet cows. 4. In the dark-blue bottle yonder is poison. 5. The snake is not poisonous. 6. The murderers of the prince have ugly faces. 7. The little son of the emperor has a leaden bullet, and is very tranquil. 8. The flowers are blue, and white, and red. 9. The blue flowers in the little‿basket are very beautiful.

Exercise 6.

Adjectives used as nouns (129) *and as adverbs* (130), *and compared* (134–40).

1. The good *man* is not always happy, but the wicked *man* is more unhappy than the good. 2. The pretty child has a little red apple in the right *hand*. 3. The Englishwoman is handsome, but the American‿woman is yet handsomer. 4. The weather is quite fine. 5. The landlord's oldest daughter is prettier than the merchant's younger sister. 6. The water in the great river yonder is not quite so clear as *it is* here in the little‿brook. 7. To-day is a remarkably fine day, and much warmer than yesterday. 8. The hero loves the noble and the dangerous. 9. The entire house is entirely finished. 10. The little hill behind the little‿forest is the highest in the vicinity; for the whole country is detestably flat. 11. A good sensible teacher loves an industrious boy. 12. The good teacher gives the industrious boy beautiful books and a little book-case; and the boy is very glad and thankful. 13. The father has heavy cares, but the son is free‿from‿care. The workman has a white house, with small cleanly rooms. 15. The grandfather is a sickly old man, but the grandmother is a strong healthy woman. 16. The grandson is a quiet well-behaved child.

Exercise 7.

Pronouns, personal and possessive (151–9).

1. I am well, but he is unwell, and she is very ill. 2. He loves them, but they love him not. 3. You give yourself unnecessary trouble. 4. Our choice is an extraordinarily happy *one.* 5. My old friend and his youngest brother are dead. 6. He gives them a costly present. 7. The merchant gives me my bill, and I give him his money. 8. The girl has a small dog, and it is very sagacious and faithful. 9. We give ourselves great trouble. 10. Have you my book? I gave it to you.

Exercise 8.

Pronouns, demonstrative, interrogative, and relative (163–77).

1. My house is not so fine as this *one*, nor as that rich merchant's house. 2. This hill is much lower than that mountain. 3. The man whose picture you have is either an Englishman or an Irishman. 4. Who gives thee this permission? 5. That

(166.3) is the brother of our new friend. 6. Which brother? the elder? 7. No, the younger; and his little‿sister, whom he greatly loves, is with him. 8. This is an old friend of my father, and a man, moreover, whom he warmly loves.

Exercise 9.

Cardinal and ordinal numerals (197–203).

1. The parson has three sons; the eldest is just sixteen years old; the second is in the twelfth year of his age, and the third is five years and three months old. 2. The professor has over seven thousand books in his library. 3. The boy has four apples, and his father gives him besides two oranges. 4. There (= es: 154.4*b*) are six hundred and seventy-three families in this town. The date is the twenty-fifth *of* (216.5*b*) January. 6. The first house on the left side of the street has only four windows, with sixty-four panes, and the door is very small.

Exercise 10.

Simple forms of the verb (236.1,2).

1. She would give (*pret. subj.*) willingly, but she has nothing. 2. When I give, I[2] give[1] publicly. 3. It is not true that they gave[3] us[1] nothing[2]. 4. The father loved his ungrateful sons, and gave them everything. 5. These men are now enemies, but formerly they[2] loved[1] one another. 6. Give, as‿often‿as (= so oft) thou hast[2] occasion[1]. 7. To give when one loves is easy; but to give without loving (= zu lieben) is difficult. 8. Those girls are loving and loved daughters. 9. Who gives more than our friends gave?

Exercise 11.

Compound forms of the verb (240, 244).

[Note the rule for arrangement 319.2*a*; 430.3.]

1. He has been *a* (66.8) soldier, and has had wounds. 2. He will not give much, for he is not generous. 3. He might have had great honor, had he (*subj.*) been true. 4. They will give a great performance. 5. When will that be? 6 It would be to-morrow evening, if they were[3] already[1] here[2]. 7. Our friends will not give the concert; and that is *a* pity, for it would have been (*plup. subj.*) very fine. 8. Thou hast the book; give it to me 9. No, I have had it, but now I[2] have[1] it[3] no longer.

Exercise 12.

Verbs of the New conjugation (245–8).

1. He has wandered far[2] to-day[1]. 2. I have always praised and loved him, but now I[2] shall[1] love him no longer. 3. She has bought the dress, and I have made it. 4. The youth hopes for the future, the man values the present, the old man loves the past. 5. He (= der: 166.2*b*) would not have said it; he is too prudent. 6. I have a cousin who talks[3] too[1] much[2], and no one heeds what he says. 7. She will have made her (= die: 161) toilette earlier than we wished.

Exercise 13.

Verbs of the Old conjugation (261–73).

1. Our parson's daughters have sung pretty songs, but they did not sing so finely as your sisters. 2. We shall sit to-day where we sat[2] yesterday[1]. 3. I fear the mad dog will bite some one before they (= man: 185) catch[2] him[1]. 4. It has already bitten some one. 5. I have read in the newspaper that the hostile army has[2] fled[1]. 6. The children were very glad, for their (= der: 161) father had come home from the war. 7. We have fought well, but many have fallen on our side. 8. Who has thrown the stone and broken this window-pane? 9. A boy who has[3] run[1] around the corner threw the stone. 10. The travellers slept on the floor, for there (= es: 154.4*b*) were not enough beds in the house.

Exercise 14.

Passive, reflexive, and impersonal verbs (274–92).

1. It is a great (= hoch) happiness to have been so loved. 2. He was loved by all who saw[2] him[1]. 3. He would be loved, if he were[4] not[1] so[2] haughty[3]. 4. Your arrival has rejoiced me much, and your friends will also rejoice. 5. The whole nation had wondered at (= über) these transactions. 6. It rained yesterday evening very hard. 7. It seems to us to[3] be[4] very[1] doubtful[2]. 8. It will be advantageous[2] to you[1]. 9. He is a self-tormentor; he worries too much.

Exercise 15.

Compound verbs (297–311).

1. It ceases to snow, and begins to rain. 2. The performance has already begun. 3. The time of their liberation draws nigh.

4. The whole family has gone‿off to Europe; and, as I hear, our neighbors will also soon depart. 5. They have the habit of taking‿a‿journey (*infin.*) every summer (*accus.:* 230.2). 6. The ship has gone down, but the passengers are saved. 7. You have begun too late; it is almost ten o'clock. 8. The servant‿girl has overturned the inkstand. 9. The king was shamefully deceived by his state-counsellor, although he had[2] honored[1] him with his confidence.

SERIES II.

EXERCISES IN THE CONSTRUCTION OF SENTENCES.

A. SIMPLE ASSERTIVE SENTENCES IN THE REGULAR ORDER (430.1–3), AND INTERROGATIVE AND OPTATIVE SENTENCES IN THE INVERTED ORDER (432.1,2).

EXERCISE 16.

Verb in simple tense, with simple subject (noun or pronoun, accompanied only by article, or by demonstrative or interrogative).

1. Frederick comes. 2. The man went. 3. Which man went? 4. This man goes. 5. Is that boy sleeping? 6. The little‿child is‿awake. 7. He ran, but I remained. 8. Let us begin. 9. Is the house burning? 10. Remain ye. 11. John, be‿silent! 12. The soldiers marched. 13. Come! 14. I am coming; is she coming too? 15. They might go. 16. Ye may be. 17. The father loved. 18. Let him talk; we hear.

EXERCISE 17.

Verb in compound tense, and compound verb (297 *etc.*; 430.3).

1. Frederick has come. 2. Anna goes away, and Louisa comes back. 3. The criminal has disappeared. 4. Would you go? 5. I should have gone. 6. The messenger will have come back. 7. Which tree was felled. 8. Had the deed been done? 9. He would have been praised. 10. Come back. 11. Will ye come back? 12. Wilt thou have come again? 13. He went back; I staid away. 14. Is a thunder-storm drawing nigh? 15. Will the child be loved? 16. It might have come. 17. They had departed.

EXERCISE 18.

Verb with single object, direct or indirect (315.1,2; 227.1; 222.II., 219.5).

1. The hunter took the gun and shot it off. 2. Which book are you reading? 3. I am reading thy book; read thou my news

papers. 4. Will ye have read the newspapers? 5. Please, take off thy overcoat. 6. The snow had covered the fields and paths. 7. The girl will have shut the windows. 8. He mocks at his chains. 9. The people need our help, and we shall help them. 10. Heed ye not the road? 11. The future is waiting for us, and we strive toward it. 12. The guide knows the road; follow *thou* after him. 13. The churches and palaces, the antiquities and ruins pleased the strangers. 14. I confess it, your friend was disagreeable to me. 15. Has he escaped his pursuers? 16. Which pupil has the teacher met? 17. Your mode of life would injure my health. 18. I know, thy brother will stand by thee. 19. He drew on his (= the: **161**) shoes, put on his (= the: **161**) hat, and began the journey. 20. Will they copy our letters? 21. The boy defied his father, and obeyed him not.

Exercise 19.

Verb with double object, direct and indirect, or remoter (**315**.3; **219**.2,3; **222**.II.,III.; **319**.2*e*,3*b*).

1. He robbed us of our repose. 2. The officer has accused a soldier of the murder. 3. Your father will relieve me of my responsibility. 4. I had acquitted myself of your commission. 5. Has he applied himself to the sciences? 6. Our friend enjoys his (**161**) life. 7. Dost thou recollect this event? 8. Has my cousin sent you back your letter? 9. He might be useful to me. 10. Your brothers and sisters resemble you. 11. Grant me my request. 12. He must render you this service. 13. Is she reading aloud to her nephews and nieces? 14. Let us assure him of our sympathy. 15. He charges his comrades with this crime. 16. The chancellor interests himself for him, and will take pity on his helplessness. 17. Has the police taken possession of his property? 18. He should be ashamed of this deed. 19. Pardon him his misdemeanor. 20. Can you lend me your dictionary? 21. I have lent it to my guardian.

Exercise 20.

Nouns with limiting adjectives (**110**.1*a*,*b*).

1. The old letter-carrier has brought me five long letters. 2. Our little cousin enclosed her photograph in her charming little letter. 3. Our neighbor is a good and provident man, and rejoices in a long and happy life. 4. He is a clever general, and will avail himself of all possible means. 5. It was a beautiful

May‿evening, clear and calm. 6. Be mindful of those times the happy *ones!* 7. The heaviest fate has its bright‿sides, and the most enviable lot its shadows. 8. The little‿brook flows noisy and rapid down. 9. May he have mercy on his unfortunate fellow-men! 10. The true hero goes‿to‿face every necessary danger.

[Exercises 5, 6 may be added as further practice.]

Exercise 21.

Verbs and adjectives with adverbial adjuncts (**317**; **144**.1; **370**; **319**.2*f*; **147**.1).

1. These peaches look well and taste badly. 2. Confess it; thy opponent has behaved excellently. 3. Why do you come so late? 4. Do you call this late? it is not[2] yet[1] seven o'clock. 5. It will not have become very late; was it not early enough? 6. Does your watch go right? 7. It has almost always gone quite right. 8. Shall you go thither to-day? 9. I am probably not going there to-day; and Henry is also not going to-day. 10. His work is getting on but slowly; thou wouldst doubtless do it more quickly. 11. His family is pretty comfortably settled there; he still remains here for‿the‿present. 12. I shall be there to-morrow very early. 13. His plan was finely devised and well executed. 14. Such a father is always fervently loved. 15. My uncle will not buy the corner-house; it is not large enough [for him]. 16. Do you do it willingly? 17. Yes, indeed; I do it very willingly. 18. Only don't tell it to her, and all will go well enough.

Exercise 22.

Noun or adjective with noun as adjunct (**111**.1; **216**.1,2,6; **217**; **223**; **145**.1,2).

1. This evil habit of his son's grows daily. 2. The number of the troops is not mentioned. 3. The rattling of the heavily laden wagon was heard afar. 4. A man of excellent character will fill the place. 5. Have you not yet seen this ornament of our city? 6. Inhabitants of all *the* cities of the realm meet together here. 7. She has felt the greatest of all earthly sufferings—the loss of her husband and her children at once. 8. I am tired of the carrying‿on. 9. He is considered guilty of the crime. 10. The manager of the property is finally weary of the incessant complaining of his workmen; he is worthy of their confidence, and they are conscious of his honesty. 11. I have examined the

house and the garden, and they just suit me. 12. The whole **affair** was for our poor Albert incomprehensible and inconceivable. 13. You and yours are always welcome to me. 14. The new boots are too tight for me, but they fit my brother excellently. 15. He stands firm, like a rock.

Exercise 23.

Noun, adjective, or verb, with prepositional phrase (**112**; **146**; **318** **373–6**; **216.**4; **219.**6; **222.**IV.; **223.**7).

1. Both parties have great hope of a good result. 2. The cities in the West increase in population very rapidly. 3. The inclination to truth is strengthened by a good education. 4. She waited in vain for the messenger. 5. I sincerely rejoice at your unexpected good‿fortune. 6. Rely in this matter completely upon me; I shall conduct it happily to *an* end. 7. The day dawns in the east. 8. He looked at me with sparkling eyes, and called to me with trembling voice. 9. A compact of so grave importance is not made in this manner. 10. The goal of my wishes lies beyond those mountains. 11. The sentinel is standing outside the gate. 12. Act in‿accordance‿with your promise. 13. Two high trees stand opposite my window. 14. I shall get through even without his assistance. 15. That is without doubt repugnant to you. 16. He seated himself upon the bench. 17. I stood beside him on the terrace. 18. He has ennui, and strolls about in the house; why does he not go to the concert? 19. Will you also go to the theatre? 20. Think upon the reward, not upon the danger. 21. The emperor drove through the streets of Paris. 22. The whole village rejoiced at his return. 23. He leaves his Bible behind for his old mother. 24. That is assuredly very unpleasant for you.

Exercise 24.

Predicate noun and adjective (**316**; **213**; **227.**3*b*,*c*; **116.**1).

1. He is called Henry, and his father and grandfather were also called Henry. 2. Would she have called me her enemy? 3. He has always been inclined to this belief. 4. This man is poor and unfortunate, but not a rogue. 5. The elder brother has always remained professor, but the younger wants rather to become *a* (**66.**8) practising physician. 6. The colonel reviled him as a coward. 7. Do you consider this Rhine‿wine genuine 8. No, I should not exactly like to call it genuine. 9. Those (=

das: 166.3) were happy days, innocent and hopeful. 10. The queen sat there sweet and mild. 11. They all[2] went[1] noiseless past. 12. You have evidently sung yourself hoarse. 13. The sunbeam has kissed the flowers awake. 14. Did you not see him surrounded by the enemy? 15. I had believed the story long since forgotten. 16. Our presence seemed to make the horse shy.

B. SIMPLE ASSERTIVE SENTENCES IN INVERTED ORDER (431*a–c*, *e–h*).

EXERCISE 25.

1. Beautiful she is not, but good and noble. 2. This estate the young duke has recently bought; the other they (= man: 185) had sold long ago. 3. That will not be done so easily, said my friend. 4. Him I have never[2] yet[1] trusted; but now I shall be obliged to trust him. 5. Proud and hopeful he went forth; sad and dejected he returns. 6. Those he has praised, these he loves. 7. We, added the others, will also accompany you. 8. Then we shall be very unhappy. 9. Assist him I shall not, for he has never been my friend, and besides, no one respects him. 10. Against that (166.4) I have something to object. 11. Thus his victims escaped him. 12. *Surely* I have told you so (= es: 154.4*e*) already. 13. Soon the other soldiers joined themselves to these.

[For further practice, the sentences of the previous exercises may be recast, in inverted order.]

C. COMPOUND SENTENCES, CONTAINING DEPENDENT CLAUSES.

EXERCISE 26.

Inverted conditional clauses (433; 332.2*b*; 438*f*; 439.6*d*).

1. If you have got what is needful (129.3), then go directly away. 2. They boast, as if their opponents had no strength. 3. He acts as if he were discontented; were he truly contented, he would not conduct thus. 4. Had he not himself insisted upon it (154.3) so obstinately, we should have consented. 5. If the children are well-behaved, I shall bring them a present. 6. Hadst thou been here, my brother had not died. 7. If you did not go too far, I should gladly go along *with you*. 8. She listens to him with rapt attention, almost as if he were a prophet. 9. If he does not soon yield, he must be forced to it (154.3). 10. The afflicted all[2] come[1] to me, as if I could help them.

Exercise 27.

Substantive dependent clauses (**436**; **113**.3).

1. I am rejoiced that he finally, after his long suffering, has got well. 2. He assured me that he would not fail‿to‿come. 3. I really do not know who is right, you or I. 4. He speaks too indistinctly; it is impossible to understand what he says. 5. That you cannot comprehend this, is incomprehensible to me. 6. Ask him minutely, how he came (*perf.*: **326**.2). 7. Where on earth the fugitive may be now, is unknown to me. 8. He who has taken the jewels must also have taken the casket. 9. He is, to‿be‿sure, not yet here; could you not, however, perhaps tell me when he is expected? 10. Whence they come and whither they go are both (*neut. sing.*) secrets. 11. Whether he comes or stays away is indifferent to me. 12. You must take care that the enemy does not surprise you. 13. It is not through our own fault that we have got into prison. 14. Our host has provided everything excellently by means of his reliable servants, without once needing to go‿there himself. 15. I do not in the least doubt of (= an) your loving me. 16. All *the* world shall learn what base means he has made‿use of. 17. The spy stepped in under the pretext that he was looking‿for something. 18. The prices in this watering-place are increased by (= durch) so many rich people staying here. 19. What I have just told you is connected with the former story. 20. What we at‿that‿time did voluntarily, [that] is now for us a forced labor. 21. I know nothing of how he has escaped. 22. When we recover what we have lost is less certain than that we shall recover it. 23. Are you quite sure that it was they (**154**.4*f*)? 24. They insisted on his turning back with them, and would hear nothing of his staying there. 25. The worthy old woman has just told me what a great misfortune has befallen her, and how no comfort is left her, save that she knows herself *to be* innocent. 26. Will you have the kindness to tell me what sort of a building that is? 27. That a new guest came in at that moment, I knew well; but who he was, I did not know. 28. She thinks only of (= auf) how she may be able to sacrifice herself to the welfare of her fellow-beings. 29. I should perhaps take this road; but I do not know whither it leads. 30. That is something which (**179**.5) the master will in no case allow. 31. What you see there is all that (**179**.5) the poor man has left in the world; and he has great apprehension that he will soon lose this also.

Exercise 28.

Adjective dependent clauses (**437**; **110.**1*c*).

1. London is a city which has an enormous extent. 2. The boys, who had been looking everywhere, finally found the place where their sister lay hidden. 3. Death is a means whereby all diseases are healed. 4. This is the second misfortune that has happened to me to-day. 5. She is speaking of a place where (= whither) I have all my life longed *to be*. 6. The vulgar *man* does not understand the goal toward which (**180**) the noble *man* strives. 7. This is the man whom he produced to me before his departure, as one upon whom I could absolutely rely. 8. Alone I should not like to go so far; but he (**166.**2*b*) is a companion with whom I could journey‿over the whole world. 9. Tell me the way in‿which (= wie) it happened. 10. The eventide, when everything betakes itself to rest, had drawn near.

Exercise 29.

Adverbial dependent clauses (**438.**1,2,3*a–c,f,g*).

1. We rested ourselves where a large oak spread‿abroad a grateful shade. 2. The railway-train goes‿roaring off while the friends at the station look after it. 3. I do it because it pleases me. 4. The company got out of the carriage, while the horses were unharnessed and led into the stable. 5. My dear friend stands now before my mind's eye exactly as I have so often seen her in reality. 6. Although he overwhelmed me with entreaties, I could not accompany him. 7. If thou art my friend, then furnish me now the proof. 8. If you do not know anything sensible (**129.**5) to say, then keep silent. 9. Henry stood still, in‿order‿that the others might pass by him. 10. The lady's answer was very low, so that it (**169.**2; **171**) scarcely reached his ears. 11. The more friendly I grow, the more repelling does he become. 12. The band played beautifully to-day, as I have never yet heard it play. 13. It is so fine an (**67**) evening that I can not‿possibly stay at home. 14. A heavy fate seems to follow him everywhere, wherever he may go. 15. No, we are not going to-day [thither] where we were day‿before‿yesterday. 16. I believe he is attached to him only [for this reason] because he hopes to gain something. 17. Your success may vary, according as you are yourself active about it or not. 18. Before they could return, we were already gone. 19. Because he is personally disagreeable to me, I do not invite him. 20. If it is you (**154.**4*f*),

do (= doch) come to me! 21. When I aimed at the little‿bird, it flew off. 22. If I can be of‿assistance to you, call upon me. 23. As the bridge is not quite‿safe, we prefer not to go over *it.* 24. He is at heart a good lad, although he does not always obey his parents. 25. Brave warriors do not give way until there is no hope left. 26. The more the clumsy *fellow* exerts himself, the ess his undertaking appears to succeed.

SERIES III.

EXERCISES ON SPECIAL POINTS IN THE GRAMMAR.

Exercise 30.

Use of the articles (66–7).

1. Patience is a rarer virtue than courage. 2. Last winter it was not very cold, and he made a journey in Turkey. 3. As a student, he lived in Charlotte St.; but now he has become a parson, and has moved to Potsdam St. 4. Then he dipped his hand into the water, passed it over his face, wiped it, and thrust it into his pocket. 5. My cousin takes *a* music-lesson twice a week. 6. He comes very often in the morning to *see* me. 7. Have you seen Lucca in Faust? 8. Jesting aside, we must be there at evening. 9. The merits of Augusta are great. 10. Otto Moltke, the bearer of this, is a colleague of mine (= me). 11. As the agent of your father, I cannot permit it.

Exercise 31.

Declension of foreign and proper names (101–8).

1. Our professor has a great collection of minerals. 2. The in habitants of New York are from all parts‿of‿the‿world. 3. Frank's portfolio and Mary's books are still lying on the sofa in the drawing-room. 4. Conrad's prospects have unfortunately grown worse. 5. In how many volumes is the edition of Heinrich Heine's works? 6. In the saloon are two sofas, a large and a small *one.* 7. The lords have all voted against it. 8. He has made the ascension of Jesus Christ [to] the subject of a painting. 9. That was formerly a castle of King Frederick the Great. 10. The influence of this climate is in many cases beneficial.

Exercise 32.

Peculiarities of adjective declension (**125–8 ; 129.5**).

1. Thou foolish man! how canst thou act so imprudently? 2. We dwelt in the beautiful open country, several long miles distant from the city. 3. It is bad weather; I believe the expected guests will stay away on that account. 4. Ye good men cannot comprehend such an injustice. 5. Below at the shore lay a pretty little wooden boat, and the children got in and went out upon the lake. 6. The temple, built of splendid white marble, stood upon an eminence. 7. He has, indeed, spoken much, but *has* said nothing good and of‿solid‿value. 8. I have just seen something beautiful and heard of something dreadful.

Exercise 33.

Specialities of use of pronouns (**154.2–4; 155.4; 161; 166.2,3, 171, 179.4,5; 181**).

1. I knew nothing of it, for no one had told me anything about it. 2. It looks very black; there is probably a storm coming; but whether it will rain or hail we can not yet say. 3. I answer for it that he does not deceive you. 4. If it is you, step nearer. 5. This moment decides whether we shall love or hate one another. 6. I have read too much; my eyes pain me. 7. Her I do not mean; I am speaking of her sister. 8. Mrs. Steinthal is in [the] town; if you want to see her, come to our house day‿after‿to-morrow. 9. I make it a (= zum: **316.2c**, *rem.;* **66.7**) principle not to believe him, whatever he may say; for all that he has said to me hitherto was false. 10. He persecutes me, who have never harmed him; and he loves thee, who canst not love him in‿return. 11. They have loved one another since [the] last summer, when they saw one another for the first time. 12. These were the considerations which moved us to it.

Exercise 34.

Expressions of measurement and of time (**211.2,3; 216.5*a,b***).

1. The baron lives alone in his castle; it lies four miles from the city, on a hill about two hundred feet high (**147.2**); he has ninety casks of wine in his cellar, and *a* thousand head of cattle in his fields; and his little army of retainers is *a* hundred and seventy-five men strong. 2. Can you tell me how many pounds that weighs? 3. We must be there punctually; the doors are

closed at eight o'clock. 4. Allow me to offer you a glass of this good wine. 5. Besides his house, a large piece of fertile land belongs to him. 6. These peasants dine at twelve o'clock, and go to bed about half past eight. 7. The whole family has been (324.3) here since the first of August; on the twentieth of September they intend to make an excursion into the country. 8. Please try a cup of this genuine Russian tea. 9. *No*, I thank you. I have already drunk two cups of tea.

Exercise 35.

Special uses of the genitive (220).

1. In the morning I write in my room; in the evening I go to walk. 2. One evening, as we sat cosily together, he told me the wonderful story‿of‿his‿life. 3. What I say to you, he said to me in all seriousness. 4. Only be of good (121.3) courage; a real danger is by‿no‿means imminent. 5. I believe, his health is perfectly restored; when I saw him last, he was in very good spirits. 6. In this case, I cannot be of your opinion. 7. My cousin Frederick has had (324.3) for years the habit of dining (345.3) with me on Sunday. 8. Alas, the fate that we have to endure! 9. I was not present, because I was unexpectedly called away shortly before the appointed time. 10. He has never, to my knowledge, been concerned in it.

Exercise 36.

Special uses of the dative (222.III*a*,*b*; 225).

1. Even if you have no inclination to it, do it to oblige your friend. 2. In honor of you the children were released from school. 3. Hail to the conquerors of our foes and defenders of our honor! 4. Alas for him! the rescue comes too late. 5. The hero, an example to us and to our children, has departed‿from‿life. 6. Welcome to every honorable guest who treads our threshold! 7. To those who follow our banner, glory and honor! 8. He looked in the eyes of one, and whispered in the ear of another; then he wiped his own eyes, and put on his spectacles.

Exercise 37.

Special constructions of the accusative (227.2; 229–30).

1. He sleeps the sleep of the righteous. 2. Now the rider gets down from his horse, and wishes to rest himself in the inn, for he has ridden himself tired. 3. He fought his way cheerfully

and courageously through life, attained a great age, and died a peaceful and painless death. 4. I should much like to take part in your mountain-excursion, but I am no longer used to such an exertion. 5. We can no longer suffer the rude, inconsiderate behavior of these men; we have at last had enough of it. 6. The travellers had to wait several minutes in this vestibule before they were let in. 7. The fellow ran rapidly down the stone steps, almost before we noticed it; and soon we had lost him from sight. 8. For ten months the leader of the band‿of‿robbers was in prison. 9. The lake is in this spot fifty feet deep. 10. We went first along a straight road, then turned to the left. 11. We were in the same town the whole summer through, without meeting each other a single time. 12. He continued standing (343.I.6) there a‿long‿time, his head bared, his eyes fixed upon the stone.

Exercise 38.

Modal auxiliaries in compound tenses, and used independently (251.4–6; 259).

1. You can have as much of it as you will; I have not wanted to reserve anything for myself. 2. William, why could you not have kept silence? you ought not to have told your father what you think of his design. 3. The hostler went to the stable in order to saddle the horse; but he could not get in, because the door was locked. 4. I am curious to know whether you can do that; I have not been able to do it. 5. If the girls knew Italian, they would more easily come to an understanding with the violinist. 6. The children may not go further; it has been [already] often forbidden them. 7. I have had to act thus, because my brother wished (*perf.*) it; in this affair I do not venture to act against his wishes. 8. The physician would gladly have decided as you wish, but his opinion differs somewhat from yours. 9. What means this standing and waiting; are you not allowed to go away? 10. We are allowed everything; but, for reasons which I cannot impart to you at this moment, we would rather not.

Exercise 39.

Passive verbs (278–82).

1. The king has received the emperor's ambassador with a discourtesy hardly to be expected. 2. Our whole family was yesterday evening at a private‿ball at Mr. Mohrenschild's; there was much dancing and eating, but remarkably little drinking 3. Is

this errand performed according to my wish? 4. Sir, it is just now performing in accordance with your wish. 5. As soon as (438.3*d*) the lamp was lighted, the interrupted work was taken up again. 6. The event *which is* to be feared has not occurred. 7. The boys who had stolen the apples were already long since discovered by the gardener, before they were driven out of the garden. 8. The professor was last night kept awake so long by some noisy boys that he feels quite weary to-day, and cannot give his promised lecture. 9. I am regularly provided by him with new books and periodicals. 10. He is provided for his journey with a pair of dark glasses, which are to protect his eyes from the dazzling snow.

Exercise 40.

Reflexive verbs (286–90).

1. The exile longs for his native country. 2. Is not the dishonest shopkeeper ashamed of his behavior? 3. Whoever risks such a thing, relies upon an accident. 4. Carefully beware of a repetition of this evil. 5. This stuff wears well; I have often worn it. 6. The little summer-house on the hill among the trees looks quite prettily. 7. Call the girls away; they are dancing themselves tired. 8. It is good walking on this handsomely levelled path. 9. I tried to recollect his name, but I positively could not *do* it. 10. Can you remember the title of the book which we read (*perf.*) together on our journey? 11. To oppose the royal dominion is difficult, but to submit to it is impossible. 12. Unawares we near the fateful hour.

Exercise 41.

Impersonal verbs (292–3).

1. Are there no Jews in this town? 2. O yes, there are some; but they are not numerous, and they all[2] live[1] in a certain quarter of the town. 3. It appears to me highly improbable that you should ever succeed in that. 4. I did not, it is true, succeed in it the time before, but methinks I shall carry it through this time. 5. How are you now? 6. I am already quite well, but you are certainly still feeling badly. 7. I am constantly getting colder; there must be a draught of air somewhere. 8. The wanderer was hungry and thirsty; the night was coming on, and he knew of no way out. 9. I wonder that my neighbors do not leave a house where they feel themselves uncomfortable. 10. There have been far fewer accidents on this railway than upon the others.

Exercise 42.

Use of the tenses (324–6).

1. The family of which you speak came to America, but went back again, and has been now for eight years in Germany. 2. How long have you been waiting for us here? 3. We had been waiting for two hours when you arrived, and we should soon have given you up. 4. Only go on‿ahead, I will follow directly. 5. We start this evening at eight o'clock; shall we not see each other at the station? 6. No, unfortunately we must take leave of each other now; I am going at seven o'clock into the suburb, and shall not come back until nine. 7. We had been there only about a quarter of an hour when they came past. 8. Did you attend the festival lately? I thought I saw you there. 9. You were not mistaken; and how did it please you on the whole? 10. The children were not in school yesterday; their mother was ill, and they staid at home to nurse her.

Exercise 43.

Optative subjunctive (331).

1. May we soon be freed from this odious imprisonment! 2. God grant that the lovers soon meet again! 3. Let him go where he will; we shall not follow him. 4. God bless our land and our people! 5. Between us be truth. 6. O that we had remained united! 7. *Long* live the young king, the friend of the people! 8. Oh, had we availed‿ourselves‿of the precious opportunity, which will never be repeated!

Exercise 44.

Conditional and potential subjunctive, and conditional (332, 335).

1. If the weather were not so hot, I should be able to work better. 2. It would have been pleasanter[1], however, if we had made the excursion‿into‿the‿country without guides. 3. What should we not have gained, had we remained faithful to our original determination! 4. O that this day were past! 5. The neighbor's child avoids us, as if it were afraid of us. 6. I would at once give you the necessary money, but I have just been paying a bill, and must first get some. 7. It might perhaps not yet be too late. 8. He has, I should think, blundered egregiously. 9. I should like myself also to have taken part in the war. 10. Put the bouquet into the water, that it may not fade. 11. It is

to be hoped (343.III.1b) that the session be soon broken up. 12. It would be imprudent to go further. 13. The wine would not suffice, if the company were increased by one person.

Exercise 45.

Subjunctive of indirect statement (333).

1. He says he has had nothing to do with it. 2. Our messenger doubts whether he can arrive at the proper time. 3. The mother cried out aloud for fear that her child would drown. 4. You will never compel your friend to confess *that* he was himself to blame for it. 5. We did not believe that the illness was so bad, and that he so much needed our help. 6. The people through (= in) the whole country complained that a downright famine threatened them. 7. Have you read to-day's paper? they say that it contains an important piece‿of‿news. 8. It is my urgent wish that he may never return. 9. Ye would have done it? If I had only known that! 10. The schoolmaster imagines he is very learned. 11. My brother writes me he has arrived safely, and will soon send me a book which our uncle has given him for me. 12. He admonished us that only those who fought bravely could hope for deliverance; but all who fled the danger must perish in it.

Exercise 46.

Infinitive constructions (343–8).

1. To be able to enjoy life is surely *a* fine *thing*. 2. It is useless to dwell upon such thoughts. 3. What shall we have for dinner to-day? 4. Whatever you choose to order will suit me. 5. I left them lying in the same spot where I found them. 6. Dost thou not hear some one call? 7. Charles was very kind to-day; he helped me copy these letters. 8. He is prepared to annihilate everything that gets into his way. 9. If you will let that happen, you must take upon yourself the whole responsibility. 10. He no longer questions and doubts anything, but accustoms himself to believe everything, even the incredible. 11. Why would you not like to have this article printed? 12. I caused the book to be read aloud to me by my brother. 13. Have the coachman called and the carriage driven up; I have an errand to attend to in the city. 14. I have caused him to be looked for everywhere, but he is not to be found. 15. Such a horse is not easily to be obtained. 16. Without heeding my express commands, he has run away, in order to amuse himself somewhere, or to attend to his own affairs.

Exercise 47.

Participial constructions (350–59).

1. The dead victims of his rage return as ghosts to plague him. 2. The high-grown trees shaded the road. 3. The foaming drink quenched our thirst and refreshed us. 4. The bystanders hastened to snatch the knife out of the hand of the madman (222.III*a*). 5. Those who had arrived knocked long at the bolted door, but in vain. 6. The exile was advised (281) to direct a petition to the Queen. 7. Filled with love and devotion, the unfortunates resigned themselves (431*d*) to their fate. 8. Engaged more and more by this pious design, he furthered it in every possible way. 9. The horses, panting and sorely wearied, bore their riders up the mountain. 10. We called both[2] the[1] (67) boys up to us; they came running. 11. I call that maturely considered.

Exercise 48.

Adverbial forms of adjectives (363).

1. He spoke well, it is true, but did not convince his hearers. 2. According to that which (179.5) I hear, the crew defended (326.2) itself bravely. 3. Will you please to reach me the butter? 4. At another time he would be exceedingly welcome, but now he comes extremely unseasonably [for me]. 5. I will tell you what has struck me most. 6. I do not feel myself in the least offended. 7. It would be pleasantest for us, if he had *dinner* served in the open air. 8. I have nothing to reproach him for; he has behaved most handsomely. 9. In‿the‿first‿place, I don't know what the fellow's name is; and secondly, he did not tell me where he lives.

Exercise 49.

Prepositions governing dative or accusative (376).

1. Henry crept behind the house, and hid himself from the soldiers. 2. Where is my book? I laid it on the table. 3. It has fallen upon the floor; it is lying there under the table. 4. Between the two houses stands a high tree. 5. I cannot think of that hour without becoming (346.1) sad. 6. The government will in no case permit that[1]. 7. The blind *man* directed his eyes upward, as if he could perceive the glorious spectacle. 8. The lad swam over the river, and his large dog swam along after him. 9 We went into his dwelling to look for him and found him in the

first room. 10. The miser buried his treasure under this flat stone. 11. The little birds hover in the air over the roofs of the houses.

SERIES IV.

Exercises founded on passages in the Reader.

Exercise 50.

Reader, p. 20, ll. 11–23.

In a certain house lived a little boy, and this boy had some tin soldiers, which had been given (281) him on his birthday. They were twenty-five in number, but they had only forty-nine legs, for one of them had to stand upon one leg, because the tin had not held out when he was moulded; but he was no less steadfast than the others who had two legs, and his remarkable history we will now read. The soldiers lay together in a box, until the boy took them out and set *them* up upon the table. There they stood now, in their splendid red and blue uniform, and each one held his musket on his arm.

Exercise 51.

Reader, p. 27, l. 3—p 28, l. 21.

When my horse at last held still, and I had seated myself properly in the saddle, I saw beside me a very strange and ugly little man. He was all yellow, and his nose was at least a foot long. He asked me for a piece of money, and said he had checked the course of my horse. That was a lie, but I gave him a gold-piece, in order to be rid of him, and trotted on. He followed after me, and cried "false money!" I galloped as fast as possible, but he was the whole time by my side. Then I stopped and wanted to give him another, but he would not take it. And he showed me the goblins under the earth, how they played with silver and gold; and he showed them my gold-piece, and they laughed and hissed and climbed up toward me, stretching out their dirty fingers. A horror seized me, and I rushed a second time madly into the wood.

Exercise 52.

Reader, p. 30.

Hast thou seen the lofty castle by the sea, with the rosy clouds that hover over it? "I have seen it; and above it stood the moon, and far around the mist." Hast thou heard the wind, and the surging sea, and festive song from the halls? "No; the wind did not blow, the waves lay quiet, and out of the castle came a song of mourning." Didst thou not see the king and queen, with their red mantles and golden crowns? and was (= went) not a maiden of splendid beauty with them? "I have indeed seen the[1] parents[1], but they wore no glittering crowns, and had put on black mourning-garments. The maiden was not there."

Exercise 53.

Reader, p. 31.

There were (**154**.4*b*,*d*) once three students, who (**438**.3*h*) crossed the Rhine, and came to an inn where they were accustomed to put up. And as they went in, the hostess came to meet them, and asked them what they would have. "Beer and wine," answered they; "and your pretty little daughter we should also[1] like to see." "Fresh beer and clear wine ye can indeed have; but my daughter is no longer living; here she lies upon the bier." Now [the] one of the three students had long loved her, and, while the others gazed sadly at her, and even began to weep, he kissed her pale mouth, and swore to love only her for ever.

Exercise 54

Reader, p. 37.

I am sad, and I cannot comprehend why I am so (**154**.4*e*). The sun is setting, and the air is cool; the Rhine flows quietly past my feet; the evening sunlight illumines the summit of the mountain, and I am thinking over and over an old legend. Up there sits a beautiful maiden; and as she combs with a golden comb her down-flowing golden hair, she sings a wondrous and mighty song. When the sailor in the little ship hears this song, a wild pain seizes him; he no longer sees the rocks about him; he no longer marks the track *on* which he has to sail. If I am not mistaken, the sailor with his boat will sink; and the Lorelei, the beautiful maiden who is singing up there, will have done it.

Exercise 55.

Reader, p. 39.

This stream is well known to me. [Already] many years ago I once crossed *it*. The castle, the weir, the whole landscape is unchanged. When I was here for the first time, I did not come alone, as I now come. In this boat two companions rode with me—an elderly, fatherly man, and a hopeful, gladsome youth. The former passed quietly through the remainder of his life, just as he had till then quietly lived: the latter, in accordance with his natural character, fell in stormy battle. Whilst I at *the* present hour transport myself back to those old happy days, I painfully feel the loss of my dear companions, snatched away by death (**147.2**). Yet Death cannot snatch away friendship from me: for he (**166.2*b***) has to do only with the body, while I am still always in communion with the spirits. Take then, ferryman, a triple fare; for with me have crossed two others, who remained invisible to thee.

Exercise 56.

Reader, p. 40.

Dost thou still remember the times when we were merry little children, and played together? Then we took a great chest which lay in the yard, and papered and furnished it, and made of it our dwelling. Often, the neighbor's cat used to visit us, and acted very courtly and aristocratic; while we curtseyed to her, and inquired most anxiously (**363.2*b,c***) after her health. And as we sat there in our cosy house, we talked together not less sensibly than old people do [it]. In our time, we lamented, everything was (**333**) better; neither coffee was dear, nor money scarce; nor had love and faith vanished from the world, as [it] was (**333.4*a***) now the case.

Exercise 57.

Reader, p. 41.

Who shall conduct us over into the Silent Land? The evening sky grows ever cloudier and darker, and on the shore where we are to land are piled up the wrecks of others' vessels. Yet we would fain *go* over, to the land where *there* is free space for the ennobling of every beautiful soul, that has faithfully endured here the struggle of life. Where the great dead live, thither will a gentle messenger, sent by our fate (**147.2**), conduct us.

Exercise 58.

Reader, p. 49.

We (**185**) have two ears and one mouth, in order to be able to hear much and say little. We have two eyes and one mouth, that we may see far more than we talk about. Likewise we have two hands and one mouth, because we are to work at least twice as much as we eat.

Exercise 59.

Reader, pp. 62–4.

In ancient times, when singers (**66.**1) still wandered through the world, two singers once came to a beautiful lofty castle, surrounded with fragrant gardens (**147.**2). In this castle ruled a rich and proud king. Gloomy and pale he sat; terrible were his thoughts and furious his looks. As the two drew near to the castle, the old man, who, sitting on a handsome steed, held in his hand a harp, spoke to the lad, who, fresh and blooming, walked at his side: "Get ready to collect all your force and to strike up your fullest tone. We must select our deepest songs, for the stony heart of this king is not easy to touch."

Now the singers stand in the splendid hall before the terrible king and the mild queen. Wonderfully the old man strikes the chords; richer and richer swells the sound upon the ear, while the clear voice of the youth blends gloriously with the hollow, ghostly singing of the old man. All scoffing dies out on the lips and in the hearts of the courtiers, the insolent warriors bow down, and the queen, deeply moved, takes the rose which she had worn upon her breast, and casts it down to the noble pair.

But the king, trembling with (vor) rage, sprang up from his throne; the singers had, he cried, enticed away from him (**222.I.**3) first his people, and now even his wife. Thereupon he hurled at (auf) the youth his flashing sword; it pierced his (**171.**2) breast; and out of the mouth from which had poured forth golden songs, gushed now a red stream of blood.

Soon the youth had breathed his last in the arms of the old man his master, and the latter, casting his mantle about him, and binding him upright upon the horse, left the castle. Yet he went not far; in the gate he stopped, and, after he had dashed his harp in pieces on one of the marble pillars, he called down from heaven with ringing voice a curse upon castle and gardens, and upon the infamous murderer.

Heaven heard the cry of the old singer; the castle, with its halls and lofty columns, is totally destroyed; even the land round about is desolate; not a tree grows there; the springs are dried up; and the king's name is forgotten.

Exercise 60.

Reader, pp. 65–70

The king casts a golden cup down from the summit of the cliff into the howling sea, and asks if any one has *the* courage to plunge into the abyss and fetch out the cup. Whoever dares *to do* this, may keep it (171) as his own.

The knights and the squires are all silent, and it appears as if (436.3*g*) no one cared to win the cup. But finally, after the king has asked a third time, one of the squires, a glorious youth, steps forth (hervor) and throws aside his cloak. And while all gaze wonderingly upon him, he steps boldly to the edge of the abyss, where the water boils and roars fearfully, and the crowding waves spurt their foam to the sky. He looks down a‿long‿time, and waits, till the waves are drawn downward again, and a bottomless chasm yawns before him: then he leaps from the rock, and quickly disappears in the dark water.

They (185) stand and linger upon the shore; they speak of the high-spirited youth, whom they never think to see again; they tell one another (155.4) *how* that the king's crown were no reward for such *a* deed;—but suddenly the flood again approaches roaring, and they see a white arm rise out of the water and joyously wave the cup. It is the brave youth, who has saved his soul alive out of the horrible abyss of waters.

He kneels down before the king and gives him the cup; the king has it filled by his lovely daughter with sparkling wine and handed to the youth; upon which the latter begins his story. He relates how the furious current had dragged him down; but God had showed him a jutting rock; this he had seized and so had escaped [an] immediate death; and so he had also found the cup, which was hanging close by on the point of a coral-branch; otherwise he would never have found it, for the bottomless depth lay there in purple darkness beneath him. Also he told what hideous monsters were there to be seen (343.III*b*); and how, terrified, he had let go the rock; but at just the time when the eddy was ready to drag him upward.

The king, astonished at this, presents him the cup, together‿ with a precious ring, and begs him to try it once more, and bring up tidings from the yet deeper bottom of the sea. But the gentle daughter‿of‿the‿king implores her father to rest content, since the noble youth had [though] already undergone what no one besides dared *undergo*.

Thereupon the king quickly seizes the cup and hurls it down into the whirlpool, with the promise *that* he will (333.3*e*) make the squire [to] the first of his knights, and give him his daughter as spouse, if he will get it (171) again.

The youth sees the maiden turn pale and sink to the ground love seizes his soul and gleams from his eyes; he determines (=

will) to win the precious prize or to die, and he plunges once more down.

The breakers come back with thundering noise, the waters rise and fall roaring, but in vain do they bend down to see the diver; the waves never bring him again.

Exercise 61.

Reader, pp. 75–6.

When two French grenadiers, who had been prisoners in Russia, heard that France had lost, and that the emperor was a prisoner, they wept together over this sad news. Then said [the] one *of them*, who was wounded: "My old wound burns again and pains me sorely; I shall not live much longer." "Thou canst die," replied the other, "for thou hast neither wife nor child at home, who would have to go begging, but for thee." "Wife or child concerns me not," said the first again, "when my emperor is taken. If thou comest to France, grant me this last request; have me buried in French earth, with my musket in my hand and the cross of honor on my breast (**230**.3), that I may lie there and listen till my emperor shall ride (**332**.5*d*) over my grave; then I will come forth armed, to protect him."

Exercise 62.

Reader, p. 104, ll. 5–21.

Within, in the house, the modest housewife governs wisely, surrounded by her children. She teaches the girls to be industrious (**343**.I.5), and controls the rude boys. Her presses become filled with treasures which she has herself made of snowy linen and of glistening wool. What is the gain of the husband without the ordering sense of the wife? What is the good that he gathers without the beauty that she adds to it?

Exercise 63.

Reader, p. 108, ll. 3–18.

Death hath dissolved forever the tender bonds of this household, in that he hath led away the faithful wife and mother into the dark land of shadows. The blooming children whom she bore to her husband, and who have grown up under her faithful management, will henceforth have to do without her care. A stranger, whose love can never equal hers, will govern in the orphaned house.

Exercise 64.

Reader, p. 154, l. 30—p. 155, l. 14.

When the signal is once given, every one begins to be foolish, yes, crazy, and to permit himself all‿sorts‿of liberties and impertinences toward high and low. The birth of Christ, the Roman thinks, has indeed been able to put off for a few weeks the ancient festival of the Saturnalia, but its (**171**.2) privileges have not by‿that‿means been altogether abolished. If thou hast thyself been present at the carnival, I shall do thee a service, in‿that I bring before thy imagination a lively depiction of its already enjoyed pleasures: if the journey is still in prospect for thee, thou wilt be able better to overlook and enjoy the crowded and noisy festival by reason of the few leaves which I now send thee.

Exercise 65.

Reader, p. 159, ll. 18–32.

An advocate, who declaims as if he were standing before *the* court, presses rapidly through the crowd. Every promenader (*dat.*) whom he can seize is threatened with a law-suit. This one is claimed to have committed sundry absurd crimes, which are rehearsed to him and to all *the* bystanders; to that one his numerous and enormous debts are exactly specified. His piercing voice and fluent tongue put every one to shame. You think perhaps *that* he will soon stop, when he has really only just got a going; he turns about and begins again when you suppose *that* he has at last gone away. While he does not address this one, whom he has gone directly at, he seizes another one, although the latter is already past. It grows maddest (**140**.2*b*), however, when two such fellows fall in with one another.

Exercise 66.

Reader, p. 165, ll. 7–18.

The practice of pelting (**345**.3) each other with *confetti* probably took its origin from some fair one's having (**346**.2) once pelted her good friend, as he went past her without noticing her, with real sugarplums; and *from* the *person* hit having then turned round, as was quite natural, and discovered her who thus assailed him. Now, however, it has become a universal custom. Real confectionery, to‿be‿sure[1], is no longer wasted in this manner; a kind *of* gypsum pellets, made specially for such use, is carried about for sale in baskets.

Exercise 67.

Reader, 168, l. 31—p. 169, l. 27.

The horses which are to run never have a covering on their bodies. When the handsomely decorated grooms lead them into the lists, they are for the most part fiery and impatient, and but for the dexterity of the grooms, they would not be to be restrained (343.III.1*b*) at all. They are unmanageable because of their eagerness to begin the race; they are skittish because of the presence of so many people. As soon as the rope falls, they start off. At first each horse seeks to get ahead of the rest, but soon they come into the narrow space, where all emulation becomes fruitless. In *a* few moments they have disappeared, and the race-course is filled up again by the in-crowding people. At the other end of the course, where they are waited for (281), they are dexterously caught, and the victor receives the prize.

Exercise 68.

Reader, pp. 201–2

What Shakspeare wished to portray, we see clearly from these words: a soul which is not equal to a great deed that is laid upon it. We see how an oak, planted in a flower-vase (147.2), destroys the vase by the expansion of its mighty roots. That which is required of him would be to a hero no heavy burden; but Hamlet is not a hero, and he cannot bear it. Neither can he throw it off, for it is to him a duty; and to a pure and noble character, such as (= wie es) Hamlet is, every duty, even the heaviest, is sacred.

The hero of the historian or the poet always acts independently, executes all that he undertakes, sets aside every obstacle, and attains infallibly to his great purpose. Life, however, teaches us differently; that the atrocious deed rolls onward in its consequences, involving *the* innocent and *the* guilty; and not until the hour of judgment comes, does the villain fall; but then the good *man* also falls with *him;* a whole race is cut down by fate, in order that another may spring up.

Exercise 69.

Reader, p. 202, l. 29–p. 203, l. 8.

Often, when one looks upon the treeless plain, lighted by the rapidly rising and sinking constellations (147.2), one believes *that* the great shoreless ocean is spreading itself out before him. The prairie, hardly less than the ocean itself, fills the mind with the feeling of infinity, and with the higher spiritual impulses which develop themselves out of this feeling. But while the ocean-surface, on account of its light-moving waves, has a friendly aspect, the prairie, on the contrary, lies stiff and desolate, almost as if it were the rocky crust of a dead planet.

Exercise 70.

Reader, p. 230, l. 18–p. 231, l. 6.

The generations of beasts arise and pass away, without (**436**.3*d*) a thought of the significance of their life and of its particular period ever arising in them. With all races of men, on the other hand, we notice that every leading event—as, for example, the birth of a child, marriage, death, and burial—is distinguished by an appropriate ceremony. The farther we look back into antiquity, the more exactly prescribed and sharply defined do the forms of such ceremonies become. The feeling lies at *the* bottom of these usages (**222**.III*a*) that nothing would be rightly done or could be looked upon as complete, if it were not legitimated in this manner.

ENGLISH-GERMAN VOCABULARY.

EXPLANATIONS.

Verbs of the Old conjugation, and of the New if irregular, are so noted (by an added *O.* or *N. irr.* respectively); their forms are to be sought in the List of Irregular Verbs. Verbs taking ſein as auxiliary have an ſ added after them. Verbs of which the character as separably or inseparably compounded would be otherwise doubtful have their accent marked (311).

Nouns have the sign of their gender appended, and the endings of their genitive singular (except of feminines) and nominative plural.

If the vowel of an adjective is modified in comparison, the fact is noted.

Adverbs in *-ly* derived from adjectives and having the same form as the adjectives (130) are not separately entered.

The case governed by a preposition, and, in many cases, by a verb or adjective, is noted in parenthesis after it.

Figures in parenthesis refer to the Grammar; others, to the Exercises.

able:—**be able**, **können** *N. irr.*

about *prep.*, (= round about) **um** (*acc.*), **um . . . her**; (a. such a time) **um** (*acc.*); (= respecting, concerning) **über** (*acc.*); **about it**, **dabei** 29.17.—*adv.* (= nearly, not far from) **etwa**, **ungefähr**; **round about**, **rings herum**; **stroll about** *etc.*, *see the verbs.*

abroad: — **spread abroad**, **verbreiten**.

absolute, **unbedingt**.

accident, (= chance) **Zufall** *m.* -ls, -älle; (= mishap) **Unglücksfall** *m.* -ls, -älle.

accompany, **begleiten**.

accordance: — **in acc. with**, **gemäß** (*dat.* 374*b*), **nach** (*dat.*) 39.4.

according:—**acc. as**, **je nachdem**; **acc. to**, **nach** (*dat.* 374*b*).

account:—**on acc. of**, **wegen** (*gen.* 373*b*); **on that acc.**, **deshalb**.

accuse, **anklagen** (*acc. gen.*).

accustom (= habituate), **gewöhnen**; **be acc'd**, **pflegen**.

acquit, **entledigen** (*acc. gen.*).

act, **handeln**; (= bear one's self) **thun** *O.* 56; (= behave) **sich betragen** *O.*

active, **thätig**.

add, **hinzufügen**.

admonish, **ermahnen**.

advantageous, **vortheilhaft** (**for**, *dat.*).

advise, **rathen** *O.*

afar, **weit**.

affair, **Sache** *f.* -en; **Geschäft** *n.* -ts, -te.

afflict, **bedrängen**.

afraid:—**be afr. of**, **sich fürchten vor** (*dat.*).

after *prep.*, **nach** (*dat.*); **along af.**, **hinter . . .** (*dat.*) **her**.—*conj.*, **nachdem**.

again, **wieder**.

against, **gegen** (*acc.*).

age, **Alter** *n.* -rs, -r.

agent, **Geschäftsträger** *m.* -rs, -r.

ago, **vor** (*prep.*, *governing in dat. the noun which* ago *follows*); **long ago**, **längst**.

ahead:—**on ah.**, **voran**.

aim *v.*, **zielen** (**at**, **auf**, *acc.*).

air, **Luft** *f.* -üfte; **draught of air**, **Luftzug** *m.* -gs, -üge; **open air**, **Frei** (*neut. adj. as noun*).

alas, **ach** (*gen.*), **wehe** (*dat.*).

Albert, **Albrecht**.

all, **all**; **all my life**, **mein Lebenlang**.

allow, **erlauben**; **be allow'd**, **dürfen** *N. irr.*

almost, **fast**, **beinahe**.

alone, **allein**.

along *prep.*, entlang (*after acc.*).—*adv.* **al. after**, *see* after.
aloud, laut; **read al.**, vorlesen *O.*
already, schon; vorhin 34.9.
also, auch.
although, obgleich, obschon.
altogether, gänzlich.
always, immer.
ambassador, Gesandt *adj. as noun.*
America, Amerika *n.* -a's.
American *noun*, Amerikaner *m.* -rs, -r; **Am. woman**, Amerikanerin *f.* -nnen.
among, zwischen (*dat. or acc.*).
amuse, unterhal'ten *O.*
an, ein.
and, und.
Anna, Anna.
annihilate, vernichten.
another, ein ander; **one another**, einander; sich, uns, euch (155.4).
answer, Antwort *f.* -ten.—*v.*, antworten; **ans. for**, stehen *O.* für (*acc.*).
antiquity, Alterthum *n.* -ms, -ümer.
any:—**anything**, etwas; **not . . . an.**, nichts; **no longer an.**, nichts mehr.
appear, scheinen *O.*
apple, Apfel *m.* -ls, Aepfel.
apply:—**ap. one's self to**, sich befleißen *O.* (*gen.*).
appoint, bestimmen.
apprehension, Angst *f.*
approach:—**ap. roaring**, heranbrausen s.
appropriate *adj.*, entsprechend.
are, sind (239.2).
aristocratic, vornehm.
around *prep.*, um (*acc.*).
army, Heer *n.* -res, -re; Armee, *f.* -en.
arrival, Ankunft *f.*
arrive, ankommen *O.* s.
article, Artikel *m.* -ls, -l.
artist, Künstler *m.* -rs, -r.
as, wie; (= as being, *or* in the shape of, *or* when) als; (= since) da; (= while) indem; (*in* twice as, not as) so; **as if**, als ob, als wenn, als *with following inverted clause.*
Ascension, Himmelfahrt *f.*
ashamed:—**be a. of**, sich schämen (*gen.*).
aside, bei Seite.
ask (= inquire), fragen; (= request) bitten *O.* (**for**, um *acc.*).
assail, angreifen *O.*
assist, unterstütz'en.
assistance, Beistand *m.* -ds; **of ass.**, behülflich *adj.*
assure, versichern (*acc. gen.*).
assuredly, gewiß.
at (at the station, a ball), auf (*dat.*); (at the brook) an (*dat.*); (wonder *or* rejoice at) über (*acc.*); (at such o'clock) um; (at this moment etc.) in (*dat.*); (at one's [house]) bei (*dat.*); (at heart) von (*dat.*); (hurl *or* aim at) auf (*acc.*); (knock at) an *acc.*); (at a time) zu.
attached, anhänglich.
attain, erreichen.
attend, (= be present at) beiwohnen (*dat.*); **att. to**, besorgen (*acc.*); nachgehen *O.* s. (*dat.*) 46.16.
attention, Aufmerksamkeit *f.*
August, August *m.* -ts.
Augusta, Augusta.
autumn:—**autumn month**, Herbstmonat *m.* -ts, -te.
avail one's self of, sich bedienen 20.4 (*gen.*); benutzen 43.8 (*acc.*).
avoid, vermeiden *O.*
awake *adj.*, wach; **be aw.**, wachen.
away, weg, fort.
axe, Axt *f.* Aexte.

back *adv.*, zurück; wieder: *see the verbs.*
bad, schlecht; schlimm 45.5.
ball:—**private b.**, Privatball *m.* -ls, -älle.
band, (of music) Kapelle *f.* -en; **b. of robbers**, Räuberbande *f.* -en.
banner, Fahne *f.* -en.
bare *v.*, entblößen.
baron, Baron *m.* -ns, -ne.
base, *adj.*, bös.
basket, Korb *m.* -bs, -örbe; **little b.** Körbchen *n.* -ns, -n.
Bavarian, Baier *m.* -rn, -rn.
be, sein (239.2); *as aux'y with pres. part., not to be rendered* (324 etc.), **be to**, sollen (257.2).
bear *v.*, tragen *O.*
bearer, Ueberbringer *m.* -rs, -r.
beautiful, schön.
beauty, Schönheit *f.* -ten.
because, weil; **bec. of**, wegen (*gen.*).
become, werden *O.* s.
bed, Bett *n.* -tes, -ten.
befal, begegnen (*dat.*) s.
before *prep.*, vor (*dat. or acc.* 376) —*conj.*, ehe, bevor.—*in adj. sense* vorig 41.4.
beg, bitten *O.*
beggar, Bettler *m.* -rs, -r.
begin, anfangen *O.*, beginnen *O*

behave, sich benehmen *O.*, sich halten *O.* 48.8.
behavior, Betragen *n.* -ns, Handlungsweise *f.* 40.2.
behind *adv.*, hinter, zurück, *see the verbs.—prep.*, hinter (*dat. or acc.* 376).
belief, Glauben *m.* -ns.
believe, glauben.
belong to, gehören (*dat.*).
below *adv.*, unten.
bench, Bank *f.* -änke.
beneficial, wohlthuend.
beside, neben (*dat. or acc.* 376).
besides *prep.*, außer (*dat.*).—*adv.* außerdem; **no one b.,** sonst niemand.
betake one's self, sich begeben *O.*
better, besser.
between, zwischen (*dat. or acc.* 376).
beware of, sich hüten vor (*dat.*).
beyond, jenseits (*gen.*).
Bible, Bibel *f.*
bill, Rechnung *f.* -gen.
bird, Vogel *m.* -ls, -ögel; **little b.,** Vögelchen *n.* -ns, -n.
bite, beißen *O.*
black, schwarz.
blame:—be to bl. for, Schuld sein an (*dat.*).
blend, sich verbinden *O.*
bless, segnen.
blind, blind.
blue, blau.
blunder, sich täuschen.
boast *v.*, sich rühmen.
boat, Boot *n.* -tes, -te; Kahn *m.* -nes, -ähne 32.5.
bolt *v.*, verriegeln.
bone, Knochen *m.* -ns, -n.
book, Buch *n.* -chs, -ücher.
book-case, Bücherschrank *m.* -ks, -änke.
boot, Stiefel *m.* -ls, -l *or* -ln.
both, beide.
bottle, Flasche *f.* -en.
bottom, Grund *m.* -des, -ünde; **at b.,** zu Grunde.
bouquet, Blumenstrauß *m.* -ßes, -äuße.
boy, Knabe *m.* -en, -en.
brave, tapfer.
break, brechen *O.*; **br. up,** aufheben *O.*
bridge, Brücke *f.* -en.
bright:—br. side, Lichtseite *f.* -en.
bring, bringen *N. irr.*; (= bring along) mitbringen 26.5.
brook, Bach *m.* -ches, -äche; **little br.,** Bächlein *n.* -ns, -n.
brooklet, Bächlein *n.* -ns, -n.
brother, Bruder *m.* -rs, -üder; **brothers and sisters,** Geschwister *pl.*

build, aufführen 32.6.
building, Gebäude *n.* -es, -e.
bullet, Kugel *f.* -ln.
burn, brennen *N. irr.*
bury, vergraben *O.*
but *conj.*, aber.—*adv.* (= only), nur; **but for,** ohne (*acc.*).
butter, Butter *f*
buy, kaufen.
by, von (*dat.*); (= by means of, as result of) durch (*acc.*); (denoting measure of difference, increase or diminution, etc.) um (*acc.*); (= beside) bei; (transition) an (*dat.*) vorüber.
bystander, Umstehend *adj. used as noun.*

call (= name), nennen *N. irr.*; (= cry out to, summon) rufen *O.*; **be called** (= have the name of) heißen; **c. down,** herabrufen; **c. away,** abrufen 35.9, fortrufen 40.7; **c. to,** zurufen (*dat.*); **c. upon** (= apply to), sich berufen auf (*acc.*).
calm, ruhig.
can, können *N. irr.*; **cannot,** nicht können *N. irr.*
care, Sorge *f.* -en; **free from c.,** sorgenfrei; **take c.,** sich in Acht nehmen *O.*
careful, sorgfältig.
carriage, Wagen *m.* -ns, -n.
carry:—c. through, durch'führen.
carrying on *n.*, Treiben *n.* -ns.
case, Fall *m.* -ls, -älle; **in no c.,** auf keinen Fall.
cask, Faß *n.* -sses, -ässer.
casket, Kästchen *n.* -ns, -n.
castle, Schloß, *n.* -sses, -össer.
catch, fangen *O.*
cattle, Rind *n.* -des, -der.
cause *v.* (*governing another verb in infin.*), lassen *O.*
cease, aufhören.
cellar, Keller *m.* -rs, -r.
certain (= sure, secure) gewiß, sicher; (= indefinite, not further specified) gewiß.
certainly, gewiß.
chain, Kette *f.* -en.
chancellor, Kanzler *m.* -rs, -r.
character, Charakter *m.* -rs, -re.
charge with, beschuldigen (*acc. gen.*)
Charles, Karl.
Charlotte St., Charlottenstraße, *f.*
charming, reizend.
cheerful, froh.
cheese, Käse *m.* -es, -e.
child, Kind *n.* -des, -der; **little ch.,** Kindlein *n.* -ns, -n.

choice, **Wahl** *f.* -len.
choose to, **wollen** *N. irr.*
church, **Kirche** *f.* -en.
city, **Stadt** *f.* -ädte.
cleanly *adj.*, **reinlich.**
clear, **klar.**
clever. **klug** (ü *in comp.*).
climate, **Klima** *n.* -a's.
close *v.*, **schließen** *O.*
close :—close by *adv.*, **daneben.**
clumsy, **ungeschickt.**
coachman, **Kutscher** *m.* -rs, -r.
cold, **kalt** (ä *in comp.*).
colleague, **College** *m.* -en, -en.
collection, **Sammlung** *f.* -gen.
colonel, **Oberst** *m.* -ten, ten.
come, **kommen** *v.* s.; **c. back, zurückkommen, wiederkommen; c. in, hereinkommen; c. on, herankommen; c. past, vorbeikommen; fail to c., ausbleiben** *O.* s.
comfort, **Trost** *m.* -tes.
comfortable, **bequem.**
command, **Befehl** *m.* -ls, -le.
commission, **Auftrag** *m.* -gs, -äge.
compact, **Vertrag** *m.* -gs, -äge.
companion, **Gefährte** *m.* -en, -en.
company, **Gesellschaft** *f.* -ten.
compel, **zwingen** *O.*
complain, **klagen.**
complaining, **Klagen** *n.* -ns.
complete, **vollständig.**
comprehend, **begreifen** *O.*
comrade, **Kamerad** *m.* -ds, -den.
concerned, **betheiligt (in, bei).**
concert, **Concert** *n.* -ts, -te.
conduct, (= guide) **führen;** (= behave) **sich betragen** *O.*
confess, **gestehen** *O.*
confidence, **Vertrauen** *n.* -ns.
connect :—be connected, zusammenhangen *O.*
conqueror, **Besieger** *m.* -rs, -r.
Conrad, **Konrad.**
conscious, **sich** (*dat.*) **bewußt.**
consent, **zusagen.**
consider (= meditate), **überle'gen;** (= regard as, deem) **erachten, halten** *O.* **für** (*acc.*) 24.7.
consideration, (= reason) **Grund** *m.* -des, -ünde.
constantly, **immer.**
contain, **enthalten** *O.*
contented, **zufrieden.**
continue, **bleiben** *O.* s.
contrary :—on the c., hingegen.
convent, **Kloster** *n.* -rs, -öster.
convince, **überzeu'gen.**
cook, **Köchin** *f.* -nnen.
copy, **abschreiben** *O.*

corner, **Ecke** *f.* -en; **c. house, Eckhaus** *n.* -ses, -äuser.
cosy, **traulich.**
costly, **kostbar.**
cough, **Husten** *m.* -ns.
counsellor :—state c., Staatsrath *m.* -ths, -äthe.
country, **Land** *n.* -des, -änder; **native c., Vaterland** *n.* -ds; **excursion into the c., Landpartie** *f.* -en.
courage, **Muth** *m.* -thes.
courageous, **muthig.**
course, **Lauf** *m.* -fes.
courtly, **höflich.**
cousin, **Vetter** *m.* -rs, -r; (female) **Cousine** *f.* -en.
cover, **verdecken.**
cow, **Kuh** *f.* -ühe.
coward, **Feigling** *m.* -gs, -ge.
creep, **kriechen** *O.*
crew, **Mannschaft** *f.* -ten.
crime, **Verbrechen** *n.* -ns, -n.
criminal, **Verbrecher** *m.* -rs, -r.
cross (= go over), **hinüberfahren** *O.* s.
cry, **Ruf** *m.* -fes, -fe.—**cry out, aufschreien** *O.*
cup, **Tasse** *f.* -en.
curious, **neugierig.**
cushion, **Kissen** *n.* -ns, -n.

daily, **täglich.**
dance *v.*, **tanzen.**
danger, **Gefahr** *f.* -ren.
dangerous, **gefährlich.**
dark, **dunkel; d. blue, dunkelblau.**
date, **Datum** *n.* -ms, -ta.
daughter, **Tochter** *f.* -öchter; **d. of the king, Königstochter** *f.* -öchter.
dawn *v.*, **grauen.**
day, **Tag** *m.* -ges, -ge.
dazzle, **blenden.**
dead, **todt, gestorben** 47.1.
death, **Tod** *m.* -des.
deceive, **hinterge'hen** *O.*, **betrügen** *O.*
decide, **entscheiden** *O.*
deed, **That** *f.* -ten.
deep, **tief.**
defend, **vertheidigen.**
defender, **Vertheidiger** *m.* -rs, -r.
defy, **trotzen** (*dat.*).
dejected, **niedergeschlagen.**
deliverance, **Rettung** *f.*
depart, **verreisen** s.; **d. from life, abscheiden** *O.* s.
departure, **Abreise** *f.*
depiction, **Schilderung** *f.* -en.
design, **Vorhaben** *n.* -ns, -n; **Absicht** *f.* -ten 47.8.
desire, **Lust** *f.*

determination, Entschluß *m.* -sses, -üsse.

detestable, abscheulich.

devise, ausdenken *N. irr.*

devotion, Ergebung *f.*

dictionary, Wörterbuch *n.* -chs, -ücher.

die, sterben *O.* s.; **die out,** verstummen s.

differ, abweichen *O.* s.

difficult, schwer.

dine, zu Mittag essen *O.*, speisen.

dinner:—for d., zu Mittag.

dip, tauchen.

direct, richten; **d. to,** einlegen bei (*dat.*) 47.6.

directly, gleich.

disagreeable, unangenehm; **be d. to,** mißfallen *O.* (*dat.*).

disappear, verschwinden *O.* s.

discontented, unzufrieden.

discourtesy, Unhöflichkeit *f.*

discover, entdecken.

disease, Krankheit *f.* -ten.

dishonest, unehrlich.

displease:—be displeasing to, mißfallen *O.* (*dat.*).

distant, entfernt.

do, thun *O.*, machen 21.10, schaffen *O.* 55; **do without,** entbehren (*gen.*); **be done,** geschehen *O.* s. 25.3; (*strengthening a request*) doch 29.20: *as aux'y in questions, negative phrases, and imperative, not to be rendered.*

doctor, Arzt *m.* -tes, Aerzte.

dog, Hund *m.* -des, -de; **little d.,** Hündchen *n.* -ns, -n.

dominion, Herrschaft *f.*

door, Thür *f.* -ren.

doubt, Zweifel *m.* -ls, -l.—*v.* bezweifeln; **d. of,** zweifeln an (*dat.*).

doubtful, zweifelhaft.

doubtless, wohl.

down, nieder, unter, hinunter, *etc.: see the verbs.*

down-flowing, herunterfließend, herniederfließend.

downright, wahr.

draught:—dr. of air, Luftzug *m.* -gs, -üge.

draw:—dr. near *or* **nigh,** heranahen s., sich nähern 59; **dr. on** (clothes etc.), anziehen *O.*

drawing-room, Gesellschaftszimmer *n.* -rs, -r.

dreadful, schrecklich.

dress, Kleid *n.* -des, -der.

drink *v.*, trinken *O.*—*noun,* Getränk *n.* -ks, -ke.

drive, (= drive away) forttreiben *O.*; (= go in a carriage) fahren *O.* s.; **be driven up,** vorfahren *O.* s.

drown, ertrinken *O.* s.

duke, Herzog *m.* -gs, -ge.

dwell, wohnen; **dw. upon,** nachhangen *O.* (*dat.*).

dwelling, Wohnung *f.* -gen.

each:—e. one, jed; **e. other,** einander; sich, uns, euch (155.4).

ear, Ohr *n.* -res, -ren.

earlier *adv.*, eher.

early, früh.

earth, Erde; **on e.,** auf Erden (95).

earthly, irdisch.

east, Osten, *m.* -ns.

easy, leicht.

eat, essen *O.*

edge, Rand *m.* -ds, -änder.

edition, Ausgabe *f.* -en.

education, Erziehung *f.*

egregiously, gewaltig.

either *conj.*, entweder.

eight, acht.

elder, älter.

elderly, ältlich.

eldest, ältest.

eminence, Anhöhe *f.* -en.

emperor, Kaiser *m.* -rs, -r.

enclose in, beilegen (*dat.*).

end, Ende *n.* -es, -en.

endure, erleiden *O.*

enemy, Feind *m.* -ds, -de; Feindin *f.* -nnen 24.2.

engaged by, ergriffen von 47.8.

Englishman, Engländer *m.* -rs, -r.

Englishwoman, Engländerin *f* -nnen.

enjoy, sich freuen (*gen.*).

ennui, Langeweile *f.*

enormous, ungeheuer.

enough, genug; **have en. of,** satt haben (*acc.*).

entire, ganz.

entreaty, Bitte *f.* -en.

enviable, beneidenswerth.

equal *v.*, gleichkommen *O.* s. (*dat.*).

errand, Auftrag *m.* -gs, -äge.

escape *v.*, entgehen *O.* s. (*dat.*), entfliehen *O.* s. (*dat.*), entlaufen *O.* s.

estate, Gut *n.* -ts, -üter.

Europe, Europa *n.* -a's.

even, auch, selbst 36.1, sogar 59.

event, Ereigniß *n.* -sses, -sse; **leading ev.,** Hauptereigniß *n.* -sses, -sse.

evening, Abend *m.* -ds, -de; **May ev.,** Maiabend *m.* -ds, -de; **this ev.,** heute Abend.

eventide, Abendzeit *f.*

ever, je, jemals.
every, jed (190); **every one,** jedermann (187); **everything,** alles; **everywhere,** überall.
evident, offenbar.
evil *adj.*, übel.—*noun*, Uebel *n.* -ls, -l.
exactly, gerade, ganz 29.5.
examine, betrachten.
example, Beispiel *n.* -ls, -le, Vorbild *n.* -ds, -der; **for ex.,** zum Beispiel.
exceedingly, höchst.
excellent, vortrefflich, ausgezeichnet.
excursion, Ausflug *m.* -gs, -üge; **exc. into the country,** Landpartie *f.* -en; **mountain-excursion,** Bergpartie *f.* -en.
execute, ausführen.
exert, bestreben.
exertion, Anstrengung *f.* -gen.
exile (= banished person), Verbannt *adj. as noun.*
expect, erwarten.
express *adj.*, ausdrücklich.
extent, Ausdehnung *f.*
extraordinary, außerordentlich.
extreme, äußerst.
eye, Auge *n.* -es, -en.

face, Gesicht *n.* -ts, -ter.—*v.* **go to face,** entgegengehen *O.* s. (*dat.*).
fade, verwelken s.
fail:—**f. to come,** ausbleiben *O.* s.
fain:—**would f.,** möchte (*pret. subj.*).
faithful, getreu.
fall, fallen *O.* s.
false, falsch.
family, Familie *f.* -en.
famine, Hungersnoth *f.*
far, weit, fern.
farther, weiter.
fate, Schicksal *n.* -ls, -le.
fateful, verhängnißvoll.
father, Vater *m.* -rs, -äter.
fault, Schuld *f.* -den.
Faust, Faust *m.* -ts.
fear *v.*, fürchten, befürchten 39.6.—*noun*, Angst *f.*
fearful, fürchterlich.
feel (= be sensible of) empfinden *O.*; (= find one's self) sich fühlen 39.8, zu Muthe sein 41.6.
fell, fällen.
fellow, Bursche *m.* -en, -en; Kerl *m.* -ls, -le 48.9.
fellow-being, fellow-man, Mitmensch *m.* -schen, -schen.
fertile, fruchtbar.
fervent, innig.
festival, Fest *n.* -tes, -te.
fetch out, herausholen.
few, wenig; **a few,** einige *pl.*
field, Feld *n.* -des, -der.
fifth, fünft.
fifty, fünfzig.
fight, fechten *O.*, streiten *O.* 45.12; **f. one's way,** sich schlagen *O.*
fill, erfüllen, (an office etc.) bekleiden 22.4.
finally, endlich.
find, finden *O.*
fine, schön.
finished, fertig.
firm, fest.
first *adj.*, erst.—*adv.* erst, zuerst 37.10, **at f.,** am Anfang 67; **in the f. place,** erstens.
fish, Fisch *m.* -sches, -sche.
fit *v.*, passen (*dat.*).
five, fünf.
fix, heften (**on,** auf).
flat, flach.
flee, fliehen *O.* s.
floor, Fußboden *m.* -ns.
flour, Mehl *n.* -les.
flow down, hinunterfließen *O.* s.
flower, Blume *f.* -en.
fly off, fortfliegen *O.* s.
foam *v.*, schäumen.
foe, Feind *m.* -des, -de.
follow, folgen s. (*dat.*), nachfolgen s (*dat.*) 43.3, nachkommen *O.* s. 42.4. **f. after,** nachfolgen s. (*dat.*).
foolish, thöricht.
foot, Fuß *m.* -ßes, -üße.
for *prep.*, für (*acc.*) 23.24; (wait, hope for) auf (*acc.*); (for fear) vor (*dat.*); (for reasons) aus (*dat.*); (for first time) zu (*dat.*); (for a certain time until now) seit (*dat.*) 35.7, 42.1; (= during) lang (*after acc.*); (ask for) um: *often to be omitted, the noun being put in the dative.*
for *conj.*, denn.
forbid, verbieten *O.*
force, zwingen; (= impose by violence) aufdringen *O.* 27.20.
forest, Wald *m.* -des, -älder; **little f.,** Wäldchen *n.* -ns, -n.
forget, vergessen *O.* (*gen. or acc.*).
former, früher; **the f.** (*opposed to* latter) jen (166.1).
formerly, früher, vormals.
forth, fort.
fortune:—**good f.,** Glück *n.* -ts.
four, vier.
Frank, Franz *m.* -zens.
Frederick, Friedrich *m.* -chs.
free *adj.*, frei; **f. from care,** sorgenfrei.—*v.*, befreien (**from,** aus).

French, franzöſiſch.
Frenchman, Franzoſe *m.* =en, =en.
friend, Freund *m.* =des, =de; Freundin *f.* =nnen.
friendly, freundlich.
from, von (*dat.*); aus (*dat.*) 31.2, 36.2; (hide, protect from) vor (*dat.*).
fugitive, Flüchtling *m.* =gs, =ge.
furious, wüthend.
furnish, (= deliver) liefern; (= provide with furniture) möbliren.
further *adv.*, weiter.—*v.* befördern.
future *noun*, Zukunft *f.*

gain *v.*, gewinnen *O.*
garden, Garten *m.* =ns, =ärten.
gardener, Gärtner *m.* =rs, =r.
gate, Thor *n.* =res, =re.
general, Feldherr *m.* =rn, =ren.
generous, freigebig.
gentle, zart (ä *in comp.*).
genuine, echt.
Germany, Deutſchland *n.* =ds.
get, (= obtain) bekommen *O.*; (= fetch) holen 44.6; (= become, grow) werden *O.* ſ.; (get into prison) kommen *O.* ſ.; (get in the way) treten *O.* ſ. 46.8; **get ready**, ſich bereit machen; **get in**, hineinſteigen *O.* ſ.; **get down**, herunterſteigen *O.* ſ.; **get on**, vorwärts gehen *O.* ſ.; **get out of**, ſteigen *O.* ſ. aus (*dat.*) 29.4; **get through**, durchkommen *O.* ſ.
ghost, Geiſt *m.* =tes, =ter.
ghostly, geiſterhaft.
girl, Mädchen *n.* =ns, =n; **servant-girl**, Dienſtmädchen *n.* =ns, =n.
give, geben *O.*; (give a lecture) halten *O.*; **give up**, aufgeben; **give way**, nachgeben.
glad, froh; **be g. to**, gern *adv.*
gladly, gerne.
gladsome, lebensfroh.
glass, Glas *n.* =ſes, =äſer; **pair of glasses**, Brille *f.* =en.
glorious, herrlich, gar herrlich 59.
glory, Ruhm *m.* =mes.
go, gehen *O.* ſ.; **go away**, fortgehen, weggehen; **go back**, zurückgehen; **go down**, untergehen; **go to face**, entgegengehen (*dat.*); **go off**, verreiſen ſ.; **go on**, weitergehen; **go on ahead**, vorangehen; **go out**, hinausfahren *O.* ſ.; **go over**, hinübergehen; **go past**, vorübergehen; **go there** *or* **thither**, hingehen 21.8, 9; **go along with one**, mitgehen; **gone**, fort 29.18.
goal, Ziel *n.* =les, =le.
God, Gott *m.* =tes.
good, gut; **g. fortune**, Glück *n.* =ks.
government, Regierung *f.* =gen.
grandfather, Großvater *m.* =rs, =äter.
grandmother, Großmutter *f.* =ütter.
grandson, Enkel *m.* =ls, =l.
grant, gewähren, geben *O.* 43.2.
grateful (= agreeable), wohlthuend.
grave *noun*, Grab *n.* =bes, =äber.
grave *adj.* (= heavy), groß (ö *in comp.*).
great, groß (ö *in comp.*), hoch (120.4, 139.1) 14.1, 37.3.
greatly, ſehr.
ground, Boden *m.* =ns.
grow, wachſen *O.* ſ.; (= become) werden; **gr. up**, aufwachſen; **gr. worse**, ſich verſchlechtern; **high-grown**, hochgewachſen.
guardian, Vormund *m.* =ds, =ünder.
guest, Gaſt *m.* =tes, =äſte.
guide, Führer *m.* =rs, =r.
guilty, ſchuldig.
gun, Büchſe *f.* =en.
gush, hervorſtrömen ſ.

habit, Gewohnheit *f.* =ten.
hail (of weather), hageln.
hail! Heil!
half, halb; **h. past eight**, halb neun.
hand, Hand *f.* =ände; **on the other h.**, dagegen.
handsome, ſchön.
happen, geſchehen *O.* ſ.; **h. to**, begegnen ſ.
happiness, Glück *n.* =ks.
happy, glücklich.
hard, ſtark (ä *in comp.*) 14.6.
hardly (= scarcely), kaum.
harm *v.*, ſchaden (*dat.*).
hasten, ſich beeilen.
hat, Hut *m.* =tes, =üte.
hate, haſſen.
haughty, hochmüthig.
have, haben *N. irr.*; *as aux'y*, haben *or* ſein *O.* ſ.; **have to** (*with infin.* 343.III.1*c*) haben zu, müſſen; (*with obj. and past part.*) laſſen *O.* (*with infin.*).
he, er (151), der (166.2*b*); **he who** wer 27.8.
head, Kopf *m.* =fes, =öpfe.
heal, heilen.
health, Geſundheit *f.*
healthy, geſund.
hear, hören.
hearer, Zuhörer *m.* =rs, =r.
heart, Herz *n.* =zens, =zen; **at heart** von Herzen.

heavy, schwer.
heed, achten (*gen.*) 18.10; achten auf (*acc.*) 12.6, 46.16.
help *v.*, helfen *O.* (*dat.*).—*noun*, Hülfe *f.*
helplessness, Hülflosigkeit *f.*
henceforth, künftig.
Henry, Heinrich.
here, hier.
hero, Held *m.* -den, -den.
herself, sich *or* selbst *or* selber (155).
hide, verbergen *O.*, verstecken (**from,** vor) 49.1.
high, hoch (120.4, 139.1); **high-grown,** hochgewachsen.
highly, höchst 41.3.
hill, Hügel *m.* -ls, -l.
himself (*refl. obj.*) sich; (*in appos'n*) selber, selbst.
his, sein (157), der (161).
history, Geschichte *f.* -en.
hitherto, bis jetzt.
hoarse, heiser.
hold:—h. still, still halten *O.*
home (= to one's home), heim; **at h.,** zu Hause.
honesty, Ehrlichkeit *f.*
honor, Ehre *f.* -en; **in h.,** zu Ehren (95); **man of h.,** Ehrenmann *m.* -ns, -änner.—*v.* beehren.
honorable, ehrbar.
hope *v.*, hoffen (**for,** auf).—*noun*, Hoffnung *f.* -gen (**of,** auf).
hopeful, hoffnungsvoll.
horse, Pferd *n.* -des, -de.
host, Wirth *m.* -thes, -the.
hostile, feindlich.
hostler, Stallknecht *m.* -ts, -te.
hot, heiß.
hour, Stunde *f.* -en; **quarter of an h.,** Viertelstunde *f.* -en.
house, Haus *n.* -ses, -äuser; **corner h.,** Eckhaus *n.* -ses, -äuser; **little h.,** Häuschen *n.* -ns, -n; **to our h.,** zu uns 33.8.
hover, schweben.
how, wie; **how many,** wieviel.
however, aber, doch 44.2.
hundred, hundert.
Hungarian, Ungar *m.* -rs, -rn.
hungry:—be h., hungern.
hunter, Jäger *m.* -rs, -r.
hurl, werfen *O.* (**at,** auf).
husband, Mann *m.* -ns, -änner.

I, ich (151).
if, wenn; *or expressed by the inverted order* (433).
ill, krank (ä *in comp.*).
illness, Krankheit *f.* -ten.
illumine, beleuchten.
imagine, sich (*dat.*) einbilden.
immediate, augenblicklich.
imminent, vorhanden.
impart, mittheilen.
implore, anflehen.
importance, Wichtigkeit *f.*
important, bedeutend.
impossible, unmöglich.
imprisonment, Gefangenschaft *f.*
improbable, unwahrscheinlich.
imprudent, unvorsichtig.
in *adv.*, (= in hither) herein.—*prep.*, in (*dat.*); (in yard, country, castle, spot) auf (*dat.*); (= in respect to) an 23.2, 50; (concerned in) bei; **in this manner** *or* **way,** auf diese Weise **in that** *conj.*, indem.
incessant, unaufhörlich.
inclination, Neigung *f.* -gen; Lust *f.* 36.1.
inclined:—be i. to, zugeneigt sein (*dat.*).
incomprehensible, unbegreiflich.
inconceivable, undenkbar.
inconsiderate, rücksichtslos.
increase, (= make higher) erhöhen; (= make more numerous) vermehren; (= become greater) zunehmen *O.*
incredible, unglaublich.
indeed, wohl, zwar 32.7, 64.
independent, selbständig.
indifferent, gleichgültig.
indistinct, undeutlich.
industrious, fleißig.
infallible, unfehlbar.
influence, Einfluß *m.* -sses, -üsse.
inhabitant, Einwohner *m.* -rs, -r 31.2, Bewohner *m.* -rs, -r 22.6.
injure, schaden (*dat.*).
injustice, Unrecht *n.* -ts.
inkstand, Tintenfaß *n.* -sses, -ässer.
inn, Wirthshaus *n.* -ses, -äuser.
innocent, unschuldig.
insist on, bestehen *O.* auf (*acc.*) 26.4, dringen auf 27.24.
intend, beabsichtigen.
interest one's self for, sich annehmen *O.* (*gen.*).
interrupt, unterbrech'en *O.*
into, in (*acc.*); (into the country) auf (*acc.*).
invisible, unsichtbar.
invite, einladen *O.*
Irishman, Irländer *m.* -rs, -r.
is, ist (239.2).
it, es, er, sie (154.1), derselbe *etc.* (171).
Italian *adj.*, italienisch.—*noun*, Italiener *m.* -rs, -r.

January, Januar *m.* =rs.
jesting *noun*, Scherz *m.* =zes, =ze.
Jesus Christ, Jesus Christus, *gen.* Jesu Christi *etc.* (107).
Jew, Jude *m.* =en, =en.
jewel, Juwel *m.* =ls, =len.
John, Johann *m.* =ns.
join one's self, sich gesellen.
journey, Reise *f.* =en; **take a j.**, verreisen.—*v.*, **j. over**, bereisen.
June, Juni *m.* =i's.
just *adv.*, (= precisely, exactly) gerade, eben; (= just now) soeben; **j. now**, soeben; **j. as**, ebenso wie 55.

keep, erhalten *O.*; **k. silent** *or* **silence**, schweigen *O.*
kind *adj.*, freundlich.
kind *noun*:—**a k. of**, eine Art *f.* =ten
kindness, Gefälligkeit *f.* =ten.
king, König *m.* =gs, =ge; **daughter of the k.**, Königstochter *f.* =öchter.
kiss *v.*, küssen.
knife, Messer *n.* =rs, =r.
knock, pochen (**at**, an *acc.*) 47.5.
know, (= be acquainted with) kennen *N. irr.*; (= be aware of, apprehend) wissen *N. irr.*; (a language) können *N. irr.*; **know of**, wissen 41.8.
known, bekannt.
knowledge, Wissen *n.* =ns, =n; **to my kn.**, meines Wissens.

labor, Arbeit *f.* =ten.
lad, Junge *m.* =en, =en.
laden, beladen.
lady, Dame *f.* =en; **young l.**, Fräulein *n.* =ns, =n.
lake, See *m.* =es, =en.
lamp, Lampe *f.* =en.
land, Land *n.* =des, =de *or* =änder.—*v.* landen.
landlord, Wirth *m.* =ths, =the.
landscape, Landschaft *f.* =ten.
large, groß (ö *in comp.*).
last, letzt; (= preceding the present, of times) vorig 30.2;—*adv.* (= the last time) zuletzt 35.5.; **at l.**, endlich.
late, spät.
lately, neulich.
lawyer, Advokat *m.* =ten, =ten.
lay, legen.
lead *v.*, führen.
leaden, bleiern.
leader, Führer *m.* =rs, =r.
leading event, Hauptereigniß *n.* =sses, =sse.
leaf, Blatt *n.* =ts, =ätter.

learn, erfahren *O.*
learned *adj.*, gelehrt.
least, mindest; **in the l.**, im mindesten; **at l.**, wenigstens.
leave, lassen *O.* 46.5; (= quit) verlassen *O.*; **l. behind**, zurücklassen —*noun*, **take l. of**, Abschied nehmen *O.* von (*dat.*).
lecture, Vorlesung *f.* =gen.
left, (= remaining) übrig; **be l.**, bleiben *O.* s.; **have l.**, noch haben *N. irr.*; (= not right) link; **to the l.** nach links.
legitimate *v.*, legitimiren.
lend, leihen *O.*
less, weniger.
let, lassen *O.*; **l. in**, einlassen; *before an infin., in imperative sense, to be rendered by imperative.*
letter, Brief *m.* =fes, =fe; **little l.**, Briefchen *n.* =ns, =n; **letter-carrier**, Briefträger *m.* =rs, =r.
level *v.*, ebnen.
liberation, Befreiung *f.*
library, Bibliothek *f.* =ken.
lie, liegen *O.*
life, Leben *n.* =ns; **all my l.**, mein Lebenlang; **mode of l.**, Lebensweise *f.*; **story of (one's) l.**, Lebensgeschichte *f.* =en.
light (= kindle), anstecken.
like *adj.*, gleich (*dat.*).—*v.* **should l.**, möchte (*pret. subj.*).
likewise, ebenfalls.
listen to, zuhören (*dat.*).
little, (= small) klein; *often to be rendered by a diminutive in* =chen *or* =lein (410.1); (= a little) wenig.
live, wohnen.
living:—**manner of l.**, Lebensweise *f.*
lock, zuschließen *O.*
London, London *n.* =ns.
long *adj.*, lang (ä *in comp.*); **l. since** *or* **l. ago**, längst, schon lange 39.7; **a l. time**, lange *adv.*
long *v.*, sich sehnen (**for**, nach *dat.*).
longer:—**no l.**, nicht mehr; **not much l.**, nicht mehr lange.
look *v.*, schauen, sehen *O.* (**in**, in *acc.*) 36.8; (= search) suchen; **l. after**, nachsehen *O.* (*dat.*); **l. at**, ansehen *O.*; **l. back**, zurückblicken; **l. for**, suchen; (= appear) aussehen *O.*, sich ausnehmen *O.* 40.6.
look *noun*, Blick *m.* =kes, =ke.
lord, Lord *m.* =ds, =ds.
lose, verlieren *O.*:—**loss**, Verlust *m.* =ts, =te.
lot, Loos *n.* =ses, =se.
Louisa, Louise *f.* =ens.

love *v.*, **lieben; l. in return, wiederlieben.**—*noun*, **Liebe** *f.*
lover, Liebend *adj. as noun.*
low, (= not high) **niedrig;** (= not loud) **leise.**
Lucca, Lucca *f.* =a's.

mad, toll.
madman, Rasend *adj. as noun.*
make, machen, machen zu 33.9; (m. a compact) **schließen** *O.*; **m. use of, sich bedienen** (*gen.*).
man, Mann *m.* =ns, =änner; (= human being, of either sex) **Mensch** *m.* =schen, =schen; **m. of honor, Ehrenmann** *m.* =ns, =änner *or* =nleute (100.2); **old m., Greis** *m.* =ses, =se.
manager, Verwalter *m.* =rs, =r.
manner, Weise *f.* =en; **m. of living, Lebensweise** *f.*; **in this m., auf diese Weise.**
many, viele *pl.*; **how m., wieviel.**
marble, Marmor *m.* =rs.
march, marschiren.
mark *v.*, **merken.**—*noun* (= peculiarity), **Eigenschaft** *f.* =ten.
Mary, Marie *f.* =ens.
master, Meister *m.* =rs, =r.
matter, Angelegenheit *f.* =ten.
maturely, reiflich.
May, Mai *m.* =aies; **May evening, Maiabend** *m.* =ds, =de.
may, (wishing, conjecture) **mögen** *N. irr.*; (possibility) **können** *N. irr.* 29.17; (permission) **dürfen** *N. irr.* 38.6: *often to be omitted, the following verb being rendered by pres.* (*or perf.*) *subj.*
mean *v.*, **meinen, sollen** *N. irr.* 38.9.
means, Mittel *n.* =ls, =l; **by m. of, durch** (*acc.*); **by no m., keineswegs; by that m., dadurch.**
medicine, Medicin *f.*
meet, begegnen s. (*dat.*); **m. again, sich wiedersehen** *O.* 43.2; **m. together, zusammentreffen** *O.* s.; **come to m., entgegenkommen** *O.* s. (*dat.*).
meeting, Zusammenkunft *f.* =ünfte.
mention, nennen *N. irr.*
merchant, Kaufmann *m.* =ns, =änner *or* =fleute (100.2).
mercy:—have m. on, sich erbarmen (*gen.*).
merit, Verdienst *m.* =tes, =te.
messenger, Bote *m.* =en, =en.
methinks, mich dünkt.
might *v.*, (possibility) **können** *N. irr.*: *often to be rendered by pret.* (*or plup.*) *subj.*; *compare* may.
mighty, mächtig.
mild, mild.
mile, Meile *f.* =en.
mind, Geist *m.* =stes.
mindful:—be m. of, gedenken (*gen.*) *N. irr.*
mineral, Mineral *n.* =ls, =lien.
minute, (of time) **Minute** *f.* =en.
minutely, genau.
misdemeanor, Vergehen *n.* =ns, =n.
miser, Geizhals *m.* =ses, =älse.
misfortune, Unglück *n.* =ks.
mistaken:—be m., sich irren.
mock at, spotten (*gen.*).
mode of life, Lebensweise *f.*
moment, Augenblick *m.* =ks, =ke.
monarch, Monarch *m.* =chen, =chen.
money, Geld *n.* =des, =der.
month, Monat *m.* =ts, =te; **autumn m., Herbstmonat** *m.* =ts, =te.
more, mehr; m. and m., immer mehr: *before adj. or adv., to be rendered by the comparative degree.*
moreover, übrigens.
morning, Morgen *m.* =ns, =n.
most, (*adv.*) **am meisten** 48.5: *before adj. or adv., to be rendered by the superlative degree.*
mother, Mutter *f.* =ütter.
mountain, Berg *m.* =ges, =ge; **m.-range, Gebirge** *n.* =es, =e; **m. excursion, Bergpartie** *f.* =en.
move, (*intr.*) **ziehen** *O.* s. 30.4; (*tr.*) **bewegen** *O.*
Mr., Herr *m.* =rn.
Mrs., Frau.
much, viel; (*adv. qualifying verb or participle*) **sehr;** (much like) **gern** 37.4.
murder, Mord *m.* =des.
murderer, Mörder *m.* =rs, =r.
music-lesson, Musikstunde *f.* =en.
musket, Gewehr *n.* =rs, =re.
must, müssen *N. irr.*
my, mein (157 *etc.*).
myself, mich *or* **selbst** *or* **selber** (155.2,5).

name, Name *m.* =ens, =en; **be n. of,** (*nom.*) **heißen** *O.*
nation, Volk *n.* =kes, =ölker.
native country, Vaterland *n.* =ds.
natural character, Natur *f.*
near *adj.*, **nah.**—*v.*, **sich nahen** (*dat.*); **draw n., herannahen** s.
necessary, nothwendig 20.10, **nöthig** 44.6.
need, *v.*, **bedürfen** *N. irr.* (*gen.*), **nöthig haben** *N. irr.* (*acc.*) 27:14.
needful, nöthig.

neighbor, Nachbar *m.* =rs, =rn.
neither *adv.*, weder, auch ... nicht 68.
nephew, Neffe, *m.* =en, =en.
never, nie, nimmermehr 60.
new, neu.
news :—piece of n., Nachricht *f.* =ten.
newspaper, Zeitung *f.* =gen.
niece, Nichte *f.* =en.
nigh :—draw nigh, herannahen s.
night, Nacht *f.* =ächte.
ninety, neunzig.
no, (negative answer) nein; *adj.*, kein (195.2); **no less,** nicht weniger; **no longer** *or* **no more,** nicht mehr; **no longer ... anything,** nichts mehr 46.10; **no one,** Niemand (186).
noble, edel.
noiseless, geräuschlos.
noisy, lärmend.
nor, noch.
not, nicht; **n. a,** kein (195.2).
nothing, nichts.
notice *v.*, gewahr werden *O.* s. (*acc.*), bemerken 66.
November, November *m.* =rs.
now, jetzt, nun 53.
number, Anzahl *f.*; **in n.,** an der Zahl.
numerous, zahlreich.
nurse, pflegen.
nut, Nuß *f.* =üsse.

oak, Eiche *f.* =en.
oar, Ruder *n.* =rs, =r.
oats, Hafer *m.* =rs.
obey, gehorchen (*dat.*).
object *v.*, einwenden.
oblige :—to ob., zu Gefallen (any one, *dat.*); **be obliged,** müssen *N. irr.*
obstinate, eigensinnig.
obtain, bekommen *O.*
occasion, Gelegenheit *f.* =ten.
occur, eintreffen *O.* s.
o'clock, Uhr (211.3).
October, October *m.* =rs.
odious, verhaßt.
of, von (*dat.*); (hope of) auf (*acc.*); (make of) aus (*dat.*): *generally to be omitted, and the governed noun put in the genitive.*
off, weg, davon; **go off,** verreisen s.; **go roaring off,** davonbrausen; **shoot off,** abschießen *O.*; **take off** (clothes), ausziehen *O.*
offend, beleidigen.
offer, anbieten *O.*
officer, Officier *m.* =rs, =re.
often, oft, öfters 40.5; **as of. as,** so oft.
old, alt (ä *in comp.*); **old man,** Greis *m.* =ses, =se.
on, auf (*acc. or dat.*, 376); (on a day) an (*dat.*); **draw on,** anziehen *O.*; **get on,** vorwärts gehen *O.* s.; **put on,** aufsetzen.
once, einmal; **o. more,** noch einmal; **at o.,** zugleich, gleich 44.6.
one, ein (198); (= they, people) man (185); **one another,** uns, euch, sich (155.4).
one's self, sich *or* selber *or* selbst (155.2,5).
only, nur.
open, frei 32.2; **op. air,** Frei, *neut. adj. as noun.*
opinion, Meinung *f.* =gen, Ansicht *f.* =ten.
opponent, Gegner *m.* =rs, =r.
opportunity, Gelegenheit *f.* =ten.
oppose, sich widersetzen (*dat.*).
opposite *prep.*, gegenüber (*dat.* 374).
or, oder.
orange, Apfelsine *f.* =en.
order *noun* :**—in o. that,** damit, um daß; **in o. to,** um ... zu.—*v.*, bestellen.
origin, Ursprung *m.* =gs.
original, ursprünglich.
ornament, Zierde *f.* =en.
other, ander.
ought, sollen *N. irr.*
our, unser (157 *etc.*).
ourselves, uns *or* selber *or* selbst (155.2,5).
out :—out of, aus (*dat.*); **get out of,** steigen *O.* s. von (*dat.*).
outside *prep.*, außerhalb (*gen.*).
over *adv.*, hinüber 29.23; **o. and o.,** fort und fort.—*prep.*, (= above) über (*dat.*); (= across) über (*acc.*); (= more than) über.
overcoat, Ueberrock *m.* =ks, =öcke.
overturn, umwer'fen *O.*
overwhelm, überhäu'fen.
own *adj.*, eigen.
owner, Besitzer *m.* =rs, =r.

pail, Eimer *m.* =rs, =r.
pain *v.*, schmerzen.
painful, schmerzlich.
painless, schmerzlos.
painting, Gemälde *n.* =es, =e.
pair of glasses, Brille *f.* =en.
palace, Palast *m.* =ts, =äste.
pane, Scheibe *f.* =en; **window-p.,** Fensterscheibe *f.* =en.
pant, keuchen.
paper, (= newspaper) Zeitung *f.* =gen

pardon, verzeihen *O.* (*dat. acc.*).
parents, Eltern *pl.*
Paris, Paris.
parson, Pfarrer *m.* =rs, =r.
part, Theil *m. or n.* =les, =le; **p. of the world,** Welttheil *m.* =ls, =le; **take p. in,** Theil nehmen *O.* an (*dat.*), mitmachen (*acc.*) 44.9.
party, Partei *f.* =eien.
pass, gehen *O.* s. 55; **p. by,** vorbeigehen an (*dat.*); **p.** [something] **over,** fahren *O.* s. mit [etwas] über (*acc.*) 30.4.
passenger, Passagier *m.* =rs, =re.
past *noun,* Vergangenheit *f.*—*adv.*, vorüber, vorbei; **go p.,** vorübergehen *O.* s.; **flow p.,** vorüberfließen *O.* s. an (*dat.*); **half p. eight,** halb neun.
path, Weg *m.* =ges, =ge.
patience, Geduld *f.*
pay, bezahlen.
peaceful, friedlich.
peach, Pfirsiche *f.* =en.
peasant, Bauer *m.* =rs, =rn.
people, (= nation) Volk *n.* =kes, =ölker; (= folks) Leute *pl.*
perceive, gewahren.
perfect *adj.*, vollständig.
perform, verrichten.
performance, Vorstellung *f.* =gen.
perhaps, vielleicht.
periodical, Zeitschrift *f.* =ten.
perish, um'kommen *O.* s.
permission, Erlaubniß *f.*
permit, zugeben *O.*, erlauben 49.6.
persecute, verfolgen.
person, Person *f.* =nen.
personal, persönlich.
petition, Bitte *f.* =en.
photograph, Photographie *f.* =en.
physician, Arzt *m.* =tes, Aerzte.
picture, Bild *n.* =des, =der.
piece, Stück *n.* =ks, =ke; **p. of news,** Nachricht *f.* =ten.
pile up, aufhäufen.
pious, fromm.
pity, (= something to be regretted) Schade; **take p. on,** sich erbarmen (*gen.*).
place, Stelle *f.* =en, Ort *m.* =tes, =te *or* Oerter; **in the first pl.,** erstens.
plague, plagen.
plan, Plan *m.* =nes, =äne.
plate, Teller *m.* =rs, =r.
play *v.*, spielen.
pleasant, angenehm.
please, (= be pleasant to) gefallen *O.* (*dat.*); (in polite request) bitte (*for* ich bitte, I beg), gefälligst *adv.* 48.3.
pocket, Tasche *f.* =en.
poison, Gift *n.* =tes, =te.
poisonous, giftig.
Pole, Pole *m.* =en, =en.
police, Polizei *f.*
poor, arm (ä *in comp.*).
population, Bevölkerung *f.*
portfolio, Mappe *f.* =en.
positively, wahrhaftig.
possession :—take p. of, sich bemächtigen (*gen.*).
possible, möglich; **not possibly,** unmöglich.
Potsdam St., Potsdamerstraße *f.*
pound, Pfund *n.* =des, =de.
practice, Gewohnheit *f.* =ten.
practising, praktisch.
praise, loben.
precious, kostbar.
prefer to, lieber *adv.* 29.23.
prepare, vorbereiten.
presence, Gegenwart *f.*
present *noun,* (time) Gegenwart *f.*, (gift) Geschenk *n.* =ks, =ke; **for the pr.,** vorläufig.—*adj.*, gegenwärtig, 55, anwesend 35.9.—*v.* (= give) schenken.
pretext, Vorwand *m.* =ds, =ände.
pretty *adj.*, niedlich, hübsch.—*adv.* (= tolerably), ziemlich.
price, Preis *m.* =ses, =se.
priest, Priester *m.* =rs, =r.
prince, Fürst *m.* =ten, =ten.
principle, Grundsatz *m.* =tzes, =ätze.
print, drucken.
prison, Gefängniß *n.* =sses, =sse.
private ball, Privatball *m.* =ls, =älle
probable, wahrscheinlich.
produce, vorführen (**to,** *dat.*).
professor, Professor *m.* =rs, =ren
promise *v.*, versprechen *O.*—*noun,* Versprechen *n.* =ns, =n.
proof, Beweis *m.* =ses, =se.
proper, recht.
property, Eigenthum *n.* =ms.
prophet, Prophet *m.* =ten, =ten.
prospect, Aussicht *f.* =ten.
protect, beschützen (**from,** vor).
proud, stolz.
provide, (= supply) versehen *O.*; (have on hand) besorgen lassen *O.*
provident, vorsichtig.
prudent, vorsichtig.
Prussian, Preuße *m.* =en, =en.
public, öffentlich.
punctual, pünktlich.
pupil, Schüler *m.* =rs, =r.
pursuer, Verfolger *m.* =rs, =r.
put, thun *O.* 44.10; **put on,** aufsetzen 18.19, 36.8, anlegen 52.

quarter:—**qu. of an hour**, Viertelstunde *f.* -en; **qu. of the town**, Stadttheil *m.* -ls, -le.
queen, Königin *f.* -nnen.
quench, stillen.
question *noun*, Frage *f.* -en.—*v.*, befragen.
quick, schnell.
quiet, friedlich, ruhig 6.16.
quite, ganz.

raft, Floß *n.* -ßes, -öße.
rage, Wuth *f.*
railway, Eisenbahn *f.* -nen; **railw. train**, Eisenbahnzug *m.* -gs, -üge.
rain *v.*, regnen.
rapid, geschwind, rasch 23.2.
rapt, gespannt.
rare, selten.
rather, lieber.
rattling, Rasseln *n.* -ns.
reach, (= hand) reichen; (= attain) erreichen.
read, lesen *O.*; **r. aloud**, vorlesen.
ready:—**get r.**, sich bereit machen.
real, wirklich.
reality:—**in r.**, leibhaftig.
realm, Reich *n.* -ches, -che.
reason, Vernunft *f.*; (= cause, motive) Grund *m.* -ds, -ünde; **for this r.**, darum.
receive, empfangen *O.*, erhalten *O.* 67.
recently, neulich.
recollect, sich entsinnen *O.* (*gen.*).
recover, wiedererlangen.
red, roth (ö *in comp.*).
refresh, erquicken.
regular, regelmäßig.
rejoice, (= give pleasure to) erfreuen; (= be glad) sich freuen (**at**, über *acc.*); **rej. in**, sich erfreuen (*gen.*); **be rejoiced**, sich freuen.
relate, erzählen.
release, entlassen *O.* (**from**, aus).
reliable, zuverläßig.
relieve, entledigen (*acc. gen.*).
rely, sich verlassen *O.* (**upon**, auf *acc.*).
remain, bleiben *O.* s.
remainder, Rest *m.* -tes.
remarkable, merkwürdig.
remember, sich besinnen *O.* auf (*acc.*) 40.10, sich erinnern (*gen.*) 56.
render, leisten.
repeat:—**be repeated**, sich wiederho'len.
repel, abstoßen *O.*
repetition, Wiederholung *f.* -gen.
reply, antworten, versetzen.
repose, Ruhe *f*
reproach one for, einem vorwerfen *O.* (*acc.*).
repugnant to, zuwider *prep.* (*dat.* 374).
request, Bitte *f.* -en.
rescue *noun*, Rettung *f.*
resemble, gleichen *O.* (*dat.*).
reserve, vorbehalten *O.* (**for**, *dat.*).
resign one's self to, sich fügen in (*acc.*).
respect *v.*, achten.
responsibility, Verantwortlichkeit *f.*
rest, Ruhe *f.*—**r. one's self**, sich ausruhen.
restore, wiederherstellen.
result, Erfolg *m.* -gs, -ge.
retainer, Vasall *m.* -len, -len.
return *v.*, zurückkehren s.—*noun*, Wiederkehr *f.*; **love in r.**, wiederlieben.
revile as, schelten *O.* (2 *acc.*).
reward, Lohn *m.* -nes, -ne.
Rhine wine, Rheinwein *m.* -ns, -ne.
rich, reich.
riches, Reichthum *m.* -ms, -ümer.
rid:—**get r. of**, los werden *O.* s. (*acc.*).
ride, (on horse) reiten *O.*; (in vehicle) fahren *O.* s.
rider, Reiter *m.* -rs, -r.
right, *adj.*, (= correct) richtig; (= not left) recht; **be r.**, Recht haben *N. irr.*
righteous, gerecht.
ring, Ring *m.* -ges, -ge.
risk, wagen.
river, Fluß *m.* -sses, -üsse.
road, Weg *m.* -ges, -ge.
roar:—**approach roaring**, heranbrausen s.; **go roaring off**, davonbrausen s.
rob, berauben (*acc. gen.*).
robber, Räuber *m.* -rs, -r; **band of r's**, Räuberbande *f.* -en.
rock, Felsen *m.* -ns, -n.
rogue, Schurke *m.* -en, -en.
roof, Dach *n.* -ches, -ächer.
room, Zimmer *n.* -rs, -r, Stube *f.* -en 6.14.
royal, königlich.
rude, roh.
ruin, Ruine *f.* -en.
rule, herrschen.
run, rennen *N. irr.*, laufen *O.* s.; **run away**, davonlaufen; **run down**, hinunterlaufen.
Russian, russisch.

sacrifice, aufopfern.
sad, traurig.
saddle *v.*, satteln.
safe, sicher.

safely, glücklich 45.11
sagacious, klug (ü *in comp.*).
sail *noun*, **Segel** *m.* -ls, -l.—*v.* **fahren** *O.* s. 54.
saloon, Saal *m.* -les, Säle.
same :—the s., derselbe (169).
save *v.*, **retten.**—*prep.*, **außer** (*dat.*) 27.25.
savings, Ersparniß *f.* -sse.
Saxon, Sachse *m.* -en, -en.
say, sagen.
scarcely, kaum.
school, Schule *f.* -en; **in s., auf der Schule.**
schoolmaster, Schulmeister *m.* -rs, -r.
science, Wissenschaft *f.* -ten.
seat *v.*, **setzen.**
second, zweit; secondly, zweitens.
secret, Geheimniß *n.* -sses, -sse.
see, sehen *O.*, **ersehen** 68.1; **see again, wiedersehen.**
seem, scheinen *O.*
select, wählen.
self-tormentor, Selbstquäler *m.* -rs, -r.
sell, verkaufen.
send, senden *N. irr.*, **schicken; send back, zurückschicken.**
sensible, verständig, gescheidt.
sentinel, Schildwache *f.* -en.
September, September, *m.* -rs.
seriousness, Ernst *m.* -tes.
servant, Diener *m.* -rs, -r; **s.-girl, Dienstmädchen** *n.* -ns, -n.
serve up, serviren.
service, Dienst *m.* -tes, -te.
session, Sitzung *f.* -gen.
set, (of sun) **un'tergehen** *O.* s.
settle, einrichten.
seven, sieben.
seventy, siebenzig.
several, mehrere *pl.*
shade, Schatten *m.* -ns, -n.—*v.*, **beschatten.**
shadow, (= dark side *or* aspect) **Schattenseite** *f.* -en.
shall, sollen *N. irr.* :—*generally to be rendered by the future tense of the verb to which* shall *is auxiliary.*
shameful, schändlich.
she, sie (151), **die** (166.2*b*) 33.7, **dieselbe** (171) 33.8.
ship, Schiff *n.* -fes, -fe.
shoe, Schuh *m.* -hes, -he.
shoot off, abschießen *O.*
shopkeeper, Krämer *m.* -rs, -r.
shore, Ufer *n.* -rs, -r.
short, kurz (ü *in comp.*).
should, sollen *N. irr.* 19.18: *generally to be rendered by cond'l: compare* shall; **sh. like, möchte** (*pret subj.*).
shut, zumachen.
shy, scheu.
sickly, kränklich.
side, Seite *f.* -en; **bright side, Lichtseite** *f.* -en.
sight, Gesicht *n.* -ts; **from s., aus dem Gesicht.**
silent :—be *or* **keep s., schweigen** *O.*
since *prep.*, **seit** (*dat.*).—*adv.*, **long s., längst.**
sincere, aufrichtig.
sink, un'tergehen *O.* s. 54.
sing, singen *O.*
single, einzig.
Sir, mein Herr.
sister, Schwester *f.* -rn; **little s., Schwesterchen** *n.* -ns, -n; **brothers and sisters, Geschwister** *pl.*
sit, sitzen *O.*
six, sechs.
sixteen, sechszehn.
sixty, sechzig.
sleep *v.*, **schlafen** *O.*—*noun*, **Schlaf** *m* -fes.
slow, langsam.
small, klein.
snake, Schlange *f.* -en.
snatch, reißen *O.*
snow, Schnee *m.* -es.—*v.*, **schneien.**
so, so, es (154.4*e*) 25.12, 54.
soldier, Soldat *m.* -ten, -ten.
solid :—of s. value, gediegen.
some, *adj. or pron.*, **ein** 66, **einige** *pl.*; *pron.* **welch** (176.2) 41.2, 44.6; **some one, Jemand** (186).
something, etwas.
somewhat, etwas.
somewhere, irgendwo.
son, Sohn *m.* -nes, -öhne.
song, Lied *n.* -des, -der; **s.-book, Liederbuch** *n.* -chs, -ücher.
soon, bald; as soon as, sobald.
sopha, Sopha *n.* -a's, -as.
sorely, schwer, heftig 61.
sort :—what s. of, was für (175); **all sorts of, allerlei** (*indecl. adj.* 415.11).
sound forth, ertönen.
spade, Spaten *m.* -ns, -n.
sparkle, funkeln.
speak, sprechen *O.*
specially, eigens.
specify, specificiren, angeben *O.*
spectacle, (= show) **Schauspiel** *n.* -ls, -le; **spectacles,** (= glasses, **Brille** *f.* -en.
speech, Sprache *f.*
spirit :—in good spirits, guter Dinge.

spirited, muthig.
splendid, prachtvoll.
splendor, Glanz *m.* -zes.
spot, Stelle *f.* -en, Fleck *m.* -kes, -ke 46.5.
spread :—sp. abroad, verbreiten; **sp. out,** ausbreiten.
spy, Spion *m.* -ns, -ne.
stable, Stall *m.* -les, -älle.
stand, stehen *O.*; **st. by,** beistehen *O.* (*dat.*); **st. still,** stehen bleiben *O.* s.
standing *noun,* Stehen *n.* -ns.
start, abfahren *O.* s.
state-counsellor, Staatsrath *m.* -ths, -äthe.
station (railway), Bahnhof *m.* -fs, -öfe.
stay, bleiben *O.* s., sich aufhalten *O.* 27.18; **st. away,** wegbleiben, fortbleiben, ausbleiben 32.3.
steal, stehlen *O.*
step *v.*, treten *O.* s.; **st. in,** eintreten. —*noun,* Stufe *f.* -en.
still *adj.* :—**stand st.,** stehen *O.* bleiben *O.* s.; **hold st.,** still halten *O.*
still *adv.* (= yet), noch.
stocking, Strumpf *m.* -fes, -ümpfe.
stone, Stein *m.* -nes, -ne.
stony, steinern.
storm, Gewitter *n.* -rs, -r.
stormy, stürmig.
story, Geschichte *f.* -en.
straight, gerade.
stranger, Fremd *adj. as noun.*
street, Straße *f.* -en.
strength, Kraft *f.* -äfte.
strengthen, stärken.
strike, (the attention of any one) auffallen *O.* s. (*dat.*).
strive, streben; **st. toward,** entgegenstreben (*dat.*).
stroll about, sich herumtreiben *O.*
strong, stark (ä *in comp.*).
student, Student *m.* -ten, -ten.
stuff, Stoff *m.* -fes, -fe.
subject, Gegenstand *m.* -ds, -ände.
submit, sich bequemen.
suburb, Vorstadt *f.* -ädte.
succeed, gelingen *O.*: *used only in third pers., e.g.*, I succeed, es gelingt mir.
success, Erfolg *m.* -gs, -ge.
such, solch (170); **s. a,** ein solcher; **s. a thing,** so etwas.
suffer, dulden.
suffering, Leiden *n.* -ns, -n.
suffice, hinreichen.
suit, recht sein *O.* s. (*dat.*).
summer, Sommer *m.* -rs, -r; **summer-house :—little s.,** Gartenhäuschen *n.* -ns, -n.

sunbeam, Sonnenstrahl *m.* -ls, -len.
Sunday, Sonntag *m.* -gs, -ge.
sure, sicher; **to be s.,** zwar, freilich 60.
surely, doch 46.1.
surprise, überrasch'en.
surround, umring'en, umge'ben *O.* 59.
swear, schwören *O.* 53.
sweet, süß.
swim, schwimmen *O.* h. *or* s.
sympathy, Theilnahme *f.*

table, Tisch *m.* -es, -e.
take, nehmen *O.*; (take a road) einschlagen *O.*; **t. care,** sich in Acht nehmen; **t. a journey,** verreisen s.; **t. off,** ausziehen *O.*; **t. out,** herausnehmen; **t. part,** Theil nehmen (**in,** an); **t. part in,** mitmachen 44.9; **t. pity on,** sich erbarmen (*gen.*); **t. possession of,** sich bemächtigen (*gen.*); **t. up,** aufnehmen.
talk, reden; **t. about,** besprechen *O.*
taste, schmecken.
tea, Thee *m.* -es.
teacher, Lehrer *m.* -rs, -r.
tell, sagen, erzählen 27.19, 28.9.
temple, Tempel *m.* -ls, -l.
ten, zehn.
tenant, Bewohner *m.* -rs, -r.
termination, Schluß *m.* -sses, -üsse.
terrace, Terrasse *f.* -en.
terrible, schrecklich.
than, als.
thank, danken (*dat.*).
thankful, dankbar.
that *pron. or pron'l adj.*, jen (*when opposed to* this, 165–6), der (166.2) 8.5, 11.5; dies 10.8; (*as antec't of a relative*) derjenige (168) 45.12.—*conj.* daß; (= in order that) damit; *in comp'n with prep'ns,* da- (365.3*b*).
the *art.*, der *etc.* (63).—*adv.*, **the . . . the . . .** (*before comparatives*), je . . . desto . . .
theatre, Theater *n.* -rs, -r.
then, dann, (*correl. to* if) so, also 55, da 56; **till th.,** bis dahin.
there, dort, da; **there is, are** *etc.* es ist *etc.* (154.4*b*,*d*), es giebt (*acc.* 232.3*a*); **go th.,** hingehen *O.*
thereupon, darauf.
they, sie (151); (= people, one) man (185).
thing :—such a th., so etwas.
think, denken *N. irr.* (**of,** auf; **upon,** an); (= entertain an opinion) halten *O.* 38.2; (= suppose one's self) glauben (*followed by infin.*).
third, dritt.

thirst, Durst *m.* -es.
thirsty :—be th., dürsten.
this, dies (165–6); der (166.2); **th. evening,** heute Abend.
thither, dahin; **go th.,** hingehen *O.* s.
thou, du (151).
thought, Gedanke *m.* -ens, -en.
thousand, tausend.
threaten, drohen (*dat. acc.*).
three, drei.
threshold, Schwelle *f.* -en.
through *prep.*, durch (*acc.*).—*adv.*, hindurch 37.11; **get th.,** durchkommen *O.* s.
throw, werfen *O.* (**at,** auf, *acc.*).
thrust, stecken.
thunderstorm, Gewitter *n.* -rs, -r.
thus, also 25.11, so 26.3.
thy, dein (154 *etc.*).
tight, eng.
till :—t. then, bis dahin.
time, Zeit *f.* -ten; (= turn, succession) Mal *n.* -ls, -le; **a long t.,** lange; **this t.,** diesmal; **at that t.,** damals.
tired, müde (**of,** *gen.*).
title, Titel *m.* -ls, -l.
to, zu (*dat.*); (to a place) nach (*dat.*); (to a concert, theatre) in (*acc.*): *very often to be omitted, the governed noun being put in the dative:* (as sign of infin.) zu; **in order to,** um . . . zu.
to-day, heute; **to-day's,** der heutige 45.7.
together, zusammen, beisammen; **meet t.,** zusammentreffen *O.* s.; **t. with,** sammt (*dat.*).
toilet, Toilette *f.* -en.
to-morrow, morgen.
too, (*qualifying adj. or adv.*) zu; (= also) auch.
totally, gänzlich.
toward, gegen (*acc.*); (toward a place) nach (*dat.*); (= to meet) entgegen; **strive t.,** entgegenstreben (*dat.*).
town, Stadt *f.* -ädte; **quarter of the t.,** Stadttheil *m.* -ls, -le.
track, Bahn *f.* -nen.
tranquil, ruhig.
transaction, Vorgang *m.* -gs, -änge.
transport back, (in thought) zurückdenken *N. irr.*
traveller, Reisend *adj. as noun.*
tread, betreten *O.*
treasure, Schatz *m.* -tzes, -ätze.
tree, Baum, *m.* -mes, -äume; **little t.,** Bäumchen *n.* -ns, -n.
treeless, baumlos.
tremble, beben.
troop, Truppe *f.* -en.
trouble, Mühe *f.*
true, wahr, (= faithful, trusty) treu; **it is t.,** zwar.
truly, wahrlich.
trunk, Koffer *m.* -rs, -r.
trust, trauen (*dat.*).
truth, Wahrheit *f.* -ten.
try, probiren 34.8, versuchen 40.9.
Turkey, Türkei *f.*
turn, biegen *O.* 37.10; **t. back,** zurückkehren.
twelfth, zwölft.
twentieth, zwanzigst.
twenty, zwanzig.
twice, zweimal.
two, zwei; **the two,** die beiden 49.4, 59.

ugly, häßlich.
unawares, unversehens.
unchanged, unverändert.
uncle, Onkel *m.* -ls, -l.
uncomfortable, unheimlich.
under, unter (*dat. or acc.* 376).
understand, verstehen *O.*; **come to an understanding,** sich verständigen.
undertaking, Unternehmen *n.* -ns, -n.
unexpected, unerwartet; **unexpectedly,** unerwarteter Weise.
unfortunate, unglücklich; **unfortunately,** leider.
ungrateful, undankbar.
unhappy, unglücklich.
unharness, ausspannen.
united, einig.
university, Universität *f.* -ten.
unknown, unbekannt.
unnecessary, unnöthig.
unpleasant, unangenehm.
unseasonable, ungelegen.
until, bis; **not until,** erst . . . wenn, erst 42.6.
unwell, unwohl.
up, hinauf 47.9; heran 47.10; herauf 60: *see the verbs.*
upon, auf (*dat. or acc.* 376); (think upon) an (*acc.*); **upon which,** worauf.
upward, in die Höhe 49.7.
urgent, inständig.
use :—make u. of, sich bedienen (*gen.*).—*v.* **use to,** pflegen zu.
used, (= accustomed) gewohnt (*acc.*).
useful :—be u. to, nützen (*dat.*).
useless, unnütz.

vain :—in v., vergebens.
valley, Thal *n.* -les, -äler.

value *v.*, **schätzen.**—*noun*; **of solid v.**, **gediegen.**
vary, verschieden sein *O.* s.
venture, dürfen *N. irr.*
very, sehr, recht 25.8.
vestibule, Vorsaal *m.* -ls, -säle.
vicinity, Nähe *f.*
victim, Opfer *n.* -rs, -r.
village, Dorf *n.* -fes, -örfer.
villain, Bösewicht *m.* -ts, -ter.
violinist, Violinspieler *m.* -rs, -r.
virtue, Tugend *f.* -den.
voice, Stimme *f.* -en.
volume, Band *m.* -des, -ände.
voluntary, freiwillig.
vote, stimmen.
vulgar, gemein.

wagon, Wagen *m.* -ns, -n.
wait, warten; **w. for**, warten (*gen.*) 18.11, warten auf (*acc.*) 23.4, 42.2.
waiting *noun*, Warten *n.* -ns.
walk, gehen *O.* s. 40.8; **go to w.**, spazieren gehen (343.I.6).
wander, wandern h. *or* s.
wanderer, Wanderer *m.* -rs, -r.
want to, wollen *N. irr.*
war, Krieg *m.* -ges, -ge.
warm, warm (ä *in comp.*); **warmly**, innig 8.8.
warrior, Krieger *m.* -rs, -r.
watch, Uhr *f.* -ren.
water, Wasser *n.* -rs, -r.
watering-place, Bad *n.* -des, -äder.
way, (= road):—**w. out**, **Ausweg** *m.* -gs, -ge; **give w.**, **nachgeben** *O.*; **fight one's w.**, **sich schlagen** *O.*; —(= manner) **Art und Weise** *f.*; **in every w.**, **auf jede Weise.**
we, **wir, man** (185) 33.2.
wear, (as clothes) **tragen** *O.*; (= last) **sich halten** *O.* 40.5.
weary *adj.*, **müde, überdrüssig** (*gen.*). —*v.* **ermüden.**
weather, **Wetter** *n.* -rs.
week, **Woche** *f.* -en.
weigh, **wiegen** *O.*
welcome *adj.*, **willkommen.**—*noun*, **Willkommen** *n.* -ns.
welfare, **Glück** *n.* -ks.
well *adv.*, **wohl, gut** 13.7, 21.1; **well-behaved, artig**; **be w.**, (einem) **wohl sein** 41.6.—*adj.*, (= healthy) **wohl** 7.1, **gesund** 27.1.
West, **Westen** *m.* -ns.
what *pron. interrog. or comp. relative*, **was** (173 *etc.*).—*adj.*, **was für** 60; **wh. sort of, was für; what is** (*before adj.*), **das** 26.1.
whatever, **was . . . auch** (179.4) 33.9, **was** 46.4.
when, *interrog. or comp. relative*, **wann**; *relative*, **wenn** 28.10, **wo** 33.11, **als** 29.21, **wie** 35.5; *conditional*, **wenn** 10.2,7.
whence, **woher.**
where, **wo**; (= whither) **wohin 43.3**; **whereby, wodurch.**
wherever, **wohin . . . auch** 29.14.
whether, **ob.**
which, **welch** (174 *etc.*); *with prepositions*, **wo-** (173.2); (way) **in wh.**, **wie** 28.9.
while *or* **whilst, während, indem.**
whisper, flüstern.
white, weiß.
whither, wohin.
who, *interrog. or comp. relative*, **wer**; *relative*, **der, welcher.**
whoever, wer 40.3.
whole, ganz; on the wh., im Ganzen.
why, warum.
wicked, bös.
will, (= want, intend) **wollen** *N. irr.*; *expressing futurity simply, to be rendered by future of the principal verb.*
William, Wilhelm *m.* -ms.
willingly, gern *or* **gerne.**
window, Fenster *n.* -rs, -r; **w.-pane, Fensterscheibe** *f.* -en.
wine, Wein *m.* -nes, -ne; **w.-bottle, Weinflasche** *f.* -en; **Rhine w., Rheinwein** *m.* -ns, -ne.
winter, Winter *m.* -rs, -r.
wipe, abwischen, wischen.
wish, Wunsch *m.* -sches, -ünsche.—*v.*, **wünschen, wollen** *N. irr.* 38.7.
with, mit; (= at the house of) **bei**; (= among) **bei** 70; (with rage) **vor.**
without, ohne; ohne daß 70.
woman, Weib *n.* -bes, -ber; **Frau** *f.* -auen 6.15, 27.25; **American w., Amerikanerin** *f.* -nnen.
wonder, sich wundern (at, über *acc.*); *impersonally*, **I wonder, es wundert mich,** *etc.*
wonderful, wunderbar.
wooden, hölzern.
work, (= labor) **Arbeit** *f.* -ten; (literary) **Werk** *n.* -kes, -ke.—*v.*, **arbeiten.**
workman, Arbeiter *m.* -rs, -r.
world, Welt *f.* -ten; **part of the w., Welttheil** *m.* -ls, -le; **in the w., auf der Welt** 27.31.
worry, sich plagen.
worse:—grow w., sich verschlechtern.
worthy, würdig (*gen.*), **werth** 27 25.

would, *as aux'y, to be rendered by pret. subj. or cond'l of principal verb;* **w. rather,** möchte *pret. subj.,* möchte lieber 38.10.
wound, Wunde *f.* =en.—*v.,* verwunden.
write, schreiben *O.*

yard, Hof *m.* =fes, =öfe.
year, Jahr *n.* =res, =re; **for years,** seit Jahren.
yes, ja; doch 41.2.
yet, noch, doch 55.
yesterday, gestern; **day before y.,** vorgestern.
yield, nachlassen *O.*
yonder, dort.
you, ihr, Sie (153).
young, jung (ü *in comp.*); **y. lady** Fräulein *n.* =ns, =n.
your, euer, Ihr (153.4).
yours, der Ihrige *etc.* (159.5).
yourself, euch, sich (155); selber *or* selbst (155.5).
youth, (= young man) Jüngling *m.* =gs, =ge.

Bake - Backen - buck - gebacken -
[illegible] - gebögen barg - geborgen
Bite - Beissen - biez - gebissen.
hide Bergen - barg geborgen
Burst - Bersten - barst - geborsten
Bend - Biegen bog. gebogen
~~[illegible]~~ Bieten bot - geboten
bind. Binden band gebunden
beg Bitten bat gebeten
blow - Blasen. ~~bliess~~ geblasen
remain Bleiben blieb geblieben
bleach Bleichen - blich geblichen
roast Braten briet gebraten
break Brechen brach gebrochen

www.ingramcontent.com/pod-product-compliance
Lightning Source LLC
LaVergne TN
LVHW020223110826
845151LV00003B/811

* 9 7 8 1 4 2 5 5 3 1 8 6 7 *